HON. HORATIO SEYMOUR.

Democratic Nominee for President.

Frank P. Blair

GEN. FRANK P. BLAIR.

Democratic Nominee for Vice President

THE LIFE

AND

PUBLIC SERVICES

OF

HORATIO SEYMOUR:

TOGETHER WITH A

COMPLETE AND AUTHENTIC LIFE

OF

FRANCIS P. BLAIR, JR.

BY

JAMES D. McCABE, JR.

NEW YORK:
UNITED STATES PUBLISHING COMPANY, 411 Broome Street.
CINCINNATI, O.; CHICAGO, ILL.; ST. LOUIS, MO.; ATLANTA, GA.
JONES BROTHERS & CO.
SAN FRANCISCO, CAL.: H. H. BANCROFT & CO.
1868.

THE TROW & SMITH
BOOK MANUFACTURING COMPANY
46, 48 & 50 Greene Street, N, Y.

TO THOSE

WHO LOVE CONSTITUTIONAL LIBERTY,

THESE HISTORIES

OF

THEIR BRAVEST DEFENDERS

ARE DEDICATED.

PREFACE.

When a citizen of the Republic is presented to the people for election by them to the highest public position in their gift, it is eminently proper that they should know the events of his previous life, in order that they may be enabled to form from them an intelligent opinion as to his qualifications for the position to which he aspires. Especially is it important that they should have this knowledge when it is proposed to place him at the head of the nation in a time like the present, when the country, almost on the brink of ruin, requires in its Chief Magistrate not only personal purity and political integrity, but also the highest and most profound wisdom, and the greatest and most unwavering firmness,—a wisdom which shall foresee and provide against the dangers which threaten our institutions and prosperity, and a firmness which, resisting all the temptations of a selfish ambition, shall keep the Republic true to itself and to its God-given mission.

The author believes that the Democratic party have presented such a man to the suffrages of the country in their nomination of Mr. Seymour, and he has endeavored to make this book a work which shall place within the reach of all, a brief, comprehensive, and convenient record of the services upon which the Democracy base their estimate of their leader, in the coming contest. He has carefully refrained from intruding his own opinions upon the reader, and his aim has been to express the view taken by the majority of the Democratic party with regard to the questions herein discussed.

It seemed but just to include in the book, a history of the life of the candidate of the party for the Vice-Presidency, as a work of this character would be incomplete without it. The Vice-Presidency has become of late years, more prominent and more important in the estimation of the public than in times gone by, and the people have been taught that it is of vital consequence to choose their high officers in such a manner, that if, in the Providence of God, the country is at any time deprived of its Executive, his Constitutional successor may be a man capable of discharging the duties of the position. The Democratic party, fully realizing this, have chosen for the second place in the Government the man best fitted for it—one whose merits as a statesman are equalled only by his genius as a soldier, whose courage and integrity, both personal and political, are without question, and whose devotion to the great principles of the Constitution has been attested upon many a hard-fought field.

With such leaders, and under the inspiration of such principles as are set forth in its platform, the Democratic party enters upon the present campaign, with a confidence which is the sure harbinger of success. It cannot fail, for, as its most eloquent historian* declares, "It represents the great principles of progress. It is onward and outward in its movements. It has a heart for action, and motives for a world. It constitutes the principle of diffusion, and is to humanity what the centrifugal force is to the revolving orbs of the universe. What motion is to them, democracy is to principle. It is the soul of action. It conforms to the providence of God. It has confidence in man and an abiding reliance in his high destiny. It seeks the largest liberty, the greatest good, and the surest happiness. It aims to build up the great interests of the many, to the least detriment of the few. It remembers the past, without neglecting the present. It establishes the present, without fearing to provide for the future. It cares for the weak, while it permits no injustice to the strong. It conquers the oppressor, and prepares the subjects of tyranny for freedom. It melts the bigot's heart to meekness, and reconciles

* *Nahum Capen.* His "History of Democracy of the United States," is soon to be published.

his mind to knowledge. It dispels the clouds of ignorance and superstition, and prepares the people for instruction and self-respect. It adds wisdom to legislation, and improved judgment to government. It favors enterprise that yields a reward to the many, and an industry that is permanent It is the pioneer of humanity, the conservator of nations. *It fails only when it ceases to be true to itself. Vox populi Vox Dei* has proved to be both a proverb and a prediction."

Copious extracts from the letters, speeches and messages, of Governor Seymour and General Blair are given in this book, in order that the reader may judge them by their own words. Their declarations are plain and not susceptible of misinterpretation, and are believed to be more interesting to the general reader than a mass of mere details could be.

The book is given to the public with the hope that it may aid, in some degree, in bringing about, in November next, the election of men who desire the perpetuation and not the destruction of our Constitution and system of Government.

J. D. McC., Jr.

New York, August 1st, 1868.

CONTENTS.

CHAPTER I.

CHAPTER II.

CHAPTER III.

CHAPTER IV.

CHAPTER V.

CHAPTER VI.

CHAPTER VII.

CHAPTER VIII.

CHAPTER IX.

CHAPTER X.

CHAPTER XI.

THE LIFE AND PUBLIC SERVICES

OF

HORATIO SEYMOUR.

THE LIFE

AND

PUBLIC SERVICES

OF

HORATIO SEYMOUR.

CHAPTER I.

The Seymour Family—Birth of Horatio Seymour—Childhood—Education—Decides to adopt the Law as his Profession—Early Studies—Entrance upon his Duties—Death of his Father, and Father-in-Law—Early Political Life—Attaches himself to the Democratic Party—Elected to the Legislature of New York—His Services in that Body—His Success in Public Life—Elected Mayor of Utica—Reëlected to the Legislature—Retires to Private Life, and resumes the Practice of the Law—The Erie Canal Question—Nominated for Governor—Defeated—Elected Governor of New York—His course as Governor sustained by the Court of Appeals.

Among the original settlers of Connecticut, was one named Richard Seymour, a just, God-fearing man, who, for conscience-sake, followed the pious Hooker through the untracked forest, to found for himself and his posterity a home in which they could worship God after the manner of their fathers, with none to molest or make them afraid. The descendants of this good man lived at Hartford, in the old homestead, until Moses Seymour, the fourth in descent from the founder of the family, grew to manhood. Moses Seymour removed

2

to Litchfield, which he represented for seventeen years in the Legislature of Connecticut. He served gallantly through the Revolution, as a Major in the Connecticut line, and established a high reputation for bravery, efficiency, and ability. He married a daughter of Colonel Marsh, of Connecticut, a distinguished officer of the Continental Army, and by her had five sons. The eldest of these sons, Henry Seymour, was born in 1780, and upon attaining his majority, removed to Onondaga County, in the State of New York. He took a leading part in the politics of the day, and was known as a man of fine abilities and unblemished integrity. He served for several terms in the State Legislature, and was for many years Canal Commissioner. He also acquired considerable property, which he left to his children. He was the father of the subject of this memoir.

HORATIO SEYMOUR was born at Pompey, Onondaga County, New York, in the year 1811. He received a liberal and thorough education in the best schools and academies of the State. No pains were spared by his parents to fit him for taking a prominent position in public affairs, to which career he seems to have been devoted from his childhood; and their efforts met with a ready and earnest coöperation on his part. He was a close and diligent student, and being possessed of fine natural abilities, took at once and maintained a leading position in his class. He was the best scholar and the readiest speaker in his classes, and from the first won the esteem and confidence of his companions.

Young Seymour at an early day decided to adopt the law as his profession, and his studies were all shaped with a view to prepare him for it. Upon the close of his collegiate course, he commenced the study of the law, which he pursued with vigor and industry. So successful was he in his efforts, that he was admitted to the bar when only a little more than twenty years old. He at once entered upon the practice of his profession in the city of Utica. The prospect before him was very flattering, and he had every reason to expect an immediate and brilliant success; but the death of his father, occurring about this period, compelled him to give the greater portion of his time to the task of settling the large and somewhat complicated estate which Henry Seymour left behind him. These duties were engrossing and numerous. Mr. John R. Bleecker, his wife's father, died some time after this, leaving a large estate, to the settlement of which Mr. Seymour devoted much time. He paid little attention to his profession, preferring to give his time to the management of his estate, which has, under his care, become one of the finest in New York. Mr. Seymour, meanwhile, kept steadily in view the great career he had marked out for himself; and realizing that he who would lead men must know man, pursued a thorough and systematic course of study, and after the close of the duties referred to above, again entered upon the practice of his profession.

In his earlier years he took very little active interest in political affairs, though his sympathies, tastes, and convictions led him to vote with the Democratic party, to which his family had been attached for several generations. His social position, his high personal character, and his acknowledged abilities, made him a valuable acquisition to the party, and efforts were not wanting on the part of its leaders to induce him to enter actively into political life. For some years he steadily refused to do this, but at length, in the fall of 1842, when not quite thirty-one years of age, he consented to accept the Democratic nomination for member of the Assembly, in the State Legislature. At this time the Whigs had a decided majority in Oneida, and the Democrats had for some years been unsuccessful in their efforts, but notwithstanding this, Mr. Seymour was elected by a handsome majority, his personal popularity having drawn off a large share of the Whig vote from the candidate of that party.

As was to be expected, Mr. Seymour took a commanding position in the Legislature. The Assembly at that day, was no insignificant body. It contained, besides Mr. Seymour, such men as John A. Dix, Michael Hoffman, David R. Floyd Jones, George R. Davis, Lemuel Stetson, and Calvin T. Hulburd. The session was one of the most memorable in the history of New York, and the debates were marked by a rare display of ability and eloquence. The Democrats were largely in the ascendency in both branches of the Legislature, and the measures of the session were important. The great question of the day was Michael Hoffman's famous bill for restoring the financial credit of the State, which was supported and passed by the entire strength of the Democracy. Mr. Seymour engaged actively in the labors of the session, speaking often and with great eloquence and force, and contributed in a marked degree to the character and success of the legislation. He began the session with a fine local reputation, but when it closed he had made himself known and honored all over the State. His success had been even greater than his warmest friends had predicted, and such as very few men have achieved during their first session.

The next spring Mr. Seymour was elected Mayor of Utica. The Whigs made strenuous efforts to defeat him, and the canvass was a warm one, but he was elected by a considerable majority.

In the fall of 1843, he was again elected a member of the Lower House of the Legislature, to which he was returned again in 1844, and in 1845. The session of 1844 was one which will be long remembered in New York. The administration of Governor Bouck met with a sharp opposition in the Legislature, and this was the cause of many exciting and skilful debates. In these discussions Mr. Seymour was pitted against the veteran Michael Hoffman, the brilliant leader of the Assembly, and a most formidable antagonist, but he fought him with such skill and effect as to win for himself the enthusiastic praise of his political associates, and the unstinted admiration of his constituents. Mr. Polk having been elected to the Presidency by a triumphant Democracy in 1844, the session of 1845 was more harmonious. At this session Mr. Seymour was nominated by his friends for the post of Speaker of the

Lower House of the Legislature, and after a sharp contest, in which he came near being defeated in consequence of some serious defections in his own party, was elected by a decisive majority. It was during this session that Daniel S. Dickinson was elected to the United States Senate, and to this election Mr. Seymour contributed in a very great degree, urging the choice of Mr. Dickinson, and exerting his entire influence in favor of it. When the question of calling a Convention to amend the Constitution of the State was brought up, he spoke earnestly and eloquently in favor of it, but voted against the bill for that purpose, as its provisions did not meet with his approval.

At the end of this session, Mr. Seymour retired to private life, and for the next five years devoted himself to his personal affairs. He took little or no part in public matters, devoting himself exclusively to his private business, taking care, however, to keep himself well informed of the drift of political events. He extended the circle of his acquaintance in other parts of the State, the fame which he had acquired in the Legislature having made him deservedly popular with the people everywhere.

In 1850, he returned to public life. In that year, the Legislature of New York passed a bill for the enlargement and improvement of the Erie Canal, and for that purpose appropriated certain revenues of the State, in direct violation of the provisions of the Constitution. This measure brought Mr. Seymour again into the field, and was opposed and denounced by him with more than his usual vigor and eloquence. His opposition to it was so marked and decided, that the Democracy solicited him to become their candidate for Governor of the State. He accepted the nomination, and at once entered upon the contest. His opponent was Mr. Washington Hunt, a gentleman of great ability and popularity. The election resulted as follows:

For Mr. Hunt, ...	214,614 votes.
For Mr. Seymour, . . .	214,352 "
Majority for Mr. Hunt, .	262 votes.

The fact that the entire Democratic ticket, with the exception of Mr. Seymour, was elected, was supposed by many to be, in a political sense, very damaging to him. That this view of the case was not correct, however, is shown by the sequel. In 1852, in spite of his defeat in 1850, Mr. Seymour was again the nominee of his party, and was this time opposed again by Governor Hunt, the Whig candidate, and also by Minthorne Tompkins, the Free Soil candidate. The canvass was a very exciting one, and was conducted with great vigor and ability by all parties. The election resulted as follows:

For Mr. Seymour, ...	264,121	votes.
For Mr. Hunt, ...	239,736	"
For Mr. Tompkins, ...	19,299	"
Seymour's majority over Hunt,	24,385	"
Seymour's majority over Hunt and Tompkins, ...	5,086	"

This splendid victory was due, in a great measure, to Mr. Seymour's personal popularity, and at once silenced all those who had predicted evil for him from his defeat in the previous canvass. His administration as Governor, now that the heat and prejudice of the times has worn away, is admitted on all sides to have been marked by ability, discretion, and sound judgment. The chief measure of it was his veto of the "Maine Liquor Law," which had passed both Houses of the Legislature. His course was based upon his conviction that the Legislature had no power to pass sumptuary laws, and his judgment convinced him that such a law would be productive of great trouble in the State, and that it would ultimately be repealed by the people. His conduct occasioned considerable surprise and feeling, but the course of the Governor has since been amply vindicated by a formal decision of the Court of Appeals that the Legislature has no power to enact such a law.

CHAPTER II.

Mr. Seymour is Re-nominated for Governor by the Democracy—Is Defeated by Mr. Clark—Resumes the Practice of the Law—His Interest in Public Affairs—His Marked Success as a Public Man—Services in behalf of the Democratic Party—Attends the Charleston Convention—Declines to be a Candidate for the Presidency—Services during the Presidential Campaign of 1860—The Secession Troubles—Mr. Seymour urges a Policy of Conciliation towards the South—The Democratic Convention at Tweddle Hall—Character of the Convention—Remarks of Judge Parker—Resolutions Adopted—Noble Speech of Gov. Seymour—His Views upon the Condition of the Country—A Plea for Justice and Humanity—A Patriotic Declaration—Mr. Seymour's Course Respecting the Troubles—The War—Mr. Seymour Retires to his home—Efforts in Behalf of the Union Cause—Serves as a Member of the County Committee for Raising and Equipping Troops—Summary of his Views Respecting the War, as drawn from his Public Speeches.

In 1854, Mr. Seymour was nominated by his party for reëlection to the Gubernatorial Chair. This time there were four candidates in the field: Mr. Seymour, the regular Democratic nominee, Myron G. Clark, Republican, Daniel Ullman, American, or Know Nothing, and Greene C. Bronson, "Hard-Shell Democrat." This unfortunate "split" in the Democratic party caused its defeat. The election resulted as follows:

For Mr. Clark, ...	156,804	votes.
For Mr. Seymour, . . .	156,495	"
For Mr. Ullman, ...	122,282	"
For Mr. Bronson, . . .	33,850	"
Mr. Clark's majority over Mr. Seymour, ...	309	"

After this defeat, Mr. Seymour returned to his home in the city of Utica. Though he did not present himself again for some years as a candidate for office, he continued to take a deep interest in the welfare of the country and the Democratic party. He was regularly sent as a delegate to the State and National Conventions of the party, in which his influence was very great. His high qualities of mind and heart had drawn to him at the outset of his political career a band of devoted friends and admirers, and every year only served to increase their numbers, until at length he came to be regarded as the foremost man of his party in his own State, and one of the purest and most gifted leaders of that party in the Union. His views were always sought on all the great questions of the day, and his voice was powerful in the Councils of the Democracy.

In the Convention of 1860, at Charleston, when it became evident that the contest between the friends of Mr. Douglas and those of Mr. Breckenridge could not be settled amicably, Mr. Seymour's name was presented by the Southern delegates, with the hope that the two wings of the party would unite upon him as a compromise. The measure might have been crowned with success, but being unwilling to relinquish the retirement of his home for the trials of office, Mr. Seymour requested his friends to withdraw his name.

During the campaign of 1860 Mr. Seymour supported the regular Democratic ticket, and when the secession movement began at once exerted himself to procure a peaceful settlement of the difficulty. He knew what untold misery a civil war would bring upon the land, and he sought by every means in his power to avert it. Though he did not think secession was the proper course for the South to pursue, he believed that section had just cause for complaint, and that her grievances demanded redress. In view of the excited condition of both sections, however, and the indisposition of either to yield its claims, he thought that the only possible settlement of the troubles lay in a compromise between the sections, and he exerted himself to bring about such a measure. His whole effort was to prevent the war, and though he may have erred in some of his views respecting the questions at issue, the people of the country will always remember with gratitude the manly efforts he made to save them from the horrors of the late war. In common with the whole Democratic party of the North, he urged the adoption of measures of conciliation and peace. His efforts were in vain, however. The extremists of the North and South applied themselves diligently to the task of bringing on the war, and the labors of the Conservative men of the country were defeated.

While matters were in this condition the Democratic State Central Committee of New York issued a call for a Convention, of four delegates from each Assembly district, to be held at Albany on the 31st of January, 1861, for the purpose of considering the state of affairs throughout the country. Mr. Seymour was sent to this body as a delegate from Utica.

The Convention met at Tweddle Hall, in Albany, on the day appointed. It was the most imposing and brilliant political body that ever assembled in the State. Thirty of the delegates had held seats in Congress, while one (Gov. Seymour) had been Governor of the State, and two others the nominees of the party for that high office. Nor was the Convention strictly a "Democratic" body, though called as such. Several of its best members had been leading Whigs, and some were "Americans." All had been drawn together by the danger which threatened the country, and they met with a solemn sense of the obligations which rested upon them, to give prudent and wise counsel, and to do nothing which should increase the peril of the nation. Sanford E. Church called the Convention to order, as temporary Chairman, and a permanent organization was speedily effected by the election of Judge Amasa J. Parker, of Albany, as President. Judge Parker, on taking the chair, said:

"This Convention has been called with no view to mere party objects. It looks only to the great interests of State. We meet here as conservative and representative men, who have differed among ourselves as to measures of governmental policy, ready, all of them, I trust, to sacrifice such differences upon the altar of our common country. He can be no true patriot who is not ready to yield his own prejudices, to surrender a favorite theory, and to clip even from his own party platform, where such omission may save his country from ruin otherwise inevitable.

"The people of this State demand the peaceful settlement of the questions that have led to disunion. They have a right to insist that there shall be conciliation, concession, compromise. While yet the pillars of our political temple lie scattered on the ground, let them be used to reconstruct the edifice. The popular sentiment is daily gathering strength, and will overwhelm in its progress alike, those who seek to stem it on the frail plank of party platforms and those who labor to pervert it to mere party advantage."

This address, which clearly and simply states the object of the Convention and the *animus* of its members, was greeted with cheers. The Convention was addressed by Governor Seymour, the venerable ex-Chancellor Walworth, and others, and unanimously adopted the following resolutions as the expression of its views respecting the national troubles:

"I. *Resolved*, That the crisis into which the country has been thrown by the conflict of sectional passions, and which has already resulted in the declared secession of six States, and the threatened coöperation of nearly all the other States of the South with them, the Seizure of Government property and of the Federal defences—the confronting of the disaffected States and of the Federal Government in the attitude and with the armament of Civil War—is of such a nature as, raising all patriotic citizens above the considerations of party, should impel them to the sacrifices by which alone these calamities may be averted or their further progress arrested.

"II. *Resolved*, That, in the opinion of this Convention, the worst and most ineffective argument that can be addressed by the Confederacy or its adhering members to the seceding States, is Civil War. *Civil war will not restore the Union, but will defeat forever, its reconstruction.*

"III. *Resolved*, That we can look for the restoration of the Union, and the reinvigoration of the Constitution, only to the continuance of that spirit of conciliation and concession in which they were founded; and that there is nothing in the nature of pending difficulties which does not render it proper to adjust them by compromises such as, by the practice of our Government, have been resorted to in the settlement of disputed claims, even with foreign nations. That while our Government, believing its title to the territories in the northeastern and northwestern portions of the Union, which were given up to Great Britain, was clear and unquestionable, yet for the purpose of saving the people from the evils of war, surrendered a portion of our original territory, and also a part of the Louisiana purchase, exceeding in value all the domain which the South demands, in joint occupation, having conceded thus much to a foreign nation in the interest of peace—it would be monstrous to refuse to settle claims between the people of our own land, and avert destruction from our common country by a similar compromise.

"IV. *Resolved*, That whereas it is obvious that the dissolution of this Union can only be prevented by the adoption of a policy which shall be satisfactory to the Border States, it is our duty to support them in their patriotic efforts to adjust those controversies. And inasmuch as these questions grow out of the acquisition of territories not provided for by the Constitution, and in regard to which the people of the South believe they are entitled to a joint occupancy, in person and property, under the Constitution, and by the decision of the Courts, while on the other hand, the dominant party at the North claim that they should be excluded therefrom, it is eminently fit that we should listen to the appeals of loyal men in the Border States, to dispose of this question by one of those measures of compromise in the spirit of which the Constitution was founded, and by which all territorial questions have from time to time been settled.

"V. *Resolved*, That inasmuch as the political convulsions which threaten the destruction of the country, were not contemplated at the time of the last election, and their continuance will be more disastrous to the interests of our citizens, involving the ruin of our commercial and laboring classes, and possibly carrying the desolation of civil war into the homes of our citizens, we hold that it is their right to be heard in regard to the adjustment of these difficulties, (which, in our opinion, can at present best be settled by the adoption of the Crittenden proposition or some other measure acceptable to the Border States,) and that a Committee of five be appointed, to prepare, in behalf of this Convention, a suitable memorial to the Legislature, urging them to submit the Crittenden Compromise to a vote of the electors of the State, at the earliest practicable day."

Mr. Seymour spoke at length in support of these resolutions. After showing clearly and irrefutably that the Republican party, and especially their leaders in Congress, were responsible for the existing troubles, he said:

"What spectacle do we present to-day? Already six States have withdrawn from this confederacy. Revolution has actually begun. The term 'secession' divests it of none of its terrors, nor do arguments to prove secession inconsistent with our Constitution stay its progress, or mitigate its evils. All virtue, patriotism, and intelligence, seem to have fled from our National Capitol; it has been well likened to the conflagration of an asylum for madmen—some look on with idiotic imbecility; some in sullen silence; and some scatter the firebrands which consume the fabric above them, and bring upon all a common destruction. Is there one revolting aspect in this scene which has not its parallel at the Capitol of your country? Do you not see there the senseless imbecility, the garrulous idiocy, the maddened rage, displayed with regard to petty personal passions and party purposes, while the glory, the honor, and the safety of the country are all forgotten? The same pervading fanaticism has brought evil upon all the institutions of our land. Our churches are torn asunder and desecrated to partisan purposes. The wrongs of our local legislation, the growing burdens of debt and taxation, the gradual destruction of the African in the Free States, which is marked by each recurring census, are all due to the neglect of our own duties, caused by the complete absorption of the public mind by a senseless, unreasoning fanaticism. The agitation of the question of Slavery has thus far brought greater social, moral, and legislative evils upon the people of the free States than it has upon the institutions of those against whom it has been excited. The wisdom of Franklin stamped upon the first coin issued by our government, the wise motto, 'Mind your business!' The violation of this homely proverb, which lies at the foundation of the doctrines of local rights, has, thus far, proved more hurtful to the meddlers in the affairs of others than to those against whom this pragmatic action is directed."

He then proceeded to show that the North had always received the greater share in the division of the Territory of the Union, and that the claims of the South were just and reasonable. He argued that the differences between the sections ought to be settled by a compromise—and declared that there were but two alternatives, compromise or civil war. Said he:

"We are advised by the conservative States of Virginia and Kentucky, that, if force is to be used, it must be exerted against the united South. It would be an act of folly and madness, in entering upon this contest, to underrate our opponents, and thus subject ourselves to the disgrace of defeat in an inglorious warfare. Let us also see if successful coërcion by the North is less revolutionary than successful secession by the South. Shall we prevent revolution by being foremost in overthrowing the principles of our Government, and all that makes it valuable to our people, and distinguishes it among the nations of the earth?"

Mr. Seymour then spoke of the valor and sagacity of the Southern people and leaders—showing that they were firm in their determination to maintain their rights out of the Union, if they could not do so within it; he referred to the extent and nature of the Southern coast line, demonstrating the impossibility of establishing a *perfect* blockade; and expressed his fear that war would bring ruin to the North as well as to the South, and that the two sections would have to compromise in the end. He said: "The question is simply this—'Shall we have compromise *after* war, or compromise *without* war?'"

A compromise, he declared, was not needed to pacify the States that had already withdrawn from the Union; but for the purpose of encouraging and strengthening the hands of the loyal men in the Border States, by which alone those States could be kept faithful to the Union. He said:

"Let us take care that *we* do not mistake passion and prejudice and partisan purposes for principle. The cry of 'no compromise' is false in morals; it is treason to the spirit of the Constitution; it is infidelity in religion—the cross itself is a compromise, and is pleaded by many who refuse all charity to their fellow-citizens. It is the vital principle of social existence; it unites the family circle; it sustains the church, and upholds nationalities.

"But the Republicans complain that, having won a victory, we ask them to surrender its fruits. We do not wish them to give up any political advantage. We urge measures which are demanded by the honor and the safety of our Union. Can it be that they are less concerned than we are? Will they admit that they have interests antagonistic to those of the whole commonwealth? Are they making sacrifices, when they do that which is required by the common welfare?"

This speech was bitterly denounced by those who were bent upon driving the country into war, as a "surrender to rebels and traitors;" but it is certainly no discredit to Governor Seymour that he desired to secure the preservation of the Union by means similar to those adopted by our forefathers for its creation. In no part of the speech did he advocate a surrender of the Union. On the contrary, his whole soul was given to the effort to save it; and that he preferred peace to war is a decided proof of that high statesmanship for which he has always been distinguished. He was a Union man in the best sense of the term. He sought to perpetuate a true Union of the States, and to avoid a resort to the sword, by which the North could do no more than reduce the South to the condition of a conquered province; and the result of the war has proved the soundness and wisdom of his views, for, after a lapse of nearly eight years, the Union is as imperfect to-day as it was when he uttered the words we have quoted.

As we have said, he earnestly desired peace; but the war came in spite of him. He was then called upon to decide whether he would cast his lot with the Union or the South. It cost him nothing to make this decision. His whole sympathy was with the Union, and he took his stand with that great party which gave McClellan, Dix, McClernand, Hancock, Buell, Meade, and even Grant, himself, with the thousands of gallant men who followed them, to support

of the War. He gave this support, however, for the preservation and restoration of the Union; and the fact that he could not and did not sanction the usurpations and despotism of the Administration during the four years of the War, does not detract from his merits as a consistent and faithful Union man.

At the beginning of the war he returned to Utica, and at once proceeded to render to the Government such aid as lay in his power in its efforts "to suppress the rebellion." He was Chairman of the War Committee in his County, and exerted himself actively in equipping and forwarding volunteers to Washington.

Some time after this, Mr. Seymour, at a public meeting in Utica, addressed his fellow citizens at some length upon the state of the country, and, among other things, said:

"We owe our duties to our Government. We must strengthen our armies and furnish it with means to conduct this war to a successful issue. The day has gone by for efforts to avert it. When the American people refuse to live together in the spirit of the Constitution, when they reject all adjustment of controversies they make the sword the only arbiter. Consistency demands that we who strove to avert the war should now strive to make it productive of those ends which we sought to reach by peaceful measures. All theories of Government, that of centralization, or that of State rights, requires that we should *stand by the standard of our Government and the standards of our State in the battle-field.*"

In January, 1862, he said at the meeting of the "State Military Association:"

"*We denounce the rebellion as most wicked because it wages war against the best Government the world has ever seen.* Remember there is guilt in negligence as well as in disobedience, and there is danger, too. We complain that the arms of the General Government were heretofore unequally distributed. This was owing in part to the treasonable purposes of officials, but it is due in part to our own neglect of our constitutional duties. Our enrolled militia should count more than five hundred thousand, but they do not exceed one-half of that number. Hence our quota of arms was diminished, and that of the Southern States increased. The want of these arms and a proper military organization has added immensely to the cost of this war, and to the burden of taxation. More than this, if we had respected our constitutional obligation we might, at the outset, *have placed in the field a force that would have put out this rebellion when it was first kindled.*"

Later in the year, he said:

"To-day we are putting forth our utmost efforts to reinforce our armies in the field. Without conditions or threats we are exerting our energies to strengthen the hands of the Government and to replace it in the commanding position in which it can either propose peace or conduct successful war. And this support is freely and generously accorded. We wish to see our Union saved, our laws vindicated, and peace once more restored to our land."

In a speech delivered in New York City in October, 1862, he said:

"I was gratified that while I was in a remote part of the great West it was in my power to promote the formation of a company of as bold and as sturdy men as ever rallied in defence of our country's flag. I recall with pride their array when drawn up before my lodgings; they expressed, through their commander, their good-will toward myself, and their obligations for such assistance as I had been able to give them."

CHAPTER III.

The War divides the people of the North into two great Parties—Political affairs in New York—Meeting of the Democratic Convention—Mr. Seymour Nominated for Governor—Platform of the New York Democracy—The Republicans Nominate General Wadsworth—Mr. Seymour is Elected—His Inaugural Address—His Message to the Legislature—Review of the Condition of the Country—He Points out the Causes of the War—Shows the Dangers which Threaten the Country—Denunciation of the Excesses of the Republicans—It is not too Late to Save the Union—Errors of the Administration—Danger to be Apprehended from a Consolidated Government—Outrages Practiced upon the People—Martial Law—The Union is Indissoluble—How it may be Saved—Eloquent Peroration—Trouble in the Legislature—A dignified Message—Governor Seymour's Speech in New York, July 4th, 1863—Review of the State of the Country—Eloquent Appeal for Mercy and Conciliation—Comments upon the Address—Mr. Seymour's Wisdom and Far-sightedness—His Candor and Intrepidity the Best Proofs of his Patriotism.

One of the effects of the war was to destroy the small parties which had existed previous to it, and to divide the people of the Union into two great parties—the Democratic and Republican. In New York the former members of the "American" party, determined to support the Democratic nominee in the contest for Governor, in the fall of 1862. They held a Convention at Troy, nominated Horatio Seymour for Governor, and adjourned. This was a high compliment, as it came from the most determined of Mr. Seymour's old political foes. A few days later the Regular Democratic Convention met at Albany, and nominated Mr. Seymour as their candidate.

It has been so often charged that Mr. Seymour was the candidate of those who wished the destruction of the Union, that we cannot do better than give the platform upon which the Democratic party went into the contest, and upon which Mr. Seymour was elected by the people of New York. It is as follows:

"*Resolved*, That the Democracy of New York, waiving the expression of their views upon questions not rendered imperative by the imperilled condition of their country, hereby declare—

"*First.* That they will continue to render the Government their sincere and united support in the use of all legitimate means to suppress the Rebellion, and restore the Union as it was and maintain the Constitution as it is—believing that that sacred instrument, founded in wisdom by our fathers, clothes the constituted authorities with full power to accomplish such purpose.

"*Second.* That by the following resolution, unanimously passed by Congress in July 1861, the Government was pledged to the policy inculcated therein, and which cannot be parted from without violation of pubic faith, viz:

"'*Resolved*, That the present deplorable Civil War has been forced upon the country by the disunionists of the Southern States, now in arms against the Constitutional Government, and in arms around the Capital; that in this national emergency, Congress, banishing all feeling of mere passion or resentment, will recollect only its duty to the whole country; that this war is not waged on their part, in any spirit of oppression, or for any purpose of conquest or subjugation, or purpose of overthrowing or interfering with the rights or established institutions of those States, but to defend and maintain the supremacy of the Constitution and to preserve the Union, with all the dignity, equality, and rights of the several States unimpaired; and that as soon as these objects are accomplished the war ought to cease.'

"*Third.* That we, having confidence in the loyalty of the citizens of New York, reiterate the sentiments heretofore expressed by the Democratic party—that the illegal and unconstitutional arrests and imprisonments of citizens of this State are without the justification of necessity, and we denounce such arrests as a usurpation and a crime, and the freedom of the press, equally protected by the Constitution, ought to be maintained.

"*Fourth.* That we are willing to act in the coming election with any class of loyal citizens who agree with us in the principles herein expressed; that we hereby invite the co-operation of all citizens in giving the most emphatic expression to these principles by supporting the ticket nominated by the Convention."

Mr. Seymour's opponent in this contest was General James Wadsworth, a gentleman of fine abilities and unblemished personal character. He was the administration Candidate, and all the influence of the Federal Government was exerted in his behalf. The election took place on the 4th of November, 1862, and resulted as follows:

For Mr. Seymour . .	306,649	Votes.
For Gen. Wadsworth . .	295,897	"
Seymour's majority over Wadsworth,	10,752	"

Governor Seymour was inaugurated at Albany on the 1st of January 1863. His Inaugural address was very brief. After complimenting the retiring Governor (Mr. Morgan) upon the manner in which he had discharged the duties of his position, he said:

"Fellow Citizens: In your presence I have solemnly sworn to support the Constitution of the United States, with all its grants, restrictions, and guarantees, and I shall support it.

"I have also sworn to support another constitution—the Constitution of the State of New York—with all its powers and rights. I shall uphold it.

"I have sworn faithfully to perform the duties of the office of Governor of this State, and with your aid they shall be faithfully performed. These Constitutions and laws are meant for the guidance of official conduct and for your protection and welfare.

"The first law I find recorded for my observance is that which declares 'it shall be the duty of the Governor to maintain and defend the sovereignty and jurisdiction of this State,' and the most marked injunction of the Constitution to the Executive is, that he 'shall take care that the laws are faithfully executed.'

"These Constitutions do not conflict; the line of separation between the responsibilities and obligations which each imposes is well defined. They do not embarrass us in the performance of our duties as citizens or officials."

The Governor then briefly alluded to the quiet transfer of political power from one party to another as a proof of the strength of our institutions, expressed the hope that in two years more the nation would be reunited, peaceful, and glorious, returned his thanks to the assemblage, and withdrew.

The Governor's message was delivered on the 6th. We have room for only a brief summary of this most excellent document.

He said that the war had taken more than 200,000 of the men of the State from the workshop into the field. Slavery was not the cause of the war, but had been made the subject of it. We must look for the cause of the war in the prevailing disregard of the laws and Constitution, and above all, in local prejudices grown up in the two extremes of the country, where remote positions and interests made them less informed regarding the condition and character of the white people than in the Central and Western States. He declared that the rights of the States must be respected, and insisted that the attempts which were being made to stifle public opinion should cease. The people, he said, demanded free discussion, and were anxious to know their true condition. His language was plain on this point. He said:

"Not only is our national life at stake, but every personal, every family, and every sacred duty and interest are involved.

"The truths of our financial and military situation must not be kept back; there must be no attempt to put down the free expression of public opinion.

"Affrighted at the ruin they have wrought, the authors of our calamities in the North and South insist that this war was caused by an unavoidable contest about slavery. This has been the subject, not the cause of the controversy. We are to look for the causes of the war in the prevailing disregard of the obligations of the law and the Constitution, in the disrespect for constituted authorities, and, above all, in the local prejudices which have grown up in the two portions of the Atlantic States—the two extremes of our country.

"There is no honest statement of our difficulties which does not teach that our people must reform themselves, as well as the conduct of the Government and the policy of our rulers. It is not too late to save our country, if we will enter upon the duty in the right spirit and in the right way.

"While it is the right of our Government to declare upon measures and policy, it is our duty to obey and give a ready support to their decisions. This is a vital maxim of liberty.

"This war should have been averted, but its floodgates were opened, and the Administration could not grasp its dimensions nor control its sweep. The Government was borne away with the current, and struggled as best it could with the resistless tide. Few seemed able to comprehend the military or financial problem.

"Hence, we are not to sit in harsh judgment upon the errors in their conduct or their policy; but, while we are to concede all these excuses for mistakes, we are not to accept errors nor sanction violations of principle.

"The same causes which estimate their faults in judgment must make us the more vigilant to guard against their usurpations."

He declared that a consolidated Government in this vast country would destroy the essential rights and privileges of the people. The sovereignty of the States can not be given up. He urged economy and integrity in the administration of affairs, as these are vital in periods of war; and said that meddling and intrigues had thwarted and paralyzed the vigor of the troops and the skill of their generals within the influence of the national capital, while those armies which operated at a distance from Washington gained victories. He denounced the outrages of the Government upon the people in making arbitrary arrests, suppressing the public journals, and establishing a system of espionage. Said he:

"The suppression of journals and the imprisonment of persons are glaringly partisan. Conscious of these gross abuses, an attempt has been made to shield the violators of law, and suppress inquiry into their routines and conduct. This attempt will fail; unconstitutional acts will not be shielded by constitutional law. I shall not inquire what rights States in rebellion have forfeited, but I deny that rebellion can destroy a single right of the citizens of a loyal State. I denounce the doctrine that civil war in the South takes away from the loyal North the benefits of one principle of civil liberty. It is a high crime to abduct citizens of this State.

"It is made my duty by the Constitution to see that the laws are enforced, and I shall investigate every alleged violation of our statutes, and see that the offenders are brought to justice. Sheriffs and district attorneys are admonished that it is their duty to take care that no persons within their respective counties are imprisoned or carried by force beyond their limits without due process of legal authority."

He denounced the establishment of *martial law* in the loyal States as opposed to the Constitution and the genius of the Government. The President, he said, holds his office, *not by the will of the majority, but by the Constitution which placed him there by a vote of* 1,800,000 *against* 2,800,000. He solemnly asserted that if the Constitution was powerless to restrain the Executive within its prescribed limits, it made him powerless to keep the States in the Union. Those who held that there was no sanctity in the Constitution, must of necessity admit that there was no guilt in rebellion.

He declared the President's emancipation proclamation a violation of the Constitution, impolitic, and unjust, and that it would have the effect of changing the object for which the war was being waged, arguing with far-seeing wisdom, that if the South must be held under military subjugation and the negroes managed by the Government, the Government must be converted into a military despotism.

He argued that the Union is indissoluble, and that the factions, both Northern and Southern, must be put down. So closely, he said, are the upper and lower valleys of the Mississippi bound together, that when cotton was burned in Louisiana, corn was used for fuel in Illinois. The war was ruining the Southern consumer and bankrupting the Northern producer.

The Union, he declared, would be restored by the Central and Western States, who are exempt from the violent passions which influence the extremes. Those of the Central Slave States which at first rejected the ordinance of secession, and which were driven off from the Union by the contemptuous and irritating policy of the Government, must be brought back. The restoration of the whole Union would only be the work of time, with such exertion as could be put forth without needlessly sacrificing the life and treasure of the North in a bloody and calamitous contest. The exercise of armed power must be accompanied by a firm and conciliatory policy, so as to restore the Union with the least possible injury to both sections.

Near the close of the message, he said:

"At this moment the fortunes of our country are influenced by the results of battles. Our armies in the field must be supported; all the constitutional demands of our General Government must be promptly responded to. Under no circumstances can a division of the Union be conceded. We will put forth every exertion of power; we will use every policy of conciliation; we will hold out every inducement to the people of the South to return to their allegiance consistent with honor; we will guarantee them every right and every consideration demanded by the Constitution alone, and by that fraternal regard which must prevail in a common country; but we can never voluntarily consent to the breaking up of the Union of these States, or the destruction of the Constitution."

The organization of the Assembly was delayed for some time by difficulties in electing a Speaker. There were efforts made by outsiders to interrupt the proceedings of that body, and the Republicans, with their usual haste and unfairness, endeavored to lay the odium of the outrage upon the Governor. The Senate adopted a resolution calling on him to perform his duty in the premises, and repress any popular disturbance. In reply to this demand, he submitted to the Senate the following message:

"Gentlemen of the Senate: I have received from your honorable body the following preamble and resolutions:

"Whereas, It has come to the knowledge of Senators that the election of a Speaker to the Assembly is delayed by the interference and threats of a mob, admitted into the lobbies of the Assembly Chamber, and which has endeavored to control the Legislative action of the Assembly by threats and by violence;

"Resolved, That it is the solemn and imperative duty of the Executive authority of this State, promptly and without hesitation, to see to it that the laws of the State be faithfully executed, and that this first attempt to coerce Legislative action by violence, and brute force and threats thereof, be promptly thwarted and punished.

"Resolved, That a committee of three be appointed by the Chair, whose duty it shall be to confer with his Excellency the Governor, and urge upon him the urgent necessity and propriety of prompt and energetic action for the protection of the Assembly from mob violence, and that the authors, aiders and abettors thereof be speedily brought to condign punishment.

"These were communicated to me by a Committee of the Senate.

"To avoid the mistaken and injurious impressions they are calculated to make, it is proper I should state that when a complaint was made on Friday last, by a member of the Assembly, that the proceedings of that body were disturbed by the disorderly conduct of persons in the lobbies and galleries, I informed him that any protection which might be called for by any member of the Assembly would be immediately afforded.

"The difficulties of the Assembly grow out of the differences of opinion among its members with respect to its organization.

"There is an obvious impropriety in any interference by one department of the Government with the proceedings of any co-ordinate branch of that Government, unless a request is made by the parties interested.

"Before the passage of the resolutions of the Senate, every member of the Assembly who spoke to me upon the subject was told that he had a right to full protection, but to avoid even apparent interference with the organization of the Assembly, which, by the Constitution, is expressly left to the exclusive control

4

of that body, my action must be based upon a request for protection from those directly concerned.

"Immediately upon being advised of the alleged disorders, I consulted with the Mayor of the city, who made adequate arrangements to prevent any outside interference. I felt it due to the Senate, as a matter of courtesy, to explain to them, that I can only act upon a request coming from members of that branch of the Legislature which is affected by any disorderly proceedings.

HORATIO SEYMOUR."

On the 4th of July, 1863, Governor Seymour addressed a large and brilliant audience in the Academy of Music, in the City of New York. We make the following extracts from this able address:

"When I accepted the invitation to speak, with others, at this meeting, we were promised the downfall of Vicksburg, the opening of the Mississippi, the probable capture of the Confederate Capital, and the exhaustion of the Rebellion. By common consent all parties had fixed upon this day, when the results of the campaign should be known, to mark out that line of policy which they felt that our country should pursue. But, in the moment of expected victory, there came the midnight cry for help from Pennsylvania to save its despoiled fields from the invading foe; and, almost within sight of this great commercial metropolis, the ships of your merchants were burned to the water's edge."

* * * * * *

"A few years ago, we stood before this community to warn them of the dangers of sectional strife; but our fears were laughed at. At a later day, when the clouds of war overhung our country, we implored those in authority to compromise that difficulty; for we had been told by that great orator and statesman, Burke, that there never yet was a revolution that might not have been prevented by a compromise opportunely and graciously made. [Great applause.] Our prayers were unheeded. Again, when the contest was opened, we invoked those who had the conduct of affairs not to underrate the powers of the adversary—not to underrate the courage, and resources, and endurance of our own sister States. This warning was treated as sympathy with treason. You have the results of these unheeded warnings and unheeded prayers; they have stained our soil with blood; they have carried mourning into thousands of homes; and to-day they have brought our country to the very verge of destruction. Once more, I come before you, to offer again an earnest prayer, and beg you to listen to a warning. Our country is not only at this time torn by one of the bloodiest wars that has ever ravaged the face of the earth, but, if we turn our faces to our own loyal States, how is it there? You find the community divided into political parties, strongly arrayed, and using with regard to each other terms of reproach and defiance. It is said by those who support more particularly the Administration, that we, who differ honestly, patriotically, sincerely, from them with regard to the line of duty, are men of treasonable purposes and enemies to our country. ['Hear, hear.'] On the other hand, the Democratic organization look upon this Administration as hostile to their rights and liberties; they look upon their opponents as men who would do them wrong in regard to their most sacred franchises. I need not call your attention to the tone of the press, or to the tone of public feeling, to show you how, at this moment, parties are thus exasperated, and stand in defiant attitudes to each other. A few years ago, we were told that sectional strife, waged in words like these, would do no harm to our country; but you have seen the sad and bloody results. Let us be admonished now in time, and take care that this irritation, this feeling which is growing up in our midst, shall not also ripen into civil troubles that shall carry the evils of war into our own homes.

"Upon one point, all are agreed, and that is this: Until we have a united North, we can have no successful war. Until we have a united, harmonious North, we can have no beneficent peace. How shall we gain harmony? How shall the unity of all be obtained? Is it to be coerced? I appeal to you, my Republican friends, when you say to us that the nation's life and existence hang upon harmony and concord here, if you yourselves, in your serious moments, believe that this is to be produced by seizing our persons, by infringing upon our rights, by insulting our homes, and by depriving us of those cherished principles for which our fathers fought, and to which we have always sworn allegiance." [Great applause.]

* * * * * *

"We only ask that you shall give to us that which you claim for yourselves, and that which every freeman, and every man who respects himself, will have, freedom of speech, the right to exercise all the franchises conferred by the Constitution upon American citizens. [Great applause.] Can you safely deny us these? Will you not trample upon your own rights if you refuse to listen? Do you not create revolution when you say that our persons may be rightfully seized, our property confiscated, our homes entered? Are you not exposing yourselves, your own interests, to as great a peril as that with which you threaten us? Remember this, that the bloody, and treasonable, and revolutionary doctrine of public necessity can be proclaimed by a mob as well as by a government." [Applause.] * * * * *

"To-day, the great masses of conservatives who still battle for time-honored principles of government, amid denunciation, contumely, and abuse, are the only barriers that stand between this Government and its own destruction. If we should acquiesce in the doctrine that, in times of war, Constitutions are suspended, and laws have lost their force, then we should accept a doctrine that the very right by which this Government administers its power has lost its virtue, and we would be brought down to the level of rebellion itself, having an existence only by virtue of material power. When men accept despotism, they may have a choice as to who the despot shall be. The struggle then will not be, Shall we have constitutional liberty? But, having accepted the doctrine that the Constitution has lost its force, every instinct of personal ambition, every instinct of personal security, will lead men to put themselves under the protection of that power which they suppose most competent to guard their persons."

* * * * * *

"We stand to-day amid new-made graves, in a land filled with mourning; upon a soil saturated with the blood of the fiercest conflict of which history gives us an account. We can, if we will, avert all these calamities, and evoke a blessing. If we will do what? Hold that Constitution, and liberties, and laws are suspended?—shrink back from the assertion of right? Will that restore them? Or shall we do as our fathers did, under circumstances of like trial, when they combated against the powers of a crown? They did not say that liberty was suspended; that men might be deprived of the right of trial by jury; that they might be torn from their homes by midnight intruders? [Tremendous and continued applause.] If you would save your country, and your liberties, begin right; begin at the hearth-stones, which are ever meant to be the foundations of American institutions; begin in your family circle; declare that your privileges shall be held sacred; and, having once proclaimed your own rights, take care that you do not invade those of your neighbor."

There are some persons who profess to see in these calm and thoughtful words the evidence that their author, at the time he spoke, was a sympathizer with the people of the South in their efforts against the Union. We are not of that number. The whole address of Mr. Seymour is marked by a deep, calm insight into the condition of the affairs of the country. He was fully aware of all that had been accomplished by the army, and was prompt to accord it his hearty praise for its services; but he held that in spite of the brilliant achievements of the army, the Administration was incompetent to profit by them. Instead of taking advantage of the Federal successes to endeavor to win back the Southern States by wise measures of conciliation, the Government expended its energy in hampering and perplexing the military commanders, and suffered every opportunity for offering terms of peace to the South to pass by unimproved. It was, therefore, against the incompetency and lack of statesmanship evinced by the Administration, that his remarks were directed, and not against the army. He held that the troops in the field had accomplished enough to make an honorable peace sure if the Government could be induced to follow up their successes by measures which would meet with a hearty response from the people of the whole country. He was not willing that the successes of the army should be allowed to go for nothing, and his strictures were directed at those who seemed to desire nothing but a continuance of the war.

In the canvass of 1864, the real issue between parties was simply this: The Republicans held that we had only to deal with a military problem; they averred that when the armies of the South were crushed out by force, and that when the life of the rebellion was stamped out by our soldiers, our difficulties would be ended, and that our Union would be restored. On the other hand, the Democratic party urged that statesmanship, as well as force, was needed to save our country from disorder, and from the fearful pressure of taxation which must grow out of the Republican policy. In a speech made by Mr. Seymour in Philadelphia, he pointed out the fact that our armies had won great and signal victories; that if the devotion of our soldiers in the field had been seconded by wisdom in the cabinet, the war would have been ended before the close of 1863; the North would have been saved from the burthen of debt and the financial troubles which now hinder its prosperity and perplex the minds of its business men. At the same time he showed the constant effort made by the Republican leaders to throw the odium of their own failures upon our armies. By declaring that it was a military problem alone, they turned the public mind away from their own imbecility and incapacity. Mr. Seymour then predicted that when every Southern army was driven from the field, and when not a man was left to raise an armed hand in resistance to the Government, it would then be found that our Union was not restored. On the other hand, all of the difficulties growing out of the malice and of the blunders of those in power, would be found to be more dangerous and difficult than the contest with armed rebellion. It would then be seen that the Republican party was not only unable to conduct public affairs in a time of war, but would prove still more incapable of governing the country with wisdom in a period of peace. It will be a problem for the future historian to solve, which faction brought the gravest evils upon the American people — those who, during four years, waged war against its Government, or that party which, during the succeeding four years, mismanaged and entangled its financial and political condition. Those who will read the speeches made by Mr. Seymour during the canvass of 1864, will find that the present condition of public affairs was clearly predicted by him. He was not thus enabled to forecast the future because he had prophetic views, but because all reason and the teachings of all history plainly foreshadowed that a policy springing from mingled corruption, malice and incapacity, could only produce, as their results, disorder, violence, and an unsettled condition of public and private affairs.

Mr. Seymour was too great a man, too wise a statesman, to confound loyalty to his country and its Constitution with fidelity to an Administration. To the former he was devoted with his whole soul, and he failed not to render to it every assistance in his power. Such aid as he could give the Government in the conscientious discharge of his duty, was promptly and faithfully given. That he did not sustain the Administration in all its acts, is to his credit and not to his discredit. He was not willing to support a war for mere conquest, and he did not desire the subjugation of the South at the expense of the freedom of the whole country. He believed that the rights secured to every citizen by the Constitution of the United States are inalienable, and he was in favor of resisting the outrages of the Government upon them. He did not believe that it was necessary to destroy freedom of speech and of the press in the North, to fill the forts and prisons of every loyal State with citizens whose only crime was a dissent from the views of the Republican party; to violate the sanctity of the telegraph and post-office, and to outrage even the most sacred relations of private life—all of which had been done, and was being done, in the loyal States by the orders of President Lincoln, and his officials. His judgment taught him that the evil seed which the Government was sowing would one day yield their fruit—that no Government can systematically violate its own laws without ultimately being destroyed; and his common sense convinced him that the Republican party, whether they desired such a state of affairs or not, were working surely and powerfully for the destruction of our free institutions and the establishment of a terrible despotism in their place; and he would have been no true patriot who could have refrained from warning his countrymen of these things. The results of the war—the complete and utter subjugation of the South, the establishment of a military despotism in that section, the effort to degrade the intelligence and worth of those States beneath their barbarism and ignorance, the vast and useless accumulation of debt in the sham efforts at reconstruction, and the unsettled and threatening condition of the loyal States—all amply vindicated the wisdom of Mr. Seymour; and the fact that he tried to avert such a state of affairs is the best guarantee of his patriotism that can be given.

CHAPTER IV.

Invasion of Pennsylvania by General Lee—Alarm in the North—Excitement in New York—The Government calls for Troops from the Border States—The President asks New York for aid—Prompt Reply of Governor Seymour—Orders of the State Authorities—Patriotic Response of the Troops—Aid sent to the Border—Statement of Troops sent by New York—Energy of Governor Seymour—Republican Testimony on this point—Messages from the Government—The President and Secretary of War thank Governor Seymour for the Prompt Assistance given by him—Testimony of Mr. Lincoln—The Official Correspondence between the State and Federal Authorities—Incontestible Proofs—Statement of the "Philadelphia Age"—Mr. Seymour triumphantly Vindicated by his own Acts from the Calumnies of his Enemies.

On the 15th of June, 1863, the Confederate army under General Lee, which had manœuvred General Hooker's army from its position on the Rappahannock and seized the upper fords of the Potomac, entered the State of Maryland, and for the second time invaded the loyal States. Marching leisurely through Maryland, Lee moved into Pennsylvania, manœuvring in such a manner as to make it uncertain whether he designed attacking Washington, Baltimore, or Philadelphia. The news of his movements filled the entire Border with alarm, and the studied reticence which the Government observed respecting the movements of the two opposing armies only tended to increase the excitement. The Government was as much excited as the people, and feeling its own incompetency to meet the crisis, refrained from trammelling General Meade, the able commander of the Army of the Potomac, with instructions. It realized one thing, however, that there was an urgent necessity for more men; and accordingly on the 15th of June, the President issued his proclamation, calling upon the States of Maryland, Pennsylvania, Ohio, and West Virginia, to furnish one hundred thousand militia, to serve for a period of six months, unless sooner discharged.

The excitement which prevailed along the Border, spread quickly to the city of New York, and this feeling was at once aroused to a positive enthusiasm when it became known that New York had been called upon to assist Pennsylvania. On the day on which the proclamation just referred to was issued, the President telegraphed to Governor Seymour, calling for twenty thousand militia, to aid in resisting the advance of the enemy. The Governor at once sent a prompt response, promising all the aid in his power, and on the same day the following orders were issued at his command:

"HEADQUARTERS FIRST BRIGADE N. Y. S. N G.
"NEW YORK, *June 15th*, 1863.

"By order of the Commander-in-Chief of the State of New York, the several regiments of this brigade will hold themselves in readiness to depart for Philadelphia at once, on short notice. By order of

"Brigadier-General C. B. SPICER.

"R. H. HOADLEY, Brigade Major and Inspector.

"WILLIAM D. DIMOCK, Aide-de-Camp."

"*Order No.* 3.

"HEADQUARTERS, 543 BROADWAY,
"NEW YORK, *June* 15*th*, 1863.

"Commandants of regiments of the Third Brigade N. Y. N. G., are hereby directed to report to General Wm. Hall, at his quarters, at six o'clock on Tuesday morning, by order of the Commander-in-Chief, Horatio Seymour, to be ready to go to Philadelphia at once, on short service.

"The brigade drill for the 17th inst. is hereby countermanded. By order, General WM. HALL.

"J. K. SMITH, Quartermaster."

Copies of these orders were at once telegraphed to Washington, where the prompt action of Governor Seymour was hailed with satisfaction and delight. The Secretary of War, at the direction of the President, telegraphed the Governor as follows:

"WASHINGTON, *June* 15*th*, 1863.

"GOVERNOR SEYMOUR: The President directs me to return his thanks, with those of the Department, for your prompt response. A strong movement of your city regiments to Philadelphia would be a very encouraging movement, and do great good in giving strength to that State.

"The call had to be for six months unless sooner discharged in order to comply with the law. It is not likely that more than thirty days' service—perhaps not so long—would be required. Can you forward your city regiments speedily? Please reply early.

"EDWIN M. STANTON, Secretary of War."

As soon as the orders were issued for the assembling of the militia, the men composing the various regiments began to assemble at their respective places of rendezvous in response to the call upon them. The utmost enthusiasm prevailed, and the preparations were pushed forward as rapidly as possible. The next day the following order was issued:

"HEADQUARTERS FIRST DIVISION N. Y. S. M.,
"NEW YORK, *June 16th*, 1863.

"The regiments of this division are directed to proceed forthwith to Harrisburg, in Pennsylvania, to assist in repelling the invasion of the State.

"The United States Quartermaster and Commissary will furnish transportation and subsistence upon the requisition of regimental quartermasters, countersigned by the colonels.

"The term of service will not exceed thirty days.

"Commandants of brigades and regiments will report to the Major-General the numbers ready for transportation, and will receive direction as to the route and time of embarkation.

"Each man will provide himself with two days' cooked provisions.

"By order of Major-Gen. CHARLES W. SANFORD.

"J. H. WILCOX, Division Inspector."

"This division consisted of four brigades. The first brigade, under Gen. C. B. Spicer, was composed of the 1st, 2d, 3d, 71st, and 73d regiments. The second brigade, under Gen. Chas. Yates, was composed of the 4th, 5th, 6th, and 12th regiments. The third brigade, under Gen. Hall, was composed of the 7th, 8th, 37th, and 55th regiments. The fourth brigade under Gen. Ewen, was composed of the 11th, 22d, and 69th regiments.

"On that day there went forward the 7th regiment, 650 men. On the 18th, the 8th, 371 men; 11th, 762 men: 23d, 626 men, and 71st, 737 men. On the 19th, the 5th, 828 men; 12th, 684 men; 22d, 568 men; 37th, 693 men; 65th, 555 men, and 74th, 504 men. On the 20th, the 4th, 560 men; 13th, 496 men; 28th, 484 men; 56th, 476 men. On the 22d, the 6th, 656 men; 52d, 351 men; 69th, 600 men. On the 23d, the 67th, 400 men. On the 24th, the 55th, 350 men; 68th, 400 men. On the 26th, the 47th, 400 men. On the 27th, the 21st, 600 men. On July 3d, the 17th, 400 men; 18th, 400 men; 84th, 480 men. The total number sent between the 15th of June and the 3d of July was 13,971 men. During the same time scattered detachments of volunteers in the State to the number of 1,827 men were organized and equipped and ordered to Harrisburg." *

Governor Seymour entered energetically upon the task of forwarding these troops. Feeling that his presence in New York would greatly encourage the men and assist the process of volunteering, he repaired to that city on the 17th of June, and gave his personal supervision to the matter.

A letter from New York, dated June 17th, and published in the *Philadelphia Inquirer*, a Republi-

* The Annual Cyclopædia, 1863, p. 95.

can journal thus describes the state of affairs in the former city at this time:

"There is a much more confident feeling visible on all hands to-day, in regard to the rebel invasion, owing partly to the reassuring character of the *Inquirer's* dispatches from the border, but mainly to the efficient measures that have been taken to beat back the rebels if their advance is persisted in. The course pursued by the several loyal Governors in reference to the crisis seems to be indicative of a unity of purpose, which is, under all circumstances, the best guarantee of efficient action. Gov. Parker, of New Jersey, and Gov. Seymour, have done well. They have shown the rebel leaders that when it comes to a Northern invasion, Democrats and Republicans occupy one and the same platform, and know no difference of opinion. Recent events raising some doubts in many minds, on that point, after all it may be the advance of the enemy to Chambersburg even may prove an advantage to us, if it has served to remove those doubts.

"The Seventh Regiment left for Harrisburg this morning, and will probably reach their destination before this is in type. On passing down Broadway they were loudly cheered.

"About three hundred of the Twenty-first New Jersey Regiment, who came home on furlough from Trenton, on Monday, received orders this afternoon to report at headquarters. They left for their destination at 3 o'clock.

"The Brooklyn regiments are rapidly recruiting. One of them is nearly full, and expects to leave to-morrow. Others, if need be, will immediately follow.

"Governor Seymour and General Sprague will be in New York to-night. A conference will be held with Major-General Sandford and the brigade Generals at the St. Nicholas Hotel at ten o'clock this evening. The Governor says, if need be, he will stay here to superintend the forwarding of the troops himself. He says when a sister State is in danger red tape must not be permitted to stand in the way.

"Brigadier-Generals Hall and Yates, of the 2d and 3d Brigades of the State Militia, have been ordered to report at Harrisburg with their commands. They will leave to-morrow. Being unable to obtain uniforms and clothing, or arms, for some of the regiments, from the United States authorities, Gov. Seymour has directed that they be drawn from the State, and requisitions are now being filled so as to enable all the regiments in this city to leave for Harrisburg to-morrow. The 8th regiment will leave this evening. Gov. Seymour arrived in this city this evening, to confer with and assist the military in a prompt movement to aid Pennsylvania.

"The military regiments throughout the State are being rapidly organized. There will be no necessity of a draft to fill them."

The President, grateful for the prompt and effective aid rendered by the Governor of New York, and for the cordial and hearty manner in which that aid was given, sent him the following despatch through the Secretary of War:

"WAR DEPARTMENT, WASHINGTON CITY,
"*June* 19*th*, 1863.

"*To Adjutant-General Sprague:*

"The President directs me to return his thanks to His Excellency Gov. Seymour, and his staff, for their energetic and prompt action. Whether any futher force is likely to be required will be communicated to you to-morrow, by which time it is expected the movements of the enemy will be more fully developed.

("Signed) "EDWIN M. STANTON,
"Secretary of War."

Again, on the 27th, the following despatch was sent to the Governor of the State by the Secretary of War:

"WAR DEPARTMENT, WASHINGTON CITY,
June 27th, 1863.

"DEAR SIR: I cannot forbear expressing to you the deep obligation I feel for the prompt and cordial support you have given the Government in the present emergency. The energy and patriotism you have exhibited I may be permitted personally and officially to acknowledge, without arrogating any personal claims on my part, to such service, or any service whatever.

"I shall be happy always to be esteemed your friend.*

"EDWIN M. STANTON.

"His Excellency HORATIO SEYMOUR."

*The following are the official telegrams relating to the action of Governor Seymour in this matter, in addition to those already given:

Not content with sending these messages, a few days before the battle of Gettysburg, when the officer of Governor Seymour's staff, who had been charged

WASHINGTON, *June 15th*, 1863.

To His Excellency GOVERNOR SEYMOUR:

The movements of the Rebel forces in Virginia are now sufficiently developed, to show that General Lee, with his whole army, is moving forward to invade the States of Maryland and Pennsylvania, and other States.

The President to repel this invasion, promptly, has called upon Ohio, Pennsylvania, Maryland, and West Virginia for one hundred thousand (100,000) militia, for six (6) months, unless sooner discharged. It is important to have the largest possible force in the least time, and if other States would furnish militia for a short time, to be ordered on the draft, it would greatly advance the object. Will you please inform me, immediately, if, in answer to a special call of the President, you can raise and forward say twenty thousand (20,000) militia, as volunteers without bounty, to be credited on the draft of your State, or what number you can probably raise? E. M. STANTON,

Secretary of War.

ALBANY, *June 15th* 1863.

Hon. E. M. STANTON, *Secretary of War, Washington:*

I will spare no efforts to send you troops at once. I have sent orders to the militia officers of the State. HORATIO SEYMOUR.

ALBANY, *June 15th*, 1863.

Hon. E. M. STANTON, *Secretary of War, Washington:*

I will order the New York and Brooklyn troops to Philadelphia at once. Where can they get arms if they are needed?

HORATIO SEYMOUR.

[Here follows Mr. Stanton's telegram of June 15th to the Governor, given above, thanking him for his promptness.]

ALBANY, *June 15th*, 1863.

Hon. E. M. STANTON, *Secretary of War, Washington:*

We have about two thousand enlisted volunteers in this State. I will have them consolidated into companies and regiments, and sent on at once. You must provide them with arms. HORATIO SEYMOUR.

with superintending the forwarding of the New York troops to Harrisburg, called to pay his respects to the President, before leaving Washington, Mr. Lincoln,

ALBANY, *June* 15*th*, 1863.

Hon. E. M. STANTON, *Secretary of War, Washington:*

Four returned volunteer regiments can be put in the field at once, for three months' service. Can arms and accoutrements be supplied in New York?

J. T. SPRAGUE,
Adjutant-General.

WASHINGTON, *June* 16*th*, 1863.

To Adjutant-General SPRAGUE:

Upon your requisition, any troops you may send to Pennsylvania will be armed and equipped in New York, with new arms. Orders have been given to the Bureau of Ordnance.

EDWIN M. STANTON.

WASHINGTON, *June* 16*th*, 1863.

To Adjutant-General SPRAGUE:

The Quartermaster-General has made provision for the clothing and equipment of the troops that may go to Pennsylvania. The issues to be made at Harrisburg. You will make requisition for subsistence and transportation as heretofore, for troops forwarded from your State.

EDWIN M. STANTON.

WASHINGTON, *June* 16*th*, 1863.

To Act. Asst. Adjutant-General STONEHOUSE:

The Quartermaster-General has been directed to clothe the volunteers from your State, upon their reaching their destination, and provision has been made for that purpose.

EDWIN M. STANTON,
Secretary of War.

ALBANY, *June* 16*th*, 1863.

GOVERNOR CURTIN, *Harrisburg:*

I am pushing forward troops as fast as possible, regiments will leave New York to-night. All will be ordered to report to General Couch.

HORATIO SEYMOUR.

ALBANY, *June* 16*th*, 1863.

Hon. E. M. STANTON, *Secretary of War, Washington, D. C.*

Officers of old organizations here will take the field with their men,

taking him by both hands, said to him earnestly, "I wish you to understand that you cannot possibly use words too warm to convey to Governor Seymour my

and will march to-morrow if they can be paid irrespective of ordnance accounts. The Government would still have a hold upon them to refund for losses.

JOHN T. SPRAGUE,
Adjutant-General.

ALBANY, *June 16th*, 1863.

Hon. E. M. STANTON, *Secretary of War, Washington:*

By request of Governor Seymour, who has called me here, I write to say that the New York city regiments can go with full ranks for any time not over three months—say from eight to ten thousand men. The shorter the period the larger will be the force. For what time will they be required? Please answer immediately.

C. W. SANDFORD,
Major-General.

WASHINGTON, *June 16th*, 1863.

To Major-General SANDFORD:

The Government will be glad to have your city regiments hasten to Pennsylvania for any time of service, it is not possible to say how long they might be useful, but it is not expected that they would be detained more than three (3) months, possibly not longer than twenty (20) or thirty (30) days.

They would be accepted for three (3) months, and discharged as soon as the present exigency is over. If aided at the present by your troops the people of that State might soon be able to raise a sufficient force to relieve your city regiments.

EDWIN M. STANTON,
Secretary of War.

ALBANY, *June 18th*, 1863.

To Hon. E. M. STANTON, *Secretary of War, Washington, D. C.*

About twelve thousand (12,000) men are now on the move for Harrisburg, in good spirits and well equipped.

The Governor says: "Shall troops continue to be forwarded?" Please answer.

Nothing from Washington since first telegrams.

JOHN T. SPRAGUE, *Adjutant-General.*

thankfulness for his prompt and efficient help given to the Government in this crisis."

Mr. Lincoln afterwards said, in grateful acknow-

ALBANY, *June 18th*, 1863.

To Governor CURTIN, *Harrisburg, Pa:*

About twelve thousand men are now moving and are under orders for Harrisburg, in good spirits and well equipped.

Governor Seymour desires to know if he shall continue to send men. He is ignorant of your real condition. JOHN T. SPRAGUE,
Adjutant-General.

WASHINGTON, *June 19th*, 1863.

To Adjutant-General SPRAGUE:

The President directs me to return his thanks to his Excellency Governor Seymour and staff for their energetic and prompt action. Whether any further force is likely to be required will be communicated to you to-morrow, by which time it is expected the movements of the enemy will be more fully developed. EDWIN M. STANTON,
Secretary of War.

ALBANY, *June 20th*, 1863.

Hon. E. M. STANTON, *Secretary of War, Washington:*

The Governor desires to be informed if he shall continue sending on the militia regiments from this State. If so, to what extent, and to what point? J. B. STONEHOUSE,
Act'g Asst. Adjutant-General.

WASHINGTON, *June 21st*, 1863.

To Act'g Asst. Adjutant-General STONEHOUSE:

The President desires Governor Seymour to forward to Baltimore all the militia regiments that he can raise. EDWIN M. STANTON,
Secretary of War.

HARRISBURG, *July 2d*, 1863.

To His Excellency, GOVERNOR SEYMOUR:

Send forward more troops as rapidly as possible. Every hour increases the necessity for large forces to protect Pennsylvania. The battles of yesterday were not decisive, and if Meade should be defeated, unless we have a large army, this State will be overrun by the rebels.
A. G. CURTIN, *Governor of Penn.*

ledgement of Governor Seymour's services, that no Governor had done more to strengthen the United States Government in the hour of its need, than Governor Seymour, of New York. Yet in the face of these facts the Republican press and speakers constantly and unblushingly assert that Mr. Seymour did his utmost to paralyze the Government and aid the Rebellion. The reckless and shameful manner in which these slanders are being circulated, and the success with which they are met and refuted by the Democracy, cannot be better shown than by giving the following editorial from the *Philadelphia Age*, of July 10th, 1868, which we present to the reader in place of any comments of our own. We ask a careful perusal of it:

"The *Press* is prompt in the work of defamation, but lacks the 'long memory' with which, according to the proverb, it ought to be provided. Here is a specimen of its efforts yesterday:

'Patriots will remember that when Judge Woodward was running for the Governorship of our State, it was openly asserted by the Democracy that, should he be elected, no Union troops should pass to the front through New York or Pennsylvania; that Seymour and Woodward would throttle the government and end the war.'

NEW YORK, *July 3d*, 1863.

To Governor CURTIN, *Harrisburg, Pa.*:

Your telegram is received. Troops will continue to be sent. One regiment leaves to-day, another to-morrow, all in good pluck.

JOHN T. SPRAGUE,
Adjutant-General.

"Not the Democracy, but the knaves who libeled them spoke thus, and in doing so, gave the best help they could to the rebellion, in flattering it with false hopes of Northern sympathy. It was by deeds, not words, that the Democracy repelled that lie. When the *Press* uttered it, in 1863, the streets of our city were glistening with the bayonets of regiments sent to the front to defend Pennsylvania, sent from New Jersey and New York—by Horatio Seymour, and by Joel Parker, the Democratic Governors of those States. Governor Curtin was in a condition of hopeless inefficiency. It was his party in this city who were slow to hear his call for troops. George W. Woodward seconded it manfully, when many a blatant Radical was dumb with terror. The candidate of the Democracy, with all his sons in the field, Judge Woodward, issued this stirring appeal, in a letter addressed to the Chairman of the Democratic State Central Committee, and published throughout the State: 'There ought to be such an instant uprising of young men in response to this call (Governor Curtin's, of July 26,) as shall be sufficient to assure the public safety, and to teach the world that no hostile foot can with impunity tread the soil of Pennsylvania (June 29, 1863).' Few can have forgotten the condition of things in this city, from which the opportune victory of Gettysburg relieved it. It cannot be better portrayed than by citing the public speech, made at that crisis by Governor Curtin, from the Continental Hotel, on the 1st day of July, 1863.

"If General Meade's army is defeated, which God forbid, I need not say to intelligent Pennsylvanians what is next to occur. Military men have concurred in the opinion, and properly, that the defence of Pennsylvania from invasion—certainly of the city—will be found upon the banks of the Susquehanna; and certainly it is pleasant for me to announce that the call made upon the people of Pennsylvania has been responded to all through the State in a manner much beyond all official anticipation, and now from her mountains and valleys, from the homes and public works, our loyal and devoted Pennsylvanians are on their way to the place of rendezvous, and will soon be in arms to protect you on the banks of her great river. I ask for 7,800 men from this city. How soon can I get them? Do not measure them by days, let it be hours. * * * * *We asked for help from New York—it has come.* We asked for help from New Jersey—it has come. New England will respond; but first let us show that we are true to our honor and protect ourselves.—*Ledger*, *July* 2, 1863.

"Here is a part of the record of Horatio Seymour, in the facts of history, from the lips of the Republican Governor: "*We asked for help from New York—and it has come.*" We thank the *Press* for uttering a calumny which we can nail to the counter with the strong, sure blows of truth. The exuberant expressions of gratitude which Mr. Lincoln sent to Governor Seymour for his energy and patriotism, we reserve for another time. We have given the Radicals to-day some of the facts of history—let them try to rail them off the record."

It is in this manner hat the enemies of Mr. Seymour try to weaken his cause. They fear the manly and formidable opposition which he opposes to their criminal schemes, and they seek to destroy his influence with the people by slandering him. Fortunately for him, his public acts have been open, and done in the full light of the day, and the record of them is so clear that his vindication is simple and easy. The infamy rests solely with the party whose favorite weapon is falsehood, for the American people are too just to sustain such attacks, and they will be prompt to reward the true friend of the Union and condemn the malice of his foes.

CHAPTER V.

A Brief History of the Conscription—The System Opposed to the Spirit of the Constitution—Congress Passes a Conscription Law—Feeling of the People of the Union upon the Subject—Unjustifiable Course of the Administration towards the Opponents of its Policy—No Necessity for a Draft—The Government decides to enforce the Draft in New York City during the Absence of the State Troops—No Notice by the Provost-Marshal—Indignation of the Citizens—The Draft begun—The First Day's Proceedings—Hostility of the Working Men to the Draft—Secret Meetings in the Laboring Districts—Resistance determined upon—Monday, July 13th—Resumption of the Draft—The First Blow—Attack upon, and Destruction of the Provost-Marshal's Office—The Riot begun—Heroism of the Firemen—Outrages of the Mob—Defenceless Condition of the City—Weakness of the Authorities—The Call for Troops—Increase of the Troubles—The Rioters defeat the U. S. Marines—Fight on Third Avenue—Burning of the Orphan Asylum—Attack on the State Armory—Gallant Defence by the Police—Burning of Buildings by the Mob—Attack on the "Tribune" Office—Rioters Defeated by the Police—Outrages upon the Negroes—Heroic Conduct of the Police—Arrival of Governor Seymour in the City—His Proclamation to the Rioters—He Declares the City in a State of Insurrection—Progress of the Riot—Attack on the Negro Quarters—Murder of Colonel O'Brien—Arrival of Troops—The Rioters Defeated by the Military—The State Troops Ordered Home—Speech of Governor Seymour to the Crowd in the Park—Effect of the Speech—Misrepresentations by the Republican Press—Disingenuousness of the "Albany Evening Journal"—Course of Archbishop Hughes—His Speech—Comments—Return of the State Troops—The Riot put down—Slanders of the Republican Party—Governor Seymour's Course Vindicated.

During the absence of the militia of the City of New York in Pennsylvania, there occurred the most terrible outbreak that has ever been known in this country.

Previous to the year 1863, the recruits for the Union army had been raised by volunteering, but the ill success which had attended the Federal arms had made it necessary that the ranks should be filled up at a more rapid rate, and the Government determined to accomplish this by a general conscription throughout the country. This determination caused considerable feeling in all the loyal States. The Constitution of the United States provides that Congress shall have power, "To provide for calling forth the militia to execute the laws of the Union, suppress insurrections, and repel invasions.

"To provide for organizing, arming, and disciplining the militia, and for governing such part of them as may be employed in the service of the United States, reserving to the States respectively, the appointment of the officers, and the authority of training the militia according to the discipline prescribed by Congress."

Under this clause, the Administration of Mr. Lincoln claimed the right of the General Government to enact and enforce the Conscription Law; and under this clause, also, there were large numbers of good and true men, earnestly devoted to the cause of the Union, who claimed that the States alone had the right to raise troops within their own limits. Unfortunately for the country, the Administration and its friends regarded and treated all difference of opinion upon this point as a crime, and were not willing to admit that any man could be a true friend of the Union who opposed their efforts to destroy the Constitutional rights of the States, and change the Government into a strong Central despotism. The leaders and men of the Democratic party, while anxious to strengthen the hands of the Government in every lawful way, were unanimously opposed to a Federal Conscription, as they believed it a violation of the Constitution, and an infringement of the rights of the States. The charge that the party was prompted to this course by hostility to the Union and sympathy with Secession, is as absurd as it is false, for thousands of Democratic soldiers and sailors were already in the service, thousands were daily following their example, and among the most gallant leaders of the Union armies and navy were many of the brightest and most popular names in the Democratic party. The truth is simply this: the party was anxious to preserve the Union as a free and liberal Government, and they believed this could be done as well by respecting and enforcing the provisions of the Constitution, as by violating and destroying them. They were willing and anxious to give, as they had done, their support to any measures for raising troops that the States might see fit to adopt, but they were unwilling that the Federal Government should enforce a draft, and as they believed such a course on its part unconstitutional, they urged that steps should be taken by the people of the respective States, to test its Constitutionality. The views of the party were well expressed by the *New York World*.

The despatches from Mr. Lincoln, the letter of Mr. Stanton, and the extracts from Republican journals, which we have given elsewhere, show the strong sense of the Republican party of the value of the services rendered by Governor Seymour in the hour of extreme peril; but the moment that this danger was dissipated by the defeat of Lee at Gettysburg, there was a change in the tone and temper of the leading Republicans towards one they had so lately lauded for his patriotism. It is one of the sad facts which will stand out in the history of the rebellion, that the party in power showed itself arrogant and tyrannical in success, but abject and fawning in moments of alarm. When our armies were defeated, and invasions threatened, they implored men to forget all party differences, to rally in support of the Union, and nothing could exceed their laudations when these appeals were responded to. When the united efforts of all parties had saved our country, again they became malignant, abusive, and threatening in their language towards their political opponents. Their treatment of Governor Seymour is a marked instance of these alternations of violent abuse and unstinted praise. Mr. Greeley and other leading Republicans felt that his conduct during the invasion of Pennsylvania had given him a strong hold upon public confidence and regard. From the hour of the defeat of Lee, on the 3d of July, they began a system of misrepresentation. Not content with distorting his speeches and misstating his position, they determined to go farther. The troops which went to the rescue of Pennsylvania were mainly from the city of New York, but forgetting every thing in their desire to hold political power, they resolved to place that city under martial law. The proposed conscription had excited deep feeling throughout the North. This feeling was naturally most intense at the great centres of population. While the military of the city were still in Pennsylvania, while its forts and its arsenals had been stripped of their men, who had been hurried away to reënforce Gen. Meade, without giving notice to Governor Seymour, or to General Wool, who was in command at that point, or to the Mayor of the city, or its police department, one of the provost-marshals commenced the draft. He began the drawing on Saturday, so that the names of the conscripts were published in the papers issued on Sunday morning.

On that day, as the citizens were not engaged in their ordinary pursuits, the draft was the topic of discussion in the groups of men who assembled in the streets or at other points where they were accustomed to meet. Most of those whose names were drawn from the wheel, were of one nationality. The draft was made in a district where the enrolment was grossly unjust. If there was no design in all this to excite disorder, there was certainly a stupid disregard of all prudence and propriety. It is certain that the riot which was brought about in this way, was made the pretext by the Republican leaders for demanding that the city should be placed under martial law, and that the rightful civil authorities should be deprived of their jurisdiction. The suspicion that mischief was designed from the outset is strengthened by the fact that the statements put forth by the Provost-Marshal General at Washington with regard to the notice of the draft were disingenuous and calculated to mislead the public. The rage and malice of the Republican journals grew higher and fiercer as the popular disturbance was put down by the civil authorities. From the first moment they labored to excite the public mind, they tried to embarrass Governor Seymour in his efforts to restore order, they indulged in gross falsehoods, and denied truths which were calculated to calm the excitement. Not content with assailing the Governor of the State, they also attacked every official of the city, or of the General Government who coöperated with him. They urged General Wool to declare martial law. When he refused to do this, they commenced intrigues for his removal, and another was put in his place because he would not become an instrument in their hands to overthrow the civil authority in a city which had done more by its contributions of men and money to uphold the Government than any other community in our broad land. The following extracts from the New York Tribune show not only the spirit that animated that journal, but also its open declarations that martial law should be declared in the city of New York at the very moment it had sent out its citizens in answer to the entreaties of the President that New York would help to turn back the invasion of a Sister State. While the policy of Governor Seymour thwarted this conspiracy, it was never entirely abandoned. After the riot was put down, statements signed by leading Republicans, were sent to Washington, charging Governor Seymour with the most absurd and criminal purposes. Before acting upon these charges, the President and the War Department determined to look into them and to find out the truth. A high official was privately sent to the city of New York to investigate the whole subject, and he reported to the President that the statements made by the leading Republicans were untrue and unfounded. The following are the extracts referred to:

"We do not know how far the Government has been made acquainted with the state of affairs in this city, or whether they know any thing about it further than is to be learned from the public press. But if they depend upon that source of information, we beg to assure them of one fact of vital moment, that is, that this district is in lamentable want of a military commander. We yield to none in respect for the past services of General Wool, but these are not times to sacrifice present interests to a respect for a reputation earned in years that are past. General Wool is now a very old man, and has neither the physical ability nor the mental resources to meet the fearful emergency into which we have been precipitated by the machinations of the treacherous 'Copperheads' and their organs. He clearly does not comprehend either the magnitude or the character of the crisis, and failing to do this, he as necessarily fails to delegate the proper authority and reponsibility to younger and more active men, who, if left to themselves even, might prove quite equal to the demands of the moment. That moment demands wisdom, energy, promptness, and above all, the courage of a true soldier, who, recognizing that a real battle is before him, with a desperate and savage, though undisciplined force, hesitates not an instant to use the means at his command to defeat and exterminate it."

"The military power of the National Government must enforce the draft. We tell the President plainly, if it is possible he can need to be told, that unless vigorous measures are adopted in season, he must expect to witness another, and beyond doubt a better organized, more extensive, and infinitely more dangerous insurrection than has yet occurred. Martial law and the means of enforcing it, soldiers, and a general of courage and capacity, will secure the execution of the draft, and they only will secure it. Will the Government be warned in time?"

The criminal folly of the Government brought about its true results. When the draft was resumed on Monday morning an attack was made on the Provost-Marshal's office, every thing in it was destroyed, and the officials were badly beaten. A cry was then raised to burn the building, and the ruffians poured camphene over the lower floor, and set fire to it, and in a few minutes the place was in flames. The alarm of fire was sounded, and the fire brigade, under Chief Engineer Decker, promply arrived on the spot, but the rioters seized the hydrant and drove the firemen away from them. Mr. Decker courageously threw himself into the crowd, and by his exertions and appeals to the mob, succeeded in inducing them to allow the engines to be worked. It was too late, however, and in two hours from the beginning of the outbreak, the entire block of which the Provost-Marshal's office was the corner building, was in ashes. Mr. Kennedy, the Chief of Police, also exerted himself gallantly to check the disorder, but was badly beaten.

While these things were going on in the upper part of the city, another mob collected lower down town, and commenced a course of indiscriminate violence and plunder. Citizens were attacked, beaten, and robbed—no mercy being shown to any one thus assailed. A reporter of the *New York Times* was cruelly beaten and robbed of his watch and valuables. He was rescued from his assailants by some firemen and taken to a neighboring engine-house. This building was immediately attacked, and had not some incident drawn the mob away from it, the unfortunate reporter would doubtless have been murdered.

Matters were serious, indeed. The city was almost defenceless. The militia regiments had been sent to Pennsylvania by the Governor, and there were no troops on the island. Officers of all grades there were in abundance, but few men to sustain them. General Wool, of the regular army, was in command of the city and its defences, and Major-General Sandford, of the militia, was the commander of the State troops of the first division, almost all of whom, as we have said, were on duty in Pennsylvania. As soon as the news of the riot became known, these gentlemen and the mayor of the city, Mr. Opdyke, met to concert measures to check the disturbance. The task before them was one of great difficulty. There were very few men in the city capable of bearing arms, who could be relied upon, and the force at the various harbor defences, and at the navy yard, was very small. The city was completely panic stricken. Business of all kinds was suspended, and the trouble was increasing. Those who knew the character of the mob, were filled with great alarm. As the best that could be done, the police were ordered to hold themselves in readiness to disperse the rioters, the commandant of the navy yard was called on for a detachment of marines, the same demand made upon the commanders of the forts, and the news of the riot and the defenceless condition of the city telegraphed to Washington and to Albany. General Wool, as commander of the Department of the East, issued the following call to "veteran volunteers:"

"The veterans who have recently returned from the field of battle, have again an opportunity of serving, not only their country, but the great emporium of New York, from the threatened dangers of a ruthless mob.

"The Commanding General of the Eastern Department trusts that those who have exhibited so much bravery in the field of battle, will not hesitate to come forward at this time, to tender their services to the mayor, to stay the ravages of the city by men who have lost all sense of obligations to their country, as well as to the city of New York.

"John E. Wool, Major-General.

"P. S.—These men are requested to report to Major-General Sandford, corner of Elm and White streets, on Tuesday, July 14th, at 10 A. M."

The Board of Aldermen of the city met at half-past one o'clock in the afternoon, but soon after adjourned, as there was no quorum present. It was generally believed that some decisive action on the part of the city authorities for the purpose of aiding the poorer conscripts in providing substitutes, would check the riot, and Alderman Hall proposed a measure to that effect; upon which, however, no action was taken that day.

Meanwhile, the mob that had burned the Provost-Marshal's office, had increased in numbers. The thieves and malefactors of the city joined themselves to the rioters in the hope of reaping a rich harvest of plunder, which expectation was fully realized. They gathered in force in the vicinity of Forty-Sixth street and Third Avenue, and detachments of the main body set fire to and plundered several fine brown-stone residences on Lexington Avenue. While this was going on, a detachment of about fifty marines from the Brooklyn Navy Yard, in charge of a lieutenant, was seen approaching in a Third Avenue horse-car. The mob at once prepared to receive them. Tearing up the rails, they rendered it impossible for the car to be drawn beyond Forty-Third street, and at that point, several thousand men, women, and children stood anxiously waiting for the storming party of fifty. Many of them, particularly the women, were armed with pieces of thick telegraph wire, which they had broken from the lines, and which, as will be seen, they used with great effect. Such a scene has rarely been witnessed; the men were sober and quiet, but malignant and fearful in their aspect; the women, on the contrary, were merry, singing and dancing; they cheered their husbands, chatted gaily with bystanders, and boasted of what should yet be done by their brawny arms. As the car, containing the marines, reached the centre of the block, the lieutenant in command ordered the men to leave and form in line. Small groups and gatherings of women and children greeted them with hisses and derisive cheers; to these they paid no attention, but marched toward the larger mob at the corner. The lieutenant called upon the crowd to disperse, but no further notice was taken of the command than a sullen refusal. He then ordered his men to fire, which they did, with blank cartridges, and of course, with blank effect. The smoke had not cleared away before the infuriated mob rushed with vengeance upon the little band, broke them into confusion, seized their muskets, trampled them under foot, beat them with sticks, punched them with the long wires, and laughed at their impotence. Several of the marines managed to escape into the side streets, but each fugitive had his gang of temporary pursuers, and quite a number were killed, while all were terribly beaten. From this moment the spirit of the mob seemed changed. Resistance was no longer thought of: attack was the watchword. A squad of police attempted to arrest some of the ringleaders at this point, but they were signally defeated, badly beaten, and one of them was killed. Elated with this triumph, excited by the spilled blood, and the instinct of passion, the mob seemed beside themselves, and proposed an immediate onslaught upon the principal streets, the hotels, and other public buildings.

Soon after this, the Colored Orphan Asylum, a handsome edifice, situated on Fifth Avenue, between Forty-third and Forty-fourth streets, was attacked by the mob. This building contained at the time between 700 and 800 children, and one would have thought that the helplessness of these little ones would have been an ample protection to them. It was not so, however. Elated by the defeat of the marines, the rioters hurried to Fifth Avenue, and surrounded the asylum. The doors and windows were broken in, and the ruffians rushed into the building. They drove the women and nurses out, kicked and beat the helpless children, seized everything they could lift, threw their plunder into the streets, where it was collected and carried off by their women, and then set fire to the building. Chief Engineer Decker, who had followed the mob from Third Avenue, now rushed into the building, extinguished the flames, and drove the rioters back. His efforts were in vain, however. The boys fired the building in another quarter, protected in their infamous work by the men, and the Asylum was soon in a mass of flames. Having accomplished this, the mob gathered up its plunder, and withdrew to another part of the city.

While this was going on another band of rioters

made a furious attack upon the State Armory, situated at the corner of Twenty-First street and Second Avenue, in the effort to get possession of the arms which the Government had stored in that building. The armory was in charge of a squad of policemen, who had orders from the city authorities to prevent the entrance of any person. The mob at this point numbered several thousand determined men, and it was plain that the police would be forced to yield. Finding the building closed against them, the rioters broke down the doors with sledge hammers and stones, and rushed in. The police received them with a discharge from their pistols, which killed two men. The mob swayed back at this, but in an instant rushed in again. The police fired another volley, killing three more men. The rioters, undismayed by this, dashed at the brave little garrison, and a severe hand to hand fight ensued, in which the police, being outnumbered, were forced to make their escape by a back door. Having thus secured the building, the mob fired it and burned it to the ground.

About noon, the office of Provost-Marshal Manierre, at the corner of Broadway and Twenty-Eighth street, was sacked and set on fire, and the entire block, of which this was the centre building, was destroyed. A demand was made upon the proprietor of the famous Bull's Head Tavern, on Forty-Fourth street, between Lexington and Fourth Avenues, that he should furnish liquor to the crowd. He refused to do so, and his house was plundered and destroyed by fire. The residences of Provost-Marshal Jenkins, Post-Master

Wakeman, and several other buildings were also burned.

About five o'clock the mob moved down from Forty-Sixth street to the City Hall Park, where they were joined by a detachment of boys and men who had gathered in front of the *Tribune* office, where they had been frightening Mr. Greeley and his associates with their yells and groans. This demonstration had been harmless, however, but now a rush was made at the office, the doors were burst open, the inmates put to flight, the furniture of the lower room broken to pieces, and preparations made to burn the building. This outrage was prevented by the sudden arrival of a detachment of police, who made a gallant charge upon the crowd, drove them off, and saved the building. This movement of the police was so sudden and vigorous that it struck terror to the rioters, and they fled in every direction.

The negroes were the especial objects of the fury of the mob. During the day at least a dozen were brutally murdered. Others were driven into the river, beaten, or forced to leave the city. Whenever a negro was so unfortunate as to fall into the hands of the mob, he was treated with the most savage cruelty. The rioters seemed to lose all humanity when dealing with the blacks. Indeed, their conduct toward all their victims, both white and black, was as cowardly as it was inhuman.

Throughout the whole day the city was practically at the mercy of the mob, and but for the police force, the only organized resistance which could be opposed to the ruffians, the damage done would have been much greater. The police did their whole duty nobly. They made frequent attacks upon the mob in the streets, always winning the victory and preventing further outrage, and during the entire day and night of the 13th they alone protected the city.

As soon as Governor Seymour was informed of the condition of affairs in New York,* he left Albany and

* The subjoined article is taken from the *Cincinnati Enquirer*. It is written, says that paper, by a gentleman who was in the employ of the Telegraph Company in New York at the time of the riots, and who speaks from his own knowledge of the facts of the case:

CINCINNATI, July 21, 1868.

To the Editor of the Enquirer:

The Radical papers of this and other cities seem to find in the July (1863) riots of New York, a sweet morsel for rolling under their tongues when all other subjects for vituperation of Governor Seymour fail. From constant contact with the virulent properties of the aforesaid tongues for falsity and misrepresentation they seem to gain new strength and comfort, and like the old gentleman famous for Munchausen stories, the oftener they repeat the tale the more they seem to believe it themselves. These journals seem to delight in fathering the riots of those days on Governor Seymour, and maliciously and falsely charging that no attempt was made by Governor Seymour to suppress the mobs. The position which I held at the time in New York State gives me the opportunity of making a statement in contradiction of these charges, which, if necessary, can be verified by several gentlemen, Republicans and Democrats, who were associated with me at the time. It is well known that among the first acts of the rioters was the destruction of all, or nearly all, the telegraph wires leading from the city to the Capital at Albany, thus hoping to cut off means of communication between the Governor and the municipal authorities from the Adjutant-General's office in Albany, from whence orders for the movement of troops would be issued. Every wire was cut, the poles thrown for a great distance through the streets, with the single exception of one wire connecting Jersey City with New York, through a cable unknown to the mob. This wire was owned by the Erie Railroad, and intended for their business alone. Governor Seymour took possession of this line, and in the language of telegraphers kept it red hot for

hastened to the scene of danger, reaching the city on Monday night. On the morning of the 14th he issued the following proclamation:

three days and nights, transmitting orders for his Adjutant-General, by the circuitous route from Jersey City *via* Binghamton to Utica, New York, and from thence back to Albany, for the organization and immediate marching orders of a sufficient force of State militia to quell the disturbance. In a very short time companies and regiments were formed and sent forward without delay, many of them composed in part or wholly of the "brutal Irishmen" that haunt our Radical friends' slumbers. Everything that was possible was done with the limited and uncertain means of communication in the hands of the Governor. While the Republican Mayor, Opdyke, was trembling in his shoes behind the City Hall doors, Governor Seymour, alone and unprotected, stood manfully forth, and by the use of calm words recalled the insane rioters to a sense of their duty as citizens, promising them that claims should be heard and their wrongs, if any existed, should be righted. His cool manner and earnest assurances of his intention to investigate any grounds they had for complaint, had the effect of quieting the passions of a populace in a manner that could not have been done by three times their number of armed men. Yet these Radical papers, from behind their breastworks of print-paper with coffee-mill rifles for defence, set up a howl of rage because this one man did not stand there and denounce the rioters as thieves, cut-throats, murderers, incendiaries, and such like invectives. The effect of such language upon a mass of people excited to feelings worse than insanity itself by real or imaginary wrongs, would have been like adding fuel to the fire. Numerous were the verbal and written expressions of gratitude received from the citizens of New York for his efforts in quelling the riot—prominent among them the names of gentlemen who, though they differed from him in political views, yet had the manliness to express their thanks and appreciation of efforts which were and are continually being denied by those who knew nothing of the facts, or perverted what they did know. The citizens of Central New York, regardless of politics, know and respect Horatio Seymour as a Christian gentleman, against whom charges of complicity in, and encouragement of, riotism and mob law rebound to the injury of the authors of such falsehoods. After the fall of Vicksburg, when the Eastern troops were being sent home *via* the New York Central Railroad, dying by the score on the route for want of proper food, rest, and medical attendance, Governor Seymour

"NEW YORK, *July* 14*th*, 1863.

"*To the People of the City of New York:*

"A riotous demonstration in your city, originating in opposition to the conscription of soldiers for the military service of the United States, has swelled into vast proportions, directing its fury against the property and lives of peaceful citizens. I know that many who have participated in these proceedings would not have allowed themselves to be carried to such extremes of violence and of wrong, except under an apprehension of injustice, but such persons are reminded that the only opposition to the conscription which can be allowed, is an appeal to the courts.

and his brother, Hon. John F. Seymour, while returning from a missionary Sunday-school, near Utica, one Sunday evening, suggested to the writer of this article and some other friends that the soldiers be fed and cared for on their passage through the city. The idea was acted upon at once. In two hours a regiment was expected. Mr. Seymour made a detail to solicit contributions of food, coffee, tea, wines, cordials, etc., for the soldiers, and by the time the regiment arrived more than sufficient was collected to feed and refresh the worn-out and haggard-looking men. Several were taken from the train and cared for in the city until they recovered, at Mr. Seymour's expense. This impromptu suggestion led to the formation of a society, with Mr. Seymour at its head, that provided refreshments and medical care for twenty-five or thirty regiments from Maine, New Hampshire, Connecticut, Rhode Island, and other States. Mr. John F. Seymour, a gentleman of the same political opinions as his brother, was State Agent for New York in the Army of the Potomac during the war, and by his care and attention to the soldiers in that army, gained for himself and the State authorities manifold blessings from the thousands whose lives were saved and health regained by his personal devotion to their wants. Hundreds of mothers and children blessed him from their hearts for restoring to their lives and homes the only ones whom they had to care for and protect them; and yet he, like his brother, was called a copperhead, traitor, and rebel sympathizer, by the Radicals, because he dared to differ from the powers that were in political views. Out upon such Pharisees!

"The right of every citizen to make such an appeal will be maintained, and the decision of the courts must be respected and obeyed by rulers and people alike. No other course is consistent with the maintenance of the laws, the peace and order of the city, and the safety of its inhabitants.

"Riotous proceedings must, and shall, be put down. The laws of the State of New York must be enforced, its peace and order maintained, and the lives and property of all its citizens protected at any and every hazard. The rights of every citizen will be properly guarded and defended by the Chief Magistrate of the State.

"I do, therefore, call upon all persons engaged in these riotous proceedings, to retire to their homes and employments, declaring to them that unless they do so at once, I shall use all the power necessary to restore the peace and order of the city. I also call upon all well-disposed persons not enrolled for the preservation of order, to pursue their ordinary avocations.

"Let all citizens stand firmly by the constituted authorities, sustaining law and order in the city, and ready to answer any such demand as circumstances may render necessary for me to make upon their services; and they may rely upon a rigid enforcement of the laws of this State against all who violate them.

"Horatio Seymour, Governor."

This proclamation produced no effect upon the mob, and it soon became evident to the Governor that he would be compelled to use more severe measures for the repression of the disorders. He at once issued the following proclamation, declaring the city in a state of insurrection:

"NEW YORK, *July* 14*th*, 1863.

"*Whereas*, It is manifest that combinations for forcible resistance to the laws of the State of New York and the execution of civil and criminal process exist in the city and county of New York, whereby the peace and safety of the city, and the lives and property of its inhabitants, are endangered; and

"*Whereas*, The power of the said city and county has been exerted and is not sufficient to enable the officers of the said city and county to maintain the laws of the State and execute the legal process of its officers; and

"*Whereas*, Application has been made to me by the sheriff of the city and county of New York, to declare the said city and county to be in a state of insurrection;

"Now therefore, I, Horatio Seymour, Governor of the State of New York, and commander-in-chief of the forces of the same, do in its name, and by its authority, issue this proclamation, in accordance with the statute in such case made and provided, and do hereby declare the city and county of New York to be in a state of insurrection, and give notice to all persons that the means provided by the laws of this State for the maintenance of law and order will be employed to whatever degree may be necessary, and that all persons who shall, after the publication of this proclamation, resist, or aid and assist in resisting, any force ordered out by the Governor to quell or suppress such insurrection, will render themselves liable to the penalties prescribed by law.

"HORATIO SEYMOUR."

This proclamation was as impotent as the other. The riot had become too formidable, and the rioters too much emboldened to be put down by any thing but brute force.

On Tuesday morning, July 14th, the city was gloomy enough. The stores were closed, business was suspended every where, and the citizens were preparing each one to make such defence of his home and property as lay in his power. The police had been indefatigable in their exertions during the night; but it was evident that these brave fellows would not be able to contend successfully with the miscreants for an indefinite time. General Wool had placed General Harvey Brown in command of the city, and had also given the same command to General Sandford; and this confusion led to difficulties during the day which were almost fatal to the cause of order. The commanding officers of the various harbor forts had sent detachments to the place of rendezvous appointed by General Sandford, and a small force of militia and volunteers had been collected, so that the authorities were now in a condition to make some progress in restoring order.

The rioters had been greatly reinforced during the night, however, and early in the morning resumed their outrages. They directed their hostility principally against the negroes. No mercy was shown to the blacks. Their neighborhoods were invaded, many buildings fired, and old men and feeble women beaten most brutally. Wherever a negro was caught by the rioters, he was murdered.

During the day, Colonel O'Brien, at the head of a detachment of his regiment succeeded in dispersing a mob on Third Avenue. In the confusion of the charge, he sprained his ankle, and went into a drug store in Thirty-Second street to rest, while his command followed up the rioters. After the troops passed on, a crowd collected around the store, and the proprietor, fearing that his property would be destroyed, requested the Colonel to leave the place. O'Brien at once complied with his request, and went out into the street alone, but undaunted. He was instantly received by the mob with abuse for his course in dispersing their friends. He answered them calmly, and urged them to go home and submit to the laws; but while he was speaking, some cowardly ruffian crept behind him and struck him a blow, which laid him senseless upon the ground. The brutal crowd instantly fell upon him and beat him unmercifully; and seizing his almost lifeless body, dragged it through the streets with shouts and groans for several hours, and finally dragged it in front of his residence, where they heaped the most brutal insults upon it. A priest of the Catholic Church, courageously forced his way through the crowd, and read over the body the prayers for the dying. This done, he ordered the remains to be taken into the house, and hastened away to another point where he hoped to do good; but he had hardly departed when a brutal savage stamped upon the corpse, which was also done by many others.

The military were very active during the day, and several conflicts occurred between them and the mob, in which the latter were invariably defeated. A crowd of about two thousand men had collected at the corner of Grand and Pitt streets. Lieutenant Wood, with one hundred and fifty regulars from Fort Lafayette, was sent to clear the street. Upon reaching the place, he ordered the crowd to disperse, and was answered with a volley of paving stones. He then caused his men to fire over the heads of the rioters, with the hope of intimidating them; but this producing no effect, he ordered the troops to fire with ball-cartridges. Twelve persons were killed and several wounded by this discharge, and the rioters fled in every direction. Two children were among the killed. In various parts of the city efforts were made by the mob to resist the troops; but as soon as ball-cartridges were used by the latter, all resistance ceased.

In this way, the trouble was made less formidable; but still, as the crowds would reassemble immediately after being dispersed, the authorities found that it would be necessary to adopt some more extensive plan of operations. The militia regiments which had been sent to Pennsylvania had been ordered home by the Secretary of War, and other troops were on their way to the city from Meade's army, as were also the militia from the interior of the State. Still, it was necessary to act promptly; for much damage might be done by the mob before this aid arrived.

About noon, a large crowd had assembled in front of the *Tribune* office. These people made no unlawful demonstration, though a man was haranguing them, and urging them to attack the *Tribune* office. At this moment, Governor Seymour, who had been urged by leading citizens to address the crowd, appeared on the steps of the City Hall, and instantly the crowd ran over to the Park, and surrounding the place where the Governor was standing, called on him for a speech. His remarks were judicious and well chosen. His first duty was to soothe the excitements then prevailing in the city; and he knew that this could be done only by the use of temperate and calm language. Threats of force would only inflame the crowd still more; and it was particularly desirable to quiet them at the cost of as little bloodshed as possible. He said:

"My Friends: I have come down here from the quiet of the country to see what was the difficulty—to learn what all this trouble was concerning the Draft. Let me assure you that I am your friend. [Uproarious cheering.] You have been my friends—[cries of 'Yes,' 'Yes,' 'That's so:' 'We are, and will be again']—and now I assure you, my fellow citizens, that I am here to show you a test of my friendship. [Cheers.] I wish to inform you that I have sent my Adjutant-General to Washington to confer with the authorities there, and to have this Draft suspended and stopped. [Vociferous cheers.] I now ask you, as good citizens, to wait for his return; and I assure you that I will do all that I can to see that there is no inequality, and no wrong done any one. I wish you to take good care of all property as good citizens, and see that every person is safe. The safe-keeping of property and persons rests with you; and I charge you to disturb neither. It is your duty to maintain the good order of the city, and I know you will do it. I wish you now to separate as good citizens, and you can assemble again whenever you wish to do so. I ask you to leave all to me now, and I will see to your rights. Wait until my Adjutant returns from Washington, and you shall be satisfied. Listen to me, and see that no harm is done to either persons or property, but retire peaceably."

He also read the following letter, showing the action he had taken respecting the draft:

"NEW YORK, *July* 13*th*, 1863.

"MY DEAR SIR: I have received your note about the draft. On Saturday last, I sent my Adjutant-General to Washington for the purpose of urging a suspension of the draft, for I know that the city of New York can furnish its full quota by volunteering. I have received a dispatch from General Sprague that the draft is suspended. There is no doubt the conscription is postponed. I learn this from a number of sources. If I get any information of a change of policy at Washington, I will let you know.

"Truly yours,

"HORATIO SEYMOUR.

"Hon. SAMUEL SLOAN, President of the Hudson River Railroad Company, New York."

The Governor was listened to with profound attention, and the reading of the above letter gave great satisfaction to his hearers. His speech was spread rapidly through the city, and there can be no doubt that it aided very greatly in inducing the men to abandon the riot.

Certain Republican politicians, anxious to destroy the influence and good name of Mr. Seymour, have affected to see in this speech a yielding to the mob, and a hostility to the Union cause. Mr. Greeley says:

"The most objectionable feature of this brief address was not its initial salutation, but its underlying assumption that order and obedience to law were suspended on the stoppage of the Draft. True, he did not in terms say, 'It would be right to riot, and burn buildings, and hunt negroes, and slaughter officers, if the Draft were to go on; but I will have it stopped and given up: so go home and keep the peace;' but, to the minds of the rioters, his speech amounted exactly to that. Hence, there was great danger that tranquillity thus attained would be broken whenever the attempt to enforce the Draft should be renewed. And it was already well understood—indeed, it had been proposed to prominent Republicans the day before—that, if they would promise that the Draft should be arrested, the riots should thereupon be stopped."

The petty malice of this attack needs no comment, yet we must say it comes in bad taste from one, the salvation of whose property was the immediate and first consequence of the speech.

The Albany Evening Journal, of July 13th, 1868, states the views of the Radicals still more strongly. It says:

"Then came the riots. Seymour went down there. Had it been Andrew Jackson, instead, there would have been no palaver with the bloody criminals. He would have dispersed them, by some other method, than by promising them all they asked. * * * Look at the scene. Rebel armies mustering; rebel conscripts hastening to the field; rebel energies gathering. On the other hand—a bleeding Union, a palsied army, brave and daring, but reduced. A nation calls for help. It decrees assistance. A yelping crew, filled with the spirit of rebellion, thirsty for blood, fired with rage, resist their country's pleas and demands, and assail the officers of the nation and the innocent poor of their city. What does Horatio Seymour do? Does he point them to the obligations of the citizen, the dangers of the nation, and their imperilled brethren of the army? Not at all."

We cannot better refute this slander than by quoting the remarks of this same *Albany Evening Journal*, printed in July, 1863, just after the occurrence of the riots. They are as follows:

"Governor Seymour, in so promptly 'declaring the city in a state of insurrection,' contributed largely to the suppression of the mob. It gave immediate legal efficiency to the military arm, and enabled the civil authorities to use that power with terrible effect. It showed also, that it was Governor Seymour's purpose to give 'no quarter' to the ruffians who seized upon the occasion of a popular excitement to rob and murder. The exercise of the power thus called into service was effective. The 'insurrection' has been quelled. The mob has been overpowered. Law and order have triumphed, and the riotously disposed everywhere have received a lesson which they will not soon forget."

The reader can form his own opinion of these attacks. To our mind, as they are the ablest that have been made, they afford the best vindication of his conduct that Mr. Seymour or his friends could desire.

The speech, as we have said, was the most judicious that could have been delivered. The reader must remember that the Governor was not addressing a parcel of rioters. The men to whom he spoke, had not been guilty, as far as could be judged, of any unlawful demonstration. They believed the draft unjust and an outrage upon them, and they were, at the time of the announcement of the Governor's presence, merely discussing what they believed to be their grievances, and their most lawless act had consisted of hissing and yelling at the *Tribune* office. This may have been a crime in the eyes of the frightened inmates of that building, but it was not so in the eyes of the law. The Governor had no reason to think them rioters, for there was no charge that they had been guilty of any outrages up to that time, whatever they might have done, but for his presence and words, and he had no right to address them otherwise than as citizens who believed themselves wronged. It was his duty to promise to investigate their grievances, and assure them that he would protect their rights, and the best proof of the wisdom of his remarks is their effect upon the crowd.

Nor was he the only person who believed conciliation the best policy. On the 16th, the following notice was placarded about the city:

"NEW YORK, *July 16th*, 1863.

"*To the men of New York, who are now called in many of the papers rioters:*

"Men! I am not able, owing to the rheumatism in my limbs, to visit you; but that is not a reason why you should not pay me a visit in your whole strength. Come, then, to-morrow (Friday) at two o'clock, to my residence, northwest corner of Madison Avenue and Thirty-Sixth street. I shall have a speech prepared for you.

"There is abundant space for the meeting around my house. I can address you from the corner of the balcony. If I should be unable to stand during its delivery, you will permit me to address you sitting; my voice is much stronger than my limbs. I take upon myself the responsibility of assuring you that, in paying me this visit, or in retiring from it, you shall not be disturbed by any exhibition of municipal or military presence. You who are Catholics, or as many of you as are, have a right to visit your bishop without molestation. + JOHN HUGHES,

"Archbishop of New York."

When, the next day, nearly five thousand persons surrounded the residence of the Archbishop, he appeared on the balcony, clad in the vestments of his high office, accompanied by many of the priests and leading Catholic citizens of New York. He began his remarks by saying, "*They call you rioters*," and proceeded to tell them he was their father. Referring to the riots, he said:

"In the case of a violent and unjust assault upon you without provocation, my notion is, that every man has a right to defend his house or his shanty at the risk of his life. The cause, however, must be just. It must be defensive, not offensive. Do you want my advice? I have been hurt by the report that you are rioters. You cannot imagine that I could hear those things without being pained grievously. Is there not some way by which you can stop these proceedings, and support the laws, of which none have been enacted against you as Irishmen and Catholics? You have suffered enough already. No Government can stand or protect itself unless it protects its citizens. Military force will be let loose on you, and you know what that is. The innocent will be shot down, and the guilty are likely to escape. Would it not be better for you to retire quietly; not to give up your principles or convictions, but to keep out of the crowd where immortal souls are launched into eternity, and, at all events, get into no trouble till you are at home? Would it not be better? There is one thing in which I would ask your advice; when these so-called riots are over, and the blame is justly laid on Irish Catholics, I wish you to tell me in what country I could claim to be born? (Voices, 'Ireland.') Yes, but what shall I say if these stories be true? Ireland, that never committed a single act of cruelty until she was oppressed —Ireland, that has been the mother of heroes and poets, but never the mother of cowards. I took upon myself to say that you should not be molested in paying me a visit. I thank you for your kindness, and I hope nothing will occur till you return home, and if, by chance, as you go thither, you should meet a police officer or military man, why just—look at him."

The effect of this speech was most happy. The five thousand men who had been drawn out of the way of mischief by the call of the Archbishop, dispersed peaceably to their homes.

Now, in what respect was the speech of the Governor more reprehensible than that of the Archbishop? Both were dictated by a profound wisdom, and the effect of each was the same. Both speakers knew that whether the grievances of the crowd were real or fancied, the only way to bring them back to the cause of order was to soothe them with kind words. The venerable Archbishop was too profound a student of human nature not to appreciate this. Further than this, his course was prompted by a direct request from Governor Seymour that he would use his influence to stop the disorders. No man will dare to charge him with cowardice, either physical or moral, for no truer specimen of pure manhood ever lived. No man will dare to charge him with disloyalty to the Union, for his whole life, and more especially his services in behalf of recruiting for the Federal armies, would give the lie to such a charge; and if his remarks were unobjectionable there is no good reason why those of the Governor should be denounced.

During the 15th several of the militia regiments returned from Pennsylvania, and these were followed the next day by others, and by regiments of veterans from Meade's Army. The ringleaders of the mob were arrested and imprisoned, and their followers disheartened and demoralized. The troops as soon as they arrived, were stationed throughout the city, and their vigilance and promptness, together with a general diffusion of the knowledge that the draft was suspended for the time, soon put a stop to the disorder. By the night of the 16th all organized resistance had ceased, but the city was patrolled by the troops for several days afterwards. The stages and cars, which had been withdrawn during the riot, were replaced on their routes on the 15th, on which day the Mayor of the City issued the following proclamation:

"MAYOR'S OFFICE, NEW YORK,
July 15th, 1863.

"*To the Citizens of New York:*

"I am happy to announce to you that the riot which has for two days disgraced our city, has been in good measure subjected to the control of the public authorities. It would not have interrupted your peace for a day but for the temporary absence of all our organized local militia. What now remains of the mob are fragments prowling about for plunder; and for the purpose of meeting these, and saving the military and police from the exhaustion of continued movements, you are invited to form voluntary associations under competent leaders, to patrol and guard your various districts. With these exceptions you are again requested to resume your accustomed daily avocations.

This is as necessary to your personal security as to the peace of the city.

"The various lines of omnibuses, railways and telegrams must be put in full operation immediately. Adequate military protection against their further interruption will be furnished on application to the military authorities of the State.

"Fellow citizens, the laws must and shall be obeyed; public order shall not be broken with impunity. Our first duty now is to restore the public peace and preserve it unbroken, and to pursue and punish the offenders against the majesty of the laws.

"GEORGE OPDYKE, Mayor."

Order was now restored. The city authorities appropriated a large sum to pay bounties to volunteers, who were immediately forthcoming, and the city's quota was soon filled without a renewal of the draft.

"The number of persons killed during these terrible riots is not known. The mortality statistics for the week, at the city inspector's office, show an increase of 450 over the average weekly mortality of the year. About 90 deaths from gunshot wounds were reported at his office. It was said—but this is, doubtless, incorrect—that the remains of many of the rioters were secretly taken into the country and buried there. A large number of wounded persons probably died during the following week. Governor Seymour in his annual message states that the 'number of killed and wounded is estimated by the police to be at least one thousand.' The police and the regular and local military forces suffered but little in comparison with the mob. With regard to the militia of the 1st Division, General Sandford gives the exact figures of their losses in a portion of the riots. He says that 'one private soldier was killed, and twenty-two men dangerously, and fifty officers and soldiers slightly, wounded, at the defeat of the mob in 42d Street, the storming of the barricade erected by the rioters in 29th Street, and in the other conflicts which followed.'

"The losses, by the destruction of buildings and other property, were originally estimated at $400,000. A committee was appointed by the county supervisors, to audit claims for damages, for all of which the county was responsible, under the law, and for the payment of which a large appropriation was made. The aggregate of the claims far surpassed the highest expectations, amounting to over $2,500,000. The committee disallowed many, and cut down most of the remainder 50 per cent. At last accounts over $1,000,000 had been paid to claimants, and it was supposed that $500,000 more would be needed for the same purpose." *

The course of Governor Seymour in these riots met the approval of all candid and unprejudiced men in the State. The better class of Republicans were warm in his praise, as will be seen by the extract from the *Albany Evening Journal*, (of July, 1863,) the leading Republican journal of the State, already given; and it was not until the heat of party passion had blinded them to the dictates of truth and honesty, that any of that party commenced, for party purposes, the sys-

* The Annual Cyclopædia, 1863, p. 816.

tematic course of slander they have of late pursued.

The charge recently brought by a distinguished Republican speaker, (Lt. Gov. Woodford), that the riots were the result of Governor Seymour's views and teachings, is distinctly refuted by the testimony of Mayor Opdyke, a Republican himself, in the proclamation given above, that they were *caused by the city being left defenceless* in consequence of "the temporary absence of all our organized local militia." Further than this, a Republican Legislature, by an almost unanimous vote, thanked Governor Seymour for his conduct during the Gettysburg excitement and the riots. Says the Veteran historian of "Democracy in the United States":

"When the war commenced, the system of slander became enlarged and intensified, and reached not only leading Democratic politicians, but the whole party as a body and all its members in detail. The Republicans erected a standard of comparison, composed exclusively of themselves, and required all mankind to conform to it, or be consigned to the ranks of 'traitors,' 'rebels,' and 'disloyalists,' 'having no rights that Republicans were bound to respect.' For the first time a political Administration was treated as the Government and the people were ignored; every one who did not approve of the acts of the Administration was denounced as disloyal and an enemy to the Union. Entering the army, fighting and losing limbs, or even life, could not remove the stain of disloyalty for questioning the wisdom, honesty, and prudence of the President, his advisers, and Congress. The Republicans assumed to sit in judgment upon every man they knew or heard of, and fixed his *status* before the world. He must not only agree with the Administration and Congress, but he must conform to the changes which almost daily occurred in their standard of faith and action. Even the insignificancy of a man did not ensure him against a military prison. Spies were dodging the heels of every man. Sufficient 'black-mail' made the contributor loyal, and the want of it usually sent him to prison, as disloyal, a rebel, or a traitor.

"No fidelity or vigilance could supply the place of the subserviency demanded. It was assumed that no Democrat performed his duty to the country, or gave efficient aid in the war, and that whatever was actually done, was by Republicans. If a riot occurred, it was charged as the work of the Democrats, and that Democratic officials did not perform their duty in suppressing it. It was charged against Governor Seymour that he had been dilatory in sending New York troops to the field. *But the records of the times show that he sent troops to Washington before any Republican State. His men were the first there. He complied with every requisition upon New York for men more promptly than any Republican State in the Union. He was never behind an hour.* It was a deep mortification to the War Department that he feretted out its wrong decisions, and especially in making distribution under different calls, and requiring at his hands suitable corrections. When the riots occurred in New York, it was charged that, instead of performing his duty in suppressing it, he secretly encouraged it. This imputation, though denied, and even disproved, was reiterated until after the election in 1864.

"Now, when all motive for further perseverance in this slander has ceased, it is nearly universally conceded that he not only performed his whole duty, but did so with untiring zeal, and unwavering perseverance, and with the most perfect success. In the Convention at Albany, Mr. Opdyke, who was then Mayor of the City of New York,* publicly refuted the accusations that had been falsely made against Governor Seymour, show-

* Mayor Opdyke in an official letter, dated June 13th, 1867, makes the following statement concerning Gov. Seymour:

* * As Governor of the State and Commander-in-Chief of its military forces, he superseded me in authority over the State militia commanded by General Sanford; but General Wool, commanding the United States military forces, continued to regard himself as under my immediate directions, subject, of course, to the approval of his own military judgment and to the commands of his superiors at Washington. It affords me pleasure to add, however, that among all those in authority no diversity of sentiment manifested itself. All co-operated in earnest efforts to restore the wonted peace and quiet of the city by the earliest possible suppression of the outbreak.

From a letter at the close of the riot, we quote the following:

Party interests and prejudices were ignored by them; their action was united and harmonious; the riot was speedily suppressed; and, considering the magnitude of the danger and the slenderness of our means of resistance, with extraordinary exemption from loss of life and property. In all my efforts I was ably and steadfastly seconded by those heads of the City Department who may be regarded as the representatives of the Democratic party, Street Commissioner Cornell, Comptroller Brennan, City Inspector Boole, Supervisors Tweed, Blunt and Purdy, and William H. Armstrong, Esq., of the Mayor's office, were faithful and courageous advisers. * * * * * * * *

GEORGE OPDYKE.

ing them to be of the highest and most worthy character." *

* *Democracy in the United States.* By Ransom H. Gillett. pp. 367, 368

CHAPTER VI.

The Draft suspended in New York City—Injustice of the Government to New York—Governor Seymour calls the Attention of the President to the Inequality in the Apportionment of Conscripts—He asks that the Draft be suspended temporarily in the State—Justice of his Demand—Reply of the President—A weak Argument—Refuses to suspend the Draft—Correspondence between the Governor and the President—Preparations for resuming the Draft in New York City and Brooklyn—Letter of General Dix to the Governor—Correspondence between Governor Seymour and General Dix—Bold and independent Course of the Governor—He maintains the Independence of his State, and fastens the Odium and Responsibility of the Draft upon the Administration—Proclamation by the Governor—Governor Seymour's Course dictated by an exalted Patriotism—Review of his Acts—His Course sustained by the Commission appointed by the War Department—He receives the Thanks of the Legislature—Letter relating to the Enlistment of Colored Troops.

The draft, as we have said, was suspended in New York city upon the filling of the city's quota by volunteers. Nevertheless, it was the purpose of the Government to enforce it in the remainder of the State. General Wool was relieved of the command of the Department, and succeeded by General Dix, who, for the purpose of overcoming any resistance to the conscription, was furnished by the Secretary of War with a force of about twenty thousand men.

The number of men ordered to be raised by conscription was one fifth of the number enrolled in each Congressional District, who belonged to the first class, or were between the ages of twenty-five and thirty-five, with the unmarried between thirty-five and forty-five. It was understood, at the first, that the burden should be equally distributed between the States according to their respective populations subject to military duty, yet when the quotas of the various States were made out, it was found that New York, which had already furnished the largest number of volunteers, was called upon to an extent entirely out of proportion to the demand made upon the other States, and it was also seen that the quota of the State was very unequally divided between its various Congressional districts.

Governor Seymour's attention was promptly called to this inequality, and he at once exerted himself to see that the people of the State were treated with justice and fairness in the matter. On the 3d of August, he addressed a letter to President Lincoln, in which he pointed out the inequalities to which we have referred, and urged a suspension of the draft until the result of the recruiting in the various portions of the State could be ascertained, and protested against the excessive quota required of the urban districts of the State. He said:

"It is just to add that the Administration owes this to itself, as these inequalities fall most heavily on those districts which have been opposed to its political views."

He called the attention of the President to that part of the conscription law which requires that the quotas should be so assigned as to equalize the number among the districts of the several States, allowing for those already furnished, and for the time of service.

He claimed that, as New York had already furnished a surplus, she was entitled to credit for them. The statement of the Provost-Marshal as to the number of troops already furnished by the State, did not agree with the records in the Adjutant-General's office at Albany, and the Governor asked that the two records might be compared.* He asked the President to suspend the draft until the constitutionality of the law could be determined by the courts. The cause of the Union would not suffer by this, as recruiting was going on actively throughout the Union. Said he:

"It is believed by at least one-half of the people of the loyal States that the Conscription Act, which they are called upon to obey because it is on the statute-book, is in itself a violation of the supreme constitutional law. There is a fear and suspicion that, while they are threatened with the severest penalties of the law, they are to be deprived of its protection. * * * I do not dwell upon what I believe would be the consequence of a violent, harsh policy before the constitutionality of the Act is tested. You can scan the immediate future as well as I. The temper of the people to-day you can readily learn."

He "earnestly urged the Government to interpose no obstructions to the earliest practical decision upon this point." He added:

"Our accustomed procedures give to our citizens the right to bring all questions affecting personal lib-

* When it is remembered how often and how plausibly records of all kinds were suppressed and altered by the officials of the War Department, some idea may be formed of the cause of this difference.

erty or compulsory service in a direct and summary manner, to the judges and courts of the State or nation. The decisions which would thus naturally be rendered within a brief period, and after full and ample discussion, would make such a current of judicial opinion as would satisfy the public mind that the act is either valid or void."

On the 7th of August, the President replied as follows:

"EXECUTIVE MANSION, WASHINGTON,
"*August 7th*, 1863.

"*His Excellency Horatio Seymour, Gov. of New York:*

"Your communication of the 3d instant has been received and attentively considered.

"I cannot consent to suspend the draft in New York, as you request, because, among other things, time is too important.

"By the figures you send, which I presume are correct, the twelve districts represented fall into two classes, of eight and four respectively. The disparity of the quotas for the draft, in these two classes, is certainly very striking, being the difference between an average 2,200 in one class, and 4,864 in the other. Assuming that the districts are equal one to another, in entire population, as required by the plan on which they were made, this disparity is such as to require attention.

"Much of it, however, I suppose, will be accounted for by the fact that so many more persons fit for soldiers are in the city than in the country, who have too recently arrived from other parts of the United States, and from Europe, to be included in the census of 1860, or to have voted in 1862. Still, making due allowance for this, I am yet unwilling to stand upon it, as an entirely sufficient explanation for the great disparity.

"I shall direct the draft to proceed in all the districts, drawing, however, at first, from each of the four districts, to wit: second, fourth, sixth, and eighth, only 2,200, being the average quota of the other class.

"After this drawing, these four districts, and also the seventeenth and twenty-ninth, shall be carefully re-enrolled, and, if you please, agents of yours may witness every step of the process. Any deficiency which may appear by the new enrolment, will be supplied by a special draft for that object, allowing due credit for volunteers who may be obtained from these districts, respectively, during the interval. And at all points, so far as consistent with practical convenience, due credit will be given for volunteers, and your excellency shall be notified of the time fixed for commencing the draft in each district.

"I do not object to abide a decision of the United States Supreme Court, or of the judges thereof, on the constitutionality of the draft law. In fact, I shall be willing to facilitate the obtaining of it, but I cannot consent to lose the time while it is being obtained. We are contending with an enemy who, as I understand, drives every able-bodied man he can reach into his ranks, very much as a butcher drives bullocks into a slaughter-pen. No time is wasted, no argument is used.

"This produces an army which will soon turn upon

our now victorious soldiers, already in the field, if they shall not be sustained by recruits as they should be. It produces an army with a rapidity not to be matched on our side, if we first waste time to reëxperiment with the volunteer system, already deemed by Congress, and palpably, in fact, so far exhausted as to be inadequate; and then more time to obtain a court decision as to whether a law is constitutional which requires a part of those not now in the service to go to the aid of those who are already in it; and still more time to determine with absolute certainty that we get those who are to go in the precisely legal proportion to those who are not to go.

"My purpose is to be in my action just and constitutional, and yet practical, in performing the important duty with which I am charged, of maintaining the unity and the free principles of our common country.

"Your obedient servant, A. LINCOLN."

On the 8th, the Governor wrote to the President expressing his regret that the draft could not be suspended until a judicial decision could be had. In this letter he forwarded a report of the Judge-Advocate General, in support of his assertions that the draft was not properly proportioned among the various districts of the State. He added:

"I wish to call your attention to the tables on pages 5, 6, 7, and 8, which show that in the nine Congressional districts in Manhattan, Long, and Staten Islands, the number of conscripts called for is 33,729, while in nineteen other districts the number of conscripts called for is only 39,626. This draft is to be made from the first class; those between the ages of twenty and thirty-five. It appears by the census of 1860, that in the first nine Congressional districts there were 164,797 males between twenty and thirty-five. They are called upon for 33,729 conscripts. In the other nineteen districts, with a population of males between twenty and thirty-five of 270,786, only 39,626 are demanded.

"Again, to show the partisan character of the enrolment, you will find in the 21st page of the Military report, that in the first nine Congressional districts, the total vote of 1860 was 151,243. The number of conscripts now demanded is 33,729. In the nineteen districts, the total vote was 457,257; yet these districts are called upon to furnish only 39,626 drafted men. Each of the nine districts gave majorities in favor of one political party, and each of the nineteen districts gave majorities in favor of the other party."

On the 11th, the President briefly replied as follows:

"EXECUTIVE MANSION, WASHINGTON,
"*August* 11*th*, 1862.

"*His Excellency Horatio Seymour, Gov. of New York:*

"Yours of the 8th inst., with Judge Advocate-Gen. Waterbury's report, was received to-day. Asking you to remember that I consider the time as being very important, both to the general cause of the country and to the soldiers in the field, I beg to remind you that I waited at your request from the 1st until the 6th inst., to receive your communication dated the 3d. In view of its great length and the known time and apparent care taken in its preparation, I did not doubt that it contained your full case as you desired to present it. It contained the figures for twelve districts, omitting the other nineteen, as I supposed, because you found nothing to complain of as to them. I answered accordingly. In doing so, I laid down the principle to which I propose adhering, which is to proceed with the draft, at the same time employing infallible means to avoid any great wrong.

"With the communication received to-day, you send figures for twenty-eight districts, including the same sent before, and still omitting three, for which I suppose the enrolments are not yet received. In looking over the fuller lists of twenty-eight districts, I find that the quotas for sixteen of them are above 2,000 and below 2,700; while of the rest six are above 2,700, and six are below 2,000.

"Applying the principle to these new facts, the 5th and 7th districts must be added to the four in which the quotas have already been reduced to 2,200 for the first draft, and with these four others must be added to those to be reënrolled. The correct case will then stand: the quotas of the 2d, 4th, 5th, 6th, 7th, and 8th districts, fixed at 2,200 for the first draft.

"The provost-marshal-general informs me that the drawing is already completed in the 16th, 17th, 18th, 22d, 24th, 26th, 27th, 28th, 29th, and 30th districts. In the others, except the three outstanding, the drawing will be made upon the quotas as now fixed. After the first draft, the 2d, 4th, 5th, 6th, 7th, 8th, 16th, 17th,

21st, 25th, 29th, and 31st, will be reënrolled, for the purpose and in the manner stated in my letter of the 7th inst. The same principle will be applied to the now outstanding districts when they shall come in. No part of my former letter is repudiated by reason of not being restated in this, or for any other cause.

"Your obedient servant. A. LINCOLN."

The Governor, in insisting upon the injustice of the proportion of conscripts demanded of New York, sent the following statement to the War Department:

"The average ratio of enrolment to the male population in the Western States, is . .	19 per ct.
In New Jersey	20 "
In Pennsylvania	$18\frac{3}{4}$ "
In the New England States, it is	17 "
In the State of New York, it is	22 "
Massachusetts, with ten Congressmen and a population of 1,231,066, has to furnish, under the recent call for 300,000 men .	15,126
The first nine Congressional districts of the State of New York, with a population of 1,218,949, are called upon for . . .	25,166
Excess in the nine Congressional districts in New York over ten Congressional districts in Massachusetts	10,040
The quota of Vermont and New Hampshire, with a united population of 641,171, and six representatives in Congress, and four senators, is	7,099

The quota of two Congressional districts in New York, the 4th and 6th, with a population of 283,229, is . . . . 7,628."

Meanwhile, as it was probable that the draft, which had been suspended in New York and Brooklyn, might have to be resumed in those cities, General Dix, then in command of the Federal troops in the Department of the East, sent the following communication to Governor Seymour:

"HEADQUARTERS, DEPARTMENT OF THE EAST,
"NEW YORK CITY, *July* 30*th*, 1863.

"SIR: As the draft under the Act of Congress of March 3d, 1863, for enrolling and calling out the national forces, will probably be resumed in this city at an early day, I am desirous of knowing whether the military power of the State may be relied on to enforce the execution of the law, in case of forcible resistance to it. I am very anxious that there should be perfect harmony of action between the Federal Government and that of the State of New York; and if under your authority to see the laws faithfully executed, I can feel assured that the Act referred to will be enforced, I need not ask the War Department to put at my disposal for the purpose, troops in the service of the United States. I am the more unwilling to make such a request as they could not be withdrawn in any considerable number from the field without prolonging the war and giving aid and encouragement to the enemies of the Union, at the very moment when our successes promise, with a vigorous effort, the speedy suppression of the rebellion.

"I have the honor to be, very respectfully, your obedient servant. JOHN A. DIX, Maj.-Gen."

To this letter, the Governor, who had written to the President, asking a suspension of the draft, and who was awaiting his answer, replied as follows:

"ALBANY, *Monday, Aug. 3d*, 1863.

"*To Maj.-General John A. Dix, Commanding Eastern Department:*

"SIR: I received your letter on Saturday. I have this day sent to the President of the United States a communication in relation to the draft in this State. I believe his answer will relieve you and me from the painful questions growing out of an armed enforcement of the Conscription law in this patriotic State, which has contributed so largely and freely to the support of the national cause during the existing war. When I receive the President's answer, I will write to you again upon the subject of your letter.

"Truly yours, &c.,

"HORATIO SEYMOUR."

On the 8th of August General Dix again addressed the Governor. He said:

"It is my duty now, as commanding officer of the troops in the service of the United States in the department, if called on by the enrolling officers, to aid them in resisting forcible opposition to the execution of the law; and it was from an earnest desire to avoid the necessity of employing for the purpose any of my forces, which have been placed here to garrison the forts and protect the public property, that I wished to see the draft enforced by the military power of the State in case of armed and organized resistance to it. But holding such resistance to the paramount law of Congress to be disorganizing and revolutionary, leading, unless effectually suppressed, to the overthrow of the Government itself, to the success of the insurgents of the seceded States, and to universal anarchy, I designed, if your coöperation could not be relied on, to ask the General Government for a force which should be adequate to ensure the execution of the law, and to meet any emergency growing out of it."

Governor Seymour, failing to procure, at the hands of the General Government, a suspension of the draft, replied as follows, on the 15th of August:

"As you state in your letter that it is your duty to enforce the act of Congress, and as you apprehend its provisions may excite popular resistance, it is proposed you should know the position which will be held by the State authorities. Of course, under no circumstances can they perform duties expressly confided to others; nor can they undertake to relieve others from their proper responsibilities. But there can be no violations of good order or riotous proceedings, no disturbances of the public peace, which are not infractions of the laws of the State, and those laws will be enforced under all circumstances. I shall take care that all the executive officers of this State perform their duties vigorously and thoroughly, and, if need be, the military power will be called into requisition.

"As you are an officer of the General Government and not of the State, it does not become me to make suggestions to you with regard to your action under a law of Congress. You will, of course, be governed by your instructions, and by your own views of duty."

On the 18th, General Dix wrote to the Governor again. He said:

"Not having received an answer from you, I applied to the Secretary of War on the 14th instant, for a force adequate to the object. The call was promptly responded to, and I shall be ready to meet all opposition to the draft."

To this letter the Governor replied on the 20th. He said he had received no notice when the draft would take place, the same course having been pursued towards him when the first order for the draft was issued, although he expected such notice, and hoped some interval would be allowed between the notice and the draft, adding:

"You will see that no time was allowed for getting credits for volunteers, for making suggestions or preparations. I do not know that the fault rests with Colonel Fry, but it is proper for me to state these facts."

On the same day, in view of the resumption of the draft, he issued the following proclamation:

"EXECUTIVE CHAMBER, ALBANY,
"*August 18th*, 1863.

"I have received information that the draft is about to be made in the cities of New York and Brooklyn, and I understand that there is danger of disorderly and riotous attacks upon those who are engaged in executing the law of Congress.

"I cannot believe that any considerable number of citizens are disposed to renew the shameful and sad scenes of the past month, in which the lives of so many, as well of the innocent as of the guilty, were destroyed. Our courts are now consigning to severe punishment many of those who were then guilty of acts destructive of the lives and property of their fellow-citizens. These events should teach all that real or imaginary wrongs cannot be corrected by unlawful violence. The liberties of our country and the rights of our citizens can only be preserved by a just regard for legal obligations, and an acquiescence in the decision of judicial tribunals.

"While I believe it would have been a wise and humane policy to have procured a judicial decision, with regard to the constitutionality of the Conscription Act, at an earlier day and by a summary process, yet the failure to do this in no degree justifies any violent opposition to the act of Congress. Until it is set aside by the decision of judicial tribunals, it must be obeyed like any other act of the State or National Legislature.

"The following rule of duty in this respect was laid down in the farewell address of Andrew Jackson. This view has always been accepted by the friends of our Union and the upholders of our Constitution:

(Unconstitutional or oppressive laws may, no doubt, be passed by Congress, either from erroneous views or the want of due consideration. If they are in reach of judicial authority, the remedy is easy and peaceful; and, if from the character of the law, it is an abuse of power not within the control of the judiciary, then free discussion and calm appeals to reason, and to the justice of the people, will not fail to redress the wrong. But until the law shall be declared void by the courts or repealed by Congress, no individual or combination of individuals can be justified in resisting its execution.)

"The antagonistic doctrine that men may rightfully resist laws opposed to their own ideas of right or duty has not only led to great disorders and violence, but is one of the chief causes of the destructive civil war which has wasted the blood and treasure of our people. Disregard for the sacredness of the Constitution, for the majesty of the law, and for the decisions of the judiciary, is, at this time, the greatest danger which threatens American liberty.

"This spirit of disloyalty must be put down. It is inconsistent with social order and social security, destructive to the safety of persons and property, and subversive of the liberty of the citizen and the freedom of the nation. Those who fear that there are designs in any quarter to overthrow the rights of the citizen, or to obstruct the accustomed administration of our laws, or to usurp any power in violation of constitutional restraints, should bear in mind that all acts of violence, all public disorders, pave the way for these very usurpations, and that they will be regarded with satisfaction by those who, for any cause, may wish to destroy either the power or rights of our National or State Governments.

"The Constitution and Statutes of the State and nation contain ample remedies for all wrongs which may be committed either by rulers or citizens, and those who wish to preserve their rights, or to punish offenders, whether in public or in private life, should themselves carefully perform their duty, abstain from all illegal acts, generously support the Government, and then calmly and resolutely claim their rights.

"I again repeat the warning which I gave to you during the riotous proceedings of the past month, that 'the only opposition to the conscription which can be allowed is an appeal to the courts. The right of every citizen to make such an appeal will be maintained, and the decision of the courts must be respected and obeyed by rulers and people alike. No other course is consistent with the maintenance of the laws, the peace and order of the city, and the safety of its inhabitants. Riotous proceedings must and shall be put down. The laws of the State of New York must be enforced, its peace and order maintained, and the lives and property of all citizens protected, at any and every hazard. The rights of every citizen will be properly guarded and defended by the chief magistrate of the State.'

"I hereby admonish all judicial and executive officers, whose duty it is to enforce the law and preserve public order, that they take vigorous and effective measures to put down any riotous or unlawful assemblages; and if they find their power insufficient for that purpose, to call upon the military in the manner pointed out by the Statutes of the State. If these measures should prove insufficient, I shall then exert the full power of the State, in order that the public order may be preserved, and the persons and properties of the citizens be fully protected.

"HORATIO SEYMOUR."

The action of Governor Seymour respecting the draft, has, of course, been denounced by the Republican press, who spare no man whose crime is a difference of opinion from them, and many good, fair-minded men, owing to a wilful misrepresentation of facts, have been led to believe that he used his power and influence to defeat the efforts of the General Government to fill up the ranks of the army. Let us look at the case for a moment. Our review of it is based solely upon the facts given herein.

Governor Seymour, in common with thousands of other true men, believed the draft to be a violation of the rights guaranteed the State of New York by the Federal Constitution. He asked its suspension at the hands of the Government until the Courts could decide upon its constitutionality, and, as the recruiting was going on briskly all over the State, he was warranted in believing that such suspension would not weaken the cause or armies of the Union. The Government refused his request, and he submitted to its decision. He pointed out the inequalities of the system which the Federal authorities proposed to inaugurate, and asked that the injustice thus done to the people of New York should be remedied. His plain duty was to protect, as far as lay in his power, the rights of the people of his State, and he would have been false to his oath of office had he not done so. It was not fair that the chief burden of the war should be made to fall upon New York, which State had already voluntarily taken the lead in filling up the army, for the war was not fought for the benefit of that State alone. All the members of the Union were interested in it, and it was but right that each one should furnish its proportionately equal share of men. Governor Seymour asked no more than this. He also pointed out the inequality of the demands made upon the various portions of the State and asked to have them equalized. He protested that it was not fair to make the heaviest demands on the Anti-Administration districts, and the fact that the War Department hoped to simplify in this way the opposition to the Administration, does not affect the justice of the Governor's plea.

When General Dix asked him to enforce the draft by using the military power of the State for that purpose, he very properly declined to do so. The Federal Government had completely ignored both the State of New York and its officials in the matter of the draft. The measure itself was a violation of the Constitutional rights of the State of New York, an outrage upon her, against which her constituted authorities and a majority of her people had protested, and it would have been simply infamous in Mr. Seymour to have complied with General Dix's request. Further than this, the Conscription bill was a Federal law. It was the duty of Federal officers alone to execute it; they alone were responsible for the manner in which it was carried out, and the officials of the State of New York could not legally take their places, or incur their responsibility. The Governor offered no opposition to the law, but manfully insisted upon its execution by the proper persons. So far, indeed, from meditating or countenancing resistance, his proclamation already given, sternly denounced any such course. This proclamation is generally passed over by his traducers, but it is certain that no more "loyal," to use a much abused term, state paper ever issued from any Republican Governor at any period before, during, or since the war.

Nor were the Governor's objections to the provisions of the draft unsupported by facts. The statement prepared by the Adjutant-General of the State showed that the draft as proposed, would throw upon the eastern portion of the State, comprising less than one third of the Congressional districts, more than one half of the burdens of the conscription. In support of his assertion that the heaviest demand was made upon the Anti-Lincoln districts, the Governor submitted the following statement, also prepared by the Adjutant-General of the State:

"The nine Anti-Lincoln districts are required to furnish nearly as many conscripts as the nineteen Lincoln districts, although the latter polled more than three times as many votes; as follows:

1860.

Lincoln Districts.			Anti-Lincoln Districts.		
District.	Total Vote.	Cons. required.	District.	Total Vote.	Cons. required.
12	22,664	2,013	1	19,194	2,212
13	19,698	2,006	2	17,169	4,146
15	25,540	2,370	3	19,297	2,697
16	17,167	1,493	4	17,253	5,881
17	20,874	1,818	5	15,731	3,390
18	27,389	2,310	6	17,056	4,538
19	29,188	2,387	7	14,832	3,452
20	28,522	2,448	8	19,440	4,892
21	21,519	1,746	9	11,271	2,521
22	23,995	2,068			
23	24,070	2,088	Totals	151,243	33,729
24	28,497	2,202			
25	22,317	1,936			
26	25,566	2,152			
27	27,673	2,419			
28	24,204	2,051			
29	22,541	1,767			
30	23,315	2,539			
31	21,518	1,753			
Totals	457,257	39,626			

The War Department referred Governor Seymour's objections to a commission, consisting of William F. Allen, of New York, John Love, of Indiana, and Chauncey Smith, of Massachusetts, for the purpose of examining them and determining upon some fair mode of correcting the inequalities complained of. These gentlemen made a formal report to the Government, *sustaining the objections of Governor Seymour as to an excess of enrolment, and an allowance of* 13,000 *men was at once made by the War Department. At the next session, the Legislature, consisting of* 103 *Administration or Republican members and* 57 *Dem-*

*ocrats, passed a vote of thanks to the Governor for his successful conduct of the affair.**

Later in the year, inquiries were made of Governor Seymour relative to the enlistment of colored troops, to which he replied as follows:

"STATE OF NEW YORK, EXECUTIVE DEPARTMENT,
"ALBANY, *Nov. 14th.*

"SIR: In answer to your inquiries about enlistment of blacks and the organization of regiments and companies, I have to say:

"1st. That, under the State laws, the bounty is paid to all without distinction, who are mustered into the service of the United States, and for whom credits are given to New York under the President's call for troops.

"2d. As to new organizations, I have no power to authorize any, either blacks or whites, which will be entitled to the bounty given by the General Government. The object at Washington is to fill up the ranks of the regiments in the field. If any new organizations for either white or black troops are made, they must be authorized by the War Department to entitle

* The following is the resolution passed by the Legislature on the 16th of April, 1864:

"*Resolved*, That the thanks of this House be, and are hereby tendered to his Excellency, Governor Seymour, for calling the attention of the General Government at Washington to the errors in the apportionment of the quota of this State, under the enrolment act of March 3, 1863, and for his prompt and efficient efforts in procuring a correction of the same.

"*Resolved*, That the Clerk of this House transmit to the Governor a copy of this report and resolution."

those who join them to the benefit of the money paid to volunteers. Yours, &c.

"HORATIO SEYMOUR.

"To JAMES RODGERS,

"No. 421 Broadway, N. Y. City."

CHAPTER VII.

Meeting of the Democratic Convention of the State—Pledges its Support to the Government in all lawful Measures for bringing the War to a successful Close—Mass Meeting at Albany to consider the unlawful Arrest of Mr. Vallandigham—Letter of the Governor—Proceedings of the Meeting—Correspondence of the Committee with the President—Meetings throughout the State—Course of Governor Seymour indorsed by all—Democratic Meeting at Syracuse—Eloquent Speech of Governor Seymour—A Plain Statement of Facts—Meeting of the Legislature—The Governor's Message—Review of the Draft, and his Action therein—Statement of his action during the Riots—Eloquent Appeal for the Union—Efforts of the Governor in behalf of the Credit of the State—His Success.

The State Democratic Convention met at Albany on the 10th of September, 1863. This body pledged the support of the Democrats of New York to the Government in "all legitimate means to suppress the Rebellion and restore the Union." It declared that the Government was pledged to conduct the war solely for the objects avowed by the resolutions of Congress in July, 1861, that illegal and arbitrary arrests were violations of the Constitution, a usurpation and a crime, that the Government should endeavor to conciliate the people of the South; that the claim of the authority of the General Government to destroy the rights and obliterate the boundaries of the States is as false and dangerous as the doctrine of secession; that the Constitution and laws do not cease to be binding in time of war; that the soldiers and sailors deserve the gratitude of the nation; that the results of conscription ought to admonish the Government "to rely upon the voluntary action of a patriotic people;" and that mob violence is a crime against a people and a Republican Government. The administration of Governor Seymour was declared worthy of the highest approval of all true friends of the Union.

On the 16th of May, 1863, a public meeting was held at Albany, to consider the unlawful arrest of Mr. Vallandigham. Governor Seymour was not able to be present, but sent the following letter to the Committee of Invitation:

"STATE OF NEW YORK, EXECUTIVE DEPARTMENT,
"ALBANY, *July* 16*th*, 1863.

"*To Peter Cagger, Solomon F. Higgins, Erastus Corning, Jr., Committee:*

"I cannot attend the meeting at the capitol this evening, but I wish to state my opinion in regard to the arrest of Mr. Vallandigham.

"It is an act which has brought dishonor upon our country; it is full of danger to our persons and to our homes; it bears upon its front a conscious violation of law and of justice. Acting upon the evidence of detailed informers, shrinking from the light of day in the darkness of night, armed men violated the home of an American citizen, and furtively bore him away to a military trial, conducted without those safeguards known to the proceedings of our judicial tribunals.

"The transaction involved a series of offences against our most sacred rights. It interfered with the freedom of speech; it violated our rights to be secure in our homes against unreasonable searches and seizures; it pronounced sentence without a trial, save one which was a mockery, which insulted as well as wronged. The perpetrators now seek to impose punishment, not for an offence against law, but for a disregard for an invalid order, put forth in an utter disregard of principles of civil liberty. If this proceeding is approved by the Government, and sanctioned by the people, it is not merely a step toward revolution, it is revolution; it will not only lead to military despotism, it establishes military despotism. In this aspect it must be accepted, or in this aspect it must be rejected.

"If it is upheld, our liberties are overthrown. The safety of our persons, the security of our property, will hereafter depend upon the arbitrary wills of such military rulers as may be placed over us, while our constitutional guarantees will be broken down. Even now the Governors and the courts of some of the great Western States have sunk into insignificance before the despotic powers claimed and exercised by military men who have been sent into their borders. It is a fearful thing to increase the danger which now overhangs us, by treating the law, the judiciary, and the authorities of States with contempt. The people of this country now wait with the deepest anxiety the decisions of the Administration upon these acts. Having given it a generous support in the conduct of the war, we now pause to see what kind of Government it is for which we are asked to pour out our blood and our treasures.

"The action of the Administration will determine in the minds of more than half of the people of the loyal States, whether this war is waged to put down rebellion at the South, or to destroy free institutions at the North. We look for its decision with the most solemn solicitude.*

"HORATIO SEYMOUR."

* The results of this meeting are so important that we append them here:

ALBANY, *May* 19*th*, 1863.

To his Excellency the President of the United States:

The undersigned, officers of a public meeting held in the city of Albany the 16th day of May instant, herewith transmit to your Excellency a copy of the resolutions adopted at the said meeting, and respectfully request your earnest consideration of them. They deem it proper on their personal responsibility to state that the meeting was one of the most respectable as to numbers and character, and one of the most earnest in support of the Union ever held in this city.

Yours, with great regard,

ERASTUS CORNING, President.

Vice-Presidents—Eli Perry, Peter Gansevoort, Peter Monteath, Samuel W. Gibbs, John Niblock, H. W. McClellan, Lemuel W. Rodgers, William Seymour, Jeremiah Osborn, William S. Paddock, J. B. Sanders, Edward Mulcahy, D. V. N. Radcliff.

Secretaries—William A. Rice, Edward Newcomb, R. W. Peckham, jr., M. A. Nolan, John R. Nessle, and others.

The resolutions were as follows:

Resolved, That the Democrats of New York point to their uniform course of action during the two years of civil war through which we have passed, to the alacrity which they have evinced in filling the ranks of the army, to their contributions and sacrifices, as the evidence of their patriotism and devotion to the cause of our imperilled country. Never in the history of civil wars has a Government been sustained with such ample resources of means and men, as the people have voluntarily placed in the hands of this Administration.

Resolved, That as Democrats, we are determined to maintain this patriotic attitude, and, despite of adverse and disheartening circumstances, to devote all our energies to sustain the cause of the Union, to secure

The Conservative citizens of New York city, at a mass meeting in Union Square, adopted the following resolutions relative to the arrest of Mr.

peace through victory, and to bring about the restoration of all the States under the safeguards of the Constitution.

Resolved, That while we will not consent to be misrepresented upon these points, we are determined not to be misunderstood in regard to others not less essential. We demand that the Administration shall be true to the Constitution, shall recognize and maintain the rights of the States and the liberties of the citizen, shall everywhere outside of the lines of necessary military occupation and the scenes of insurrection, exert all its powers to maintain the supremacy of the civil over military law.

Resolved, That in view of these principles we denounce the recent assumption of a military commander to seize and try a citizen of Ohio, Clement L. Vallandigham, for no other reason than words addressed to a public meeting, in criticism of the course of the Administration, and in condemnation of the military orders of that general.

Resolved, That this assumption of power by a military tribunal, if successfully asserted, not only abrogates the right of the people to assemble and discuss the affairs of Government, the liberty of speech and of the press, the right of trial by jury, the law of evidence, and the privilege of habeas corpus, but it strikes a fatal blow at the supremacy of law, and the authority of the State and Federal Constitutions.

Resolved, That the Constitution of the United States—the supreme law of the land—has defined the crime of treason against the United States to consist "only in levying war against them, or adhering to their enemies, giving them aid and comfort;" and has provided that "no person shall be convicted of treason, unless on the testimony of two witnesses to the same overt act, or on confession in open court." And it further provides that "no person shall be held to answer for a capital or otherwise infamous crime, unless on a presentment or indictment of a grand jury; except in cases arising in the land and naval forces, or in the militia, when in actual service in time of war or public danger;" and further, that "in all criminal prosecutions, the accused shall enjoy the right of a speedy and public trial, by an impartial jury of the State and district wherein the crime was committed."

Resolved, That these safeguards of the rights of the citizen against the pretensions of arbitrary power, were intended more especially for his protection in times of civil commotion. They were secured substantially

Vallandigham and the letter of Governor Seymour:

"*Whereas*, within a State where the Courts of law

to the English people, after years of protracted civil war, and were adopted into our own Constitution at the close of the Revolution. They have stood the test of seventy-six years of trial under our republican system, under circumstances which show that while they constitute the foundation of all free government, they are the elements of the enduring stability of the republic.

Resolved, That in adopting the language of Daniel Webster, we declare, "it is the ancient and undoubted prerogative of this people to canvass public measures and the merits of public men. It is a 'homebred right,' a fireside privilege. It has been enjoyed in every house, cottage, and cabin in the nation. It is as undoubted as the right of breathing the air or walking on the earth. Belonging to private life as a right, it belongs to public life as a duty, and it is the last duty which those whose representatives we are shall find us to abandon. Aiming at all times to be courteous and temperate in its use, except when the right itself is questioned, we shall place ourselves on the extreme boundary of our own right, and bid defiance to any arm that would move us from our ground. This high constitutional privilege we shall defend and exercise in all places; in time of peace, in time of war, and at all times. Living, we shall assert it; and should we leave no other inheritance to our children, by the blessing of God we will leave them the inheritance of free principles and the example of a manly, independent, and constitutional defence of them."

Resolved, That in the election of Gov. Seymour, the people of this State, by an emphatic majority, declared their condemnation of the system of arbitrary arrests, and their determination to stand by the Constitution. That the revival of this lawless system can have but one result, to divide and distract the North, and destroy its confidence in the purposes of the Administration. That we deprecate it as an element of confusion at home, of weakness to our armies in the field, and as calculated to lower the estimate of American character and magnify the apparent peril of our cause abroad. And that, regarding the blow struck at a citizen of Ohio as aimed at the rights of every citizen of the North, we denounce it as against the spirit of our laws and Constitution, and most earnestly call upon the President of the United States to reverse the action of the military tribunal which has passed a "cruel and unusual pun-

are open and their process unimpeded, soldiers under the command of officers of the United States army have broken into the residence and forcibly abducted

ishment" upon the party arrested, prohibited in terms by the Constitution, and to restore him to the liberty of which he has been deprived.

Resolved, That the president, vice-presidents, and secretary of this meeting be requested to transmit a copy of these resolutions to his Excellency the President of the United States, with the assurance of this meeting of their hearty and earnest desire to support the Government in every constitutional and lawful measure to suppress the existing rebellion.

EXECUTIVE MANSION, WASHINGTON,
June 12*th*, 1863.

Hon. Erastus Corning, and others:

GENTLEMEN: Your letter of May 19th, enclosing the resolutions of a public meeting held in Albany, N. Y., on the 16th of the same month, was received several days ago.

The resolutions, as I understand them, are resolvable into two propositions—first, the expression of a purpose to sustain the cause of the Union, to secure peace through victory, and to support the Administration in every constitutional and lawful measure to suppress the rebellion; and, secondly, a declaration of censure upon the Administration for supposed unconstitutional action, such as the making of military arrests. And from the two propositions a third is deduced, which is, that the gentlemen composing the meeting are resolved on doing their part to maintain our common Government and country, despite the folly or wickedness, as they may conceive, of any Administration. This position is eminently patriotic, and as such I thank the meeting, and congratulate the nation for it. My own purpose is the same, so that the meeting and myself have a common object, and can have no difference, except in the choice of means or measures for effecting that object.

And here I ought to close this paper, and would close it, if there were no apprehension that more injurious consequences than any merely personal to myself might follow the censures systematically cast upon me for doing what, in my view of duty, I could not forbear. The resolutions promise to support me in every constitutional and lawful measure to suppress the rebellion; and I have not knowingly employed, nor shall knowingly employ, any other.

from his home, the Hon. Clement L. Vallandigham; and whereas, a body of men, styled a military commission, have arraigned before them and tried the said

But the meeting, by their resolutions, assert and argue that certain military arrests, and proceedings following them, for which I am ultimately responsible, are unconstitutional. I think they are not. The resolutions quote from the Constitution the definition of treason, and also the limiting safeguards and guarantees therein provided for the citizen on trial for treason, and on his being held to answer for capital or otherwise infamous crimes, and in criminal prosecutions, his right to a speedy and public trial by an impartial jury. They proceed to resolve "that these safeguards of the rights of the citizen against the pretensions of arbitrary power were intended more especially for his protection in times of civil commotion." And, apparently to demonstrate the proposition, the resolutions proceed, "they were secured substantially to the English people after years of protracted civil war, and were adopted into our Constitution at the close of the Revolution." Would not the demonstration have been better if it could have been truly said that these safeguards had been adopted and applied during the civil wars and during our Revolution, instead of after the one and at the close of the other? I, too, am devotedly for them after civil war and before civil war, and at all times, "except when, in cases of rebellion and invasion, the public safety may require" their suspension. The resolutions proceed to tell us that these safeguards "have stood the test of seventy-six years of trial, under our republican system, under circumstances which show that while they constitute the foundation of all free government, they are the elements of the enduring stability of the republic." No one denies that they have so stood the test up to the beginning of the present rebellion, if we except a certain occurrence at New Orleans; nor does any one question that they will stand the same test much longer after the rebellion closes. But these provisions of the Constitution have no application to the case we have in hand, because the arrests complained of were not made for treason—that is, not for the treason defined in the Constitution, and upon the conviction of which the punishment is death; nor yet were they made to hold persons to answer for any capital or otherwise infamous crimes; nor were the proceedings following, in any constitutional or legal sense, "criminal prosecutions." The arrests were made on totally different grounds, and the proceedings following accorded with the grounds of the arrests.

Hon. C. L. Vallandigham, a civilian and eminent public man, for words spoken in the discussion of public questions before an assemblage of his fellow-citizens;

Let us consider the real case with which we are dealing, and apply to it the parts of the Constitution plainly made for such cases.

Prior to my installation here it had been inculcated that any State had a lawful right to secede from the national Union, and that it would be expedient to exercise the right whenever the devotees of the doctrine should fail to elect a President to their own liking. I was elected contrary to their liking; and, accordingly, so far as it was legally possible, they had taken seven States out of the Union, had seized many of the United States forts, and had fired upon the United States flag, all before I was inaugurated, and, of course, before I had done any official act whatever. The rebellion thus begun soon ran into the present civil war; and, in certain respects, it began on very unequal terms between the parties. The insurgents had been preparing for it for more than thirty years, while the Government had taken no steps to resist them. The former had carefully considered all the means which could be turned to their account. It undoubtedly was a well-pondered reliance with them that in their own unrestricted efforts to destroy Union, Constitution, and law, all together, the Government would, in a great degree, be restrained by the same Constitution and law from arresting their progress. Their sympathizers pervaded all departments of the Government and nearly all communities of the people. From this material, under cover of "liberty of speech," "liberty of the press," and "habeas corpus," they hoped to keep on foot amongst us a most efficient corps of spies, informers, suppliers, and aiders and abettors of their cause in a thousand ways. They knew that in times such as they were inaugurating, by the Constitution itself, the habeas corpus might be suspended; but they also knew they had friends who would make a question as to who was to suspend it; meanwhile their spies and others might remain at large to help on their cause. Or if, as has happened, the executive should suspend the writ, without ruinous waste of time, instances of arresting innocent persons might occur, as are always likely to occur in such cases; and then a clamor could be raised in regard to this, which might be, at least, of some service to the insurgent cause. It needed no very keen perception to discover this part of the enemy's programme, so soon as by open hostilities their machinery was fairly put in motion. Yet thoroughly imbued with a reverence for the guaranteed rights of individuals, I was slow to

and whereas, the said military commission has sentenced him to a punishment as yet unknown, but which is to be announced in some military order promulgated hereafter, therefore

adopt the strong measures which by degrees I have been forced to regard as being within the exceptions of the Constitution, and as indispensable to the public safety. Nothing is better known to history than that courts of justice are utterly incompetent to such cases. Civil courts are organized chiefly for trials of individuals, or, at most, a few individuals acting in concert, and this in quiet times, and on charges of crimes well defined in the law. Even in times of peace bands of horse thieves and robbers frequently grow too numerous and powerful for the ordinary courts of justice. But what comparison in numbers have such bands ever borne to the insurgent sympathizers, even in many of the loyal States? Again, a jury too frequently has at least one member more ready to hang the panel than to hang the traitor. And yet, again, he who dissuades one man from volunteering, or induces one soldier to desert, weakens the Union cause as much as he who kills a Union soldier in battle. Yet this disuasion or inducement may be so conducted as to be no defined crime of which any civil court would take cognizance.

Ours is a case of rebellion—so called by the resolution before me—in fact, a clear, flagrant, and gigantic case of rebellion; and the provision of the Constitution that "the privilege of the writ of habeas corpus shall not be suspended unless when in case of rebellion or invasion the public safety may require it," is the provision which specially applies to our present case. This provision plainly attests the understanding of those who made the Constitution that ordinary courts of justice are inadequate to "cases of rebellion"—attests their purpose that, in such cases, men may be held in custody whom the courts, acting on ordinary rules, would discharge. Habeas corpus does not discharge men who are proved to be guilty of defined crime; and its suspension is allowed by the Constitution on purpose that men may be arrested and held who cannot be proved to be guilty of defined crime, "when, in case of rebellion or invasion, the public safety may require it." This is precisely our present case—a case of rebellion, wherein the public safety does require the suspension. Indeed, arrests by process of courts and arrests in cases of rebellion do not proceed altogether upon the same basis. The former is directed at the small percentage of ordinary and continuous perpetration of crime, while the latter is directed at sudden and extensive uprisings against the Gov-

"*Resolved*, That we, the citizens of the city of New York, here assembled, denounce the arrest of Hon. Clement L. Vallandigham, and his trial and sentence

ernment, which, at most, will succeed or fail in no great length of time. In the latter case arrests are made not so much for what has been done, as for what probably would be done. The latter is more for the preventive and less for the vindictive than the former. In such cases the purposes of men are much more easily understood than in cases of ordinary crime. The man who stands by and says nothing when the peril of his Government is discussed cannot be misunderstood. If not hindered, he is sure to help the enemy; much more if he talks ambiguously—talks for his country with "buts" and "ifs" and "ands." Of how little value the constitutional provisions I have quoted will be rendered, if arrests shall never be made until defined crimes shall have been committed, may be illustrated by a few notable examples. Gen. John C. Breckinridge, Gen. Robert E. Lee, Gen. Joseph E. Johnston, Gen. John B. Magruder, Gen. William B. Preston, Gen. Simon B. Buckner, and Com. Franklin Buchanan, now occupying the very highest places in the rebel war service, were all within the power of the Government since the rebellion began, and were nearly as well known to be traitors then as now. Unquestionably, if we had seized and held them, the insurgent cause would be much weaker. But no one of them had committed any crime defined in the law. Every one of them, if arrested, would have been discharged on habeas corpus, were the writ allowed to operate. In view of these and similar cases, I think the time not unlikely to come when I shall be blamed for having made too few arrests rather than too many.

By the third resolution the meeting indicate their opinion that military arrests may be constitutional in localities where rebellion actually exists, but that such arrests are unconstitutional in localities where rebellion or insurrection does not actually exist. They insist that such arrests shall not be made "outside of the lines of necessary occupation, and the scenes of insurrection." Inasmuch, however, as the Constitution itself makes no such distinction, I am unable to believe that there is any such constitutional distinction. I concede that the class of arrests complained of can be constitutional only when, in cases of rebellion or invasion, the public safety may require them; and I insist that in such cases they are constitutional wherever the public safety does require them; as well in places to which they may prevent the rebellion extending, as in those where it may be already prevailing; as well where they may restrain

by a military commission, as a startling outrage upon the hitherto sacred rights of American citizenship.

"*Resolved*, That exigencies of civil war require the

mischievous interference with the raising and supplying of armies to suppress the rebellion, as where the rebellion may actually be; as well where they may restrain the enticing men out of the army, as where they would prevent mutiny in the army; equally constitutional at all places where they will conduce to the public safety, as against the dangers of rebellion or invasion. Take the particular case mentioned by the meeting. It is asserted, in substance, that Mr. Vallandigham was, by a military commander, seized and tried "for no other reason than words addressed to a public meeting in criticism of the course of the Administration, and in condemnation of the military orders of the general." Now, if there be no mistake about this; if this assertion is the truth, and the whole truth; if there was no other reason for the arrest, then I concede that the arrest was wrong. But the arrest, as I understand, was made for a very different reason. Mr. Vallandigham avows his hostility to the war on the part of the Union; and his arrest was made because he was laboring, with some effect, to prevent the raising of troops; to encourage desertion from the army; and to leave the rebellion without an adequate military force to suppress it. He was not arrested because he was damaging the political prospects of the Administration, or the personal interests of the commanding general, but because he was damaging the army, upon the existence and vigor of which the life of the nation depends. He was warring upon the military, and this gave the military constitutional jurisdiction to lay hands upon him. If Mr. Vallandigham was not damaging the military power of the country, then his arrest was made on mistake of fact, which I would be glad to correct on reasonable satisfactory evidence. I understand the meeting whose resolutions I am considering, to be in favor of suppressing the rebellion by military force—by armies. Long experience has shown that armies cannot be maintained unless desertion shall be punished by the severe penalty of death. The case requires, and the law and the Constitution sanction, this punishment. Must I shoot a simple-minded soldier-boy who deserts, while I must not touch a hair of a wily agitator who induces him to desert? This is none the less injurious when effected by getting a father, a brother, or friend, into a public meeting, and there working upon his feelings until he is persuaded to write the soldier-boy that he is fighting in a bad cause, for a wicked Administration of a contemptible

fullest and freest discussion of public questions by the American people, to the end that their temporary public servants may not forget that they are the crea-

Government, too weak to arrest and punish him if he shall desert. I think that in such a case, to silence the agitator and to save the boy, is not only constitutional, but withal a great mercy.

If I be wrong on this question of constitutional power, my error lies in believing that certain proceedings are constitutional when, in cases of rebellion or invasion, the public safety requires them, which would not be constitutional when, in absence of rebellion or invasion, the public safety does not require them; in other words, that the Constitution is not, in its application, in all respects the same, in cases of rebellion or invasion involving the public safety, as it is in times of profound peace and public security. The Constitution itself makes the distinction; and I can no more be persuaded that the Government can constitutionally take no strong measures in time of rebellion, because it can be shown that the same could not be lawfully taken in time of peace, than I can be persuaded that a particular drug is not good medicine for a sick man, because it can be shown not to be good food for a well one. Nor am I able to appreciate the danger apprehended by the meeting that the American people will, by means of military arrests during the rebellion, lose the right of public discussion, the liberty of speech and the press, the law of evidence, trial by jury, and habeas corpus, throughout the indefinite peaceful future which I trust lies before them, any more than I am able to believe that a man could contract so strong an appetite for emetics during temporary illness, as to persist in feeding upon them during the remainder of his healthful life.

In giving the resolutions that earnest consideration which you request of me, I cannot overlook the fact that the meeting speak as "Democrats." Nor can I, with full respect for their known intelligence, and the fairly presumed deliberation with which they prepared their resolutions, be permitted to suppose that this occurred by accident, or in any way other than that they preferred to designate themselves "Democrats" rather than "American citizens." In this time of national peril, I would have preferred to meet you upon a level one step higher than any party platform; because I am sure that, from such more elevated position, we could do better battle for the country we all love than we possibly can from those lower ones where, from the force of habit, the prejudices of the past, and selfish hopes of the future, we are sure to expend much of our

tures of the public will, and must respect the obligations and duties imposed upon them by the Constitution of their country, which is the authentic, solemn

ingenuity and strength in finding fault with and aiming blows at each other. But, since you have denied me this, I will yet be thankful, for the country's sake, that not all Democrats have done so. He on whose discretionary judgment Mr. Vallandigham was arrested and tried is a Democrat, having no old party affinity with me; and the judge who rejected the constitutional view expressed in these resolutions, by refusing to discharge Mr. Vallandigham on habeas corpus, is a Democrat of better days than these, having received his judicial mantle at the hands of President Jackson. And still more, of all those Democrats who are nobly exposing their lives and shedding their blood on the battle-field, I have learned that many approve the course taken with Mr. Vallandigham, while I have not heard of a single one condemning it. I can assert that there are none such. And the name of President Jackson recalls an incident of pertinent history. After the battle of New Orleans, and while the fact that the treaty of peace had been concluded was well known in the city, but before official knowledge of it had arrived, Gen. Jackson still maintained martial or military law. Now that it could be said the war was over, the clamor against martial law, which had existed from the first, grew more furious. Among other things, a Mr. Louaillier published a denunciatory newspaper article. Gen. Jackson arrested him. A lawyer, by the name of Morel, procured the United States Judge (Hall) to order a writ of habeas corpus to relieve Mr. Louaillier. Gen. Jackson arrested both the lawyer and the Judge. A Mr. Hollander ventured to say of some part of the matter that "it was a dirty trick." Gen. Jackson arrested him. When the officer undertook to serve the writ of habeas corpus, Gen. Jackson took it from him, and sent him away with a copy. Holding the Judge in custody a few days, the General sent him beyond the limits of his encampment, and set him at liberty, with an order to remain till the ratification of peace should be regularly announced, or until the British should have left the Southern coast. A day or two more elapsed, the ratification of the treaty of peace was regularly announced, and the Judge and others were fully liberated. A few days more, and the Judge called Gen. Jackson into court and fined him a thousand dollars for having arrested him and the others named. The General paid the fine, and there the matter rested for nearly thirty years, when Congress refunded principal and interest. The late Senator Douglas, then in

expression of that will; and that whenever, upon the orders of military commanders, and from fear of their spies and informers, American citizens not in the

the House of Representatives, took a leading part in the debates, in which the constitutional question was much discussed. I am not prepared to say whom the journals would show to have voted for the measure.

It may be remarked: First, that we had the same Constitution then as now; secondly, that we then had a case of invasion, and now we have a case of rebellion; and, thirdly, that the permanent right of the people to public discussion, the liberty of speech and of the press, the trial by jury, the law of evidence, and the habeas corpus suffered no detriment whatever by that conduct of Gen. Jackson, or its subsequent approval by the American Congress.

And yet, let me say, that, in my own discretion, I do not know whether I would have ordered the arrest of Mr. Vallandigham. While I cannot shift the responsibility from myself, I hold that, as a general rule, the commander in the field is the better judge of the necessity in any particular case. Of course I must practise a general directory and revisory power in the matter.

One of the resolutions expresses the opinion of the meeting that arbitrary arrests will have the effect to divide and distract those who should be united in suppressing the rebellion, and I am specially called on to discharge Mr. Vallandigham. I regard this act as at least a fair appeal to me on the expediency of exercising a constitutional power which I think exists. In response to such appeal, I have to say it gave me pain when I learned that Mr. Vallandigham had been arrested—that is, I was pained that there should have seemed to be a necessity for arresting him —and that it will afford me great pleasure to discharge him so soon as I can, by any means, believe the public safety will not suffer by it. I further say that, as the war progresses, it appears to me that opinion and action, which were in great confusion at first, take shape and fall into more regular channels, so that the necessity for strong dealing with them gradually decreases. I have every reason to desire that it should cease altogether, and far from the least is my regard for the opinions and wishes of those who, like the meeting at Albany, declare their purpose to sustain the Government in every constitutional and lawful measure to suppress the rebellion. Still I must continue to do so much as may seem to be required by the public safety.

A. LINCOLN.

military service shall be denied the right to approve or disapprove measures of public policy, to denounce or applaud the Commander-in-Chief, and to advocate

ALBANY, *June 30th*, 1863.

To his Excellency the President of the United States:

SIR: The undersigned, officers of the public meeting held in this city on the 16th day of May last, to whom your communication of the 12th of this month, commenting on the resolutions adopted at that meeting, was addressed, have the honor to send to your Excellency a reply to that communication by the committee who reported the resolutions. The great importance to the people of this country of the questions discussed, must be our apology, if any be needed, for saying, that we fully concur in this reply, and believe it to be in entire harmony with the views and sentiments of the meeting referred to.

We are, with great respect, very truly yours,

ERASTUS CORNING, President.

The following extracts from the reply of the committee contain the points presented in that document:

The fact has already passed into history that the sacred rights and immunities which were designed to be protected by these constitutional guarantees, have not been preserved to the people during your Administration. In violation of the first of them, the freedom of the press has been denied. In repeated instances newspapers have been suppressed in the loyal States, because they criticized, as constitutionally they might, those fatal errors of policy which have characterized the conduct of public affairs since your advent to power. In violation of the second of them, hundreds, and we believe, thousands of men, have been seized and immured in prisons and bastiles, not only without warrant upon probable cause, but without any warrant, and for no other cause than a constitutional exercise of freedom of speech. In violation of all these guarantees, a distinguished citizen of a peaceful and loyal State has been torn from his home at midnight by a band of soldiers, acting under the orders of one of your generals, tried before a military commission, without judge or jury, convicted and sentenced without even the suggestion of any offence known to the Constitution or laws of this country. For all these acts you avow yourself ultimately responsible. In the special case of Mr. Vallandigham, the injustice commenced by your subordinate was consummated by a sentence of exile from his home, pronounced by you.

peace or war, as their judgments may dictate, they have ceased to be freemen and have already become slaves.

That great wrong, more than any other which preceded it, asserts the principles of a supreme despotism.

These repeated and continued invasions of constitutional liberty and private right, have occasioned profound anxiety in the public mind. The apprehension and alarm which they are calculated to produce, have been greatly enhanced by your attempt to justify them, because in that attempt you assume to yourself a rightful authority possessed by no constitutional monarch on earth. We accept the declaration that you prefer to exercise this authority with a moderation not hitherto exhibited. But, believing, as we do, that your forbearance is not the tenure by which liberty is enjoyed in this country, we propose to challenge the grounds on which your claim of supreme power is based. While yielding to you as a constitutional magistrate the deference to which you are entitled, we cannot accord to you the despotic power you claim, however indulgent and gracious you may promise to be in wielding it.

We have carefully considered the grounds on which your pretensions to more than regal authority are claimed to rest; and if we do not misinterpret the misty and cloudy forms of expression in which those pretensions are set forth, your meaning is, that while the rights of the citizens are protected by the Constitution in time of peace, they are suspended or lost in time of war, when invasion or rebellion exists. You do not, like many others in whose minds reason and the love of regulated liberty seem to be overthrown by the excitements of the hour, attempt to base this conclusion upon a supposed military necessity existing outside of, and transcending the Constitution, a military necessity behind which the Constitution itself disappears in a total eclipse. We do not find this gigantic and monstrous heresy put forth in your plea for absolute power, but we do find another equally subversive of liberty and law, and quite as certainly tending to the establishment of despotism. You claim to have found, not outside, but within the Constitution, a principle or germ of arbitrary power, which in time of war expands at once into an absolute sovereignty, wielded by one man; so that liberty perishes, or is dependent on his will, his discretion, or his caprice. This extraordinary doctrine you claim to derive wholly from that clause of the Constitution which in case of invasion or rebellion, permits the writ of habeas corpus to be suspended. Upon this ground your whole argument is based.

"*Resolved*, That we reverently cherish that great body of constitutions, laws, precedents, and traditions which constitute us a free people, and that we hold those who designedly and persistently violate them as public enemies.

"*Resolved*, That we are devotedly attached to the Union of these States, and can see nothing but calamity and weakness in its disruption, and shall continue to advocate whatever policy we believe will result in the restoration of that Union.

"*Resolved*, That at a time when our fellow-citizens are falling by thousands upon the battle-field, and human carnage has become familiar, we implore the Federal authorities not to adopt the fatal error that a system of imprisonment and terrorism will subjugate the minds and stifle the voices of the American people.

"*Resolved*, That we call upon the Governor of the State of New York and all others in authority, as they value organized society and stable institutions, to save us from the humiliation and peril of the arrest and trial before Military Commissions of citizens whose only crime shall be the exercise of a right without which life is intolerable and republican citizenship a false name and a false pretence.

"*Resolved*, That the refusal of the Judge of the district within which the Hon. C. L. Vallandigham is incarcerated to grant a writ of *habeas corpus*, is itself a nullification of the Constitution and an infamous outrage upon the clearly defined rights of the citizen.

"*Resolved*, That we fully and heartily endorse the

language of our noble and patriotic Governor, addressed to the meeting assembled at Albany on Saturday, the 16th inst., that the arbitrary arrest and imprisonment of Mr. Vallandigham is "an act which has brought dishonor on our country, which is full of danger to our persons and homes, and which bears upon its front a conscious violation of law and justice."

"*Resolved*, That while fully and heartily endorsing the manly and outspoken sentiments of the Governor of New York, we shall do all in our power to sustain him in his determination to preserve inviolate the sovereignty of our State and the rights of its people against Federal encroachments and usurpations."

At a meeting held in Troy—the largest ever seen in that city, and made all the more important by the fact that it was officered and attended to a considerable extent by gentlemen who had never before acted with the Democratic party—the following resolution, endorsing the Governor, was adopted:

"*Resolved*, That we fully and heartily endorse the language of our noble and truly patriotic Governor, addressed to the meeting assembled at Albany, on Saturday, the 16th inst., that the arbitrary arrest and imprisonment of Mr. Vallandigham is 'an act which has brought dishonor upon our country, which is full of danger to our persons and homes, and which bears upon its front a conscious violation of law and justice.'"

The New York resolutions given above were unanimously readopted.

Similar meetings were held, and resolutions of a like character adopted, all over the State.

The election for State officers and members of the Legislature was held in November. On the 30th of October, a large and enthusiastic Democratic meeting was held at Syracuse, at which several gentlemen acted as Vice-Presidents who had voted for Mr. Lincoln for President, and for Gen. Wadsworth for Governor, the year before. Governor Seymour addressed the meeting at considerable length. We make the following extracts from his speech:

"One year ago we were a people united in purpose—to-day we are distracted and paralyzed. Why? To-day the South, which was then ready to fall to pieces, is united, and apparently as strong as ever. Why? That party most endangers the public welfare which not only refuses to use every influence that can be brought to bear, but opposes obstacles in the way of a successful completion of the contest in which we are engaged. That man who, not content with restoring the Union and upholding the Constitution, adds further objects more difficult of attainment, hinders the success of the war. I appeal to you, men of Onondaga, men of Central New York, if they are not making success more difficult, more unattainable, if in any event they are not postponing the end, until you are brought nearer and nearer those calamities which lie straight in our pathway—national bankruptcy and national ruin. They say we must fight until slavery is extinguished; they say we must fight until the States shall assume new relationships to the Federal Government—until it becomes revolutionary in its aspects and influences. We are to unsettle what eighty years of experience had settled; we are to upturn the foundations of our Constitution. At this very moment, when the fate of the nation and of individuals trembles in the balance, these madmen ask us to plunge into a bottomless pit of controversy upon indefinite purposes. Does not every man know that we must have a united North to triumph? Can we get a united North upon a theory that proposes to centralize the power of the General Government upon propositions that you shall not have the great right and liberty of protecting your own person? that the Constitution can be set aside at the will of one man, because, forsooth, he judges it to be a military necessity? ['No, no.'] I never heard yet that Abraham Lincoln was a military necessity. [Great laughter.] If military necessities are to govern, let us at least be consistent, and ask that military men shall judge what these necessities are—men who can marshal armies in the field and fight great battles. The very proposition disfranchises you. If you assent to it, you men of Central New York, give up your Constitutional right to your own judgment.

"Now I propose to inquire, What has taken place since I stood here one year ago? What were the circumstances of our country then? At that moment the people of the United States had given, voluntarily, under the calls of our Government, six hundred thousand men to swell the ranks of your armies. Before that time our political opponents, through their journals and speakers, had said that the Administration had failed in the conduct of the war. Therefore it was that at the last November election, when you did me the honor to place me in the Gubernatorial chair, you decided that they had failed in meeting the just expectations of the American people. You gave them 600,-000 more, 600,000 living men—somebody's sons, somebody's brothers, somebody's husbands. They went from the homes of our land; they constituted the wealth and power of the nation. Where are they? What has been done? Is our country saved? Is the war terminated? To-day, when we ought to rejoice at the full completion of our heart's desire, we are met—not by assurances that peace is restored to our land, not by the fact that rebellion is put down; no, my friends, we are met by another call for 600,000 men. This moment everywhere our armies are on the defensive. The question to-day is—not 'What are we doing?' but 'What are the enemy doing?' The question is—not 'Where do our Generals attack?' but 'Where are we threatened?' Look at the Potomac. Look at the Cumberland and Tennessee. Notwithstanding the vast contributions of blood, and men, and treasure, to-day we are called upon to furnish 600,000 more, including the number embraced under the Conscription act, and you, the people of New York, to-day are called upon to furnish 108,000 men before the 5th of January next. Now, there are some things about which there is no difference of opinion among candid men of all parties.

"It is agreed that there is a limit in the expenditure of money when the nation must be whelmed in national bankruptcy, and that there is a limit in the prosecution of the war when the nation will go to ruin.

Every day's expenditure of life and money brings us nearer to these calamities. We agree that the war must be brought to the speediest possible honorable conclusion. Now, which of the two parties asking your support is the one most likely to reach this result before we reach national bankruptcy, ruin, and disgrace? Let the past go. We will leave it to the judgment of the future to say who has been right and who has been wrong. Let us now confront the duties of the hour boldly and patriotically. We are to decide by our votes what shall be the future policy of the Government, for I tell you the voice of New York will be potential in the end. If the people of this State shall decide in favor of the radical policy, which is to prolong the war for indefinite issues, we are lost forever. On the contrary, if the people of this State decide in favor of a policy which can be reached and which will bring the war to a successful conclusion, there is yet a glorious future for our land. Where do the two parties differ? The Republicans say, 'We want to put forth all the material powers of our land to bring the war to a close.' We say so, too. We are upon the brink of a cataract, without time to inquire into the past; we must put forth every material power to secure success to our cause. But we say more than that; we say that we will add to the power of force the influences of wise statesmanship, of conciliation, of Christian charity, of patriotic purpose. [Cheers.]

"The draft has been the first great attempt to exercise this power, and it has miserably failed. Instead of strengthening the Government, it has immeasurably weakened it. I do not fear for the States, but for the Federal Government. The great State of New York can maintain her rights when the little men who insult her are passed away and forgotten. [Great cheering.] You remember how gloriously the State responded to the calls for volunteers. Our rulers, when they saw the mighty armies they had marshalled, thought it had been done by their own power, instead of by the spontaneous patriotism of the people. They said we will pass around the hat no more when we want men or money, but we will pass a law and send out force, so that when we want men we will take them out of the houses of the nation by compulsion. New York sent out of itself one hundred and twenty thousand volunteers. Now look at the result of the draft for sixty-eight thousand men. They gave you credit under that draft for twenty-one thousand men. How is this twenty-one thousand made up? Well, you are valued as being worth about three hundred dollars apiece, and of these twenty-one thousand men which have been rendered, twelve or thirteen thousand are three hundred dollar bills—not men of muscles and sinews ready to do service; and that act has not sent out from this State eight thousand men. I do not believe it has more than six thousand, and more than half of these are substitutes, which is another name for volunteers. So much for the centralization policy.

"You are to decide the most momentous questions ever submitted to a people; questions that come home to each man of you in all the relationships of life. The mighty debt that is being rolled up is an encumbrance upon your property, and now equals one-fourth of the value of the whole property of the country. So far as it is necessary to spend for proper purposes, let it be poured forth; but if it is to gratify the theories of fanatics and bigoted men, we should express our disapproval of those theories that are mortgaging our lands. We are willing to sustain them in all constitutional purposes; we dedicate ourselves and all we have to the preservation of our country; but when they ask of us sacrifices for the purpose of trampling down the Constitution and destroying the great principles of liberty, then we must at least have the poor privilege of raising our voices in terms of expostulation against a policy so fatal and ruinous. We love that flag [pointing to the stars and stripes] with the whole love of our life; and every star that glitters on its blue field is sacred. And let me conclude with the sentiment of a citizen of another State, declaring that we will preserve the Constitution. We will preserve the Union; we will preserve our flag, with every star that glitters upon it, and we will see to it that there is a State for every star." [Continued cheering.]

The meeting then adjourned, and Gov. Seymour, arriving again at the hotel, shook hands and conversed with citizens and friends until the hour for dinner.

The Legislature met at Albany on the 5th of January, 1864. The Governor's Message was sent in on the same day. After dealing with matters relating purely to the State, such as the common schools, the prisons, banks, finances, trade, canal, immigration, and the Constitutional amendment, the Governor proceeded to speak of the draft. He said:

"Congress, at its last session, passed an act for drafting citizens into the army. It wrought a change in the public feeling with regard to military service, and all, without respect to political views, tried to evade its operations. It has proved injurious to the civil, industrial, and military interests of the country.

"I called the attention of the President of the United States to the inequality in the enrolment. The wrong was partially corrected by reducing the numbers called for in those districts where they were excessive, to the average number in the other districts of the State. New York is required to furnish more than other States in proportion to its population."

The Governor then submitted a statement which we have already given in another chapter, showing the truth of his assertion. He then related the action of the War Department, and gave the result of the volunteering which had been going on in the State during the past year, with great success. He declared the draft a failure. Said he:

"It not only fails to fill our armies, but it produces discontent in the service; it is opposed to the genius of our political system; it alienates our people from the Government; it is injurious to the industrial pursuits of the country.

"The difficulty in getting recruits is owing in part to the exhausting demands which have been made for that purpose. But it is also owing to other reasons; and among them attempted coercion is foremost. Congress attempted to keep up the number of men in the field without regard to State or local Government, and it set aside those numerous minor local organizations, whose united contributions of men have made up our vast armies. By efforts to make itself independent of popular and local influences, the General Government impaired its power to get recruits."

He argued that as long as the people and Govenment are financially prosperous, recruits ought to be raised by bounties, and not by coercion, and demonstrated that the system inaugurated by the Federal Government was extravagant, unpopular, and calculated to do great injury to the cause and to the *morale* of the army, He said that the army should not be allowed to run down until it was inefficient, and then be refilled by a violent and revolting effort. Recruiting should go on all the time, with such reasonable bounties as would draw volunteers. The militia of the States should be kept up to an efficient standard at all times, and would thus constitute a reserve force, ready for any emergency. Had this been done in the past, Ohio and Pennsylvania would not have been invaded, nor would New York be then insulted by threatening attacks upon her border cities and towns. The sympathy which ought to exist between the army and people, ought to be fostered by the Government. The armies should feel that they are upholding a just, paternal Government, which respects their personal rights, the happiness of their families, the sanctity of their homes. Such a feeling is not likely to exist in an army of conscripts, dragged from their homes and forced into the service against their will.

The Governor related the incidents connected with the call for aid from Pennsylvania, and the sending of the militia to her assistance, and referred to the draft riots as follows:

"While the militia were thus absent from the city, and its forts and harbor unprotected, on Saturday, the 11th day of July, the draft, under the act of the last Congress, was commenced in one of the wards of the city. *I was not advised of the step, and I believe the Mayor of the city was equally ignorant of the proceeding.* A despatch was sent to me by the Mayor of New York, informing me of a popular outbreak, on Monday evening, the 13th day of July, and on the following morning I reached the city and found it agitated with wild excitement and riotous violence. The militia were ordered to return immediately from Pennsylvania. * * * * *

"For the purpose of legalizing the most extreme exertion of force to put down violent resistance to law, I declared the city in a state of insurrection. It was divided into districts, which were placed under the control of persons of influence or military experience, who were directed to organize the citizens. Three thousand stand of arms were issued to these and other organizations. I endeavored by these arrangements to enable the police and the military to act against the masses of the rioters, and to relieve them from the fatigue of marching to distant points to check minor disorders.

"To prevent the spread of violence, I obtained from the Collector of the port the service of an armed vessel, to traverse the rivers and bays in the vicinity of New York, and I also authorized the Police Commissioners to charter another steamer, which could be used to carry policemen and soldiers to any point on the shores or islands where disturbances were threatened. * * * * *

* * * "I do not underrate the value of the services rendered by the military and naval officers of the General Government who were stationed in the city, or those of Gen. Sandford, for the public are under great obligations to them for their courage and prudent counsels. But they had at their command only a handful of troops, who alone were entirely unequal to the duty of defending the vast amount of public property that was endangered. The rioters were subdued by the exertions of the city officials, civil and military, the people, the police, the firemen, and a small body of only twelve hundred men, composed equally of the State and National forces."

The Governor then stated that, in consequence of an appeal from General Wool, showing that there was not force enough in his command to properly garrison the forts about the city, he ordered the militia from the interior of the State to repair at once to New York to man the fortifications, but that Gen. Wool subsequently requested him to rescind the order.

The remainder of the message was devoted to national affairs. The lawless and unprincipled conduct of the Administration was severely condemned, and the outrages practised upon citizens of the loyal States denounced as revolutionary. The issues of the war were discussed temperately and practically. The language of the message was calm and dignified, and the whole paper breathed forth an earnest devotion to the Constitution and the Union. The Governor declared that the war ought to be waged only for the restoration of the Union, which Union ought to be preserved as a free Government, not as a military despotism. The message closed as follows:

"Wise statesmanship can now bring this war to a close, upon the terms solemnly avowed at the outset of the contest. Good faith to the public creditors; to all classes of citizens of our country; to the world, demands that this be done.

"The triumph won by the soldiers in the field should be followed up and secured by the peace-making policy of the statesmen in the Cabinet. In no other way can we save our Union.

"The fearful struggle which has taught the North and South the courage, the endurance, and the resources of our people, have made a basis of mutual respect upon which a generous and magnanimous policy can build lasting relationships of union, intercourse, and fraternal regard. If our course is to be shaped by narrow and vindictive passions, by venal purposes, or by partisan objects, then a patriotic people have poured out their blood and treasure in vain, and the future is full of disaster and ruin.

"We should seek not the disorganization but the pacification of that section of our country devastated by civil war. In this hour of triumph appeals should be made to States, which are identified with the growth and greatness of our country, and with some of which are associated the patriotic memories of our revolutionary struggle. Every generous mind revolts at the thought of destroying all those memories that cling about the better days of the Republic; that are connected with the sacrifices of the men who have made our history glorious by their services in the Cabinet, in the forum and in the field.

"The victories which have given our Government its present commanding position were won by men who rallied around and fought beneath the folds of a flag whose stars represent each State in our Union. If we strike out of existence a single State, we make that flag a falsehood. When we extinguish the name of any one of the original thirteen States, we dishonor the historic stripes of our national banner. Let the treasonable task of defacing our flag be left to those who war upon our Government, and who would destroy the unity of our country.

"Faith to our armies and to our citizens demands that we keep sacred the solemn pledge made to our people and to the civilized world when we engaged in this bloody war, 'that it was not waged in any spirit of oppression, or for any purpose of conquest or subjugation, or purpose of overthrowing or interfering with the rights of established institutions in those States, but to defend and maintain the supremacy of the Constitution and to preserve the Union with all the dignity, equality and rights of the several States unimpaired;

and that as soon as these objects are accomplished the war ought to cease.' "

Early in the year, the Legislature adopted a resolution declaring that no distinction should be made between the foreign and domestic creditor in the payment of interest on the State debt. This action of that body drew forth the following message from the Governor:

" EXECUTIVE DEPARTMENT,
" *Albany, April* 22, 1864.

" *To the Legislature :*

" My attention has been called to a concurrent resolution which has passed both branches of the Legislature, in the following words:

" ' *Whereas,* All the stocks issued by this State were made payable and negotiable in this State; therefore,

" ' *Resolved,* That no distinction should be made between the foreign and domestic holders of such bonds as to the currency in which the principal and interest thereon should be paid.'

" To the principle laid down in this resolution, in terms, there can be no objection offered. All the creditors of the State, whether they be of our own people or foreign, should be alike paid; paid promptly and in full all that was promised them.

" The Legislature, last year, adopted a concurrent resolution on this subject in the following words:

" ' *Resolved,* That the interest accruing on so much of the State debt on the first day of April as was, on the 1st day of March, 1863, held by persons residing out of the United States, and is still held by them, be paid in gold or its equivalent.'

"And an appropriation was made for the purchase of coin to an extent sufficient to enable the Comptroller to pay in gold the interest on the stocks of New York held by persons residing abroad; and only to that extent. Although the resolution of last year did not in terms forbid the payment of the interest due to our creditors residing in this country, in coin, yet the absence of any appropriation for the purpose obliged the Comptroller to forego such payment.

"In practice, a distinction was thus made between the non-resident creditor and the resident creditor. We kept faith with the stranger who had trusted us; we broke faith only with those of our own household.

"The effect of the resolution of this year, in the absence of any appropriation, will be that no part of the interest will be paid, to wit, in coin or its equivalent.

"When we sought the markets of the world with our securities, we pledged ourselves to redeem them in the currency of the world. The partial neglect of plighted faith last year is now to be followed by an open refusal to pay any of our promises according to their plain sense. The disgrace of last year was limited; it was kept within ourselves; now our shame and dishonor are to be borne in the face of the world.

"I look upon this matter as of so much moment to the welfare and to the character of New York and of its people that I feel constrained to ask you to give the subject a reconsideration; and to urge you to pass a concurrent resolution that shall enable the Comptroller to pay all the interest which may fall due before the next session of the Legislature, in coin. In this way your resolution of this year can be carried into effect consistently with the good credit of the State, and 'no distinction' will 'be made between foreign and domestic holders' of the bonds. If you do not do this, let me urge you to provide, at least, for the interest that is due residents of other countries being paid in coin.

"The refusal to pay in coin to our own citizens may justify itself to some minds, although not to mine, as a measure of *quasi* taxation; special, discriminating, and unfair, but excused by our present extraordinary condition. In dealing with our creditors in other countries no such considerations can come in. We have over them no legitimate power of taxation; these creditors of ours have no voice nor part in our political action; we have no claim upon them that they should take a share in the misfortunes that befall us in our career. They are not of our household, nor bound to take part of our domestic calamities upon themselves. The burdens and the misfortunes of this war belong to us; it is ungenerous to shift any portion of them upon others who are not a part of us. These foreign creditors of ours are strangers who lent us their money when we wanted it; upon no security but our word of honor. If we do not pay them back their money to the strict letter of our bargain, we incur a shame that can never be removed from us. We deprive New York of an element of strength which heretofore has been wisely used, and which its people have found profitable, to wit, its unquestioned credit.

"Principle and policy unite to urge the action I recommend to you. It is the only way in which the State can, in truth, fulfil its contracts. It is the only way in which the State can keep itself in a position to go into the market hereafter decently as a borrower.

"The State is even now in the market for money to pay its bounties to volunteers. The whole amount of the appropriation I urge upon you will be more than repaid in the first negotiation the State may make, by the enhanced price of its securities. We shall lose more in our immediate transactions, than the cost of providing the coin for this interest. Not only our future profit but our immediate gain will be served by adhering now to the strictest letter of our contracts.

"The saving proposed by not paying in coin is small and temporary, while the dishonor is lasting; and the pecuniary loss consequent upon this dishonor, will be in the end enormous.

"Bad faith on the part of New York, the leading member of our Confederacy, must, inevitably, weaken very greatly, if it does not destroy the credit of our Government security in foreign markets. Compared with the importance of this State action in its effect upon the credit of the Government, the cost of paying our interest in coin is insignificant.

"Aside from the consideration of interest or policy, our duty, in my judgment, is plain. It is to pay the debts of the State; to pay them in precisely the mode in which they were promised to be paid; to keep the honor of the State unsullied; and to this plain duty we should be true, cost what it may.

"Horatio Seymour."

On the same day Governor Seymour issued an appeal "to men of capital, the bankers, the merchants, and others of the people of the State who have its honor at heart, whereby at least so much of the interest as belongs to non-resident creditors, if not the whole," might be paid in coin or its equivalent. The appeal was unsuccessful, and the efforts of the patriotic Governor to keep pure the honor of the State were fruitless.

CHAPTER VIII.

The Bogus Proclamation of Mr. Lincoln—Deception practised upon Democratic Newspapers—Suppression of the "World" and "Journal of Commerce"—Highhanded Measures of the Administration—Governor Seymour's Action in the Case—His Instructions to the District Attorney—Action in the Case—Refusal of the Grand Jury to do its Duty—The Governor's Instructions to Mr. Hall—Proceedings against General Dix and his Officers—Trial of the Case before Judge Russell—Decision of the Court—The Sequel—Meeting of the Chicago Convention—Mr. Seymour chosen President of that Body—His Services during the Presidential Campaign—He procures the Passage of a Law for Collecting the Votes of the State Troops in the Field—Statement of the Provisions of this Law—Mr. Seymour again nominated for Governor by the Democratic State Convention—His Circular to the Officers of the New York Troops in the Federal Service—His Anxiety for a fair Election—Measures on the part of the Government to control the Election—The Reign of Terror—Proclamation by the Governor—The Election—How the Administration carried it—Mr. Seymour defeated by Mr. Fenton.

On the 18th of May, 1864, there appeared in the *Journal of Commerce* and *The World*, of New York City, a proclamation purporting to have been issued by President Lincoln, setting apart the 26th of May as a day of fasting and prayer, and calling 400,000 men into the service of the United States. This paper was delivered at the offices of these journals late on the night of the 17th, and in such a manner as to induce the belief that it was a genuine "Washington despatch." Soon after its publication, it was discovered to be a forgery, whereupon the fact was announced by the journals on their bulletin-boards, and a reward of five hundred dollars offered for the author of the paper. The editors of *The World* and *Journal of Commerce*, at once informed General Dix of the forgery, and gave him such information as they thought would be of service in his efforts to discover the author. As soon as the Government received information of the matter, orders were issued to General Dix to seize the offices of *The World* and *Journal of Commerce*, to suppress the publication of those papers, and imprison the editors and proprietors in Fort Layfayette—the American Bastile. The order for the arrest and imprisonment of these gentlemen was rescinded on the same day, but the publication of their papers was suspended for two days. The author of the proclamation was discovered, arrested and imprisoned in Fort Lafayette, however, before the printing offices which had been seized were restored to their owners. He was detained in the fort several months, and then discharged without any further investigation of his offence.

The outrage upon the newspapers excited the deepest indignation on the part of the conservative citizens of the State; and the conduct of the Government was seen to be all the more atrocious as the victims were entirely innocent of intentional wrong.

Governor Seymour determined to make it the occasion of testing the power of the General Government to outrage the liberties and rights of the citizens of his State, and on the 22d of May addressed the following letter to the District Attorney:

"STATE OF NEW YORK, EXECUTIVE DEPARTMENT,
"ALBANY, *May 22d*, 1864.

"*To A. Oakey Hall, District Attorney of the County of New York:*

"SIR: I am advised that on the 19th inst., the office of the *Journal of Commerce* and that of the *New York World* were entered by armed men, the property of the owners seized, and the premises held by force for several days. It is charged that these acts of violence were done without due legal process, and without the sanction of the State or national laws.

"If this be true, the offenders must be punished.

"In the month of July last, when New York was a scene of violence, I gave warning that 'the laws of the State must be enforced, its peace and order maintained, and the property of its citizens protected at every hazard.' The laws were enforced at a fearful cost of blood and life.

"The declaration I then made was not intended for that occasion merely or against any class of men. It is one of an enduring character, to be asserted at all times, against all conditions of citizens, without favor or distinction. Unless all are made to bow to the law, it will be respected by none. Unless all are made secure in their rights of person and property, none can be protected. If the owners of the above-named journals have violated State or national laws, they must be proceeded against and punished by those laws. Any action against them outside of legal procedures is criminal. At this time of civil war and disorder, the majesty of the law must be upheld, or society will sink into anarchy.

"Our soldiers in the field will battle in vain for constitutional liberty, if persons, or property, or opinions are trampled on at home. We must not give up home freedom, and thus disgrace American characters while our citizens in the army are pouring out their blood to maintain the national honor. They must not find, when they come back, that their personal and fireside rights have been despoiled.

"In addition to the general obligation to enforce the laws of the land, there are local reasons why they must be upheld in the city of New York. If they are not, its commerce and greatness will be broken down. If this great centre of wealth, business, and enterprise is thrown into disorder and bankruptcy, the National Government will be paralyzed. What makes New York the heart of our country? Why are its pulsations felt at the extremities of our land? Not through its position alone, but because of the world-wide belief that property is safe within its limits from waste by mobs and spoliation by Government. The laborers in the workshop, the mine, and in the field, on this continent and in every other part of the globe, send to its merchants, for sale or exchange, the products of their toil. These merchants are made the trustees of the wealth of millions living in every land, because it is believed that in their hands property is safe under the shield of laws administered upon principles and according to known usages.

"This great confidence has grown up in many

years by virtue of painstaking honest performance of duty by the business men of your city. In this they have been aided by the enforcement of laws based upon solemnly-recorded pledges that 'the people's right to be secure in their persons, houses, papers, and effects against unreasonable searches and seizures, shall not be violated, and that no one shall be deprived of liberty or property without the process of law.' For more than eighty years have we as a people been building up this universal faith in the sanctity of our jurisprudence. It is this which carries our commerce upon every ocean, and brings back to our merchants the wealth of every clime. It is now charged that in utter disregard of the sanctity of that faith, at a moment when the national credit is undergoing a fearful trial, the organs of commerce are seized and held, in violation of Constitutional pledges; that this act was thus done in a public mart of your great city, and was thus forced upon the notice of the commercial agents of the world, and they were shown in an offensive way that property is seized by military force and arbitrary orders. These things are more hurtful to the national honor and strength than the loss of battles.

"The world will confound such acts with the principles of our Government, and the folly and crimes of officials will be looked upon as the natural results of the spirit of our institutions. Our State and local authorities must repel this ruinous interference. If the merchants of New York are not willing to have their harbor sealed up and their commerce paralyzed, they must unite in this demand for the security of persons and property. If this is not done, the world will withdraw from their keeping its treasures and its commerce. History has taught all, that official violation of civil law and order goes before acts of spoliation and other measures which destroy the safeguards of commerce.

"I call upon you to look into the acts connected with the seizure of the *Journal of Commerce* and of the *New York World*. If these acts were illegal, the offenders must be punished. In making your inquiries and in prosecuting the parties implicated, you will call upon the Sheriff of the County and the heads of the police department for any needed force or assistance. The failure to give this by any official under my control, will be deemed a sufficient cause for his removal.

"Very respectfully, yours, &c.,

"HORATIO SEYMOUR."

Upon receipt of these instructions, the District Attorney laid the matter before the Grand Jury, who reported that it was "inexpedient to examine into the subject." The Governor thereupon sent Mr. Hall these further instructions:

"EXECUTIVE CHAMBER,
ALBANY, *June* 25*th*, 1864.

"*A. Oakey Hall, Esq., Dist. Attorney of the City and County of New York:*

"SIR: In the matter of the seizure of the offices of the *World* and *Journal of Commerce*, the Grand Jury, in disregard of their oaths 'to diligently inquire into and make the presentment of all such matters and things as should be given them in charge,' have refused to make such inquiries, and declare that 'it is inexpedient to examine into the subject referred to in the charge of the court,' with respect to such seizures. It becomes my duty under the express requirements of the Constitution 'to take care that the laws of the State are faithfully executed.' If the Grand Jury, in pursuance of the demands of the law and the obligations of their oaths, had inquired into the matter given them in charge by the Court and the Public Prosecutor, their decision, whatever it might have been, would have been entitled to respect. As they have refused to do their duty, the subject of the seizure of these journals should at once be brought before some proper magistrate. If you wish any assistance in the prosecution of these investigations, it will be given to you.

"As it is a matter of public interest that violations of the laws of the State be punished, the views or wishes of the parties immediately affected must not be suffered to influence the action of public officers. If through fear or other motives, they are unwilling to aid you in getting at facts, it will be your duty to compel their attendance as witnesses in behalf of the people. "Respectfully yours,

"HORATIO SEYMOUR."

On the 28th of June, the District Attorney made an affidavit before Judge Russell, of the City and County, who issued subpœnas for witnesses. After hearing the testimony of the witnesses, Judge Russell issued warrants for the arrest of Major-General John A. Dix, Capt. Barstow, Major Bowles, Capt. Cundy, and Lieut. Tuthill, and placed these warrants in the hands of the Sheriff.

The parties voluntarily appeared in Court by their counsel on the 6th of July, and were relieved from custody on the parole of General Dix. The argument of the case was ordered to be made on the 9th. The Counsel for the defence announced that the President had ordered General Dix to disregard the process of the Court and not to allow himself to be arrested or deprived of his liberty. Information of this was at once telegraphed to Governor Seymour, who, on the 7th of July, ordered the District Attorney to enforce the law of the State without regard to the President's order to General Dix to resist the process of the Court.

The case was heard on July 9th, Judge Pierrepont and Mr. Evarts, the present Attorney-General of the United States, arguing in favor of the right of the President to order the suppression of the journals by General Dix, and Mr. Hall, and Gen. Cochrane, the Attorney-General of the State, sustaining the view of the case taken by the Governor. On the 1st of August, the judge delivered his decision. He said that, after a careful examination of the matter, he had concluded to hold General Dix and the other parties to the acts complained of, subject to the action of the Grand Jury of the City and County. He said:

"It is unnecessary for me, in deciding this matter, to rehearse the facts of the case. The defendants, through their counsel, place themselves under the protection of Section 4 of the Act of Congress of March 3, 1863, entitled 'An Act relating to Habeas Corpus, and regulating judicial proceedings in certain cases.' If that provision is constitutional, it assimilates the President of the United States during the existence of the present rebellion, to an absolute monarch, and makes him incapable of doing any wrong. This is a very novel and startling doctrine to advance under a republican form of government.

"I have given the case a most careful consideration; on the one hand, seeking to avoid an undue interference with the agents of the Government in the performance of their duty, and, on the other, keeping before me my own obligation to uphold and enforce the laws of this State. I do not deem it proper to state in detail the view I entertain upon the legal principles so ably discussed before me by counsel upon both sides. Such an exposition of the law would be more appropriate should the case come before the Court for trial."

The efforts of the Governor in behalf of the freedom of his fellow-citizens were successful. The military authorities were made to recognize the supremacy of the civil law by their appearance in Court, though the President had ordered them not to appear.

The National Democratic Convention met at Chicago on the 29th of August, 1864, for the purpose of nominating candidates for the offices of President and Vice-President of the United States. It was organized by the election of Mr. Seymour as President of the

Convention. His friends had insisted on placing his name before the Convention for the nomination for the Presidency of the United States; but on the day before the organization of that body, he announced positively that he would not be a candidate. The Convention nominated General McClellan for the Presidency, and Hon. Geo. H. Pendleton for the Vice-Presidency.

The campaign was an ardent and exciting contest, in which the Administration gave unmistakable evidence of its determination to carry the elections in its favor at any risk.

As there were thousands of legal voters of the State of New York serving in the army, Governor Seymour had some time before this procured the passage of a Constitutional amendment by the Legislature, which was submitted to and approved by the people, authorizing the soldiers of the State in the service of the Union, who were legal voters, to take part in the election without returning home. In consequence of this authority from the people, a law was passed by the Legislature, and approved by the Governor on the 21st of April, 1864, prescribing the manner in which the elections should be held in the army and navy.

This law extends the right to vote in time of war, to qualified electors "in the actual military service of the United States, in the army or navy thereof, who shall be absent from the State of New York on the day of election." The right thus extended is by the terms of the law expressly restricted to the officers and enlisted men actually in the military service, and is not granted to sutlers, clerks, teamsters, officers' servants, and other camp followers. They could vote only at their own homes in the State. If any soldier or sailor is in the State on election day, he can vote only at the precinct in which he resides. The right given to volunteers is also extended to qualified citizens of the State who are members of the regular army, and to those who may be members of the militia regiments absent from the State at the time, in the service of the United States.

"An elector authorized to vote by the provisions of the law, can do so at any time within the sixty days next previous to the election. For that purpose, he must execute a proxy, authorizing any elector of the town or city in which he resides, whom he may name in the proxy, to deliver his vote to the inspectors of the election district in which the voter resides, on the day of the election. The proxy must be signed by the person voting, and must also be attested by a subscribing witness and sworn to before any field-officer, captain, adjutant, or commandant of any company or detachment on detached service, in the service of the United States, and commissioned as officers in the volunteer force of the State of New York; or, if the absent elector is in the navy, before 'the captain or commandant of any vessel in the naval service of the United States to which the said absent elector may belong or be attached.' The voter is also required to make and subscribe before any such officer an affidavit of his qualification as an elector.

"The elector can vote 'for all officers for whom he would have a right to vote if he were present' at the election. He must fold his ballots and inclose them with his proxy in an envelope, duly sealed, on the outside of which must be his affidavit of qualification as an elector. The envelope must be enclosed in another envelope, which must be sealed and directed to the person authorized by the proxy to cast the vote, and transmitted to him 'by mail or otherwise.'

"The person to whom the proxy is directed may open the outer envelope, but not the inner one. On the day of the election he must deliver the inner envelope to the inspectors at the polls. If the name of the soldier making the affidavit of qualification as a voter, endorsed on the envelope, is on the list of registered electors, the inspectors will open the envelope and deposit the ballots in the appropriate boxes. If the name is not on the list, an affidavit must be made by 'a householder of the district,' that he knows the soldier to be 'a resident of the district,' or the envelope will not be opened, and the soldier will lose his vote. The affidavit required is only to prove residence, and the law provides no separate affidavit of qualification of colored men, as required by the Constitution." *

During the month of September, the Democratic State Convention nominated Mr. Seymour for reëlection to the Governor's chair, and the Republicans put forward the Hon. Rueben E. Fenton as their candidate. The election was held in November together with the Presidential election.

As the political campaign progressed, Governor Seymour addressed the following circular, with refer-

* Annual Cyclopædia, 1864, pp. 581–582.

ence to the act to authorize soldiers to vote, to the commandants and surgeons of New York regiments in the field:

"STATE OF NEW YORK, EXECUTIVE DEPARTMENT,
"ALBANY, *Sept.* 30, 1864.

"*To ——— of N. Y. S. Vols.:*

"The Legislature of this State, at its last session, passed an act which received my signature and became a law, on the 21st of April, 1864, entitled 'an act to enable the qualified electors of this State, absent therefrom in the military service of the United States, in the army or navy thereof, to vote.'

"This act inaugurates a new feature in our system of elective franchise, and I feel it incumbent upon me to call your attention to its provisions, and to ask that you see it faithfully and impartially carried out. The act provides for this in the following section:

"'SEC. 13. *Any officer of the State or of the United States, or any other person, who shall directly control or attempt to control any such enlisted elector in the exercise of any of his rights under this act, by menace, bribery, fear of punishment, hope of reward, or any other corrupt or arbitrary measure, or resort whatever, to annoy, infure, or otherwise punish any such officer or man, for the manner in which he may have exercised any such right, shall be deemed guilty of an offence against the sovereignty of this State, which shall be punished as a misdemeanor, and for which he may be indicted and tried at any future time, when he may be found within the limits of the State; and upon con-*

viction he shall be imprisoned for a term not exceeding one year, and fined in a sum not exceeding one thousand dollars, and he shall also thenceforth be ineligible, after conviction, to hold any office in this State.'

"The twelfth section of the act herein referred to, provides for the preparation, by the Secretary of State, of blank forms and envelopes, which, together with copies of the soldiers' voting act, have been forwarded by express to the different regiments and battalions of New York State volunteers in the United States service, and to the sick and wounded New York soldiers in U. S. hospitals, under the following order:

'WAR DEPARTMENT, ADJUTANT GENERAL'S OFFICE,
'WASHINGTON, *August* 8, 1864.

'SPECIAL ORDERS NO. 262.

'19. *All officers in the military service of the United States will render every facility to such Express Companies as may be charged by the Governor of New York with the delivery of the necessary forms and blanks required to secure the votes of soldiers of that State in the field, with a view to the blanks being delivered with the least practical delay.*

'*By order of the Secretary of War.*

'E. D. TOWNSEND,
'[*Official.*] *Assistant Adjutant General.*
'E. D. TOWNSEND, *Assistant Adjutant General.*'

"I send you a set of ballots prepared by the friends of General McClellan, and have requested the Secretary of State to forward to you a set prepared by the friends of Mr. Lincoln.

"The State and Local Committees of the two political parties will send you the necessary number of ballots.

"You can do much towards securing to your officers and men a fair expression of their political preferences, if you will detail one or more officers of your command of each political party, to distribute the ballots and to aid soldiers and commissioners in filling up the requisite powers of attorney. You are also requested to use every effort to send forward the envelopes, containing the powers of attorney and ballots, to the electors in the several election districts of this State, named on the back thereof—either by express or mail, or through such reliable commissioners as may visit your command.

"I feel confident that every officer from New York will feel an honorable pride in seeing that the laws of his State are carried out according to their letter and spirit, and that they will protect all under their care in the full and free exercise of their personal and political rights. Truly yours, &c.,

"HORATIO SEYMOUR."

On the 28th of October, General Dix issued an order, warning all persons from attempting to interfere with the elections, and taking measures to prevent the incursions of any armed partisans of the enemy into the State from Canada, as the Government affected to believe there was danger of this. The true motive of the Administration was doubtless to inspire terror in the hearts of the timid members of the Democratic party, and keep them away from the polls on election day. Other orders, having the same object in view, were issued, and good care was taken by the Administration to let it be known that it would regard voting the Democratic ticket as an "act of disloyalty." So thoroughly, indeed, was this understood that many persons feared the election would be controlled by armed force. To calm this state of feeling and encourage every citizen to assert his right, the Governor issued the following proclamation:

"EXECUTIVE CHAMBER, ALBANY,
"*November 2d*, 1864.

"In a few days the citizens of this country are to exercise their constitutional duty of electing a President and Vice-President of the United States, at a time when the condition of our country excites the deepest interest.

"The questions of the day not only affect the personal welfare of all, and the happiness of their homes, but also are of a character to arouse the passions and lead to angry controversies between parties.

"The existence of a terrible civil war and the assertion of the right of military commanders in some sections of our country to interfere with elections, have caused painful and exciting doubts in the minds of many with regard to the free and untrammelled exercise of the elective franchise. I therefore appeal to all men of all political parties to unite with those holding official positions, in their efforts to allay undue excitement, soften the harshness of party prejudices and passions, and to avoid all measures which tend to strife or disorder.

"However we may differ in our views of public policy, we are alike interested in the maintaining of order, in the preservation of the rights and the promotion of the prosperity of our State.

"While we do not agree as to the methods by which these ends are to be gained, they are earnestly sought by all.

"It is certain they cannot be reached by angry controversies, unreasonable suspicions or disorderly actions.

"There are no well-grounded facts that the rights of the citizens of New York will be trampled upon at the polls.

"The power of this State is ample to protect all classes in the free exercise of their political duties. In doing this the public authorities will be upheld by good citizens of all parties.

"There is no reason to doubt that the coming election will be conducted with the usual quiet and order.

"Sheriffs of counties, and all other officers whose duty it is to keep the peace and protect our citizens, will take care that every voter shall have a free ballot in the manner secured to him by the Constitution and laws. It will be their duty to see that no military or other organized forces shall be allowed to show themselves in the vicinity of the places where elections are held, with any view of menacing or intimidating citizens in attendance thereon. Against any such interference they must exercise the full force of the law, and call forth, if need be, the power of their districts.

"In witness whereof I have hereunto signed my name, and affixed the Privy Seal of the [L. S.] State, at the city of Albany, this 2d day of November, in the year of Our Lord 1864.

"HORATIO SEYMOUR.

"By the Governor:

"D. WILLERS, Jr., Private Secretary."

Governor Seymour made frequent and eloquent addresses during the Presidential campaign, in favor of the choice of General McClellan by the people. The election was held on the 8th of November, and through the indirect interference of the Government, resulted in the reëlection of President Lincoln by a majority of 406,812 in a poll of 4,004,850 votes. Had there been a fair election, there is no doubt General McClellan would have been successful, but so great was the terror inspired by the Government, that many Democrats stayed away from the polls, and in the Border States, at least, many were prevented from exercising their right of suffrage on the ground that voting for McClellan was "an act of disloyalty." In this way the Republicans carried the country, and forced upon an unwilling people a continuance of their rule.

In the contest for Governor, Mr. Seymour was defeated by Mr. Fenton, by keeping back the soldiers' votes. More than enough ballots to change the result were delivered at the post-offices after the election was over.

CHAPTER IX.

Efforts of the Governor to secure a fair Vote in the Army—Alleged Fraud on the part of State Agents—Arrest of Colonel North and others—They are imprisoned in the Old Capitol—Governor Seymour resolved to defend their Rights as Citizens of New York — Commissioners sent to Washington — His Letter of Instructions—Action of the Commissioners—Their Interview with the Secretary of War—Their first Requests complied with—They Visit the Prisoners—Inhuman Treatment of its Prisoners by the Administration—No Charges made against them—The Letter of the Commissioners to the Secretary of War—Statement of the Case—The Government without Jurisdiction in the matter—Reply of the War Department—The Sovereignty of New York outraged by the Administration—Departure of the Commissioners—Persecution of Colonel North and his Companions—Their Acquittal and subsequent Captivity—Slanders of the Republicans upon Governor Seymour—Their Shallowness—Mr. Seymour retires to Private Life—The Democratic State Convention—Tribute to President Johnson—Mr. Seymour's Speech at Cooper Institute in June, 1868—A magnificent Effort—Review and Denunciation of the Republican Policy—The Radicals exposed to the Public Scorn.

In order to carry out the law for the casting of the ballots of the New York troops in the field, Governor Seymour appointed agents on the part of the State, and sent them to various points where the New York troops were serving, to collect and forward the ballots.

On the 27th of October, in order to make sure of the success of its schemes for carrying the Presidential election, the Government determined to take measures to prevent the full vote of the State of New York from being cast in that contest. On that day the New York Agency at Washington City was closed, and Colonel Samuel North, Levi Cohn, and M. M. Jones, the parties in charge of it, were seized and imprisoned in the Old Capitol prison, by order of the War Department.

This high-handed outrage excited the deepest indignation on the part of the Democrats. It was well known that the gentlemen referred to were entirely innocent of any crime, and the fact that the Government brought no charges against them, was convincing proof that it knew them to be guiltless of wrong when it arrested them.

Thousands of ballots, *en route* from the army to the State of New York, to be cast by the proxies of the men in the field, were seized by the Government and detained until after the election, when they were delivered with the most unblushing impudence.

A military commission was called to meet in Washington to try Colonel North and his associates in the State Agency, but neither those gentlemen nor their friends were allowed to know the nature of the offences with which they were accused. They were thus openly made the victims of a deliberate and undisguised persecution, which has no parallel in our history. The charges on which they were finally tried were, conduct prejudicial to good order and military discipline, and fraud toward the New York State electors in that they forged the names of officers and soldiers to what purported to be ballots of said soldiers, to be used at the election. They were also charged with falsely and fraudulently issuing divers and sundry blanks, which purported to be signed by officers and soldiers in the military service of the United States, authorizing certain parties to cast their votes at the ensuing State and national election, with the intent to defraud the true elector of his rights.

The Government, as we have said, had no ground for suspecting Col. North or his companions, and was influenced solely by a wicked and reckless determination to carry the election in New York by withholding the ballots of the soldiers, producing confusion in the election, and thus depriving by force the citizens of a free State of the rights guaranteed them by the Constitution which those engaged in the outrage had sworn to support. Colonel North was the duly accredited agent of the State of New York, appointed to look after the interests of the volunteers from that State in Washington; Mr. Cohn was the paymaster of the State, temporarily in Washington for the purpose of paying the State bounties to reënlisted men; and Mr. Jones, was connected with the State agency as Visitor of Hospitals. All these gentlemen had well and faithfully discharged their duties to the satisfaction of the State authorities, and the Government had no just cause of complaint against them. Their arrest was dictated by partisan hostility on the part of the Secretary of War. Had the charges brought against them been true, the Government would have had no power to try or punish them, as the offence was one against the State of New York, and not against the United States.

Feeling that the rights of these victims of the War Department, who were citizens of New York, and entitled to the protection of that State, had been infringed, Governor Seymour, who was well aware of the despotic manner in which the War Department treated its victims, determined to send a commission, composed of three of the leading men of the State, to Washington, to look into the matter, and also to endeavor to procure and forward the soldiers' ballots which had been seized by the Government, in order that such as were legal might be cast at the approaching election. Accordingly, on the 30th of October, he issued the following order:

"ALBANY, *October* 30.

"*To Amasa J. Parker, William F. Allen, and William Kelly, greeting:*

"It being reported that Col. Samuel North, agent of the State of New York at Washington, together with certain other citizens of this State, not in the military or naval service of the United States, have been placed in arrest by the military authorities of the United States, and no reason for such arrest having been given to me, and being anxious to learn the fact of such arrest and the grounds therefor, to the end that no innocent persons may be imprisoned without a fair and speedy trial, and that no obstacle may be put in the way of soldiers of this State having a fair ballot, according to its laws;

"Know you that I, Horatio Seymour, Governor of the State of New York, do hereby appoint you,

Amasa J. Parker, William F. Allen, and William Kelly, Commissioners for and in behalf of the State of New York, and do authorize and direct you and each of you forthwith to proceed to the City of Washington as such Commissioners, there to inquire into the facts and circumstances relating to such arrests and alleged causes thereof, and to take such action in the premises as will vindicate the laws of the State and the rights and liberties of its citizens, to the end that justice may be done, and that all attempts to prevent soldiers from this State, in service of the United States, from voting, or to defraud them, to coerce their action in voting, or to detain or alter the votes already cast by them in pursuance of the laws of this State, may be exposed and punished, and that you report your proceedings to me with all convenient speed.

"Horatio Seymour.

"D. Willers, Jr., Private Secretary."

The gentlemen thus appointed at once repaired to Washington, reaching that city on the 31st of October, when they immediately entered upon their duties. They sought and obtained a preliminary interview with the Secretary of War, in which they stated their business, after which they submitted to him the following written request:

"The undersigned request the Secretary of War that he will give them an order to receive the soldiers' votes which have been taken and are now in the custody of the Provost-Marshal at the New York agency in this city, as further delay to forward the votes may make it too late to use them at the approaching election.

"They also request that the blanks in the office of the New York agency in this city may be handed over to an agent of the State of New York, to be used, and that the agents may be permitted to proceed and take further soldiers' ballots, to be forwarded to the State of New York; and that a military officer of the New York volunteers may be designated by the Department to attend at the New York agency to administer oaths to voters.

"The undersigned also request a copy of the charges against Col. North, and the others in custody.

"Also, a permit for the undersigned to see Colonel North and the others in custody, and to make provision for furnishing counsel to defend them."

The Secretary granted the requests, and gave the necessary orders to his subordinates for their compliance. Several hundred ballots which had been detained five days, which were all that had been seized, were recovered, and the Commissioners were allowed to visit the victims of the War Department in their prison. Their account of the condition in which they found these *innocent* men is so fair a picture of the manner in which the Government treated its political prisoners during the war, that we quote the following from their report to the Governor.

"The undersigned availed themselves of the permit granted them to visit Colonel North, M. M. Jones, and Levi Cohn. *They found them in the 'Carroll prison,' in close confinement. They then learned that Messrs.*

North and Cohn had been confined together in one room, and had not been permitted to leave it for a moment during the four days they had been prisoners, even for the purpose of answering the calls of nature. They had been supplied with meagre and coarse prison rations, to be eaten in their room where they constantly breathed the foul atmosphere arising from the standing odor. They had no vessel out of which to drink water, except the one furnished them for purposes of urination. They had but one chair, and had slept three of the nights of their confinement upon a sack of straw on the floor. They had not been permitted to see a newspaper, and were ignorant of the cause of their arrest. All communication between them and the outer world had been denied them, and no friend had been allowed to see them. The undersigned complained to the acting superintendent, who seemed humanely disposed, *but justified his course by the prison rules and the instruction of his superiors.* The undersigned afterwards complained of the treatment of these persons to the Judge Advocate, and also the Secretary of War and the Assistant Secretary, and were happy to learn at subsequent visits to the prisoners that the severities were relaxed and their condition made more tolerable. *But at neither of these visits made to the prisoners by the undersigned, were they permitted to see them without a special permit and only in the presence of an officer of the prison.*"

The Commissioners next made application to the Judge Advocate for a copy of the charges against Colonel North, but without success. They reported to the Governor upon this point, as follows:

"From the best investigations the undersigned have been able to make, though there may have been irregularities, they have found no evidence that any frauds, either against any elector or the elective franchise, have been committed by any person connected with the New York agency."

The Commissioners then delivered to the Secretary of War the following communication as presenting their case, together with a copy of their commission, and asked that the papers might be filed with the papers of the War Department.

"WILLARD'S HOTEL,
WASHINGTON, *Nov.* 1*st.*

"TO HON. EDWIN M. STANTON, *Secretary of War:*

"SIR: We beg leave to submit to and leave with you a copy of the commission from his Excellency the Governor of the State of New York, under which we act in behalf of that State. From it you will perceive the nature of the duties assigned to us.

"In accordance with the suggestion made by yourself at our first interview yesterday, we take the liberty of submitting in writing our claims in respect to the imprisonment of Col. Samuel North, Mr. Levi Cohn, and Mr. Morven M. Jones, now and since Thursday last in close confinement in the Old Capitol prison.

"You are aware that they were, at the time of their arrest, in this city (Washington) as agents of the State under authority from the proper departments, to look after the interests and care for the soldiers from the State of New York in the service of the United States. They were not in the military or naval service of the United States, and by no law of which we are aware were they subject to the martial and military laws of the United States, or to the orders of the War Department.

"Since our interview with yourself yesterday, we have seen Col. North in the presence of his keeper. By an inadvertent omission in our permit, we did not see the other prisoners.

"We have also had interviews with Col. Forster, the Judge Advocate, having, as we understand, charge of the cases of the persons named, and have endeavored to learn the character of the offences charged against Col. North and the others named, and the nature of the charges made against them, and the character of the proofs. This was important to enable us to inquire into and prevent any attempt or anticipated frauds upon the election laws of our State, if any such were threatened. The proofs are withheld from us.

"The charges, so far as we can learn, are not for the violation of any law of the United States, but relate to acts purporting to have been done under the law of the State of New York concerning elections, and making provisions for soldiers voting in that State, it being claimed that certain irregularities have intervened which give reason to suspect that frauds and forgeries are intended, and may be consummated.

"The suspected and anticipated fraud have respects solely to the election laws of the State of New York, and the action of the Government in making the arrest is claimed to be justified upon the ground that unless thus prevented frauds will be perpetrated against the ballot-box at the approaching election in the State of New York.

"We beg leave, in behalf of the State, respectfully to protest against this jurisdiction, assumed as well over the alleged offence as over the persons of the accused, who are citizens of the State, in its employ, and entitled to its protection.

"The proper business of the State agency is greatly interfered with by the arrest and detention of the agents, and the State is deprived of its proper jurisdiction and its agents and citizens, over offences against its laws, and over its own ballot-box, and the exercise of the elective franchise within its limits.

"We therefore must earnestly, and at the same time most respectfully, demand, as we think we may properly do in behalf of the State, the release of the persons named from arrest, that they may resume their business at the agency, if the Governor shall see fit to continue them.

"We also ask and would urge a compliance with our request that all the proofs in possession of the Government of the United States tending to show any wrongful acts or irregularities on the part of these agents may be furnished us, that we may report them to the Governor or other proper authority, to the end that the unfaithful agents may be removed, and if guilty of any offence, that they may be properly punished.

"We do not consider this a proper occasion to

argue the question of jurisdiction, but it may be fit and proper to suggest some grounds upon which we think the arrests are without jurisdiction, that you may have them before you when you pass upon our demands.

"1st. We claim that the military authorities of the United States have no jurisdiction of the persons of the individuals named; that they are not in the military service of the United States, or in any way subject to the orders of the military authorities; that they are the servants of the State of New York, subject to its authority and amenable to its laws.

"2d. We claim that the acts charged, if proved to have been committed, are not offences against any law of Congress or any rule or order of the War Department made by authority of law.

"3d. We claim that the acts, if offences at all, are only offences against the laws of the State of New York, and punished by those laws only.

"4th. The papers, whether incomplete and irregular, and simply giving evidence, as is claimed, of an intended violation of the laws of New York, or complete in form, although forgeries in fact (if it is claimed there are any such, of which we are not informed), are evidence of no crime against the United States, and are of no value anywhere except in New York, where alone they can be used in the perpetration of any fraud, and that fraud would be against the sovereignty, the laws, and the people of that State.

"5th. It is not to be presumed that the laws of New York are insufficient to guard against fraud of the character anticipated, or that they would be so badly administered that the frauds can be successfully accomplished, or if accomplished that the guilty would gc unpunished.

"But if this were not so, and it were morally certain that the frauds could and would be accomplished with impunity, the General Government would have no jurisdiction in the premises.

"6th. The alleged fraudulent act would not be an offence against the soldier in the field. He cannot be deprived of his proper vote by any number of forgeries, and the presentation and reception of fictitious votes affect the whole people of the State and not the soldier alone.

"7th. If the acts alleged could deprive the soldier of any right, it would be a right pertaining to him as a citizen and not as a soldier. He votes, if he votes at all, as a citizen of the State, and not as a soldier of the United States. For protection in his rights as a citizen he looks to the State only.

"We will add that the laws of the State provide that parties guilty of the acts of which the parties named are suspected, shall upon their return to the State be punished.

"In this connection we would refer to the cases of Ferry and Donohue, who, we learn, have been recently tried at Baltimore for acts to some extent of the same character as those charged upon Messrs. North, Cohn, and Jones.

"Ferry and Donohue were, at the time of their arrest, in Baltimore, in the capacity of State agents, under authority from Governor Seymour, and if we are not entirely mistaken in our views of the case, their trial was a nullity, for want of jurisdiction in the court or commission by which they were tried.

"We therefore ask that these men be surrendered by the United States Government to the State Government, that they may be tried, and if guilty of any offence against the laws, be suitably punished.

"Permit us also respectfully to suggest, without desiring to reflect upon any of the agents of the Departments, that the haste with which such trials were pressed through, and their *ex parte* character, the accused being without counsel, especially in a time of intense partisan feeling like the present, and before a court of supposed party bias, without at all bringing in question the integrity of the court, may well lead the public to distrust the fairness of the trial. We submit that if jurisdiction of the alleged offences is to be assumed and exercised by a military tribunal, it should not be the means of depriving the accused of the presumption of innocence, or the aid of counsel, or of ample time to prepare for the defence.

"The undersigned beg leave to ask for an early reply; and are, respectfully,

"Your obedient servants,

"AMASA J. PARKER,
"W. F. ALLEN,
"WILLIAM KELLY."

The Secretary of War referred this communication to the Judge Advocate General, Mr. Holt. The Commissioners then asked that the trial might be postponed until after the election; and that if their request for the surrender of the prisoners to the State of New York should be refused, they might be released on parole. On the same day, the Secretary of War replied to the Commissioners, through Colonel Hardie, of the Department, that Judge Holt had reported on the communication given above, as follows:

"The within paper is not regarded as presenting any legal grounds for postponing the trials referred to. It is believed that the cases should be allowed to take the ordinary course. * * * It is expected that the trials of these parties will be proceeded with to-morrow. No reason is perceived, therefore, for paroling them."

"Such being the view of the Chief of the Bureau of Military Justice," continued Colonel Hardie, "the Secretary of War does not feel authorized to pursue a different course on the applications presented by you."

After some further correspondence with the Government, the Commissioners left the city for Albany. They wrote to the Governor, reviewing their course, and concluded their report as follows:

"Under these circumstances, after having retained counsel for the persons accused, the labors of the undersigned are brought to a close, their power is exhausted, and nothing remains but to report their proceedings.

"The demands made in behalf of the State of New York are thus refused. The persons arrested are to be summarily tried before a military commission, clearly, in our opinion, without jurisdiction, in violation of their personal rights, in usurpation of the just powers of our State, and in the midst of an exciting political contest; and though, up to this time, the morning of Thursday the 3d of November, when we are leaving Washington, no charges have been served on the accused, and perhaps none have yet been framed, yet we are told the trial shall proceed immediately, and that the time asked for to procure witnesses for the defence shall not be afforded."

This "speedy trial" was prolonged by the Government for many weeks, and the victims of the tyranny of the War Department were subjected to an imprisonment of three months, during which time they suffered many privations and hardships. The Court or Commission acquitted Colonel North, and Messrs. Cohn and Jones, of the charges brought against them, completely exonerating them from all blame in their conduct; *but the Government arbitrarily forced them, with the full proof of their innocence in its possession, to submit to their barbarous imprisonment for nineteen days after the verdict of the Court was formally rendered.*

The Republicans labored hard to induce the people of the State to believe that Governor Seymour had encouraged and assisted certain parties in their efforts to obtain fraudulent soldiers' votes; but the trial of Col. North, and his companions, showed the utter falsity of these charges. It was also shown that the Governor endeavored, by every means in his power, to have a full and fair vote polled by the troops; and that he urged the Secretary of State, a Republican, to appoint agencies "consisting of one Democrat and one Republican to visit the army together and receive the soldiers votes in a public manner, so as to avoid all possibility of fraud, and that no notice was taken of Governor Seymour's letters. The inference that the Republicans preferred separate secret action, to aid in obtaining fraudulent votes, is clearly to be drawn from the recorded evidence on file in the War Department. The facilities for accomplishing such purposes were in proportion to the number of Republican commissioned officers. Although it is well known that two thirds of the rank and file of the army were Democrats, the Republicans held three fourths of all the commissions. In this lay the power of that party to control what should be returned as the soldier-vote. Governor Seymour's action on this occasion was honorable and just, and above suspicion." *

Fortunately for Mr. Seymour, his acts have all been open and frank. They have never required concealment, and he has never desired any for them, and when his enemies assail him he has only to point to them for his vindication.

Mr. Seymour retired from the Governor's chair on the 1st of January, 1865, and was succeeded by Governor Fenton. From that time he devoted himself to his private affairs, presenting himself to the people for no public office. He gave his best efforts, however, to the cause of the Democratic party in his State, and contributed in no slight degree to the glorious victories which have marked the recent history of the New York Democracy.

In the Democratic State Convention, which met in

* Democracy in the United States, p. 368.

March, 1868, he delivered an address of great eloquence and force, in which he paid the following tribute to that lion-hearted defender of the Constitution who now fills the Executive Chair of the nation:

"I have no political prejudices in favor of Mr. Johnson. I have never seen him. He is not one I helped to place in office, nor have I ever advised him or been consulted by him as to his policy. I know he has been cheated and betrayed by those about him, who plotted his destruction from the outset. But while he has been most unhappy in his friends, no man has been so fortunate in his enemies. They have given him a high place in history as one who suffered for the rights of the American people. And when he shall go to his final account, and his friends seek in clear, terse, and lasting terms to tell that he was a man who loved his country, and was hated by the corrupt and treasonable, they have but to chisel upon his tombstone that he was impeached by this House of Representatives and condemned by this Senate."

This Convention nominated Mr. Seymour as a delegate from his district to the National Democratic Convention to meet in New York on the 4th of July, 1868.

On the 25th of June, 1868, a mass meeting of the Jackson Central Association, and the Democracy in general of New York, was held at Cooper Institute. The immense hall was crowded to excess, as it was known that Governor Seymour would address the meeting.

Shortly after eight o'clock, Mr. Thomas J. Creamer, the President of the Association, rose and introduced the orator of the evening, Ex-Governor Seymour. Mr. Seymour was received with enthusiastic applause. He said:

"We see in every part of our land proofs of a wide-spread change in political feeling. As the evils of misgovernment unfold themselves, the best men of the Republican Party are driven from its ranks. At its late Convention its policy was shaped in a great degree by those who are most violent in their passions and most brutal in the policy they urge upon the people. While the ablest Republicans refuse to go on with a party which tramples upon the judiciary, usurps power, and is unsettling all ideas of political morality, and unhinging all the business machinery of our land, we are laboring under some embarrassments from the great volume of the change in our favor. Those who are rallying around the standard of constitutional rights have heretofore held conflicting views with regard to the events of the past eight years, and the question is, how can we set this great majority in the field so arrayed that they can drive out of place the disciplined and desperate horde of office-holders who now misgovern our country? This is the only problem to be settled. The American people are disgusted with the conduct of the Congressional party. Can we mark out a policy which will unite the majority of our standard? This can only be done by a thoughtful, forbearing, unselfish course. At the same time we must be outspoken and must confront all the questions which perplex us. Men look forward with hope and fear to the action of the National Convention on the Fourth of July. I shall not speak of candidates. Let the claims of each one be considered in a courteous and kindly spirit, and let us take care that no personal partisanship shall draw us aside from our duty to our country. We should support, with hearty zeal, every upholder of constitutional rights. It is upon discord in our ranks that our opponents build their hopes. A party born of strife naturally looks to selfish passions to keep it alive. Let this hope be crushed out by our action. It will, in the present state of our country, be an unholy thing to go into the July Convention with any purpose which shall not have in view the rescue of our Government from the men who now have it in hand. The next election will be controlled by thoughtful, business and laboring men. No party can gain their support unless its tone and temper show that it seeks to get our country out of its troubled condition. Appeals to prejudice and passion will have no weight. These were tried at the late Republican Convention. I need not say with what cold indifference they have been received by the public. The quiet, watchful citizens who seek for the protection of a wise administration of government, now turn their eyes upon us. We must look to it that we take no position which will not bear the closest scrutiny.

"The financial condition of our country forces itself upon our attention. Among the evil results of our moneyed and tax policy, the most hurtful is the jealousies it has made between the sections of our country. It has divided our Union into debtor and cred itor States. It builds up favored interests and crushes out the industry of other classes. It taxes toil and lets some forms of wealth go free from the cost of the Government. It gives to labor and business a debased money and to the untaxed bond-holder sterling coin. These curses upon honest industry have grown up like ill weeds among the sacred interests of contracts, trusts, and the fruits of labor, until we are troubled how to root out the tares sown by evil spirits, without killing the crops planted and tilled by honest industry. Lest it should be felt that what I have to say on this point springs from any views about the candidates or action of the National Convention, I will go back to the first years of the civil war, when the Democratic Party of New York took its position upon the financial policy of Government. In the elections of 1862 it was discussed before our people. We then pointed out the great evils which now trouble us as the sure results of the errors of those who were shaping our moneyed system. To show clearly how we then tried to avoid these dangers, let me read some passages from the messages of a Democratic Governor to the Legislature, in January, 1863. In his position he spoke, after a general consultation, for the great party which had just placed him in the Executive chair. Positions taken many years ago could have no reference to the personal wishes or purposes of this day. I will speak of the questions which now agitate our country in the light of the warning we then uttered. In the Convention of 1862, the nominee of the Democratic Party of the State of New York, for the office of Governor, used the words:

'The vast debt growing out of the war will give rise to new and angry discussions. It will be held almost exclusively in a few Atlantic States. Look upon the map of the Union, and see how small is the territory in which it will be owned. We are to be divided into creditor and debtor States, and the last will have a vast preponderance of power and strength. Unfortunately, there is no taxation upon this national debt, and its share is thrown off upon other property. It is held where many of the Government contracts have been executed, and where, in some instances, gross frauds have been practised. It is held largely where the constitution gives a disproportional share of political power.'

"In his message to the Legislature, in 1863, the Democratic Governor, speaking of the public credit, foreshadowed our dishonored condition at the time in these words:

'Extravagance and corruption are violations of the faith pledged to the public creditors. The money loaned to the National Treasury was not brought forward at a time of peace, but in a time of doubt and danger. These claims are held by the rich and poor. The amount held by corporations represents the interests of women and children, the aged and infirm. The right of our soldiers to demand integrity is of the most sacred character. A fearful crime will be done by those who suffer national bankruptcy to turn into dust and ashes the pensioners' bounties thus gained at the cost of blood and health and exposure. It is worse that a government should be overturned by corruption than by violence. A virtuous people will regain their rights if torn from them, but there is no hope for those who suffer corruption to sop and rot away the fabric of their freedom.'

"These are the positions we took years ago in the darkest hour of the war; these are the positions we hold now, and they cover every question of public and party agitation. To show the anxiety we felt to avoid all sectional controversies, and our sense of the value of intercourse with the Western States, I will quote from the message of the same Democratic Governor in 1864:

'A deep interest is felt with regard to our commerce with the Western States. Its growing value and the loss of our trade with the Southern States makes us dependent for commercial prosperity upon that section of our country which sustains our domestic and foreign commerce, and which adds so largely to the imports and business prosperity of the City of New York. This State will be untrue to itself if it fails to control this great source of wealth by a vigorous and generous policy. Rather than suffer its diversion into other channels, we should strike off all tolls upon Western produce. New York should exhibit that degree of interest in all measures designed to benefit the West which will show our purpose to keep up the most intimate commercial relationship with that portion of our Union.'

"These words are quoted—not because the words

of any one man are of consequence, but to show the record of the great party which inspired them. The Democratic Party saw the evil in the beginning; they are the party to cure it. They have always kept our public finances out of confusion, when in power. Years ago we pointed out the wrong done to the West by making them send nearly twice as many soldiers to the war from each Congressional war district as were demanded from Vermont or Massachusetts, while the currency given to them under the banking system was not one quarter as great, although the Western States needed currency the most. The act authorizing the banks of New York to organize under a general Banking law was not signed, because the currency was unjustly divided, and because the system made a useless tax upon the people of $18,000,000 in gold each year. Thus we tried at an early day to save our country from sectional questions. In vain we warned the East and West against an unwise policy. The East and West upheld the policy of the Administration, and we have now to deal with the results. What are some of them? All of the States are heavily taxed, but some of them get back as much, some more than they pay out, while others get but little. In the case of the heaviest item of expense—the military and naval system—the Western States get nothing back except the cost of Indian war, while large sums are spent at the South. The next heaviest item is the interest on the debt. The West get but a small sum back; most of it is paid to the North Atlantic States. The indirect taxes, tariffs, are still more hurtful to the West, as they are practically premiums given to Eastern manufacturers. The division of the favors of Government in distributing banking currency is startling in its injustice. But the most offensive distinction is that of having two kinds of currency. Good money for the bondholder, and bad money for the laborer, the pensioner and the business man. Every paper dollar now put out is a Government falsehood, for it claims to be worth more than its real value, and it goes about the country defrauding the laborer, the pensioner, the mechanic and the farmer. An indignant chief of one of the tribes from whom we bought land at an early day by a pledge of moneyed annuity, said the Government was a cheat. It got land from the Indians by promising them so many dollars each year, that now it paid them in money which was a lie, which said on its face it was a dollar when it was but little more than a half dollar. The red man told the simple truth. Of all the devices to cheat honest labor, to paralyze industry, to degrade public morals and to turn business pursuits into reckless gambling, none has been so hurtful as a shifting standard of value, a debased and lying currency. I have not thus set forth the condition of our country for the purpose of indulging in invectives against the party in power, but for another object. Many Republicans who admit the wrong doing of their leaders say that we have no plans for the relief of our country, that pointing out wrongs is of no use unless we can point out remedies. This we propose to do, and we probe the ulcers to the quick because we mean to meet the case and cure the malady. Among other things which have caused anxiety in the disordered state of our Union, is the fact that our Government bonds are mainly held in one section of our country. The labor of the West puts its earnings in a large degree into lands, which are tax-burdened. The labor of the East puts its earnings into savings banks, life insurance, or in other forms of moneyed investment. Thus they are deeply interested in Government bonds. The amount in savings banks in this State alone is $140,000,000. This shows that there must be at least $300,000,000 of money thus deposited in all the States. The average of the deposits in 1867 in the State of New York was $270. The number of depositors in the State of New York is about five hundred thousand (487,479,) and in the City they number more than one third of the population. This will make the number of depositors in the Union more than 1,800,000. In the State of Connecticut, in 1865, one quarter of its population had deposits in the savings banks. It is now usual for men of small property to insure their lives. The number of policies given out by all the life insurance companies are about four hundred and fifty thousand, and the amount of insurance about one thousand and two hundred and fifty millions. The money invested is held as a sacred trust, as it is a fund laid aside for their families when the insurers die. All of the funds of savings banks and the insurance companies are not put in Government bonds, but they hold an amount which would cripple or ruin them if the bonds are not paid, or if they are paid in debased paper. If we add the trusts for widows and orphans we find 2,500,000 persons are interested in Government bonds, who are not capitalists, and who are compulsory owners, at present prices, under the operations of our laws. There is a fear that this state of things will make a clashing of interests between the labor of the East and the labor of the West. It is clear that our opponents hope that it will hinder us from going into the contest with compact ranks and with one battle-cry.

However alarming this aspect may be, I am sure there is a policy to be marked out which will harmonize all jarring interests. It can be shown that the dangers spring from an unwise conduct of public affairs. They have come up like fogs at night from foul fens; they rise from unwholesome darkened counsels, and will fade away before the light and life of a clear and honest policy. Is it true that the laborer, the pensioner, the tax-payers and the bondholders have conflicting interests which will hinder them from acting together in upholding constitutional right? Why are the tax-payers laboring under a debt which bears an interest of six per cent., while other Governments can borrow money at three per cent., and at this low interest their bonds sell for better prices than ours? Why is the laborer, the farmer, the mechanic and the pensioner paid in bad money, so that they get one-quarter less than they are entitled to on every paper dollar paid to them? Why is the bondholder wronged by the tainted credit of the Government, so that he cannot sell his bond for as much by one-third as the citizen of Great Britain gets for the bond of his Government, which bears a lower interest; and why is his claim made odious in the eyes of the people by the fact that his interest is paid in specie, while they are compelled to take debased paper? It is clear to every thoughtful man that public safety and honor will not admit of our having two kinds of currency for any length of time. We must have a uniform currency for all classes. There is but one question to be settled. Shall our currency be uniformly good or uniformly bad? Are we to force the bondholder to take bad money? Are we to have an honest standard of value for all, or is industry, enterprise and morality to be perplexed and disordered by a shifting and dishonest standard? If it can be shown that all these evils under which we labor, spring from a common source, then it is clear that all classes should join in a common effort to root out the policy which sheds such wide-spread curses. There are two ways of making our paper money as good as coin. One is to contract its volume by calling in the legal tenders. This will make them scarce and will force a specie standard, but it will carry ruin and bankruptcy into every part of our country. It will bear down the prices of property and of labor. It is a policy which cannot be carried through, for the country will not consent to it. There is another way of lifting up our greenbacks to par which will not harm any, but will help all, which will bring back confidence, will revive business and enterprise, will lighten taxation, will give to labor honest money and will do justice to the public creditor. And that way is to give to all the world full faith in the honor and wisdom of the American Government. Our paper money is not its par in coin, because the national credit is dishonored. How can the notes of our Government, which pay no interest, be worth their face in gold or silver, when the bonds of Government, which pay six per cent. interest, are worth only eighty cents on the dollar? You cannot make the notes put out by banks worth more than the bonds which secure these notes. It is a sad thing to say that our credit is dishonest in the markets of the world, but it is true, and it must be said, if we are to find a remedy. It is humiliating to find that when Great Britain borrows $1,000 for twenty years, it pays the lender but $1,700, when, if we make the same loan, we have to pay $2,700 to the lender. If we wish to help the tax-payer—if we wish to get at the cause of debased currency in the hands of the laborer—we must first find out why our credit is dishonored; for it is a tainted credit that sinks alike the value of bonds, of greenbacks and bank notes. Make the credit of the United States as good as that of Great Britain, or of a merchant in good standing, or of a mortgage on a farm, and our troubles would disappear. If we make our paper money good by a harsh system of contraction, we shall cripple the energies of the country and make bankruptcy and ruin. If, on the other hand, we debase the currency by unwise issues, we shall equally perplex business and destroy sober industry, and make all prices mere matters of gambling tricks and chances. This will end as it did in the Southern Confederacy. At the outset the citizens of Richmond went to market with their money in their vest pockets and brought back their dinners in their baskets, in the end they took their money in their baskets and took home their dinners in their vest pockets. Make our money good by an honest and wise course, and when this is done it will be worth twenty-five per cent. more than it is now, which will be equal to an increase of one-quarter in the amount of currency. Business will be strengthened, industry will be encouraged, prices will be regular, and men will then dare to go on with useful enterprises. We find right here the cause of our troubles, perplexities and national disgrace. Our credit is tainted. But for that we could borrow money as Britain does, at three per cent., and cut down taxation. But for that our paper money would be good, and gold and silver would glitter in the hands of labor. But for that fact there would be no question how the bonds are to be paid, and we never should have heard of the greenback issue. But for the national discredit business men would not be perplexed, and the disquiet and fears which now disturb the public mind would not exist. Now if this dishonor cannot be helped, we must bear it in the best way we can, and we must get on with the sectional and social and political troubles growing out of it until time and events shall bring some cure. But if it can be shown to be the work of those in power, then all sections, all classes and all interests should unite and turn them out. Fortunately, we have official statements to guide us in our inquiries. We take the showing of the very portion under impeachment to show where the guilt lies.

"To show the waste of those in power let us compare the cost of Government during the four years of peace before 1861, and the four years of peace following the 1st of July, 1865. For the fiscal year ending July 1st, 1869, I will take the estimate just made by the Committee of Ways and Means. Bear in mind that this is the best promise the Republicans can make on the eve of a Presidential election. It will prove to be many millions short of what they will spend, but we will give them the benefit of their own statements. After the close of the war, and up to the 1st of July, 1865, the War Department spent $165,000,000—which is $75,000,000 more than was spent by the same department in the four years of Mr. Polk's administration, and which included the cost of the Mexican war. It took nearly twice as much to stop a war under Republican policy as it did to carry on a war under the Democratic management. But I will not take this $165,000,000 into account. Let us close the war. Since July 1st, 1865, about three months after the surrender of Lee, up to July 1st, 1868, the cost of Government will be, by official reports and estimates, $820,390,208. Up to July 1st, 1869, by the estimate of the Chairman of the Committee of Ways and Means, it will be $197,973,366, making the cost of Government for four years $1,018,363,574. This does not include one cent paid or to be paid for interest or principal of the debt. The cost of Government during the four years before the war (leaving out interest on debt) was $256,226,414. This shows that the Republicans have spent, in a time of peace, four dollars where the Democrats spent one. But the cost of Government grows greater, and we will allow them to spend two dollars where the Democrats spent one. This will make $512,452,828. But they spent $505,910,646 beyond this. What did they do with the money? During the four years of Mr. Polk's term, which included the Mexican war, the cost of the War Department was only $90,540,788 21. We find that the cost of the War Department, taking their own statements and estimates, will be in those four years of peace $541,613,619. And this follows an expenditure of more than $3,000,000,000 during the war. The cost of the Navy Department in the four years ending July 1st, 1869, will be, by Republican statements and estimates, $117,471,802; and this follows an expenditure of $314,186,742 during the war. In the four years before the war the navy cost only $62,910,534. We then stood in the front rank of commercial Powers. Our ships were on every sea and were to be found in every port. American shipping is now by our tariff policy swept from the ocean, but the cost of the navy is nearly doubled. The year ending July 1, 1868, is the third year of peace. But the War Department cost $128,858,494, which is more than its cost during the four years of Mr. Polk's term, which covered the expenses of the Mexican war. Not only does one year of peace cost more than four years of war then did, but the third year of peace costs more than the second, for in the year ending July 1, 1867, the War Department spent only $95,224,415. In these statements we have given the Republicans the full benefit of their promises for the fiscal year ending July 1, 1869, but we should like to ask a few questions. If $38,081,013 is enough for the War Department in that year, why and how did you spend $123,858,490 this year? If $17,500,000 is enough for the navy in 1869, why did you spend upon it $43,324,111 in 1866, and $31,024,011 in 1867? You have not cut down the numbers of the army. Did you waste money this year, or are your statements for next year untrue? We ask Republicans to read the estimates for the future, for they show the profligacy of the past. If $500,000,000 of the money paid for military, naval, and other expenses had been used to pay the debt, to-day the credit of the United States would have been as good as that of Great Britain. The rapid payment, and the proof it would have given of good faith, would have carried the national credit to the highest point. The bonds would be worth much more in the hands of holders, and yet the taxpayer would seem better off, for the cost of Government would be cut down as its credit rose. We could put out new bonds bearing less interest, which would not have the odious exemption from taxation. Our debt would have been less, our interest lower, and our taxes reduced. The hours of labor could be shortened. What now lengthens the time of toil? If we were free from any form of taxation, direct or indirect, six hours of work would earn as much as ten do now. One hour more of work ought to meet a laborer's share, of the cost of government, another hour should pay his share of the national debt. He now works two hours more each day than he ought to pay for the military and negro policy of Congress and its corrupt schemes. It has just passed a law that eight hours make a day's labor, while it piles up a load of taxation which forces the laborer to work ten more or starve. But the wise and honest use of this $500,000,000 would not have stopped here. When it carried our bonds to the level of specie value, it would have carried up our currency to the value of specie. The plan of making our currency as good as gold by contracting its volume carries with it great distress and suffering. But if we lift up its value, by getting rid of the taint upon the national credit, it harms no one, it blesses all. Now our legal tender and bank currency must be debased while our national bonds stand discredited. They must rise and fall together. They are all based upon the national credit. Bank notes cannot be worth more than the bonds which secure them. If, then, the $500,000,000 had been duly and honestly used to pay our debt, to-day the tax-payers would have been relieved, the mechanic, laborer and pensioner would be paid in coin, or money good as coin, and would not be cheated out of one-quarter of their dues by false dollars. The holders of bonds in savings banks or life insurance would be better off, as their securities would be safer and worth more. There would be no question how they should be paid, for this question grows out of the follies of those in power, and will disappear when they disappear from the places they now hold. The bondholder would no longer stand in an odious light. He would not be charged with the taxation which has been used to hurt, not to help, his claim. If a wise, an honest use of the public money would have done this good in the past, it will do it in the future.

"But the Republican party, at Chicago, pledged itself, by its nominations and resolutions, to keep up its negro policy. It is impossible to give untutored Africans at the South uncontrolled power over the government, the property, and laws of the people of ten States, by excluding white votes, without military despotism. You cannot give to three millions of negroes more Senators than are allowed to fifteen millions of white men living in New York, Pennsylvania, Ohio, Illinois, Indiana, Wisconsin, Iowa, Kentucky, Missouri, and Michigan, without keeping up great standing armies. Without a general amnesty, and the restoration of the suffrage to all the whites in the South, a great standing army must be a permanent institution. In order to curse the South with military despotism, negro rule, and disorganized labor and industry, they cursed the farmers of the North with taxation, the mechanics with more hours of toil, the laborers and pensioners with debased paper, the merchant with a shifting standard, and the public creditor with a dishonored and tainted national faith. Are these classes to turn and see how each can push the burdens upon each other, or are they to make common cause and do away with the curses of a bad Government? If the Republican policy prevails, this struggle must begin. Either the laborer or the capitalist must go down. Both cannot live under it, and men must choose between. If, on the other hand, the policy of selfish ambition and of sectional hate is put down, our country will start upon a new course of prosperity, and all classes will reap in common the fruits of good Government. The next election will turn upon this question—can the Congressional party succeed in their efforts to excite and array the industrial and monied interests against each other, or will these unite and turn out the authors of the mischief under which they are all suffering? The only hope of our opponents is discord where there should be harmony and concert of action. In our State, at the last election, we appealed to all classes to help us save New York from misgovernment; and all came up to the rescue, and we made a change of 70,000. Let us again appeal to all classes of interests throughout the Union; let us go before the people with these facts, and we will make a change which will sweep the wrong-doers from their places. We say to the bondholders and to the laborer who has put his money into savings bank: "We do not wish to harm you; we do not seek to give you bad money, but to get a good currency for all. It will not help us to break down the credit of your bonds—it hurts us; it keeps up our taxes by making us pay high interest; but we ask you to help save us, as tax-payers, from the cost of the negro and military policy at the South. It is hard for us to pay you if you let men in power take the money we give in taxes to reduce your claims and use it to uphold military despotism. We see clearly that a state of affairs which will compel you to take a debased currency will force every laborer, farmer, mechanic, and creditor, to take a debased currency as well. If your claims were all wiped out to-morrow by an issue of greenbacks, it would not relieve the fear of patriots; labor would still be cheated by false dollars, our standard of value would still be shifting. Taxation would be kept up by the reconstruction policy; for it is despotism more than debt that makes taxation so heavy. Nothing would be settled. The Judiciary would still be trampled under foot; the Executive would still be manacled so that it could not punish crime nor protect innocence. But strike down the Congressional policy and all will be set right. Since the war closed in 1865, the Government has spent for its expenses, in addition to payments on principal or interest of the public debt, the sum of more than $1,000,000,000. Of this sum there has been spent nearly $800,000,000 on the army and navy, and for military purposes. This is nearly one-third of the national debt. This was spent in the time of peace. The cost of our navy before the war was about $13,000,000 each year. Since the war, when our shipping has been swept from the ocean by taxation, the annual average cost has been $30,000,000, although we have now no carrying trade to protect. While money is thus wasted without scruple upon the army and navy, if any aid is sought to lessen the cost of transportation for the farmers of the West or to cheapen food for the laborers of the East, we are at once treated with Congressional speeches upon the virtues of economy. If from this amount there had been saved and paid upon the debt the sum of $500,000,000, how changed would our condition have been. With this payment, which would have cut down the debt to about $2,000,000,000, our credit would at least have been as good as that of Great Britain. It is because we did not thus apply this money to this purpose, but spent it upon the negro policy, the military despotism, and other abuses of Government, that our credit is so low. The world saw we were violating our faith with the public creditors and the tax-payers alike, when the money was used for the partisan purpose of keeping the South out of the Union until sham governments could be manufactured by military violence and Congressional action. The world not only saw the monstrous diversion of the money, wrung from the people by taxation, but it also saw that it made, through a long series of years, still greater annual expenses unavoidable. When the entire control of the Southern States is given over, unchecked by the intelligence of the white race, to untutored negroes, whom the people of the North have said were unfit to be voters, when the unfortunate Africans, drunk with unusual power and goaded on by bad and designing men, shall make life and property unsafe, and shall shock and disgust the world with outrages, we shall be forced to raise and pay still greater armies. Up to this time the South has had at least an intelligent tyranny in military officers. Every man who is not blinded by hate or bigotry looks forward with horror to the condition of the South under negro domination. The bad faith to the public creditor and tax-payer in thus unsettling our Union, of keeping the South in a condition where it cannot help the national prosperity, but is made a heavy load upon the country, is the real cause of our debased credit. The tax-payer was told the burdens put upon him were to pay the debt, but the money was not used in good faith to him, for the debt still stands; nor in good faith to the creditor, for he was not paid what he should have been; but it was used in a way which harmed both, in a way that tainted the nation's credit, kept up taxation by keeping up the rate of interest, while it sunk the value of the bonds, and with them carried down the paper currency, and thus wronged the laborer and pensioner. But for the policy of bad faith, of partisan purposes, mad folly, we could to-day borrow money as cheaply as Great Britain; but we have cursed the tax-payers, the laborer, the pensioner, the public creditor, for the sake of cursing the people of the South with military despotism and negro domination. Every one must see, if we paid off one-fifth of our debt, had kept down the cost of Government, had given peace to our Union, had built up industry and good order in the South, not one of the evils which now afflict us could have existed. Our whole condition would have been changed. We demand that our currency shall be made as good as gold, not by contracting the amount, but by contracting the expenses of Government. We are against measures which will pull down business credit, and call for those which shall lift up the national credit. When we stop the waste which forces us to pay a usury of ten per cent, and take a course which will enable us to borrow money upon the rates paid by other nations, we shall add to the dignity and power of our Union. When we give value to our bonds by using the money drawn by taxation to the payment of our debt, and not to the military and negro scheme, we shall relieve the tax-payer, the bill-holder, and give strength and value to the claims of the public creditor. We have seen the mischief wrought out by the policy of the past three years. It will be as hurtful in the future as it has been in the past. Yet the Republican Party has approved it and is pledged to it. We have shown how the policy of using our money to pay our debts would have helped us in the past. It will do the same for us in the future. To that policy we are pledged. There is not one man in our party in this broad land who doubts upon this point. It was never charged that a single Democrat in these United States ever favored the military and negro policy upon which the credit of the country has wrecked. Our remedy is to use the public money to pay the public debt. It is a simple, brief, but a certain remedy for our national malady. Our ailment is debt, aggravated by despotism. In another way the Republicans do a constant wrong to the bondholders. In answer to complaints of heavy taxation, they say it cannot be helped with our heavy debt, and thus throw the whole odium on the debt. Why do they not tell the truth, and say one-third of our taxation is made by our debt? Then they will be asked, what makes the two-thirds? This question they do not want to have asked, and they do not want to answer. When they do answer, the eyes of all classes with be opened. They will be forced to say that last year they spent, by reports of Committee of Ways and Means, $379,178,066 83, and this in the third year of peace. Well, say our well-meaning Republican friends, we suppose the interest of the debt took most of it. Oh, no; that took $149,418,-383 87, not quite as much as was spent by the War and Navy Departments, which was $149,472,165 35, and besides this we spent $80,292,513 14 for other things. Why, that is $20,000,000 more than the Democrats spent for army and navy and all expenses of Government put together. But why do you spend $25,613,673 53 on the navy, when it formerly cost $12,000,000 annually? Has American shipping grown so much that we have to keep up vast navies to protect it? Oh, no; our tariffs have swept away American ships from the ocean; we have lost the carrying trade; the British have got that. Then why don't you give the builders of merchant ships the money spent on the navy, by way of drawback on duties? Would that start work at our ship-yards? Oh, yes, half the cost would do it. Then, why is it not done? We did not think of it; really, we have been so busy with the impeachment and negro questions, that we forgot our sailors and mechanics. But we see that the War Department this year spent $128,858,466, when the year before it spent about $95,000,000. The longer we have peace the more the army costs. How is this? Well, it costs a great deal to keep soldiers and Freedmen's Bureau agents, and to feed and clothe negroes at the South. But why do you do it? Let the negroes support themselves as we do. You make the laborers at the North work to feed and clothe these idle Africans. True, but by so doing we get their votes, and they will send our travelling agents to Congress; we shall get twenty Senators in this way, while a majority of the people of the United States living in nine States, have only eighteen. The people may vote as they please, but they cannot get the Senate, nor repeal any of the laws we got through for our advantage; we have managed it so that one-quarter of the people have more power in the Senate than the three-quarters. We now own the negroes of the South. Did we not buy them by your blood and money? We now see where the money goes; we now see why the credit of our country is so tainted; we now see why the value of our paper money is sinking. It was only at twenty-one per cent. discount in 1866; is now at a discount of about twenty-nine per cent.; we now see why our laborers and pensioners are cheated by false dollars. If the mechanic cares to know why he works so many hours, let him study the reports of the Secretary of the Treasury. It is clear why business is hindered and business men perplexed. We now know why the public creditor is harassed by our dishonest credit, and the tax-payer is hunted down by the tax-gatherer. The negro military policy of the Republican Party is at the bottom of all these troubles. We now get at the real issues between parties. The Republicans, by their nominations and resolutions, are pledged to keep up the negro and military policy, with all its cost and taxations. These will be greater hereafter. The government of the South is to go into the hands of the negroes. We have said they are unfit to be voters at the North. The Republicans say they shall be governors at the South. We are clearly opposed to this policy. We have seen how much it costs the tax-payer, the bondholder and the laborer in the past three years. It will be as hurtful in the future. We have also seen how our policy of using the money to pay our debts would have helped the tax-payer, the bondholder and the laborer in the past. It will do as much in the future. The whole question is brought down to this clear point: shall we use our money to pay our debts, relieve the tax-payer, make our money good in the hand of the laborers or pensioner, and help the bondholder? or shall we use it to keep up military despotism, feed idle negroes, break down the Judiciary, shackle the Executive and destroy all constitutional rights?

"I have said nothing in behalf of, or against the views of any one who is spoken of as a candidate for the Presidency on the Democratic side. I have only said what each one agrees to and is in favor of. No man has been named who is not in favor of reducing expenses, and then making our paper as good as gold. No man has been named who is not in favor of cutting down military expenses. No man has been named who is not in favor of using the money drawn from the tax-payers to pay the public debt. No man has been named who is not in favor of a general amnesty to the people of the South. No man has been named who is not an upholder of constitutional rights. No man has been named by the Democratic party whose election would not help the tax-payer, the pensioner, the laborer, and the bondholder. On the other hand, the candidates of the Republican party are pledged to their past policy, which has sunk the value of our currency more than eight per cent. in the past two years. The discount upon our paper money was twenty per cent. in April, 1866; it is now about twenty-nine per cent. It will continue to go down under the same policy. As it sinks it will increase taxes, it will curse all labor and business, it will endanger still more the public credit; for the greater the premium on gold the harder it becomes to pay specie to the bondholder, and his claims become more odious. What claim have the Republicans upon our soldiers? They take away from him one-quarter of his pension, by paying him in false money, which is worth less than seventy-five cents on the dollar. A wise and honest administration would have made it worth its face in gold. What right have they to call upon the mechanic and laborer? They have lengthened out the hours of their toil to feed swarms of office-holders at the North, and to support armies and hordes of negroes at the South. How can they look the tax-payers in the face, when they have wrung from them so many millions upon the pretext that the debt compelled them to do so, while they were using the money thus collected to support standing armies and to trample upon the rights and liberties of the American people? Can they, with decency, appeal to the bondholder, after tainting the national credit and sinking to the level of the Turks, and endangering their securities by throwing upon them the whole odium of taxation? Then let the East and West, the North and the South, the soldier, the sailor—in ships or in the field—the tax-payer and the bondholder, by one united effort, drive from power the common enemies of liberty, honesty, honor, rights, and constitutional laws."

CHAPTER X.

The National Democratic Convention of 1868—Arrival of Delegates in New York—Scenes in the City—Preparations for the Convention—Review of the Prospects of Candidates—Noble Letter from Mr. Pendleton—Mr. Seymour Declines to be a Candidate—The "New York Citizen" on Mr. Seymour—Patriotism of the Pendleton Men—The Convention—The North and the South Renew their old Harmony—Organization of the Convention—Mr. Seymour Chosen its President—Reception by the Convention—His Speech—A Scathing Review of Radicalism—Adoption of the Platform—Eloquent Statement of the Principles of the Party—Adoption of the "Two-Thirds Rule"—Nominations—The Balloting—A "Dead-Lock"—Withdrawal of Mr. Pendleton—His Friends Insist upon the Nomination of Governor Seymour—He Declines the Honor—Scene in the Convention—Mr. Seymour is compelled to Submit to the Will of the Party—Enthusiasm—He is Declared the Unanimous Choice of the Convention for the Presidency—Nomination of General Blair for the Vice-Presidency—Statement of the Ballots for President—Final Adjournment of the Convention.

THE National Democratic Convention met in Tammany Hall, in New York City, on the 4th of July, 1868. For several days previous, the city had been filling up rapidly with the arriving delegates and their friends, and great enthusiasm prevailed among the new-comers. The most extensive preparations had been made for the assembling of the Convention. The new hall of the Tammany Society, which was just fresh from the builder's hands, had been fitted up and decorated with a taste and magnificence which excited the admiration of all beholders.

Previous to the assembling of the Convention, the

friends of Mr. Seymour had repeatedly urged him to allow his name to be presented as a candidate for the nomination; but he modestly but firmly refused to grant their request. The peaceful retirement of his home had more attractions for him than the Presidency, and he was determined not to abandon it unless he should be called from it by some cause more urgent than any which then presented itself to him. It being understood, therefore, that Mr. Seymour would not be a candidate for the nomination, the choice at the first seemed to lie between the Hon. George H. Pendleton, of Ohio, and General Hancock. The former, having the almost unbroken strength of the Western delegations, and many friends among the Eastern to sustain him was undoubtedly the strongest of all the competitors for the prize, and it was feared by some that his friends would insist upon his nomination with a persistency which would cause serious trouble in the Convention. Those who entertained this feeling, however, knew little of Mr. Pendleton. No purer or more unselfish patriot is to be found in the land. Ever prompt to assert his principles, always prepared to defend them, he is the first to sacrifice his own personal interests to their success. Before the Ohio delegation, his staunchest friends, left their homes for New York, he addressed the following manly and generous letter to one of the members:

"CINCINNATI, *Thursday*, *June* 25, 1868.

"MY DEAR SIR: You left my office this morning before I was aware of it. I seek you at home but you are not here. I must say what I want by note.

"As soon as you get to New York, see Governor Seymour. You know well my affection and admiration for him. You know well what was my feeling before and after I heard from him last fall. He is to-day the foremost man in our party in the United States. His ability, cultivation, and experience put him at the head of our statesmen. He commands my entire confidence—I would rather trust him than myself with the delicate duties of the next four years. You know I am sincere.

"Make him feel this, and that he can rely on me and my friends. I have a natural pride—an honest pride, I believe—in the good-will of my countrymen; but you, better than any one else, know that it is neither egotistical nor over-ruling, and that I am ready, anxious, to give up the nomination to any body who can get one single vote more than myself.

"Express all this frankly to the Governor, but delicately, and let him understand my views of men and measures as I have frequently given them to you. Good-bye. God bless you!

"Very truly,

"GEORGE H. PENDLETON.

"*To Washington McLean, Esq.*"

* *The New York Citizen*, in an editorial published on the 25th of August, 1866, nearly two years ago, thus expressed its views concerning Mr. Seymour, which are interesting, as confirming the opinion held by Mr. Pendleton and the rest of the Democratic party:

"The time is fast approaching, if not already fully come, in which independent men may do justice to the character and conduct of ex-Gov-

There was no real prospect then that the Pendleton men of the West would be influenced by any other feeling than the pure and disinterested patriotism

ernor Horatio Seymour—to-day the most brilliant and accomplished member of the Democratic party, the best beloved son of New York, and with a rarer and more genial faculty for making and retaining friends than any other public man of our acquaintance, since the death of Judge Stephen A. Douglas.

"While the recent civil war was in progress, Seymour labored under a cloud of Radical misrepresentation from which no efforts of himself, or of his loyal friends, could relieve his attitude. He had farther vision than most men—a larger knowledge of the past, and consequently a better prevision of the future. And he foresaw, that while we were asserting the Constitution by force of arms against the temporary rebels of the South, the Radical Jacobins in Congress were seeking to establish a permanent tyranny which must forever nullify all rights under the Constitution both in the Northern and Southern States.

"But during the hot days of the war, to question any act of the General Government was to be 'disloyal;' and to cast a doubt upon the infallibility or perfect patriotism of Congress, was the 'unspeakable sin' in political religion. When Governor Seymour denounced the conduct and management of the Provost Marshal General's department, he was regarded as a 'traitor;' and for asserting and offering to prove that some of the subordinates in that department were perjured villains, who were attempting to operate the draft with illegal severity in some of the Democratic districts of our city, he was held up to odium in the Radical press as one deserving a cell in Fort Lafayette, if not summary execution on the parade-ground of Governor's Island.

"It was all in vain, therefore, for Governor Seymour to organize regiments, and to strain every practical power of his position for the support of the Union cause, while the morbid and feverish state of public opinion lasted. For openly daring to doubt the sincerity of the so-called 'Union party's' professed devotion to the Union and the Constitution, and for this crime alone, he was condemned to suffer the major anathema and excommunication of the whole loyal church. But how stands this matter to-day? Was he wright or wrong?

"Is it not now admitted, even by the most reckless partisans of the Radical cause, that the management of our Provost Marshal's department during the war, was a disgrace to our country and century? That

which swayed their leader, and when the delegates began to assemble in caucuses, previous to the opening of the Convention, it was found that there was no

many of its subordinates—in fact nearly all—were scoundrels capable of every crime conceivable; and that the excessive drafts upon the Democratic city of New York, which Judge Waterbury exposed and Governor Seymour resisted, were only some atrocious parts of a great plot for striking down all resistance to the Radical programme at the point of the bayonet? Should any conservative Republican be disposed to question this fact, he is respectfully referred to the present infamous notoriety of Lafayette C. Baker, whose name nearly blisters every lip that breathes it; or to the report made by Congress, and echoed in the *Tribune*, of the disclosures resulting from the difficulty between General James B. Fry and Congressman Roscoe Conklin.

"Again: all must remember how the agents appointed by Governor Seymour for collecting the votes of our soldiers in the various armies, were denounced by the Radical press, and finally flung into the Old Capitol prison and other bastiles of the General Government, under charges of making fraudulent returns. This course was pursued just prior to, and had its effect upon the last Presidential election; but when that struggle was over, and the Radical authorities were called upon to substantiate their charges against Col. North and his associate agents by some form of trial—even one before a Military Commission packed to convict—do we not also remember how the Government shrank back from its false accusations, and was compelled to acknowledge their falsehood by liberating without trial, or even formal arraignment, Governor Seymour's agents?

"And lastly—at least for the present week—was Horatio Seymour right or wrong in denouncing the Republican party as false to the Constitution and not sincerely desirous for a return of the Union? Let President Andrew Johnson answer this, and let all the conservative Republicans who met at Philadelphia take part in his reply. That party is now openly arrayed against the reconstruction of the Union, and it is on the eve of impeaching President Johnson for his attempt to arrest its illegal usurpations and exactions. It has thrown off the mask it wore when soliciting Democrats to fight the battle for its existence, under a delusion that they were fighting the battle of the country; and it is to-day—as Governor Seymour always knew it to be, and pronounced it—the revolutionary and usurpational party of the country, endeavoring to

doubt that the session would be marked by greater harmony than had been known in the party for years.

The occasion was indeed an interesting one. It was the first National Convention of the Democratic

hold the Southern States as conquered provinces wherein its satraps may pillage at discretion; and ready even to plunge the whole country back into the seething caldron of civil war, rather than resign the illegal powers and profits which it seized during the busy and half delirious days of our recent contest.

"For men like Horatio Seymour, the reverses of to-day are nothing —the future is the promised land of justice; and that future has arrived. Traduced and vilified during the war, his course has been nobly vindicated by the subsequent actions of his slanderers; and to-day he occupies a proud pedestal before the whole American people as one who was wisely and greatly true to the Union and the Constitution, in the very darkest days we have seen and in the best sense of truth; an asserter of individual liberty and the liberty of the press against the arbitrary usurpations of Radical power; a fearless and faithful guardian of the people's liberties and rights; and one who could better afford to be overcome and vituperated in a course he knew to be right, than to accept all the honors and rewards of government while acquiescing in concessions to the illegal demands of a fanatical and usurping junta.

"While Seymour was Governor of our State, his worst enemies made no suggestion of corruption. His hands were pure, and he had pure men in his councils. For vetoing the Broadway Railroad Bill and other measures of like iniquity and rapacious fraud, he was defeated two years ago by the machinations of the friends of the bill; but the day is fast approaching in which the rascals who took part in that treachery, and boasted of their share in its success, will call upon the rocks and mountains to cover them so that their sight may not be blasted by the glory of Mr. Seymour's vindication. Warm and deep in the heart of every honest Democrat in the State of New York, the image of Horatio Seymour has its home. He is our ablest, most faithful and most beloved representative. He is the man of widest grasp and highest culture in our party. He is the statesman who might nobly and bravely fill that seat which Seward's imbecility disgraces; and he, of all men we know, could most certainly and easily assert for our State its just ascendency in the great council of the nation, if he were elected next Winter to the seat in the United States Senate now occupied by Mr. Ira Harris."

party since the close of the war—the first in which the Southern States had participated since 1860. The representatives of that great Democracy of the North and West that had carried the war to a successful close, met once more as brothers in a common cause, those who for four years had resisted them with a valor and skill which no true American need feel otherwise than proud of. The North here met the South in a spirit of frank and generous forgetfulness of the past and hopefulness for the future, and the South, saddened and wiser by its reverses, came forward manfully to renew its allegiance to the Constitution and laws of the Union. Both came to do what lay in their power to save that Constitution and those laws from the ruin and infamy which the fanaticism of the party in power sought to bring upon them, and here was laid the firm foundation of that mutual esteem and brotherly love which is once more to bind together the great conservative elements of the two sections.

At precisely twelve o'clock on the 4th of July, 1868, the Convention was called to order by the Honorable August Belmont, the Chairman of the Democratic National Committee, who, after a few well-timed remarks, nominated the Honorable Henry L. Palmer of Wisconsin, as temporary Chairman. Mr. Palmer accepted the position in a brief address, after which the proceedings of the Convention were opened with a prayer by the Rev. Dr. Morgan of the Episcopal Church. After transacting the usual preliminary business, the Convention adjourned until Monday, July 6th.

The Convention was formally organized on Monday by the election of Governor Seymour as President. The nomination was received with the wildest enthusiasm and was carried by acclamation. A committee, consisting of Senator Bigler, of Pennsylvania, and Governor Hammond, of South Carolina, was then appointed to conduct Mr. Seymour to the chair. His appearance on the platform in company with these gentlemen was hailed with loud and repeated cheers. The whole convention rose and greeted him with the utmost enthusiasm, in which the ladies and the spectators in the galleries joined. The cheering continued for several minutes, and when quiet was restored Mr. Seymour came forward and said:

"GENTLEMEN OF THE CONVENTION: I thank you for the honor you have done me in making me your presiding officer. (Cheers.) This Convention is made up of a large number of delegates from all parts of our broad land. To a great degree we are strangers to each other, and view the subjects which agitate our country from different standpoints. We cannot, at once, learn each other's modes of thought, or grasp all the facts which bear upon the minds of others. Yet our session must be brief, and we are forced to act without delay upon questions of an exciting character and of deep import to our country. (Applause.) To maintain order, to restrain all exhibitions of passion, to drive out of our minds all unkind suspicions is, at this time, a great duty. (Cheers.) I rely upon your sense of this duty and not upon my own ability to sustain me in the station in which I am placed by your kind partiality. Men never met under greater responsibilities than those which now weigh upon us. (Applause.) It is not a mere party triumph which we seek. We are trying to save our country from the dangers which overhang it. (Cheers.) We wish to lift off the perplexities and the shackles which, in the shape of bad laws and of crushing taxation, now paralyze the business and labor of our land. (Loud cheers.) We hope, too, that we can give order, prosperity, and happiness to those sections of our country which suffer so deeply to-day in their homes and in all the fields of their industry from the unhappy events of the last eight years. I trust that our actions will show that we are governed by an earnest purpose to help all classes of our citizens. Avoiding harsh invectives against men, we should keep the public mind fixed upon the questions which must now be met and solved. (Cheers.) Let us leave the past to the calm judgment of the future and confront the perils of the day. (Cheers.) We are forced to meet the assertions of the resolutions put forth by the late Republican Convention. I aver there is not in this body one man who has it in his heart to excite so much of angry feeling against the Republican party as must be stirred up in the minds of those who read these declarations in the light of recent events and in view of the condition of our country. (Applause.) In the first place, they congratulate the perplexed man of business, the burdened tax-payer, the laborer whose hours of toil are lengthened out by the growing cost of the necessaries of life, upon the success of that reconstruction policy, which has brought all these evils upon them by the cost of its military despotism and the corruption of its bureau agencies. In one resolution they '*denounce all forms of repudiation as a national crime.*' Then why did they put upon the statute books of the nation the laws which invite the citizens who borrow coin to force their creditor to take debased paper, and thus wrong him of a large share of his claim in violation of the most solemn compact? (Cheers.) If repudiation is a national crime, is it no crime to invite all the citizens of this country thus to repudiate their individual promises? (Applause.) Was it not a crime to force the creditors of this and other States to take a currency at times worth no more than 40 cents on the dollar in repayment for the sterling coin they gave to build roads and canals which yield such ample returns of wealth and prosperity? (Applause.) Again they say, '*It is due to the laborer of the nation that taxation should be equalized.*' Then why did they make taxation unequal? Beyond the injustice of making one class of citizens pay for another their share of the cost of schools, of roads, of the local laws which protect their lives and property, it was an unwise and hurtful thing. (Cheers.) It sunk the credit of the country, as unusual terms are always hurtful to the credit of the borrower. They also declare, '*The best policy to diminish our burden of debt is to improve our credit that capitalists will seek to loan us money at lower rates of interest than we now pay and we must continue to pay so long as repudiation, partial or total, open or covert is threatened or suspected.*' Then why have they used full five hundred millions of the taxes drawn from the people of this country to uphold a despotic military authority and to crush out the life of the States, when, if this money had been used to pay our debts, capitalists would now seek to lend us money at lower rates of interest. (Cheers.) But for this "covert repudiation" our national credit would not be tainted in the markets of the world. Again, they declare, 'Of all who were faithful in the trials of the late war, there were none entitled to more especial honor than the brave soldiers and seamen who endured the hardships of campaign and cruise, and imperiled their lives in the service of the country; the bounties and pensions provided by the laws for these brave defenders of the nation are obligations never to be forgotten; the widows and orphans of the gallant dead are the wards of the people—a sacred legacy bequeathed to the nation's protecting care.' How have these sacred duties been performed; they pay to the maimed man, to the widow, or the orphan, a currency which they have sunk one-quarter below its rightful value by their policy of hate, of waste, and of military despotism. The pittances paid to the wounded soldiers is pinched down twenty-five per cent. below the value of that coin which he had a right to expect. (Loud cheering.) Is there no covert repudiation in this? (Applause.) Again they say, '*Foreign immigration, which has added so much to the wealth, development, and resources and increase of power to this Republic, the asylum of the oppressed of all nations, should be fostered and encouraged by a liberal and just policy.*' Is this foreign immigration fostered by policy which, in cruel mockery of laws just passed declaring eight hours to be a legal day's labor, by the cost of government and of swarms of officials, so swells the cost of living that men must toil on to meet the exactions? (Cheers.) The time was when we could not only invite the European to share with us the material blessings of our great country, but more than that, we could tell those who fled from oppression that we lived under a government of laws administered by the Judiciary, which kept the bayonet and the sword in due subordination. (Cheers.) We could point to a written constitution which not only marked out the powers of government, but with anxious care secured to the humblest men the rights of property, of person and of conscience. Is immigration encouraged by trampling that Constitution in the dust; treating it with contempt; shackling the Judiciary; insulting the Executive, and giving all the world to understand that the great guarantees of political and social rights are destroyed? (Great applause.) But the crowning indictment against the follies and crimes of those in power is in these words: 'That we recognize the great principles laid down in the immortal Declaration of Independence as the true foundation of democratic government, and we hail with gladness every effort towards making these principles a living reality on every inch of American soil.' If within the limits of ten States of this Union an American citizen, stung by a sense of his wrongs, should publicly and truthfully denounce the men in power because, in the very language of this Declaration of Independence, '*They have erected a multitude of new offi-*

ces and sent forth swarms of officers to harass our people and eat out their substance,' he would in all human probability be dragged to a prison. Or if, in the indignant language of our fathers, he should exclaim, '*They have affected to render the military independent of and superior to the civil power, they have abolished the free system of English laws, and established herein an arbitrary government;*' for the offence of asserting these principles he would be tried and punished by a military tribunal. (Great cheering.) Having declared that the principles of the Declaration of Independence should be made a '*living reality on every inch of American soil,*' they put in nomination a military chieftain who stands at the head of that system of despotisms that crushes beneath its feet the greatest principles of the Declaration of Independence. (Cheers.) To-day, in some States, it is held by military orders to be a crime to speak out the indignation and contempt which burn within the bosoms of patriotic men. If to-morrow a military order should be put forth in that State where the ashes of Washington are entombed, that it should be an offence to declare that the military should ever be subordinate to the civil authority—to speak out the sentiment that it was a disgrace to our country to let the hordes of officials eat up the substance of the people—he who uttered these words could be dragged to prison from the very grave where lie the remains of the author of the Declaration of Independence—(loud cheers)—from this outrage there could be no appeal to the courts; and the Republican candidate for the Presidency has accepted a position which makes the rights and liberties of a large share of our people dependent upon his will. (Applause.) In view of these things, can there be one man in this Convention who can let a personal ambition, a passion, a prejudice, turn him aside one hair's breadth in his efforts to wipe out the wrongs and outrages which disgrace our country? (Cheers.) Can there be one man here whose heart is so dead to all that is great and noble in patriotism that he will not gladly sacrifice all other things for the sake of his country, its liberties, and its greatness? Can we suffer any prejudices, growing out of past differences of opinion, to hinder us from uniting now with all who will act with us to save our country? (Cheers.) We meet to-day to see what measures can be taken to arrest the dangers which threaten our country, and to retrieve it from the evils and burdens resulting from bad government and unwise counsels. I thank God that the strife of arms has ceased, and that once more in the great Conventions of our party we can call through the whole roll of States and find men to answer for each. (Tremendous and continued cheering.) Time and events in their great cycles have brought us to this spot to renew and invigorate that Constitutional Government which nearly eighty years ago was inaugurated in this city. (Loud cheers.) It was here that George Washington, the first President, swore to "preserve, protect, and defend" the Constitution of these United States. (Cheers.) And here, this day, we as solemnly pledge ourselves to uphold the rights and liberties of the American people. Then, as now, a great war which has desolated our land had ceased. Then, as now, there was in every patriotic breast a longing for the blessings of a good government, for the protection of laws, and for sentiments of fraternal regard and affection among the inhabitants of all the States of this Union. When our Government, in 1780, was inaugurated in this city, there were glad processions of men, and those manifestations of great joy which a people show when they feel that an event has happened which is to give lasting blessing to the land. (Cheers.) To-day in this same spirit this vast assemblage meets, and the streets are thronged with men who have come from the utmost borders of our continent. They are filled with the hope that we are about, by our actions and our policy, to bring back the blessings of good government. It is among the happiest omens which inspirit us now that those who fought bravely in our late civil war are foremost in their demands that there shall be peace in our land. The passions of hate and malice may linger in meaner breasts, but we find ourselves upheld in our generous purposes by those who showed true courage and manhood on the field of battle. (Cheers.) In the spirit, then, of George Washington and of the patriots of the revolution, let us take the steps to reinaugurate our Government, to start it once again on its course to greatness and prosperity. (Loud cheers.) May Almighty God give us the wisdom to carry out our purposes, to give to every State of our Union the blessings of peace, good order, and fraternal affection."

Mr. Seymour closed amid long-continued and tremendous cheering.

The Convention then proceeded to transact its business. A number of resolutions were adopted, and it was resolved that no balloting for a candidate for the Presidency or Vice-Presidency should be had until a platform was adopted.

The Committee on Resolutions were busily engaged during the day in preparing the platform, and did not make their report until Tuesday morning, when the platform, as reported by them, through their Chairman Mr. Murphy, was unanimously adopted. It is as follows:

"The Democratic Party in National Convention assembled, reposing its trust in the intelligence, patriotism, and discriminating justice of the people, standing upon the Constitution as the foundation and limitation of the powers of the Government, and the guarantee of the liberties of the citizen; and recognizing the questions of slavery and secession as having been settled for all time to come—(tremendous cheering)—by the war or the voluntary action of the Southern States in Constitutional Convention assembled, and never to be renewed or re-agitated, do with the return of peace demand:

"*First*—Immediate restoration of all the States to their rights in the Union under the Constitution, and of civil government to the American people. (Cheers.)

"*Second*—Amnesty for all past political offences, and the regulation of the elective franchise in the States by their citizens. (Cheers.)

"*Third*—Payment of the public debt of the United States as rapidly as practicable; all moneys drawn from the people by taxation, except so much as is requisite for the necessities of the Government, economically administered, being honestly applied to such payment; and where the obligations of the Government do not expressly state upon their face, or the law under which they were issued does not provide, that they shall be paid in coin, they ought, in right and in justice, to be paid in the lawful money of the United States. (Thunders of applause.)

"*Fourth*—Equal taxation of every species of property according to its real value, including Government bonds and other public securities. (Renewed cheering and cries of 'Read it again.')

"*Fifth*—One currency for the Government and the people, the laborer and the office-holder, the pensioner and the soldier, the producer and the bondholder. (Great cheering and cries of 'Read it again.') The fifth resolution was again read and again cheered.

"*Sixth*—Economy in the administration of the Government; the reduction of the standing army and navy; the abolition of the Freedmen's Bureau—(great cheering)—and all political instrumentalities designed to secure negro supremacy; simplification of the system, and discontinuance of inquisitorial modes of assessing and collecting Internal Revenue, so that the burden of taxation may be equalized and lessened; the credit of the Government and the currency made good; the repeal of all enactments for enrolling the State militia into national forces in time of peace; and a tariff for revenue upon foreign imports, and such equal taxation under the Internal Revenue laws as will afford incidental protection to domestic manufactures, and as will, without impairing the revenue, impose the least burden upon, and yet promote and encourage the great industrial interests of the country.

"*Seventh*—Reform of abuses in the administration, the expulsion of corrupt men from office, the abrogation of useless offices, the restoration of rightful authority to, and the independence of, the executive and judicial departments of the Government, the subordination of the military to the civil power, to the end that the usurpation of Congress and the despotism of the sword may cease. (Cheers.)

"*Eighth*—Equal rights and protection for naturalized and native-born citizens at home and abroad, the assertion of American nationality which shall command the respect of foreign powers, and furnish an example and encouragement to people struggling for national integrity, constitutional liberty and individual rights, and the maintenance of the rights of naturalized citizens against the absolute doctrine of immutable allegiance, and the claims of foreign powers to punish them for alleged crime committed beyond their jurisdiction. (Loud applause.)

"In demanding these measures and reforms, we arraign the Radical party for its disregard of right and the unparalleled oppression and tyranny which have marked its career.

"After the most solemn and unanimous pledge of both Houses of Congress to prosecute the war exclusively for the maintenance of the Government and the preservation of the Union under the Constitution, it has repeatedly violated that most sacred pledge under which alone was rallied that noble volunteer army which carried our flag to victory. (Cheers.) Instead of restoring the Union it has, so far as in its power, dissolved it, and subjected ten States, in time of profound peace, to military despotism and negro supremacy. It has nullified there the right of trial by jury; it has abolished the *habeas corpus*, that most sacred writ of liberty; it has overthrown the freedom of speech and the press; it has substituted arbitrary seizures and arrests, and military trials and secret star-chamber inquisitions for the constitutional tribunals; it has disregarded in time of peace the right of the people to be free from searches and seizures; it has entered the post and telegraph offices, and even the private rooms of individuals, and seized their private papers and letters without any specific charge or notice of affidavit, as required by the organic law; it has converted the American capitol into a bastile; it has established a system of spies and official espionage to which no constitutional monarchy of Europe would now dare to resort—(cheers), it would abolish the right of appeal on important constitutional questions to the supreme judicial tribunal, and threatens to curtail or destroy its original jurisdiction which is irrevocably vested by the Constitution, while the learned Chief-Justice—(loud cheering)—has been subjected to the most atrocious calumnies, merely because he would not prostitute his high office to the support of the false and partisan charges preferred against the President. Its corruption and extravagance have exceeded everything known in history, and by its frauds and monopolies it has nearly doubled the burden of the debt created by the war. It has stripped the President of his constitutional power of appointment, even of his own Cabinet. Under its repeated assaults the pillars of the Government are rocking on their base, and should it succeed in November next and inaugurate its President, we will meet as a subjected and conquered people amid the ruins of liberty and scattered fragments of the Constitution.

"And we do declare and resolve that ever since the people of the United States threw off all subjection to the British crown, the privilege and trust of suffrage have belonged to the several States, and have been granted, regulated, and controlled exclusively by the political power of each State respectively, and that any attempt by Congress, on any pretext whatever, to deprive any State of this right, or interfere with its exercise, is a flagrant usurpation of power which can find no warrant in the Constitution, and if sanctioned by the people will subvert our form of Government, and can only end in a single centralized and consolidated government in which the separate existence of the States will be entirely absorbed, and an unqualified despotism be established in place of a Federal Union of coequal States.

"And that we regard the Reconstruction acts (so-called) of Congress, as such, as usurpations and unconstitutional, revolutionary and void.

"That our soldiers and sailors who carried the flag of our country to victory against a most gallant and determined foe must ever be gratefully remembered, and all the guarantees given in their favor must be faithfully carried into execution. (Cheers.)

"That the public lands should be distributed as widely as possible among the people, and should be disposed of either under the preëmption of homestead lands, or sold in reasonable quantities, and to none but actual occupants, at the minimum price established by the Government. When grants of public lands may be allowed, necessary for the encouragement of important public improvements, the proceeds of the sale of such lands, and not the lands themselves, should be applied. (Cheers.)

"That the President of the United States, Andrew Johnson—(applause)—in exercising the power of his high office in resisting the aggressions of Congress upon the constitutional rights of the States and the people, is entitled to the gratitude of the whole American people, and in behalf of the Democratic party we tender him our thanks for his patriotic efforts in that regard. (Great applause.)

"Upon this platform the Democratic party appeal to every patriot, including the conservative element and all who desire to support the Constitution and restore the Union, forgetting all past differences of opinion, to unite with us in the present great struggle for the liberties of the people—(cheers)—and that to all such, to whatever party they may have heretofore belonged, we extend the right hand of fellowship, and hail all such coöperating with us as friends and breth ren. (Loud cheering.)"

Mr. Murphy stated to the Convention that the Committee had given this platform their unanimous approval, and in view of this unanimity, he moved the previous question upon the adoption of the resolutions. The previous question was seconded, and the Chair put the question upon the adoption of the platform. A unanimous vote was given, *viva voce*, in the affirmative. When the call was made for those opposed to the resolutions, a dead silence prevailed in the hall. Not a voice was raised against them. Then burst forth a storm of cheers and applause that fairly shook the building to its foundations. This continued for several minutes.

Upon this bold and fearless enunciation of their principles, the Democracy of the Union intend to carry the country with them in the coming election. Their cause is the cause of the country, of economy, of justice, and of liberty; and not even the strong arm of the military power upon which their adversaries rely, can prevent their success.

The Convention then adopted the "two thirds rule" of the former Conventions of the party; and after a slight delay, the Secretary proceeded to call the roll of States for nominations for a candidate for the Presidency.

The State of Connecticut presented the name of Governor Jas. E. English; Maine nominated Major-General W. S. Hancock; Ohio, her favorite son, George H. Pendleton; New Jersey, Ex-Governor Parker; New

York, Sandford E. Church; Pennsylvania, Asa Packer; Tennessee, President Andrew Johnson; and Wisconsin, Jas. R. Doolittle.

The balloting was then begun. On the first ballot, nearly all the Southern States cast their votes for Andrew Johnson, of Tennessee, as a mark of their gratitude for his noble efforts in their behalf. Six ballots were taken without any thing definite being accomplished, when the Convention adjourned for the day. On Wednesday, the 8th, the National Executive Committee for the ensuing year was appointed, and the balloting resumed. Twelve ballots were taken during the day. The eighth ballot stood thus:

Whole number of votes cast, 317.

James E. English	6
W. S. Hancock	28
George H. Pendleton	156½
Joel Parker	7
Asa Packer	26
Andrew Johnson	6
James R. Doolittle	12
Thomas A. Hendricks	75
Frank P. Blair	½

The full strength of Mr. Pendleton was drawn out by this ballot, and from that time it became evident that his friends would have more difficulty in securing his nomination than they expected. When the eighteenth ballot was taken, at the close of the day's proceedings, Mr. Pendleton's vote had declined to 56½.

The Convention met again on Thursday morning.

Two days had now been consumed in fruitless balloting, and in order to bring about a speedy choice on the part of the Convention, Mr. Pendleton's friends, in obedience to his instructions, withdrew his name as a candidate for the Presidency. Soon after the opening of the morning session, Mr. Vallandigham, of Ohio, rose and said:

"Mr. President, I have a communication in writing to make to this Convention. By permission of the Chair I will read it from the stand. (Applause.) During which Mr. Vallandigham made his way to the rostrum.

"The Chair.—Mr. Vallandigham, of Ohio, will make a communication to the Convention.

"Mr. Vallandigham.—The following is the communication to which I refer:

'CINCINNATI, July 2, 1868.

'*Washington McLean, Fifth Avenue Hotel, New York:*

'MY DEAR SIR: You know better than any one the feelings and principles which have guided my conduct since the suggestion of my name for the Presidential nomination. You know that while I covet the good opinion of my countrymen, and would feel an honest pride in so distinguished a mark of their confidence, I do not desire it at the expense of one electoral vote—(great applause)—or of the least disturbance of the harmony of our party. I consider the success of the Democratic party in the next election of far greater importance than the gratification of any personal ambition, however pure and lofty it might be. (Loud cheers.) If, therefore, at any time a man shall be suggested which, in the opinion of yourself and those friends who have shared our confidence, shall be stronger before the country, or which can more thoroughly unite our own party, I beg that you will instantly withdraw my name, and pledge to the Convention my hearty and zealous and active support for its nominee.

'Yours very truly,

'GEORGE H. PENDLETON.'

(Great cheering.)

"Mr. Vallandigham.—At the request of the gentleman to whom this letter is addressed, I submit it to this Convention. It was his desire that it should have been done very early in the afternoon of yesterday; but the earnest zeal and fidelity of the Ohio delegation, and the distinguished son of Ohio whom they had presented to the Convention for the office of President, precluded their consent to any such proposition. This morning his request has been renewed, and in conformity with it I have produced and read the letter, and submit that the spirit of magnanimity, unselfishness, and of patriotic devotion to the interests of the country, speak in terms of far higher eulogy in behalf of this distinguished gentleman than any words I could utter. (Great applause.) Pursuant, therefore, to the authority of Mr. McLean, and acting under the advice of Mr. Pendleton, I withdraw his name with hearty thanks to the multitude of earnest, zealous, and devoted friends who have adhered to him with so great fidelity. (Applause long continued, and cheers for Pendleton.)

"The Chairman.—Mr. Vallandigham, by the instruction of the Ohio delegation, withdraws the name of George H. Pendleton as a candidate for the Presidency before the Convention, and he does so by the direction of Mr. Pendleton himself. We will now proceed with the nineteenth ballot."

Two more ballots were then taken, Judge Field and Gen. F. P. Blair having been placed in nomination, but without a choice being made.

Mr. Pendleton, in the letter we have given at the commencement of this chapter, had, as the reader will remember, plainly declared his preference for Governor Seymour as the candidate of the party, and his friends in the Convention now resolved to be guided by his wishes, and urge the nomination of Mr. Seymour in such a manner as would make it plain to that gentleman that it was his duty to the conservative element of the country to lay aside his personal wishes and yield to the judgment of the Convention. They had stood by Mr. Pendleton faithfully, until his disinterested devotion to the country had forced them to withdraw his name, and they now determined to rally upon the leader whom their own beloved chief had offered them. The movement was entirely without premeditation, and was the result of one of those happy inspirations which are the sure harbingers of victory.

Upon the announcement of the twenty-first ballot, General McCook rose, and to the surprise of the Convention, spoke as follows:

"Mr. Chairman: I arise at the unanimous request and the demand of the delegation from Ohio, and with the consent and approval of every public man in the

State, including the Hon. George H. Pendleton, to again place in nomination, against his inclination, but no longer against his honor, the name of Horatio Seymour, of New York. (Rousing cheers and long-continued applause.) Let us vote, Mr. Chairman, and gentlemen of the Convention, for a man whom the Presidency has sought, but who has not sought the Presidency. (Applause.) I believe in my heart that it is the solution of the problem which has been engaging the minds of the Democrats and Conservative men of this nation for the last six months. ("Good," "good.") I believe it will have a solution which will drive from power the Vandals who now possess the Capitol of the nation. (Applause.) I believe it will receive the unanimous assent and approval of the great belt of States from the Atlantic—New York, New Jersey, Pennsylvania, Ohio, Indiana, Michigan, Illinois, and Missouri, and away West for quantity—to the Pacific Ocean. (Applause.) I say that he has not sought the Presidency, and I ask—not demand—I ask that this Convention shall demand of him that, sinking his own inclination and the well-known desires on his part, he shall yield to what we believe to be the almost unanimous wish and desire of the delegates to this Convention. (Great applause and three cheers.) In my earnestness and enthusiasm, I had almost forgotten to cast the twenty-one votes of Ohio for Horatio Seymour. (Tremendous excitement, and nine cheers for Horatio Seymour.)"

The nomination was hailed with the wildest applause, and the surprise of the Convention at this sudden move of the Pendleton men changed at once to the greatest delight.

Mr. Seymour was taken completely by surprise. His refusal to be a candidate had been so emphatic that he had not the least idea that any one would venture to place him in nomination, and as soon as the applause which followed General McCook's remarks subsided, he advanced to the front of the platform to decline the honor thus proffered him. He said, in a voice unsteady with the grateful emotions which this unexpected and overwhelming tribute of the Convention had aroused in his heart:

"GENTLEMEN OF THE CONVENTION: (Cheers)—The motion just made by the gentleman from Ohio excites in my mind the most mingled emotions. (Applause.) I have no terms in which to express my gratitude—(cheers)—for the magnanimity of his State and for the generosity of this Convention. (Cheers.) I have no terms in which to tell of my regret that my name has been brought before this Convention. God knows that my life and all that I value most in life I would give for the good of my country, which I believe to be identified with our own party. (Applause, and cries of "Take the nomination then.") I do not stand here as a man proud of his opinions, or obstinate in his purposes, but upon a question of duty and of honor I must stand upon my own convictions against the world. (Applause, and a voice, "God bless you, Horatio Seymour.") Gentlemen, when I said here at an early day, that honor forbade my accepting a nomination by this Convention, I *meant* it. When, in the course of my intercourse with those of my own delegation and my friends, I said to them that I could not be a candidate, I *meant* it. And now permit me here to say that I know, after all that has taken place, I could not receive the nomination without placing, not only myself, but the great Democratic party, in a false position. But, gentlemen of the Convention, more than that, we have had to-day an exhibition from the distinguished citizen of Ohio, that has touched my heart, as it has touched yours. (Cheers.) I thank God, and I congratulate this country, that there is in the great State of Ohio, whose magnificent position give it so great a control over the action of our country, a young man, rising fast into fame, whose future is all glorious, who has told the world he could tread beneath his feet every other consideration than that of duty, and when he expressed to his delegation, and expressed in more direct terms, that he was willing that I should be nominated, who stood in such a position of marked opposition to his own nomination, I should feel a dishonored man if I could not tread in the far distance, and in a feeble way, the same honorable pathway which he has marked out. (Great applause.) Gentlemen, I thank you, and may God bless you for your kindness to me; but your candidate I cannot be." (Three cheers for Horatio Seymour.)

This plain refusal did not in the least abate the enthusiasm of the Convention or lessen the determination of the delegates. As Mr. Seymour resumed his seat, Mr. Vallandigham rose, and in clear sonorous tones declared that the Governor had no right to decline the nomination in view of the unusual circumstances of the case. Said he:

"In times of great public exigency, and especially in times of great public calamity, every personal consideration must be yielded to the public good. (Applause.) The safety of the people is the supreme law, and the safety of the American Republic demands the nomination of Horatio Seymour, of New York. (Cheers.) Ohio cannot; Ohio will not accept his declination, and her twenty-one votes shall stand recorded in his name. (Cries of "good, good," and cheers.) And now I call upon the delegations from all the States represented on this floor; upon the delegations from all the States of this Union, from the Atlantic to the Pacific, from the great lakes to the gulf, disregarding those minor considerations which justly, it may be, properly I know, tend to sway them in casting their ballots, to make this nomination unanimous; and before God, I believe that in November, the judgment of this Convention will be confirmed and ratified by the people of all the United States. (Applause.) Let the vote of Ohio stand recorded then—twenty-one votes for Horatio Seymour. (Immense and continued applause.)

"Mr. Kernan (New York)—Mr. President: Belonging to the delegation from the State of New York, and coming from the district where the President of this Convention lives, I cannot, as an individual delegate, refrain from asking the indulgence of this Convention in making one or two observations. And in order that we may relieve every body, in order that we may relieve our Chairman from every bit of sensitiveness on the question of honor, I desire to say, on behalf of the delegation from the State of New York, that they have had neither lot nor part in the motion, which in our hearts we yet rejoice to hear from the State of Ohio. (Applause.) We heard but recently that some such movement was thought, by wise and good men, necessary for the safety of our country, but our hearts were coerced out of deference to the sensitiveness of the gentleman who presides over this Convention, and we told them we could have neither lot nor part in it, unless others overcome that which we had never been able to do. Now, sir, let me say another word; we have balloted two or three days; we have balloted, thank God, in the best of temper and of spirits; we have resolved, and we required the judgment of two-thirds of the delegates of this Convention for our nominee, to the end that we might be sure, for the sake of our country, that we would have a majority of the electors next November. And after striving hard, after striving long, and after consulting as well as we could in reference to the various names brought before us, we have not been able yet to convince the judgment of two-thirds of the Convention for the candidates we have supported. New York has steadily voted her judgment with kind feelings to other candidates. We have pronounced as our second choice for a distinguished citizen of Indiana. But it seems to me that after this long struggle, and in this crisis of our affairs, and in view of what is so important to every man, woman and child in this

Union—that we should succeed in November—it seems to me now, in reference to our distinguished Chairman, that his honor is entirely safe. No one can doubt that he has steadily and in good faith declined; but now his honor is safe, and his duty to his country, his duty to his fellow-citizens, to all that shall come after us, requires that he shall let the judgment of the delegates of this Convention prevail; and if it should select him as the standard-bearer, most certain, in their opinion, to win a triumph for the country next November. (Applause.) We leave it in the hands of others, as we are constrained to do; but I give it as my judgment, for the past, the present, and the future, that if we should select him as the man, in our judgment, upon whom we can all unite, New York will fall in and give a majority of a hundred thousand without a canvass. (Great cheers.)"

The Secretary then continued to call the roll of the States, each delegation answering with a unanimous vote for Horatio Seymour. The States which had already voted now changed their votes to Seymour, and it required no prophet to foresee that there would be no division of the vote this time. The balloting was carried on amidst the wildest excitement. Cheer after cheer rang through the vast building; the audience and delegates sprang to their feet and waved their hats and handkerchiefs, and Mr. Seymour, seeing that he could not in justice to himself or the country, refuse longer to yield to the current which was sweeping every thing before it, relinquished the chair to a Vice-President, and withdrew to the body of the hall. Order being partially restored, the Chairman said:

"The Honorable Horatio Seymour having received the unanimous vote of this Convention, I therefore declare him candidate, and the standardbearer of the Democratic party in the ensuing election."

Again the hall rang with cheers. The enthusiasm of the Convention spread to the crowds in the street without, and cheer after cheer greeted the annnouncement.

Never was the nomination of any public man for any position more enthusiastically made or received than was that of Mr. Seymour.*

* The following card from Mr. Vallandigham, which appeared in the *New York Herald* of July 26th, sets at rest the slanders which the enemies of Mr. Seymour have set on foot.

"THE TAMMANY NOMINATIONS—LETTER FROM MR. VALLANDIGHAM.

VALLANDIGHAM AND TWO NEW YORK DELEGATES RESPONSIBLE FOR SEYMOUR'S NOMINATION.

'Every day brings to light some new feature in the conduct of the managers of the Democratic Convention. It is now understood that the night preceding the nomination the Ohio delegation met, and having carefully canvassed the situation, again determined to support Pendleton. With this understanding the delegation adjourned. Later in the night Vallandigham and two New York delegates had a consultation, which lasted until daylight.

'When the Convention met, Ohio instead of voting for Pendleton, withdrew his name, and before the delegation knew what they were about the name of Seymour was hoisted and carried through with a rush. When this trick was discovered there was great outcry among the Ohioans, and Vallandigham, General McCook, Pugh and Thurman, who were discovered to have been the perpetrators, were alluded to in no very temperate epithets.

'These men the democratic party must hold responsible for the humiliating attitude it holds before the eyes of the nation, and at their door should be laid the blame of the sacrifice of so fair a prospect of success.'—*Washington correspondence of New York Herald, July* 16.'

"In the above are many inaccuracies.

After the announcement of the nomination, the Convention adjourned until the afternoon.

"1. The Ohio delegation did not the night before the nomination determine to continue to support Pendleton. On the contrary, McLean gave distinct notice to the delegation that in the morning he would present Mr. Pendleton's letter of declination. Some time later than midnight the delegation, after a hot debate, adjourned, without agreeing upon a candidate. In the morning they met; Hancock received a majority of the votes; there was much excitement, and finally it was resolved to cast the first ballot for Packer. Seymour was canvassed and found to be acceptable whenever it should be deemed advisable to present his name.

"2. Vallandigham did not meet with two delegates, nor with one or any, from New York, at all that night, much less consult with them till daylight. In the morning, upon the assembling of the Convention, he learned personally and definitely that the New York delegation did not feel at liberty to support Seymour, and replied that if necessary he would be put in nomination notwithstanding.

"3. Seymour's name was not 'hoisted' before the Ohio delegation knew what they were about. Colonel McCook called the delegation out, and by vote was instructed to put Seymour in nomination.

"4. There was no 'trick,' and therefore no 'discovery,' and, of course, no 'outcry' from Ohioans on the subject.

"5. Neither Mr. Pugh nor Judge Thurman was present nor had knowledge of the movement, and no epithets, 'temperate' or otherwise, were applied to them, nor to any body else.

"6. The men who were responsible for the nomination of Governor Seymour rejoice, no doubt, in the responsibility, especially in view of the strong and rapidly increasing probabilities of his election.

"7. As a matter of opinion I believe that had New York withheld her vote from Mr. Hendricks, Judge Chase would have been nominated within an hour.

"So much by way of correction. As to the manner in which the nomination was partly brought about and partly happened it is not proper that any thing be said further, except that positively Governor Seymour had no knowledge or intimation of the movement till twenty minutes previous to his nomination, and acted in good faith throughout, and, moreover, will go into the Presidential office without a single pledge or promise of any kind made to any one previous to his nomination.

"As to the pretended exultation of a part of the Republican press over the Democratic nominations, pay no heed to it. It is an old trick

In the afternoon the Convention re-assembled, and on the first ballot chose Major General Francis P. Blair, of Missouri, as the Democratic candidate for the office of Vice-President of the United States, after which the Convention adjourned *sine die*.

The Convention was the most harmonious and enthusiastic the party has ever seen, and its labors have met with an endorsement from the people which promises a brilliant success for its nominees in November. Everywhere our cause is triumphing over Radicalism, and Americans of all classes are waiting for the day when they shall have an opportunity of following the old Democratic flag to the most glorious victory it has ever gleamed upon.

and very shallow. The more sagacious and candid Republican organs, such as the New York *Times* and *Commercial Advertiser*, advise their friends 'to stop trifling and boasting and set to work without delay.' And the *Advertiser* declares that 'Seymour is the most popular man in the democratic party.'

"Elections already held within a year show that the Democracy are almost in the ascendency in States enough to give a majority of electoral votes to Seymour and Blair. Add now to these that vast multitude of burdened, wronged, oppressed and discontented people among the Republican masses, and who are determined to 'have a change,' and success in November is certain.

"I have now myself been in New York, New Jersey, Pennsylvania, Maryland and Delaware, and can say with truth that among the Democratic masses no nominations have been made for years which are received with so much satisfaction, and that I have never known a time when among these masses there was such universal confidence in success. Nothing now is needed but combined wisdom and boldness in planning and conducting the campaign.

"C. L. V.

"NEWARK, Del., July 18, 1868."

The following is a statement of all the ballots cast for the nominee for the Presidency:

CANDIDATES.	1	2	3	4	5	6	7	8	9	10	11	12	13	14	15	16	17	18	19	20	21	22
Pendleton	105	104	119½	118½	122	122½	137½	156½	144	147½	144½	145½	134½	130	129½	107½	70½	56½	—	—	—	—
Andrew Johnson	65	52	34½	32	24	21	12½	6	5½	6½	5½	4½	4½	—	5½	5½	6	10	—	—	5	—
Hancock	33½	40½	45½	43½	46	47	42½	28	34½	34	32½	30	48½	56	79½	113½	137½	144½	135½	142½	135½	—
Church	33	33	33	33	33	33	33	—	—	—	—	—	—	—	—	—	—	—	—	—	—	—
Packer	26	26	26	26	27	27	26	26	26½	27	26	26	26	26	—	—	—	—	22	—	—	—
Joel Parker	13	15½	13	13	13	13	7	7	7	7		7	7	7	7	7	7	3½	—	—	—	—
English	16	12½	7½	7½	7	6	6	6	6	—	—	—	—	—	—	—	—	—	6	16	19	—
Doolittle	13	12½	12	12	15	12	17	12	—	12	12½	12½	13	13	12	12	12	12	12	12	12	—
Reverdy Johnson	8½	8	11	8	—	—	—	—	12	—	—	—	—	—	—	—	—	—	—	—	—	—
Hendricks	2½	2	9½	11½	19½	30	34½	75	80½	82½	88	89	81	84½	82½	70½	80	87	107½	121	132	—
F. P. Blair, Jr.	½	10½	4½	2	9½	5	½	½	½			½		—	—	—	—	—	13½	13	—	—
Ewing	—	½	1	1	—	—	—	—	—	—	—	—	—	—	—	—	—	—	—	—	—	—
Horatio Seymour	—	—	—	9	—	—	—	—	—	—	—	—	—	—	—	—	—	—	—	—	—	317
J. Q. Adams	—	—	—	—	—	—	—	—	—	—	—	—	—	—	—	—	—	—	—	—	—	—
McClellan	—	—	—	—	—	—	—	—	—	—	—	1	—	—	—	—	—	—	—	—	½	—
Chase	—	—	—	—	—	—	—	—	—	—	—	½	½	—	—	—	½	½	½	—	4	—
Franklin Pierce	—	—	—	—	—	—	—	—	—	—	—	—	1	—	—	—	—	—	—	—	—	—
John T. Hoffman	—	—	—	—	—	—	—	—	—	—	—	—	—	—	—	—	3	3	—	2	½	—

CHAPTER XI.

Mr. Seymour Decides to Accept the Nomination conferred upon him by the Convention—The Motives of his Action—Formal Tender of the Nomination—Scene in Tammany Hall—Speech of General Morgan —Reply of Mr. Seymour—Enthusiasm of the Audience—The Meeting in Fourteenth Street—Speech of Mr. Seymour—How the News was received throughout the Country—Comments of the Press—Tributes from Republicans—Governor Seymour returns Home—Scenes along the Route—Arrival at Utica—His Welcome Home—An overwhelming Demonstration—His Speech at Utica—Retires to his Home—His Letter of Acceptance.

Mr. Seymour, as we have said, had declined to allow his name to be presented to the Convention for the nomination, upon the assembling of that body, and had refused to accept the nomination when it was tendered to him by General McCook, of Ohio, and many persons were in doubt after the adjournment of the Convention, as to whether he would still persist in his refusal. Had he followed his own impulses, he would most likely have done so, but the unusual circumstances of his nomination made him no longer a free agent in the matter. He had been chosen against his wishes and repeated requests not to be put in nomination, and the overwhelming and resistless enthusiasm of the Convention made it plain beyond all doubt that he was the free and genuine choice of the Democratic party. In the position in which he had been placed, he would have been ungrateful to his friends, and untrue to his country, had he still refused to sacrifice his personal preference to the wishes of the party as expressed so emphatically by the Convention. His first duty was to the country, and the unhappy condition of public affairs at this time made that duty doubly binding upon him. The great conservative masses of the nation had chosen him as the one best fitted to the task of restoring our lost prosperity and the good feeling between the various sections of the Union, and it was his duty as a patriot to bow to the decision thus made, and accept the honor thus conferred upon him.

Taking this view of the matter, Mr. Seymour expressed his willingness to accept the nomination of the Convention whenever it should be formally tendered to him.

As a fitting *finale* to the proceedings of the Convention, it was resolved to make a formal public tender of the nominations to the candidates on the night after the adjournment of that body, and accordingly on Friday night, July 10th, a large and brilliant audience assembled in Tammany Hall to take part in this interesting proceeding. The hall was densely crowded, and Fourteenth street, in front of the building, was thronged with an enthusiastic multitude. The meeting in the hall was organized by the choice of Mr. S. J. Tilden as President. Mr. Tilden announced the object of the meeting in a few well-chosen remarks, and presented to the audience Mr. Seymour, who advanced to the front of the platform. The vast audience sprang to their feet simultaneously, and cheer after cheer burst from them, and was caught up and reëchoed by the crowd in the street. Scarcely would one round of applause die away before it would be succeeded by another, and for fully five minutes the scene was thrilling beyond description. When order was restored, General Morgan, the Chairman of the Committee charged with the duty of tendering the nominations, turned to Mr. Seymour and said:

"Governor Seymour—On behalf of the committee appointed for that purpose, I have the pleasure, Sir, of presenting to you a communication announcing your unanimous nomination as the candidate for the office of the President of the United States, by the National Democratic Convention; and on behalf, Sir, of the Conservative and Democratic people of the States whom we have the honor to represent, we here pledge their united and cordial efforts in securing relief to the country from the thraldom which now possesses it, and in placing you, Sir, as the Chief Magistrate of the United States, in the Executive chair."

Tremendous cheering followed this address. When this had subsided, Governour Seymour replied as follows:

"Mr. Chairman and Gentlemen of the Committee: I thank you for the courteous terms in which you have communicated to me the action of the Democratic National Convention. (Cheers.) I have no words adequate to express my gratitude for the good will and kindness which that body has shown to me. Its nomination was unsought, and unexpected. It was my ambition to take an active part, from which I am now excluded, in the great struggle going on for the restoration of good government, of peace and prosperity to our country. (Great cheering.) But I have been caught up by the whelming tide that is bearing us on to a great political change, and I find myself unable to resist its pressure. (Loud cheers.) You have also given to me a copy of the resolutions put forth by the Convention, showing its position upon all the great questions which now agitate the country. As the presiding officer of that Convention, I am familiar with their scope and import, and as one of its members I am a party to their terms; they are in accord with my views, and I stand upon them in the contest upon which we are now entering; and I shall strive to carry them out in future wherever I may be placed, in public or private life. (Cheers.) I congratulate you, and all conservative men, who seek to restore order, peace, prosperity, and good government to our land, upon the evidences everywhere shown, that we are to triumph at the next election. (Prolonged cheering.) Those who are politically opposed to us flattered themselves there would be discord in our councils; they mistook the uncertainties of our views as to the best methods of carrying out our purposes for difference of opinion with regard to those purposes. They mistook an intense anxiety to do no act which should not be wise and judicious for a spirit of discord, but during the lengthened proceedings and earnest discussions of the Convention there has prevailed an entire harmony of intercourse, a patient forbearance, and a self-sacrificing spirit, which are the sure tokens of a coming victory. Accept for yourselves, gentlemen, my wishes for your future welfare and happiness. (Cheers.) In a few days I will answer the communication you have just handed me by letter, as is the customary form." (Tremendous and long-continued cheering.)

The nomination of Vice President was then formally tendered to General Blair, who accepted it in an eloquent address.

During all this while the crowd in the street had been calling impatiently for Mr. Seymour, and at the close of the ceremonies in the hall he appeared on the balcony, and addressed them as follows:

"Fellow-citizens: I am unable with my broken voice and exhausted frame to do more than return you my sincere thanks for the compliment which you now pay me. May God bless you, and may he bless our country, and may he give us in the pending contest that triumph which will tend to secure constitutional law, good order, peace, and prosperity to our land. I can say no more, but to bid you good night, and once more to thank you for your kindness to me."

The nomination of Mr. Seymour was everywhere hailed with delight by the party. The following comments of the Democratic press will show this. *The Cincinnati Inquirer*, Mr. Pendleton's organ, in its issue of July 10th, said:

"As we stated yesterday, the Democratic ticket is one of which not only the party but the country may well be proud. It has been long since there was so strong a combination of intellectual vigor, force of character, and statesmanlike experience presented to the suffrages of the American people. The name of Horatio Seymour is a tower of strength, and challenges not only the warm admiration of his political friends, but the respect, if not esteem, of his opponents. If there is a man who is eminently qualified for the Presidential office, who would fill it with dignity, with consummate tact, who would honor the place, it is Horatio Seymour. There is no qualification in which he is deficient. He is a ripe scholar, a polished writer, a splendid orator, a profound thinker, who has made the science of government his lifelong study; and in addition, he has every personal grace and accomplishment that are properly associated with so exalted an office. He has a national fame and reputation as extensive as that of any man in the Union. More than all, he is devotedly attached to the Constitution as it was made by the fathers, and would administer it strictly upon the principles of Jefferson and Madison. Not the least flaw or defect can be found with his general political record. No man has fought more gallantly the battles of the Democracy and the Union. He has wielded an intellectual weapon in their behalf as keen as a Damascus blade.

"The selection of Mr. Seymour is peculiarly fortunate at this time, for the practice has latterly been to select mediocrity and inexperience for Presidential honors, rather than consummate talent and ripe experience. The election of Mr. Seymour would redeem us from the reproach that has been cast upon us, that it is impossible to place a first-class statesman in the Presidential office. The delegates from Ohio and the

West faithfully discharged their duty when, Mr. Pendleton being no longer in the field, they gave their votes to the distinguished statesman of the Empire State. It is true there has been a divergence of views to some extent in the sentiments of Mr. Seymour and Mr. Pendleton, upon the greenback question, but the adoption of a platform which is a substantial affirmation of Mr. Pendleton's creed, and the acceptance by Mr. Seymour of a nomination upon it, will remove all difficulty, and be generally acceptable to the entire Democracy of the country. Mr. Seymour being a man of high personal honor, may be safely trusted to carry out and give administrative enforcement to all the doctrines of the platform upon which he is running, and in behalf of which the suffrages of the people are solicited. On the negro suffrage issue, and on all the points involved in the so-called Congressional reconstruction, Mr. Seymour occupies the most advanced Democratic ground, as is well known to every one who has read his many magnificent addresses denunciatory of the whole Radical Congressional scheme. Mr. Seymour's sentiments on this question render him particularly acceptable to the Democracy of the Great West.

"General Frank P. Blair, the nominee for Vice-President, is another selection which possesses eminent fitness at this time. General Blair comes of good Democratic stock, and his name is redolent with a Jacksonian and Bentonian flavor that is exceedingly pleasant to the Old-line Democracy. His father was the confidential friend of President Jackson, and conducted the Washington *Globe*, the official organ, during the twelve years' administration of Jackson and Van Buren. His son Frank has inherited the force of character and the intellectual vigor of his father, which was always remarkable, and which has been evinced during his long and eventful life. General Blair is the soul of honor, as fine a representative of true and genuine manhood as the country affords. There was no better, no more gallant soldier in the late war than General Blair, none who received higher encomiums for distinguished and meritorious services. He was for a long period the commanding officer of the fighting Seventeenth Corps in Sherman's army, which performed prodigies of valor on all the battle-fields from the Ohio to the sea. The Radical press, who now affect to disparage this gallant officer, were then warm and enthusiastic in his praise. Their abuse of to-day is answered by their compliments to him then. It is true that General Blair for a time acted with the Republican party, but, like thousands of others, he became disgusted with its excesses, and returned again to the old Democratic household. But even when acting with the Republicans, he never gave any countenance or favor to the atrocious doctrine of negro equality, but always favored the supremacy of the white race, and insisted that to it alone should be intrusted the destinies of the country. But Mr. Blair's merits as a citizen soldier are not his only claims to public favor. He, too, possesses civic experience, and long and intimate acquaintance with American politics. He has been in Congress, and would make an accomplished officer in the Senate.

"Almost every element of strength is combined in this ticket of Seymour and Blair. One comes from the extreme East, the other from the extreme West. It unites, as we have shown, both civil and military talent and experience. If the Old-line Democrats hail with rapture the nomination of Horatio Seymour, the dissatisfied Republicans, together with the soldiers and sailors, recognize in General Blair's selection a compliment to them, and a testimonial of the liberality of the Democratic organization. This ticket was nominated to be elected; and elected it will be, by one of the most triumphant majorities known in the history of modern Presidential campaigns. Every thing indicates this. We regard it as certain as any event in the future can possibly be. The hour has arrived for political deliverance from the most intolerable oppression and misgovernment which has so long afflicted the country. The people are ripe for a change, and a change in November we shall have. Messrs. Seymour and Blair are the next President and Vice-President of the United States."

The Portland (Maine) *Argus* said:

"Horatio Seymour is the foremost living statesman of our country. In private life he is the pure, upright citizen; in public life he has ever been distinguished for enlarged and liberal views, and for devoted patriotism. No man in the country is better qualified for the wise discharge of the responsible duties of President; and if elected, his whole mighty energies will be expended in endeavors to bring to our country peace, union and prosperity."

The Hartford (Connecticut) *Times* said:

"Governor Seymour's reputation is wider than the Union, and his ability and integrity are believed to be fully equal to the high duties which he will be called upon to discharge. We need not say that the nomination has fallen upon a true and reliable representative of the Democratic party. Without derogation of the patriotism or the power of the eminent man who wears the robes of the Chief Justice, we may say that at this juncture it required a Democrat to unite the great party of the people, and to win. This does win. Governor Seymour will be elected. The platform is as sound and strong as the nomination. Both will sweep the West like a whirlwind, and indeed carry nearly all the Northern States, as well as some of the Southern."

The Rochester (N. Y.) *Union* said:

"It would be sheer affectation in us to say that we are overjoyed at the nomination of New York's favorite son, the first statesman of the day, for the first office in earthly government, by the Democratic National Convention. The circumstance and the manner of this nomination render it doubly gratifying—especially gratifying in this, that it wipes away every semblance of antagonism in the Democratic and Conservative ranks, and unites them in solid column. * * * The East and the West, the North and the South, meet upon the common platform of principles laid down with such striking force and unanimity, and following the lead of Horatio Seymour we will march to triumph at the ballot-box. Yielding to General Grant all that is claimed for him, the people know and feel that for the high civil station of Chief Magistrate of this country, he is as the mole-hill to the mountain compared to Governor Seymour. Their interests, their honor, their every thing demands a statesman in the Presidential chair—a man who will command the respect of the world at home and the world abroad; and who will administer the Executive office with an intelligence, with a dignity, and with a success that will restore the once proud prestige of the United States. Such a man is Horatio Seymour, the scholar, the statesman, the Christian gentleman, whose private character is spotless, and whose public record has withstood the assaults of every foe and still defies them. Is General Grant such a man? We put this question home to our Republican fellow-citizens, whose interests and honor in the Government are identical with those of their Democratic fellow-citizens. As a soldier General Grant has been successful, and he has been rewarded—he holds the highest military command in the world, settled upon him for life, with an income attached that renders himself and his family independent. As a civilian he has been a failure in every avocation that he has tried; and repeatedly he has confessed, and by his acts has given evidence, that he is not fitted by either education or taste for a political station. We cannot doubt the verdict of the people—that they will call Horatio Seymour to the Presidency, and leave General Grant to wear the laurels and enjoy the emoluments of the only office for which he is fitted. No happier choice for the second place upon the ticket could have been made than that of Major-General

Francis P. Blair, of Missouri, the great soldier of the West, and a statesman of national reputation. He represents the volunteer army, which enlisted to put down the rebellion that peace and Union might be restored, combining the private in the ranks and the general in command; as he also represents the old anti-Slavery element which warred against the 'peculiar institution' of the South, and which, now that that institution has gone to its grave with the rubbish of the past, demands that we shall have a Union of States in fact as well as in name, according to our constitutional system and upon the basis of universal freedom."

The fair-minded Republicans were equally frank in their tributes. *The New York Sun*, an able and independent journal, said of the nomination :

"We but repeat what we have repeatedly said, when we assert that Governor Seymour is the most distinguished member of the Democratic party. Though he was clearly entitled to its nomination, the extraordinary unanimity with which it was conferred upon him amid the most intense excitement and unbounded enthusiasm, must be extremely gratifying to his feelings. He is the fair representative of the average sentiments of the Democracy upon all the leading issues of the canvass. He is the most popular candidate that could have been selected to command the vote of the party on this side of the Alleghanies. On all the questions that agitate this section of the Union, his views, so often and so recently expressed, are fully understood. General Blair is a man of fair talents and great force of character. He did good service in the field during the war, and has had some experience in civil life. Though coming of a pure Democratic stock, he acted with the Republicans from the organization of that party down to about the period of the death of Mr. Lincoln, when his political course became somewhat wayward and fitful. In his recent letter he takes far higher ground than that laid down in the Democratic platform in favor of overturning the reconstruction policy of Congress and remanding the Southern States to their condition at the close of the war. General Blair is a gentleman of strict temperance principles, and popular among his personal friends."

Governor Seymour left New York for his home in Utica on the 11th of July, taking the night boat to Albany, where he remained during Sunday, the 12th. On Monday he resumed his journey home, passing over the New York Central Railway. He had suffered on Sunday from a severe attack of diphtheria, and was anxious that no demonstration should be made along the route to his home. The news of his journey, however, had preceded him, and at every town he was met and welcomed by enthusiastic crowds. The demonstrations were very hearty, and touched the Governor deeply. He was too unwell to speak, however, and his thanks were returned through other persons.

Upon reaching Utica, he was received with a perfect ovation. The depot, the hotels, the stores, and many of the private residences, were handsomely decorated with flags. The Governor was formally received by the Mayor of the town and a Committee of citizens, and escorted to a platform tastefully festooned with flags, passing through a double row of young girls from the "Christian Brothers' School" and the Sisters of Charity Orphan Asylum. These little ones had frequently enjoyed the hospitalities of Mr. Seymour in their pic-nics on his grounds, and were enthusiastic in their reception of him. The church and factory bells were rung, and a salute fired from a battery of artillery. Upon reaching the platform, Mr. Seymour was greeted with hearty cheers. He was then addressed, on behalf of his fellow-citizens, by Hon. Hiram Denio, late Chief Justice of the State of New York. Mr. Denio said:

"GOVERNOR SEYMOUR:—A number of your townsmen and fellow-citizens casually assembled here tender you a hearty welcome to your home. Our meeting to-day is especially interesting on account of the events of the last week. They have placed you in a peculiar position before the country. (Cheers.) As a candidate for the highest position in the nation, your name is made a rallying point of that large portion of our people who, with me, attribute the difficulties and dangers of our political and financial situation—which cannot well be exaggerated—to the unwise proceedings, amounting to infatuation, of the existing legislative branch of our national Government. We are gratified that the choice of the Convention has fallen upon you, and we anticipate with confidence that their nomination will be ratified by the people. (Great cheering.)"

Amid tremendous cheering Governor Seymour responded as follows:

"I have been very grateful for the marks of good will which I have received from the representatives of the Democratic party of all the States in this Union, but this exhibition of kindness and partiality from my own townsmen impresses itself upon my heart most deeply of all. (Cheers.) During the whole course of my life I have received from them, without distinction of party, proofs of good will that I shall ever cherish with gratitude during the remainder of my existence. (Cheers.) I am now suffering from a violent inflammation in my throat which, my physician advises me, makes it dangerous to speak in the open air, but at the risk of my life I must thank you for this striking and gratifying proof of your good will and partiality towards me. (Loud cheering.)"

After this reception, Mr. Seymour retired to his residence near the town, where he received the congratulations of his neighbors.

On the 4th of August, Mr. Seymour sent to the Committee appointed by the Convention, the following letter of acceptance:

"UTICA, August 4.

"GENTLEMEN: When in the City of New York on the 11th of July, in the presence of a vast multitude, on behalf of the National Democratic Convention, you tendered to me its unanimous nomination as its candidate for the office of President of the United States, I stated I had no words 'adequate to express my gratitude for the good will and kindness which that body had shown to me. Its nomination was unsought and unexpected. It was my ambition to take an active part, from which I am now excluded, in the great struggle now going on for the restoration of good government, of peace and prosperity to our country. But I have been caught up by the whelming tide which is bearing us on to a great political change, and I find myself unable to resist its pressure. You have also given me a copy of the resolutions put forth by the Convention, showing its position upon all the great questions which now agitate the country. As the presiding officer of that Convention, I am familiar with their scope and import; as one of its members, I am a party to their terms. They are in accord with my views, and I stand upon them in the contest upon which we are now entering, and shall strive to carry them out in future, wherever I may be placed, in political or private life.'

"I then stated that I would send you these words of acceptance in a letter, as is the customary form. I see no reason, upon reflection, to change or qualify the terms of my approval of the resolutions of the Convention.

"I have delayed the mere formal act of communicating to you in writing what I thus publicly said, for the purpose of seeing what light the action of Congress would throw upon the interests of the country. Its acts since the adjournment of the Convention show an alarm lest a change of political power will give to the people what they ought to have—a clear statement of what has been done with the money drawn from them during the past eight years. Thoughtful men feel that there have been wrongs in the financial management which have been kept from the public knowledge. The Congressional party has not only allied itself with military power, which is to be brought to bear directly upon the elections in many States, but it also holds itself in perpetual session, with the avowed purpose of making such laws as it shall see fit, in view of the elections which will take place within a few weeks. It did not, therefore, adjourn, but took a recess, to meet again if its partisan interests shall demand its reassembling. Never before in the history of our country has Congress thus taken a menacing attitude towards its electors. Under its influence some of the States organized by its agents are proposing to deprive the people of the right to vote for Presidential electors, and the first bold steps are taken to destroy the rights of suffrage. It is not strange, therefore, that thoughtful men see in such action the proof that there is with those who shape the policy of the Republican party, motives stronger and deeper than the mere wish to hold political power; that there is a dread of some exposure which drives them on to acts so desperate and impolitic.

"Many of the ablest leaders and journals of the Republican party have openly deplored the violence of Congressional action and its tendency to keep up discord in our country. The great interests of our Union demand peace, order, and a return to those industrial pursuits without which we cannot maintain the faith or honor of our Government. The minds of business men are perplexed by uncertainties. The hours of toil of our laborers are lengthened by the costs of living made by the direct and indirect exactions of Government. Our people are harassed by the heavy and frequent demands of the tax-gatherer. Without distinction of party there is a strong feeling in favor of that line of action which shall restore order and confidence, and shall lift off the burdens which now hinder and vex the industry of the country. Yet at this moment those in power have thrown into the Senate Chamber and Congressional Hall new elements of discord and violence. Men have been admitted as Representatives of some of the Southern States, with the declaration upon their lips that they cannot live in the States they claim to represent without military protection. These men are to make laws for the North as well as the South. These men, who a few days since were seeking as suppliants that Congress would give them power within their respective States, are to-day the masters and controllers of the actions of those bodies. Entering them with minds filled with passions, their first demands have been that Congress shall look upon the States from which they come as in conditions of civil war; that the majority of their populations, embracing their intelligence, shall be treated as public enemies; that military forces shall be kept up at the cost of the people of the North, and that there shall be no peace and order at the South save that which is made by arbitrary power. Every intelligent man knows that these men owe their seats in Congress to the disorder in the South; every man knows that they not only owe their present positions to disorder, but that every motive springing from the love of power, of gain, of a desire for vengeance, prompts them to keep the South in anarchy. While that exists, they are independent of the wills or wishes of their follow-citizens. While confusion reigns, they are the dispensers of the profits and the honors which grow out of the government of mere force. These men are now placed in positions where they cannot urge their views of policy, but where they can enforce them. When others shall be admitted in this manner from the remaining Southern States, although they will have in truth no constituents, they will have more power in the Senate than a majority of the people of this Union living in nine of the great States. In vain the wisest members of the Republican party protested against the policy that led to this result. While the chiefs of the late rebellion have submitted to the results of the war, and are now quietly engaged in useful pursuits for the support of themselves and their families, and are trying by the force of their example to lead back the people of the South to the order and industry, not only essential to their well-being, but to the greatness and prosperity of our common country, we see that those who, without ability or influence, have been thrown by the agitations of civil convulsion into positions of honor and profit, are striving to keep alive the passions to which they owe their elevation. And they clamorously insist that they are the only friends of our Union—a Union that can only have a sure foundation in fraternal regard and a common desire to promote the peace, the order and the happiness of all sections of our land.

"Events in Congress since the adjournment of the Convention have vastly increased the importance of a political victory, by those who are seeking to bring back economy, simplicity, and justice in the administration of our national affairs. Many Republicans have heretofore clung to their party who have regretted the extremes of violence to which it has run. They have cherished a faith that while the action of their political friends has been mistaken, their motives have been good. They must now see that the Republican party is in that condition that it cannot carry out a wise and peaceful policy, whatever its motives may be. It is a misfortune, not only to a country but to a governing party itself, when its action is unchecked by any form of opposition. It has been the misfortune of the Republican party that the events of the past few years have given it so much power that it has been able to shackle the Executive, to trammel the Judiciary, and to carry out the views of the most unwise and violent of its members. When this state of things exists in any party, it has ever been found that the sober judgments of its ablest leaders do not control. There is hardly an able man who helped to build up the Republican organization who has not, within the past three years, warned it against its excesses, who has not been borne down and forced to give up his convictions of what the interests of the country called for: or, if too patriotic to do this, who has not been driven from its ranks. If this has been the case heretofore, what will be its action now with this new infusion of men who, without a decent respect for the views of those who had just given them their positions, begin their legislative career with calls for arms, with demands that their States shall be regarded as in a condition of civil war, and with a declaration that they are ready and anxious to degrade the President of the United States whenever they can persuade or force Congress to bring forward new articles of impeachment.

"The Republican party, as well as we, are interested in putting some check upon this violence. It must be clear to every thinking man that a division of political power tends to check the violence of party action and to assure the peace and good order of society. The election of a Democratic Executive, and a majority of Democratic members to the House of Representatives would not give to that party organization the power to make sudden or violent changes, but it would serve to check those extreme measures which have been deplored by the best men of both political organizations. The result would most certainly lead to that peaceful restoration of the Union and re-establishment of fraternal relationship which the country desires. I am sure that the best men of the Republican party deplore as deeply as I do the spirit of violence shown by those recently admitted to seats in Congress from the South. The condition of civil war which they comtemplate must be abhorrent to every right thinking man.

"I have no mere personal wishes which mislead my judgment in regard to the pending election. No man who has weighed and measured the duties of the office of President of the United States, can fail to be impressed with the cares and toils of him who is to meet its demands. It is not merely to float with popular currents, without a policy or a purpose. On the contrary, while our Constitution gives just weight to the public will, its distinguishing feature is that it seeks to protect the rights of minorities. Its greatest glory is that it puts restraints upon power. It gives force and form to those maxims and principles of civil liberty for which the martyrs of freedom have struggled through ages. It declares the right of the people—'to be secure in their persons, houses, and papers against unreasonable searches and seizures. That Congress shall make no law respecting an establishment of religion or the free exercise thereof, or abridging the freedom of speech or of the press, or the right of the people to petition for redress of grievances. It secures the right of a speedy and public trial by an impartial jury.'

"No man can rightfully enter upon the duties of the Presidential office, unless he is not only willing to carry out the wishes of the people expressed in a constitutional way, but is also prepared to stand up for the rights of minorities. He must be ready to uphold the free exercise of religion. He must denounce measures which would wrong personal or home rights, or the religious conscience of the humblest citizen of the land. He must maintain, without distinction of creed or nationality, all the privileges of American citizenship.

"The experience of every public man who has been faithful to his trust teaches him that no one can do the duties of the office of President, unless he is ready not only to undergo the falsehoods and abuse of the bad, but to suffer from the censure of the good who are misled by prejudices and misrepresentations. There are no attractions in such positions, which deceive my judgment, when I say that a great change is going on in the public mind. The mass of the Republican party are more thoughtful, temperate and just than they were during the excitements which attended the progress and close of the civil war. As the energy of the Democratic party springs from their devotion to their cause and not to their candidates, I may with propriety speak of the fact that never in the political history of our country has the action of any like body been hailed with such universal and widespread enthusiasm as that which has been shown in relation to the position of the National Democratic Convention. With this the candidates had nothing to do. Had any others of those named been selected, this spirit would have been, perhaps, more marked. The zeal and energy of the conservative masses spring from a desire to make a change of political policy, and from the confidence that they can carry out their purpose.

"In this faith they are strengthened by the cooperation of the great body of those who served in the Union army and navy during the war. Having given nearly sixteen thousand commissions to the officers of that army, I know their views and wishes. They demand the Union for which they fought. The largest meeting of these gallant soldiers which ever assembled was held in New York, and indorsed the action of the National Convention. In words instinct with meaning, they called upon the Government to stop in its policy of hate, discord and disunion, and in terms of fervid eloquence they demanded the restoration of the rights and liberties of the American people.

"When there is such accord between those who proved themselves brave and self-sacrificing in war, and those who are thoughtful and patriotic in council, I cannot doubt we shall gain a political triumph which will restore our Union, bring back peace and prosperity to our land, and will give us once more the blessings of a wise, economical and honest government.

"I am, gentlemen, truly yours, &c.,

"HORATIO SEYMOUR.

To General G. W. Morgan, and others, Committee," &c., &c.

LIFE

OF

FRANCIS PRESTON BLAIR, JR.

CONTENTS.

CHAPTER I.

CHAPTER II.

CHAPTER III.

CHAPTER IV.

CHAPTER V.

CHAPTER VI.

LIFE

OF

FRANCIS P. BLAIR, JR.

CHAPTER I.

Birth—Childhood—A Favorite with General Jackson—Attends Princeton College—Studies Law—Removes to St. Louis—Failure of his Health—Makes a Journey to the Rocky Mountains—Volunteers for the Mexican War—His Services during that Struggle—Political Life—Supports Mr. Van Buren—Acts with the Republican Party—His Opposition to Slavery—Elected to the Legislature—Elected to the 35th Congress—His Career in Congress—His Plan for Relieving the Country of the Negroes—A Remarkable Speech—The Scheme both Wise and Practicable—Speech on the Volunteer Bill—Opposes the Introduction of Slavery into the Territories—Free *vs.* Slave Labor—Advocates the Building of the Pacific Railroad.

FRANCIS PRESTON BLAIR, JR., was born in the town of Lexington, Kentucky, on the 19th of February, 1821. He is the son of Francis P. Blair, Sr., at present a citizen of the State of Maryland, and a gentleman who has filled a distinguished and conspicuous place in the political history of the country. Soon after the birth of young Frank, Mr. Blair, Sr., removed to Washington City, where the childhood of the former was spent. Mr. Blair, Sr., was an intimate friend of General Jackson, and was honored with the confidence of the old hero to an extent rarely enjoyed by any one, and young Frank was a frequent visitor at the White House and a favorite with its distinguished occupant. The boy received a careful education at the best schools in the District, and as soon as he was prepared, was placed in Princeton College, New Jersey, where he graduated in his twentieth year with distinction. Returning to Lexington, he studied law, and was admitted to the bar, after which he removed to St. Louis, in 1843, and began the practice of his profession, in which he achieved a rapid and brilliant success. He applied himself so closely to his work that his severe labor began to tell on his strong constitution, and in 1845, being then in his twenty-fifth year, he made a journey to the Rocky Mountains, in company with a party of trappers, for the benefit of his health, which was completely restored by the trip. Returning to St. Louis, he resumed his practice.

The Mexican War now broke out, and Mr. Blair, abandoning the law for a time, was among the first to volunteer his services for the defence of the country. He served through the struggle as a lieutenant of volunteers, and took part in the expedition to New Mexico under Kearney and Doniphan. He gained a high reputation for bravery and efficiency in this war, and gave the first evidences of the military genius he has since displayed in such a marked degree.

After the peace, he returned to St. Louis and resumed the practice of his profession. His hereditary predilection for politics now caused him to enter zealously into the Presidential campaign of 1848, in which he ardently supported the nomination of Mr. Van Buren, the candidate of the Buffalo Free Soil, or

Republican Convention, and vigorously opposed the extension of Slavery in the Territories. Thenceforward he always acted in concert with the Republican party, the position of the Democracy with regard to slavery preventing him from uniting himself with them. In 1852 he was elected to the Missouri Legislature, as an avowed Free Soiler, representing the county of St. Louis, and in 1854 was returned to that body, although Thomas H. Benton, the candidate of his party for Congress, was defeated. Mr. Blair was for some time an editor and writer for the *Missouri Democrat*, and his articles were among the most successful and popular published in that journal.

In the fall of 1856, Mr. Blair was nominated to Congress by the Republicans of St. Louis, and elected over Mr. Kennett, the Democratic candidate who had two years previous defeated Colonel Benton. He took his seat in the Thirty-fifth Congress, which met on the 7th of December 1857, the only Republican from Missouri. He took a commanding position in the House from the first, and was regarded as one of the ablest and most fearless members of that body. He was an uncompromising adversary of the system of slavery, but his hostility to the institution, which was founded on high principle, did not degenerate into hatred of the slaveholders, among whom were many of his warmest personal friends. Besides condemning slavery upon grounds of morality, he believed it to be an element of weakness not only to the South, but to the whole country, and he was anxious to get rid of it by all lawful means; and as a sure way of accomplishing this, he was in favor of preventing its extension and confining it within its then existing limits. As a means of getting rid of the system, he proposed a plan which is set forth in the following Resolution, offered by him in the House of Representatives, on the 14th of January, 1858:

"*Resolved*, That a select committee, to consist of — members, be appointed by the Speaker, with instructions to inquire into the expediency of providing for the acquisition of territory either in the Central or South American States, to be colonized with colored persons from the United States who are now free, or who may hereafter become free, and who may be willing to settle in such territory as a dependency of the United States, with ample guarantees of their personal and political rights."

Mr. Blair addressed the House in support of this resolution, in a speech of considerable length and great force. We make the following extracts from the speech, as it is a full and clear statement of the views of its author:

"It was remarked by a gentleman from Tennessee [Mr. MAYNARD] the other day, on this floor, that he had hoped and believed that this question would be discussed and disposed of without reference to the subject of slavery, because, he said, there were no slaves in Central America. The inquiry was made immediately, by many around me, 'How long will it be before there are slaves there?' This inquiry shows, what is almost universally felt to be true, that the slavery question is at the bottom of this whole movement.

There is a party in this country who go for the extension of slavery ; and these predatory incursions against our neighbors are the means by which territory is to be seized, planted with slavery, annexed to this Union, and, in combination with the present slaveholding States, made to dominate this Government, and the entire continent; or, failing in the policy of annexation, to unite with the slave States in a southern slaveholding Republic. I believe that there are those who entertain such a purpose. I am opposed to the whole scheme, and to every part of it; and, in order to oppose it successfully, I think we should recur to the plans cherished by the great men who founded this Republic. I think we ought to put it out of the power of any body of men to plant slavery anywhere on this continent, by taking immediate steps to give to all of these countries that require it, and especially to the Central American States, the power to sustain free institutions under stable governments; and, as one method of doing this, we might plant those countries with a class of men who are worse than useless to us, who would prove themselves to be of immense advantage to those countries, who would attract the wealth and energy of our best men to aid and direct them in developing the incredible riches of those regions, and thus open them to our commerce, and the commerce of the whole world. I refer to our enfranchised slaves, all of that class who would willingly embrace the offer to form themselves into a colony under the protection of our flag, and the guarantee of the Republic of every personal and political right necessary to their safety and prosperity.

"What I propose is not new; it is bottomed on the reasoning and recommendation of Mr. Jefferson. Speaking of a proposition, similar in many respects, urged by him upon the Legislature of his native State, he says:

'It was, however, found that the public mind would not yet bear the proposition, nor will it bear it even at this day; yet the day is not far distant when it must bear it, and adopt it, or worse will follow. Nothing is more certainly written in the book of fate, than that these people (the negroes) are to be free; nor is it less certain that the two races, equally free, cannot live in the same Government. Nature, habit, opinion, have drawn indelible lines of distinction between them. It is still in our power to direct the process of EMANCIPATION AND DEPORTATION, and in such slow degree as that the evil will wear off insensibly, and their place be *pari passu* filled up by free white laborers. If, on the contrary, it is left to force itself on, human nature must shudder at the prospect held up. We should in vain look for an example in the Spanish deportation or deletion of the Moors.'

"The time has ripened for the execution of Mr. Jefferson's plan. By adopting it, we may relieve ourselves of a people who are a burden to us; give to them an amount of happiness and comfort they can never realize here, where they are treated as a degraded class; reinvigorate the feeble people of the southern Republics, and open up to the enterprise of our merchants the untold wealth of the intertropical region, containing a greater amount of productive land than all the balance of the continent; put a stop to the African slave trade, which is created and kept up by the demand for tropical productions; by supplying that demand by the labor of the only class of freemen capable of exertion in that climate. I make this proposition to meet, oppose, and defeat that which seeks by violence to re-establish slavery, reopen the African slave trade, subject those regions, in Walker's own language, "*to military rule*," and exclude from them the people of the northern States. I shall discuss and compare these propositions as fully as the time limited will allow me.

"Mr. Randolph, in one of his most celebrated speeches in the Senate, addressing himself to Mr. Calhoun, said:

'Sir, I know there are gentlemen, not only from the southern, but the northern States, who think that this unhappy question—for such it is—of negro slavery, which the Constitution has vainly attempted to blink by not using the term, should never be brought into public notice, more especially into that of Congress, and most especially here. Sir, with every due respect for the gentlemen who think so, I differ with them *toto cœlo*. Sir, it is a thing which cannot be hid. It is not a dry rot that you can cover with a carpet until the house tumbles about your ears. You might as well try to hide a volcano in full operation. It cannot be hid; it is a cancer on your face, and must not be tampered with by quacks, who never saw the disease or the patient, and prescribe across the Atlantic. It must be, if you will, let alone.

'But no, sir; the politico-religious quacks, like the quack in medicine and in everything else, will hear of nothing but his nostrum; all is to be forced—nothing can be trusted to time or to nature. The disease has run its course; it has run its course in the northern States, it is beginning to run its course in Maryland. The natural death of slavery is the unprofitableness of its most expensive labor. It is also beginning in the meadow and grain country of Virginia—among those people there who have no staple that can pay for slave labor.'

"He then points his conclusion in a way to make it stick in the memories of the masters of slaves, to whom he addressed himself:

'The moment the labor of the slave ceases to be profitable to the master, or very soon after it has reached that stage, *if the slave will not run away from the master, the master will run away from the slave.*'

"Mr. Chairman, I am Mr. Randolph's proselyte; he was no Abolitionist, although aware that slavery was sapping the very foundations of the free institutions of his country—a cancer on the face, which, unless removed, would eat into the vitals of the Republic. I concur in his opinion, that the master must run away from his slaves, unless they run away from him. Unhappily for the slave States, many of their enterprising young men leave their native land for those States where individual ability and exertion are sufficient to confer wealth and eminence; and all of that oppressed class who are compelled to labor with their naked hands, and struggle for existence in competition with the monopolizing slave power that holds the soil, and bands together, by a common interest, the capital, the intelligence, and influence of the order controlling the government of the Commonwealth to make it paramount, would also fly, if they had the means of flight, or a spot on earth they could call their own to receive them. Although the time has not yet come when the masters are ready to run away from their slaves, it will doubtless come, if ever that great mass of freemen who feel the weight of the institution pressing them to the earth, should have the means of reaching homesteads in happier regions, where their labor might render them independent. Can any condition be more lamentable for a State than that which makes it the obvious interest of the mass of its free population to abandon it? and if poverty prevents this desertion, the cause of detention, constantly increasing, must in the end grow into a frightful calamity.

"Every statesman who has looked into the condition of the slave States, has always found it full of difficulties. Mr. Randolph's solution does not end them, unless we go a step further. Where would the slaves go if they could run away? The North may receive an absconding straggler here and there, but what States would receive five million of slaves? or how would the runaways be anywhere provided for? The free States which have put an interdict, so far away as remote Oregon, upon the admission of free blacks, even in the stinted number which might come from the limited emancipation permitted in the South, would hardly receive millions upon a general jail delivery. Nor can the masters run away from their slaves, unless the North is ready to become a St. Domingo; nor emancipate them *en masse* without making it a St. Domingo."

* * * * * *

"Mr. Chairman, there is nothing in the comparative progress of the slave and free States, since the illustrious patriots of Virginia, in the last and most solemn act of their lives, bore their testimony against the institution which now convulses the Confederacy, tending to condemn their policy. There is much in the aspect now given to our affairs by that fatal element, against which their forecast gave warning, to prove that their solicitude to remove it had its root in that sound judgment and devoted love to the country, which made the strongest features of their characters. One great difficulty obstructed these efforts. Emancipation was easy, but the amalgamation of the white and black races was abhorrent, and their existence as equals, under the same Government, was for that reason impossible. They were, nevertheless, resolved to make the experiment of the gradual abolition of slavery, hoping that time would make some outlet to the degraded caste. I believe the existing circumstances on this continent now justify that hope. The attempt of African colonization, to relieve us of the load, has failed. The immense distance, and the barbarous state of the mother country, to which we would restore its improved race that has arisen among us, has paralyzed all the efforts of the benevolent society that has labored so long in vain to form a community in

Liberia which would draw hence its kindred emancipated population, and establish a nation there to spread civilization and religion over Africa. Time has shown that the causes which have produced races, never to improve Africa, or to be improved there, but to abandon it and give their vigor and derive their advancement in other climes, are not to be reversed by the best efforts of the best of men. 'Westward the star of empire takes its way,' is a prophesy which will find its accomplishment within the tropics as well as outside of them on this continent. Liberty and security promote enterprise and industry, and so create that intelligence which brings in its train civilization and Christianity. Africa is a desert, in which every effort to propagate the elements which lead to such results have proved failures; and for ages Africa has ever been 'the house of bondage.'

"As Americans, it is our first interest to take care of this continent, and provide for the races on whose faculties and labor its advancement depends. In my opinion, the door is now open in Central America to receive the enfranchised colored race born amongst us, and which has received, with our language and the habits contracted under our institutions, much that adapts it to sustain a part in giving stability to the institutions copied from ours in the Central American Republics." * * * *

Mr. Blair then declared that it was the intention of the Pro-Slavery party to force slavery upon Central America, and that President Buchanan had lent himself to the scheme. Said he:

"The purpose of subjecting Central America to slavery has been boldly proclaimed; and the opening of the African slave trade is relied upon to fill up the void in the laboring population which must be made by the war and the expulsion of dangerous classes. Is it not a degradation of the nation which stands on this continent as the first asserter of its freedom and independence, and the great exemplar of popular sovereignty in the world, to have a Chief Magistrate and controlling councils harboring designs which they dare not avow, and seeking by sly intrigues to involve it in a war, to accomplish schemes which the people would spurn with disgust, if promulgated before they became committed in the conflict? I have no doubt my countrymen would regard with just indignation, and resist an attempt by England to turn our flank on the Gulf of Mexico. That she spreads her dominion across this continent, from the Gulf of the St. Lawrence to Vancouver's Island on the Pacific, bringing its pressure to bear upon our whole northern frontier, is as much constraint as can be endured. The nation would be willing to close this century as it began—in hostility with England—rather than to submit to encroachment in our southern quarter. For this reason our Government insisted that Great Britain should abandon the assumed protectorate claimed over the coasts of Central America. She relinquished it; but she stipulated with Honduras that the subjects left by her in the Bay Islands should continue to enjoy the free institutions which she had planted there. Our own citizen, Mr. Wells, looking to the establishment of our influence through our institutions in this quarter, hails this step as '*the establishment in Central America of Republican institutions, which are not to be overthrown at the caprice of temporary rulers.*'

"Can Mr. Buchanan summon hardihood to involve this country in a war to expel the freedom guarantied to the Bay Islands by the treaty made with the dictator Guardiola, and subject them to his absolute authority? I would rather hope that our Government, if not now, may yet, under another Presidency, extend its influence over the mainland of Central America, by giving its support to maintain Governments there based upon its own republican principles. To do this, we must, like England in the case of the Bay Islands, *send our people into the country, protect our merchants in their enterprises there, and make an honest demonstration of the fixed purpose of our Government to build up the prosperity of Central America for its own and our advantage.*"

* * * * * *

He avowed his belief that the only permanent and peaceful solution of the negro question lay in colonizing them in some other country—a suggestion richly worth the consideration of our people at the present day. He said, in support of this proposition:

"Mr. Chairman, it is evident to every man of thought that the freed blacks hold a place in this country which cannot be maintained. Those who have fled to the North are most unwelcome visitors. The strong repugnance of the free white laborer to be yoked with the negro refugee breeds an enmity between races, which must end in the expulsion of the latter Centuries could not reconcile the Spaniards to the Moors; and although the latter were the most useful people in Spain, their expulsion was the only way to peace. In spite of all that reason or religion can urge, nature has put a badge upon the African, making amalgamation revolting to our race. Centuries have shown that even the aboriginal race of this continent, although approaching our species in every respect more nearly, perish from contiguity with the white man. But I will not argue the point. The law of the North has put its ban upon immigration of negroes into the free States.

"In the South, causes more potent still make it impossible that the emancipated blacks can remain there. The multiplication of slaves and freed men of the same caste in the section where the dominant race must become proportionately fewer from emigration, has already compelled the latter to prohibit emancipation within the States, and to seek means of deliverance from the free blacks. The Northern States will not receive them; the Southern States dare not retain them. What is to be done? What was done with the native population which it was found incompatible with the interests of Georgia and the States southwest of the Ohio, and the States northwest, to indulge with homes within their limits? The United States held it to be a national duty to purchase their lands from them, acquire homes for them in other regions, and to hold out inducements and provide the means for their removal to them. Have not the negroes, born on our soil, who have grown up among us, and although fated to be a burden and obstruction to our progress—yet always in amity and laboring to render service—equal claims upon us with the savages, against whom we have had to fight our way for centuries, resisting all attempts to bring them within the pale of civilization?

"The President, in his late message, proposes to gather these savages in colonies, and at an early day raise them to the dignity of forming States, and assuming equality with the States of the Union. The Africans, bred and educated within civilized communities, who speak our language, are listeners at our canvasses, lookers-on at the elections, worshipers in our churches, and constantly witness the processes of improvement in our society, in the field, the workshop, and every domestic scene—one would think quite as capable of being disciplined in colonies, and fitted to take part in the Government of the Union as the Shawnees, Pottawatomies, Winnebagoes, the Sacs and Foxes, removed from the northwest, or the Cherokees, Choctaws, Creeks, and Seminoles, from the southwest. As far as respects the Sioux, Pawnees, Cheyennes, Utahs, Camanches, and Blackfeet, the President might have spared his recommendation until they are caught. I believe the people who constitute this Confederacy will forever scout the idea of blending either Indian or negro States with it. The aboriginal or imported tribes which cannot amalgamate with our race, can never share in its Government in equal sovereignties. In the benevolent design of colonizing the Indians, protecting and aiding their efforts to gain a subsistence by cultivating the soil set apart for them, I most heartily concur; but I think, whatever form of society they may assume, they must always be held as dependencies—not upon the footing of equality with the States.

"And ought not the Government to be equally provident for such portions of the unfortunate race born to slavery, but who, having attained freedom, find that it renders them a burden to those among whom they live—a burden that will not be borne? This is the question which absolute necessity now forces on the consideration of the country—one deeply affecting the interests and feelings of slaveholders and non-slaveholders of the superior race, and of more than half a million already manumitted inferiors pressed down by their weight."

The Liberal party of Central America, he said, would gladly welcome those negroes who would settle among them; and he urged upon the House that such a colonization would increase and strengthen the influence of the United States in Central America more than anything else could, and declared that it was far wiser and honester to plant our influence in that country in such a way, than to encourage such expeditions as Walker's. Near the close of the speech, he said:

"In my opinion, the propagation of slavery can only be successfully resisted by the propagation of freedom. It is this mission, arrogated by Great Britain as peculiarly hers, which has conferred on her the preponderance she holds in almost every portion of the earth. She has swayed it with an iron hand, but everywhere of late years Anglo-Saxon justice, civilization, and Christianity, wherever they prevailed, have allowed every man to feel the comfort of laboring for himself, and he has labored all the better for his country.

"Great Britain has her hands full in Christianizing, civilizing, and improving, for commercial usefulness, the old continents. She must leave to us the regeneration of the new one; and this I find, from a paper in a late Westminster Review, marked by the editor with an unusual notification ascribing it to '*an able and distinguished contributor*,' seems to be the opinion of some of the great men of England. This eloquent writer, describing the missions of what he calls 'the four Empires,' RUSSIA, FRANCE, GREAT BRITAIN, and the UNITED STATES, assigns its office to the latter in the following passage:

'And it may once for all be assumed that the human race, whatever Cabinets or Parliaments may think of it, will not be driven from their inevitable course. The work which has begun so largely will go forward. The Asiatic independence which survives will narrow down and grow feebler, and at last die. The will and the intellect of the more advanced races will rule in due time over that whole continent. The genius of France will follow the shores of the Mediterranean; the line of kingdoms which divides the empires of England and Russia will grow thinner, till their frontiers touch. In spite of Clayton-Bulwer treaties, and Dallas-Clarendon interpretations of them, the United States will stretch their shadow ever further south. Revolution will cease to tear the empire of

Montezuma. The failing Republics of Central America will not forever be a temptation, by their weakness, to the attacks of lawless ruffians. The valley of the mighty Amazon, which would grow corn enough to feed a thousand million mouths, must fall at last to those who will force it to yield its treasures. The ships which carry the commerce of America into the Pacific, carry, too, American justice and American cannon as the preachers of it. The Emperor of Japan supposed, that by Divine right, doing as he would with his own, he might close his country against his kind; that when vessels in distress were driven into his port, he might seize their crews as slaves, or kill them as unlicensed trespassers. An armed squadron, with the star-spangled banner flying, found its way into the Japan waters, and his serene Majesty was instructed that in nature's statute-book there is no right conferred on any man to act unrighteously, because it is his pleasure; that in their own time and by their own means, the upper powers will compel him, whether he pleases or not, to bring his customs in conformity with wiser usage.'

"The starting-point in this new career, is the resumption of the progress which received its impulse in the revolution tending to the deliverance of the white laboring class of this country from the superincumbent weight of African slavery. This redemption of our own race from its vassalage under slavery has been brought to a stand-still, and six millions of our free white kindred endure deprivation, corporeal and intellectual, from the slave occupation of the soil and of the pursuits which would add to their means of living and their sources of mental improvement. Neither the slave owners, nor the slave States, are responsible for the arrest of the enfranchisement which promised blessings to the toilers of both races. For, whether as a slave or free man, the presence of multitudes of the black race is found to be fatal to the interests of our race: their antagonism is as strong as that of oil and water, and so long as no convenient outlet, through which the manumitted slave can reach a congenial climate and country willing to receive him, is afforded, the institution of slavery stands on compulsion. But let me suppose Central America—tempting in gold and every production of the tropical soil to stimulate exertion, with a climate innoxious only to the black man—were opened up to him, under circumstances to advance him in the scale of humanity, how long before masters in all the temperate slave States would make compositions to liberate them on terms that would indemnify them for transplantation? Hundreds of more benevolent owners would, from a sense of public good and for conscience sake, by wills, or by deeds of emancipation, make this deliverance, if the General Government would take the charge of the deportation to the region it might acquire for them—a gradual and voluntary emancipation by individuals, if not by States, would thus in time be accomplished. I hold that it is the duty of the nation to offer this boon to slaveholders and to the slave States to enable them to have complete control of the subject, which is the source of so much anxiety and mischief to them."

This speech attracted great attention throughout the country, and there are to-day many who agree with its author that the plan proposed by him was and is still both wise and practicable.

On the 16th of March, 1858, Mr. Blair introduced a bill making an appropriation for the improvement of the Mississippi, Missouri, Ohio, and Arkansas Rivers by contract, which was read a first and second time, and referred to the Committee on Commerce.

On the 18th of March, 1858, the House having under consideration the bill for raising additional volunteer regiments, Mr. Blair addressed the House at some length in support of the bill, showing that the Government was in absolute need of a more efficient force for the protection of the distant Territories. He made a clear and forcible exposition of the outrages of the Mormons upon the "Gentile" settlers in Utah; of their bitter and rebellious hostility to the Constitution and laws of the Union; and of the audacity with which they assumed to dictate terms to the Government. He said, in conclusion:

"Now, Mr. Speaker, I think it is due to the exigency that we should at least place these troops at the disposal of the President, so that if there should arise any emergency in Utah, requiring the troops, he may have them. * * *

"I know of no difficulty—none at all—on the subject of the power of the President to move the Army into the Territories of this Government. Nor have I difficulties about the power of this Government over the Territories; and I trust that if no other good thing comes out of this unfortunate affair—so to characterize it—it will give the last and fatal blow to that heresy of Squatter Sovereignty that has grown up in this land. I am one of those who believe as strongly in the doctrine of popular sovereignty as any man on this floor; but it is the sovereignty of the whole people of the country in regard to their Territories. It is the right of the people of the country to govern what belongs to them; and I say it is rank cowardice to abdicate a power conferred on Congress by the Constitution, to shirk it off upon the first two or three hundred individuals that may reach a Territory to be organized by this Government. * * * *

"I shall therefore vote for the bill to place five regiments of volunteers at the disposal of the President, but I will not, under any consideration, vote to add a single man to the Regular Army."

On the 23d of March, 1858, Mr. Blair addressed the House in opposition to the Lecompton Constitution of Kansas, and in behalf of free labor in that Territory. His speech was able and forcible, and attracted considerable attention at the time. Near the close of his remarks, he said:

"The oligarchy say they have the right to take their Slaves into the Territories of the Union. * * They demand that they shall be allowed to put their slaves to work side by side with mechanics and laborers, and, in the same breath, they claim that no slave shall be allowed to degrade the employments in which they condescend to engage. I contend that they have no more right to inflict this degradation on mechanics, by placing slave labor in competition with their free labor Not a whit more; and, as they exercise the right of excluding slaves from the professions in which they are themselves engaged, (as they do by inhibiting their education,) I say they admit the right of others to exclude them from the mechanical trades, and from competition with every freeman who follows an honest calling.

"There was a time when this Democratic party was not Democratic in name alone. There was a time when this party took ground against privileged classes, and against every attempt on the part of Capitalists to usurp the power of this Government, and pervert it to their own purposes. I instance the case of the United States Bank, where the Stockholders undertook to force this Government to allow them to bank on the national revenue, the Democratic party took issue with them, and put them down. Since that time we have had the tariff discussion, where the manufacturing interests of the country—a vast aggregation of wealth—undertook to influence legislation, and effect the passage of laws for their especial benefit, in derogation of the rights and interests of the working classes of the country, the Democratic party took ground against the high protective tariff, and defeated it.

"And now here is another question in which this struggle between capital and labor is presented in its most odious and revolting form. Here is a colossal aggregation of wealth invested in negroes, which undertakes to seize this Government to pervert it to its own purpose, and to prevent the freemen of the country from entering the Territories except in competition with slave labor; and the Democratic party, instead of standing where it used to stand, in opposition to these Anti-Democratic measures, is as servile a tool of the oligarchy as are the negro slaves themselves.

"This is no question between North and South. It is a question between those who contend for caste and privilege, and those who neither have nor desire to have, privileges beyond their fellows. It is the old question that has always in all free countries, subsisted—the question of the wealthy and the crafty few endeavoring to steal from the masses of the people all the political power of the Government. These gentlemen are wrong who say that it is a question of North and South. If there is one class of people on this Continent more interested than another in putting a stop to the extension of slavery in the Territories, it is the free white laborers of the South. They have infinitely more interest in the matter than any other class of the people, because they have felt the pressure of the institution. They have been shut out from all ownership in the soil, and driven out of all employment in the States where Slavery now exists; and should we allow the Territories of the Government to be closed against them, they will have no escape from the oppression which has ground them to the dust. No, Sir, it is not a question between the North and South. It is a question which commends itself especially to the non-slaveholding and laboring white men of the South.

"Now, Sir, this controversy will, in my opinion,

end in great good. In the struggle which terminated the American Revolution, the principles of liberty were so deeply instilled in the heart of the people, that when that struggle ended, the slaves were emancipated in a large number of the States, from the impulse which the love of liberty received in that contest. This struggle, which is on the same principle, will terminate in the same way. I know that there are as good men in the South now as there were in the days of the Revolution. There are men—slaveholders—now there who burn to emulate the noble examples of the illustrious men of the Revolution; and the noble State which I have the honor, in part, to represent on this floor, will, in my opinion, have the glory of leading the way in this magnanimous career. Her honor and interest alike beckon her, and that she will not be insensible to these high motives, nor regardless of the glorious destiny which awaits her, the legend which she bears upon her shield, '*Salus populi suprema lex esto*,' sufficiently attests."

The scheme for the construction of a railroad from the Missouri to the Pacific found an early and true friend in him. His knowledge of the West taught him that such a system of communication was the only means of building up the great West, and maintaining the influence and power of the Government over the Pacific Coast. He also gave his support to the measures looking to the establishment of the "Overland Mail" route, using his influence in favor of it, both in public and private. On the 25th of May, 1858, he addressed the House in favor of the Pacific Railroad bill, arguing in behalf of the central route, which he deemed the most practicable. His speech was a clear statement of the scheme, and of the necessity for, and advantages of, the proposed system of communication with the Pacific. He was listened to with marked attention, and made a decided impression upon his hearers.

Mr. Blair was regularly returned to Congress in 1858 and 1860, and during the memorable sessions of the Thirty-Sixth Congress maintained the reputation won by him during his first session.

CHAPTER II.

Rëelected to Congress in 1860—Advocates the Election of Mr. Lincoln—The Secession Troubles—Mr. Blair takes his Position as a Union Man—The War—He is the First Union Volunteer—Condition of Affairs in Missouri—Services of Mr. Blair—He Raises Troops in St. Louis—Assists Capt. Lyon—Removal of the Arms from the Arsenal—Capture of Camp Jackson—Interview with Governor Jackson—The Capture of Jefferson City—Battle of Booneville—Gallant Conduct of Colonel Blair—He Leaves for Washington—Effect of his Absence—Meeting of Congress in July, 1861—Colonel Blair declines the Speakership—Is made Chairman of the Military Committee—Procures the expulsion of Mr. Clark—Speech on the Battle of Bull Run—Defence of the President—Returns to Missouri—Quarrel with General Fremont.

In 1860 Mr. Blair contested the seat of Mr. Barrett, from the St. Louis district.

He was successful in this effort, after which he resigned his seat. An election was held in the summer of 1860, to fill the vacancy, at which Mr. Blair, through an unfairness in counting the vote, was defeated. This election was to fill the vacancy in the unexpired term. Mr. Blair was a candidate again at the regular election in November, and was elected by a large majority.

The Republican party had nominated Mr. Lincoln for the Presidency, and in the canvass of 1860, Mr. Blair warmly supported this nomination. This party in Missouri did not number over twenty thousand men, but it had the advantage of being determined in its efforts, compact, and perfectly harmonious. It was thoroughly hated by the Southern men of the State, and won its advantages only by the most energetic and persistent efforts.

"The leading spirit and chief adviser of the Republicans in 1860 and 1861," says Col. Peckham, in his valuable biography of Gen. Lyon, "was FRANK PRESTON BLAIR, JR., who, in the canvass of 1856, had whispered the magic word EMANCIPATION. No history of Missouri in the momentous crisis of 1861 can possibly be complete without having that name stamped upon its pages in characters of splendid coloring. Himself a Southerner, *and* a slaveholder, the stereotyped cry of 'Yankee prejudice,' 'New England education,' and 'negro equality' could not be raised against him in efforts to intensify passion and excite hate. His own personal courage and coolness silenced the pretensions of the insolent, and forced opponents from the employment of abuse into the arena of debate, and there, before his exhaustive arguments and array of facts, the mailed squires of slavery were speedily unhorsed. Even in his personal intercourse with opposing partisans, in whose breasts were lurking the twin-passions of hate and fear, he exhibited not only the courteousness of an affable gentleman, but an equanimity of temperament and apparent forgetfulness really wonderful. The antagonist who expected at the first meeting a rupture, because of bitter attacks made upon Mr. Blair in recent speeches, was surprised, in passing, at the placid countenance and nonchalance of manner of his political foe. This power over self, made Mr. Blair powerful with others. Serving a great cause in the interests of humanity, warring against an institution deep-seated in the hearts and purposes of a powerful class, he knew exactly the work before him, and the depths he would necessarily stir into fermentation. He made it his purpose to disregard passion, to answer declamation with argument, and to *act* in *self-defence* against ruffianly attacks. His example was infused into his partisans. The effect was visible in the rapidly increasing growth of the Republican brotherhood and the permanent radiancy of the Republican idea." *

Mr. Blair spoke frequently in various parts of Missouri in behalf of Mr. Lincoln, his speeches being justly considered the ablest and most forcible delivered in the State. His ability and earnestness drew upon him from the first the hostility of the pro-Slavery men, and he was frequently interrupted in his speeches, and the meetings he addressed broken up by mobs sympathizing with the opposition. In order to put a stop to such demonstrations, the Republicans organized clubs of "Wide Awakes," whose duty it was to preserve order at their public meetings and protect the speaker. Detachments of these clubs sometimes ac-

* The author is indebted to Col. Peckham for the assistance kindly furnished by him. His *General Nathaniel Lyon and Missouri in* 1861, has been the guide and authority for the statements of this narrative concerning Gen. Blair's services in Missouri, and the reader is referred to that valuable work for a more perfect account of those services.

The author's thanks are especially due to Major Arden R. Smith, of St. Louis, private secretary to Gen. Blair, for much valuable information furnished him, which has contributed in no slight degree to the task of preparing this work.

companied Mr. Blair in his visits to the interior, and compelled his opponents to let him speak without molestation.

Mr. Lincoln having been elected to the Presidency in November, 1860, his election was made the occasion of a withdrawal of the Southern States from the Union. It is not my purpose to discuss the secession troubles, or the causes which led to them—the reader being familiar with them—but simply to relate that portion of them with which the subject of this memoir was associated.

The Missouri Legislature met on the 31st of December, 1860. Political feeling ran very high at the time, and it was found upon the assembling of the Legislature, that a majority of that body were undisguised friends of the South. The Governor and Lieutenant-Governor, and two-thirds of the State officers were Southern sympathizers, and the Union men concerned in the government of the Commonwealth were in a decided minority. Conscious of their power, the Secessionists in the two Houses of the Legislature prepared a series of measures for placing themselves in unlimited control of the State, for the purpose of uniting the destinies of Missouri with those of the South in case of a war between the two sections.

"The only real friends"—says Colonel Peckham, "those who were known as unconditionally such—of the Union, in St. Louis, in January, 1861, were the Republicans. They were called Blair-men, and the party hate of years was still cherished for their leader. It required the utmost prudence and skilful management on the part of Mr. Blair to break down this prejudice in the minds of many and induce them to coöperate with him in patriotic effort. This he succeeded in doing to quite an extent, and prepared the way for success at the February polls." *

In view of the strength and determination manifested by the Secessionists, Mr. Blair, who was by common consent regarded as the head of the Union party in Missouri, advised his friends to revive the "Wide Awake" organizations which had been disbanded after the Presidential election in 1860. This advice was promptly acted upon, and by the middle of January, 1861, the "Wide Awakes" were formally reorganized into a Union club. All Union men were invited to join this club, but very few outside the Republican party responded to the invitation.

There were many persons in Missouri, as elsewhere, who believed that the troubles would pass by, and the country return to its old condition of peace; but Mr. Blair was not among the number. He read the signs of the times more clearly, and his judgment convinced him that the war was inevitable. He had reliable information that the Southern men of the State were secretly preparing to follow the example of the people of the far South, and he knew that if the Union men of Missouri would keep the State true to the Union they must prepare to meet force with force. Though he believed the Southern leaders to be misguided and wrong in their views and designs, he knew them to be brave, resolute, and capable, and this knowledge

* *Gen. Nathaniel Lyon and Missouri in* 1861, p. 30.

caused him to resolve that nothing should be left undone to baffle them. He at once called together the most influential members of the Union party in St. Louis, and in secret meetings explained to them the necessity for prompt action on their part. As the Southern men were organizing and arming secretly, he declared the Union men must do the same. After some hesitation, it was decided to act upon this advice, and a military organization was formed and preparations made for a secret drill. Mr. Blair undertook to raise the first company, which was done secretly and promptly, and of this company he was the first volunteer and was elected captain. His company numbered seventy-three men, officers included. His example was at once followed by others, and in a short time the Union force of St. Louis, thus secretly organized, numbered eleven companies. In order to have a common head for this organization, Mr. Blair was elected its colonel; and by his advice a Committee of Safety, consisting of five of the leading Republicans of the city, was appointed to look after the interests of the Union men of St. Louis. Besides forming the military force, the Union men constituted themselves an "inside organization," of which Mr. Blair was elected President. The military force was for active service in case of necessity; the "inside organization" was charged with the duty of controlling that force and providing for whatever emergency might arise. The meetings and drills were conducted with the utmost secrecy, in order that the Secessionists might not learn of them. The floors of the drill-rooms were strewn with sawdust to deaden the tramp of the men, and the places themselves were strongly guarded to prevent surprise. Passwords and signs by which members could know each other and gain access to their meetings, were adopted; and the whole system carried on with such success that it was not even suspected by the uninitiated. As the time passed on, the organization was extended by the rapid enlistment of new members.

The organization having been effected, it was necessary to provide the men with arms. There was considerable difficulty in the way of this, as the purchase and distribution of the arms would have to be made in secret, but Mr. Blair resolved that the effort should at least be made. The Southern men had set detectives to watch the movements of the Republicans, and it was necessary to act with the utmost caution. Mr. Blair was equal to the emergency. Communicating his design to several of the leading Union men of the city, he succeeded in raising a sum of money sufficient for arming his own company and providing it with a supply of ammunition. He did not stop here, however. He exerted his every effort to increase the force of which he was a member, and to procure arms and money. He was aided by energetic Union men of his own selection, and quiet but successful appeals were made in Missouri and elsewhere, with such success that by the last of February, 1861, the secret Union force in St. Louis consisted of four regiments, armed and equipped. Money was contributed liberally by citizens of other States for the support of the Union cause in Missouri, and at length a fund of thirty thousand dol lars was raised for this purpose. These results were due to the energy and fertility of resource of Mr. Blair, who conceived the plans and infused a part of his own spirit into the persons appointed to carry them out.

Meanwhile the Secessionists were not idle. They had formed secret associations in St. Louis, under the leadership of Gen. D. M. Frost, the commander of the militia of the first district, a brave and able officer, and could rely with certainty upon the co-operation of the State authorities in the event of a collision with the Union men. Their principal object was to seize the United States arsenal at St. Louis, and, having armed their partisans with the weapons thus secured, to take possession of and hold the city, which they justly regarded as the most important strategic point in the South-West. The arsenal was of great value, and its stores consisted of 60,000 stand of arms of the best and latest patterns, 1,500,000 ball cartridges, a number of cannon of all sizes, many valuable machine shops with their full equipments, and an ample supply of all kinds of munitions of war including nearly 100,000 pounds of powder. This valuable property was in charge of three or four officers, about twice as many detailed soldiers, and the unarmed workmen in the machine shops ; in other words, it was defenceless. Major Bell, the officer in command, was ready at any moment to surrender the post to the State authorities, who refrained from seizing it merely because they were confident of their ability to do so at any moment. Gen. Frost secretly made his preparations to take the arsenal, and as a means of calling his men together, made arrangements with the representative of the Archbishop of St. Louis, who was absent from the city, for the purpose of sounding his signal from the bells of the Catholic churches of the city. He communicated this arrangement to his subordinates in a secret circular, which fell into the hands of Mr. Blair. In consequence of this discovery, Messrs. Filley and Foy, friends of Mr. Blair—the former the Mayor of the city—called upon Archbishop Kendrick and asked if the information they had gained was true. The Archbishop replied that it was, but that he had already given orders that the bells of his churches should not be used for any such purpose.

Mr. Blair at once sent the circular of Gen. Frost to Gen. Scott, and urged him to transfer the command of the arsenal from Major Bell to some one upon whom the Government could rely, and also to send troops to that post for its protection. Gen. Scott, about the last of January, sent a detachment of troops to the arsenal, and issued an order to Major Bell to report for duty at the headquarters of the Department of the East. Major Bell declined to obey the order on account of his large property interests in St. Louis, and tendered his resignation, which was accepted. Major Hagner was then placed in command of the arsenal.

Early in January, the force at Jefferson Barracks, near the city, was increased. On the 11th, the United States funds at the Custom House were removed, under the protection of a strong guard, from the arsenal. These events created great indignation among the Southern men of St. Louis.

Meanwhile, Mr. Blair labored earnestly to bring all the friends of the Union into one party. He was willing to make any honorable concession to effect this, and urged his friends to drop the title of "Republicans," and call themselves Union men, in order that the old partyisms of the past might not defeat the end he had in view. His efforts were not successful, however. The men who had been his political foes for years, and who were really true to the Union, could not forget their old party prejudices; and, while they desired the preservation of the Union, did not wish to follow in the lead of the man who had dealt them such hard blows in old times. Mr. Blair was not discouraged. He had resolved that Missouri should be saved to the Union, and he felt himself competent to effect this. The Union men had unanimously chosen him their leader, and it was fortunate for them that their choice was so wisely made.

"The most admirable of all the personal incidents of that time was the perfect confidence and trust reposed in each other by individual Republicans, and the supreme reliance placed in their leader. Between Mr. Blair and others of prominence in the party (men of great abilities and solid judgment as well), there existed the most thorough personal sympathy and harmony. Indeed, it was no time to cater to ambition. The positive character, untiring energy, and undaunted courage of Mr. Blair, capacitated him for leadership in such a crisis. His fertile brain devised every expedient, his indomitable will carried out every plan. While the rebels threatened, they found the work of a master on every hand. In activity and vigilance, he was more than a match for the whole batch of conspirators. In council with his co-laborers, he accepted their suggestions, strengthened their plans, discouraged contentious debate, when indulged in by some young and unthinking friends, by mild remark or gentle reproof, and rendered strict homage to age and ability. No spirit of jealousy, no desire for notoriety, interfered with his authority, and no personal ambition prompted him to encounter popular prejudice." *

As we have said, Mr. Blair was very anxious to draw into one organization all the friends of the Union. The Legislature of the State had called a Convention to consider the troubles which were agitating the country, and both parties were desirous of gaining the control of that body. The Republican party, as a general rule, were in favor of putting forth a simple Republican ticket, but Mr. Blair and a few others opposed the idea. He said he was very anxious to secure the aid of the State generally in behalf of the Union men, but he feared the prejudice against the Republican party was so strong in the State, that numbers of good Union men would refuse to support a Republican ticket, no matter who were the candidates. He was for nominating an *unconditional Union* ticket, the candidates to be taken from all parties. He met with considerable opposition.

* Col. Peckham.

One of his friends, an ardent Republican, said he did not believe in breaking up the Republican party under any circumstances. "Let us have a COUNTRY first," responded Blair, "and then we can talk about parties." *

He worked unceasingly to accomplish the end he had in view, and at length succeeded in procuring, by a meeting of the *unconditional Union men* of all parties, the nomination of a ticket for candidates for the Convention from the City of St. Louis. Of these candidates three were Douglas Democrats, seven Bell-Everett men, and four Republicans. At the meeting which nominated these gentlemen, Mr. Blair made a speech of great power and eloquence. He said he did not care what party the candidates belonged to. He wanted a new party—an unconditional Union party—which would remain faithful to the Union under any circumstances, and that he should support the ticket nominated. He said he meant to remain in the Union whether the State went out or not, and that he meant to remain in St. Louis, too. If Missouri seceded from the Union, he wanted St. Louis to secede from Missouri. The city must be saved to the Union under any circumstances. It was no time to talk about party, but it was the duty of all good men to forget all party considerations in their devotion to their common country.

The elections for the Convention were held on the 18th of February, and Mr. Blair had the satisfaction of seeing the ticket for which he had labored, elected.

* Col. Peckham.

The Union ticket throughout the State was successful by about 80,000 majority.

The month of January, 1861, witnessed great activity on the part of the Union men of Missouri. The secret organizations were rapidly pushed forward to an effective footing, and spies were employed to watch and report the movements of the Secessionists. A strict watch was kept over the arsenal, the Union men holding themselves in readiness to march to its aid at any moment. Lieutenant Sweeney, of the regular army, had been placed in charge of the troops at that post, and he had avowed his determination to blow up the building rather than yield it to any one. Letters poured in upon Mr. Blair from all parts of the State, from Union men asking for advice, aid, and comfort, and his private secretary was kept busy replying to them. The cause of secession seemed prosperous in all parts of the State.

On the 6th of February a company of eighty enlisted men of the regular army reached the St. Louis arsenal from Fort Riley. The officer in charge of this force succeeded, by virtue of his rank, to the command of all the troops at the arsenal. He was Captain Nathaniel Lyon, a distinguished officer of the regular army, and it was not long before it came to be understood that he was just the man for whom the Union men of St. Louis had been wishing so long.

"Upon his arrival in St. Louis, Captain Lyon at once called upon Mr. Blair, and from him learned the exact condition of affairs, both in the city and throughout the State. Thus between these two men was formed an intimacy which speedily ripened into the warmest friendship and the most profound mutual respect and confidence. As the plot thickened, and the changing days developed new conditions, Blair was the trusted, confidential adviser, sought for in every instance, and in every instance upholding and sustaining. This confidence, this reliance, this friendship was never weakened by the clashing of opposing opinions, or by the selfishness which generally obtains in men flattered by official position and power." *

Captain Lyon was introduced to the leading Union men of the city, and made acquainted with all their movements. He visited the armories and secret drills of the Union guards, and frequently aided in instructing the men and establishing the necessary discipline. He at once set to work to put in force measures for the defence of the arsenal, but found himself greatly hindered by the conduct of Major Hagner, who threw every obstacle in his way. Indeed, so studied was Hagner's course that Lyon could not doubt that he was secretly in favor of giving up the arsenal to the Secessionists.

In order to remove this fatal opposition on the part of Major Hagner, Mr. Blair wrote repeatedly to Washington, laying the case before the Government, but failing to get a prompt response to his letters, he concluded to see the President in person, and accordingly set out at once for Washington, stopping at Springfield, Illinois, to see Mr. Lincoln, the President elect,

* *Gen. Nathaniel Lyon and Missouri in* 1861. By Lt. Col. James Peckham. P. 58.

to whom he explained the situation and plans of the Union men of Missouri. He failed to accomplish any thing during Mr. Buchanan's administration, but after the inauguration of Mr. Lincoln procured an order from the War Department placing Captain Lyon in command of the defences of the arsenal. This order was at once sent to Gen. Harney, the commander of the Department, and reached him about the middle of March. Harney interpreted it literally, and placed Lyon in command of the troops and defences of the post, but left Hagner in charge of the arsenal. This made matters really very little better, as Hagner still had the power to thwart all of Lyon's measures for resisting an attack upon the arsenal. About the same time Captain Lyon was ordered to go to Fort Leavenworth on court martial duty, but this order was revoked by Gen. Scott as soon as he learned the true state of the case. Lyon, in spite of the obstacles before him, fortified the arsenal as well as the means at his command would permit, and posted sentinels at all its entrances with orders to refuse admittance to all persons not connected with the post. He assured a committee of Union men who called upon him to warn him of a rumored attack upon him, that he would defend the post to the last; that if he found Hagner attempting to play into the hands of the Secessionists, he would throw him into the river; and that if the Union men of the city were attacked he would take the responsibility of arming them from the arsenal.

In the excited condition of feeling in Missouri at this time, it was very difficult to prevent a collision between the Union men and Secessionists. Mr. Blair exerted himself on all occasions to prevent an outbreak. He urged his friends to submit to any thing rather than bring on a conflict. He was influenced by no hatred of his political foes; his motives were high and pure; and he believed his cause too sacred to be sullied by violence. His influence triumphed, and in spite of the unusual excitement, there was no bloodshed.

Mr. Blair returned from Washington on the 17th of April, after the fall of Fort Sumter. On the day of his arrival, the Governor of the State replied to President Lincoln's call for troops, refusing to furnish the aid asked for. Mr. Blair denounced this act in unmeasured terms, and "telegraphed at once to Washington, offering to raise immediately four regiments for active duty, and urging their acceptance and the appointment of an officer to muster them into the service. That there might be no failure in securing the attention of the Government to this matter, as well as to the general wants of the loyalists of Missouri, Captain Barton Able visited Washington City for the purpose of representing Missouri affairs to the President and Cabinet. Mr. Blair also advised those officers of the militia who called upon him and announced their desire to identify themselves with the Union, to withdraw from the Jackson militia at once. He also advised the immediate recruiting of companies, and inspired confidence of their speedy muster. It is true, and in justice should be said, that Mr. Blair at that day was himself a host. Wherever loyal men met in council he was there; whenever loyal men received the word of command it was from him." *

On the 20th of April the Western Arsenal of the United States, at Liberty, Missouri, was seized by the State authorities. This was at once reported to Capt. Lyon, who was also warned that the command of Gen. Frost was contemplating an attack upon the St. Louis Arsenal. He made his arrangements to defend the post, and the Union men of St. Louis prepared to march to his assistance at the first signal of danger.

On the 21st of April, Mr. Blair received a despatch from Washington accepting the four regiments he had offered. On the same day Captain Lyon informed him that Lieutenant (now Major-General) Schofield was in St. Louis with authority to muster volunteers into the service. Mr. Blair at once sought an interview with Lieut. Schofield, who informed him that he was ready to muster in the four regiments. Schofield then proceeded to the arsenal for the purpose of receiving the recruits, but, arriving there, found himself stopped by orders from General Harney, prohibiting the entrance of volunteers into the arsenal, and also their subsistence and arming. He returned to Mr. Blair with this report, and the two at once called upon Gen. Harney and urged him to countermand his order, but he refused to do so. Mr. Blair then returned home, and sending for a telegraph operator, Mr. Lucien Barnes, upon whose fidelity and discretion he knew he could rely, sent the following telegram to the Governor of Pennsylvania:

* *Gen. Nathaniel Lyon and Missouri in* 1861, p. 103.

ST. LOUIS, *April* 21, 1861.

"*Governor* A. G. CURTIN, *Harrisburg*, *Pennsylvania:*

"An officer of the army here, has received an order to muster in Missouri regiments. General Harney refuses to let them remain in the arsenal grounds or permit them to be armed. I wish these facts to be communicated to the Secretary of War by special messenger, and instructions sent immediately to Harney to receive the troops at the arsenal, and arm them. Our friends distrust Harney very much. He should be superseded immediately by putting another commander in this district. The object of the Secessionists is to seize the arsenal here, with its seventy-five thousand stand of arms, and he refuses the means of defending it. We have plenty of men but no arms.

"FRANK P. BLAIR, Jr."

While in Washington, Mr. Blair had procured from the War Department an order to Capt. Lyon to issue five thousand stand of arms from the arsenal to the Union men, in case it became necessary to defend the arsenal or to resort to force to protect their lives. Two days previous to the occurrence related above, Mr. Blair, finding that Harney would not allow the execution of the order, despatched his friend, Dr. Hazlett, to Washington with the following letter to his brother, the Postmaster-General:

"ST. LOUIS, *April* 19, 1861.

"DEAR JUDGE: Dr. Hazlett will hand you this letter. He goes to Washington for the purpose of urging the removal of General Harney from this post, and giving us some one to command who will not obstruct the orders of Government intended for our assistance. Harney has issued orders, at the instance of the Secessionists, refusing to allow us to have the guns which the Government had ordered to be given to us. We also want an order to Captain Lyon to swear in the four regiments assigned to Missouri. I have already written and telegraphed to this effect; but in these days we do not know what to rely upon, and therefore we have deemed it advisable to send a special messenger. If you will send General Wool, or some one who is not to be doubted, to take command in this district, and designate an officer to swear in our volunteers, and arm the rest of our people, who are willing to act as a civic or home guard, I think we shall be able to hold our ground here. But the man sent to supersede Harney should reach here before Harney is apprised of his removal; and the order to swear in our volunteers should come as soon as possible, and should be sent to Lyon by telegraph, if not already sent, and should be repeated, even if the order has been sent already. I consider these matters of vital importance, otherwise would not urge them upon your attention. I ask you to see Cameron immediately in regard to the business.

"Yours, FRANK P. BLAIR, JR.

"Hon. Montgomery Blair."

After sending his telegram to Washington, on the 21st, Mr. Blair went to the arsenal to see Lyon. He found three of the Committee of Safety there in consultation with the Captain. The course of General Harney and the situation of affairs were gravely discussed, and it was unanimously resolved that the arsenal should be reinforced by the volunteers that night, General Harney's order to the contrary notwithstanding. These recruits were successfully introduced into the building, and armed at the appointed time.

On the same day, being apprehensive of a collision in the city, Mr. Blair sent his family away from St. Louis. The Southern men were constantly making offensive demonstrations in front of his residence, and as he did not know how long it would be before these insults would be changed into violence, he thought it best to send his family beyond the reach of danger.

On the 23d, General Harney was summoned by the Secretary of War to report at Washington without delay, and he at once complied with the order. In four days four regiments were mustered into the Federal service. Their Colonels were Blair (1st Regt.), Boernstein (2d Regt.), Sigel (3d Regt.), and Schuttner (4th Regt.). Colonel Blair was not formally mustered into the Federal service at this time, as he did not wish to forfeit his seat in Congress. All these regiments were full to the maximum limit, and more men were offered, but could not be received. The officers were anxious to elect Colonel Blair their Brigadier-General, but he declined to comply with their wishes, declaring that Captain Lyon was entitled by his services, skill, and devotion to the cause, to the honor Lyon at once urged Blair to accept the position, and assured him of his earnest desire to serve under him; but Blair was firm in his decision. He told Lyon that it was likely the old political prejudice against him as a Republican might keep some men out of the service of the Union if he assumed the command of the brigade, and assured him he would consider the honor too dearly bought if it kept back a single man.* Lyon was finally chosen the General of the brigade, and at once commenced to act as such, though he was not officially confirmed in his command until some weeks later. The rush of volunteers was so great, that Lyon accepted and mustered in a fifth regiment, under Colonel Stifel, trusting to Colonel Blair to make good his action with the Government. In addition to this force of five thousand men, five thousand Home Guards were organized and armed, and still it was necessary to decline many volunteers.

Having armed this force, Lyon determined to send the remainder of the arms and stores away from the arsenal, in order to make sure of their being safe from betrayal or capture. On the nights of the 26th of April and 1st of May, he sent away by steamer every thing of value to Alton, whence the precious freight was transferred to Springfield, Illinois.

On the 3d of May, the militia force under the command of Brigadier-General D. M. Frost, of the State service, established a camp of instruction on the outskirts of the city, which was called Camp Jackson, in honor of the Governor of the State. This camp

* Colonel Peckham.

was established for the ostensible purpose of instructing the militia which had been called into the State service by the Governor, but really for the purpose of capturing the arsenal, which the Southern leaders supposed to be still furnished with its usual amount of arms and stores. The presence of the force at Camp Jackson was regarded by Captain Lyon and Colonel Blair as a formidable menace against the authority of the General Government. The designs of General Frost and his friends were fully known to them, and they agreed that something ought to be done to check the evil before it grew too great. Captain Lyon visited the camp in the disguise of a woman on the 9th of May, and informed himself as to its position, strength, &c., and returning to his quarters, sent for Colonel Blair, and told him he had resolved to capture Frost's whole force before he could be reinforced. The Committee of Safety was then sent for, and the plan, which had received Blair's hearty approval, was sanctioned by them after some hesitation.*

Lyon made his preparations promptly, and on the afternoon of May 10th, suddenly surrounded Camp Jackson with his five regiments and a battery of artillery, and demanded of Gen. Frost an immediate surrender of his camp and forces. Being completely surprised and outnumbered, Frost had no alternative but a compliance with this demand, and at once surrendered his whole force, camp, and equipments.

* The sanction of this Committee was necessary, inasmuch as the President had directed Lyon to be guided by the advice of its members.

A large crowd of citizens had collected to witness the movements of the Union troops, and the great part of these spectators were friends of, and sympathizers with the militia. Infuriated by the capture of their friends, the crowd made an attack on company F. of the Third Regiment of Missouri Volunteers. At first stones and bricks were used, and finally several pistol shots were fired by the mob. Captain Blandowski, commanding the company, urged his men to refrain from returning the attack of the mob, but, when one of his men had been killed, several wounded, and himself mortally wounded, he ordered his command to fire upon the mob. The order was obeyed with fatal effect, and the crowd was driven back with a loss of twenty killed and wounded. On the return of the troops to the arsenal with their prisoners, they were followed by the crowd for some distance, and one or two more conflicts occurred, in which the citizens suffered severely. The total loss of the citizens was about 40 killed and wounded. One federal soldier was killed, one (Capt. Blandowski) mortally wounded, and several more or less injured. Lyon and Blair exerted themselves to the utmost to keep the troops from firing. During the whole affair not a single shot was fired from Blair's regiment, though his men were subjected to the most galling taunts and insults from the prisoners and the mob. The prisoners were conveyed to the arsenal, where they were parolled and sent back to the city the next evening.

Gen. Harney returned to St. Louis on the 11th of May, and announced his intention to disband the

Home Guards, a declaration which greatly elated the Southern leaders. The next day Gen. Harney called on Col. Blair and informed him of this design. Blair replied that he (Gen. Harney) had no right to do so. He showed him the President's order authorizing the organization of the Home Guards, and assured him that an order for their dispersion would not be submitted to in the face of this authority. A lengthy interview ensued, which resulted in General Harney's promising not to interfere with the Home Guard. Blair, after the General's departure, was fearful that he might still attempt to break up this force, and resolved with Lyon and the officers of the regular army on duty at the arsenal, to arrest Harney in case he tried to put such an order into execution. Harney, however, was faithful to his promise, and issued a proclamation stating that he had no authority to disband or disarm the Home Guards.

About this time certain citizens of St. Louis went to Washington with the hope of having Capt. Lyon removed. They gained over the Attorney General by their misrepresentations, and came near being successful. To counteract their influence, Col. Blair sent his brother-in-law, Mr. F. A. Dick, to Washington, to lay the real state of affairs before the President. This special messenger was soon followed by a statement from the Committee of Safety, prepared by Col. Blair, fully sustaining Lyon in all his acts. Mr. Dick's mission was successful, and resulted in the promotion of Lyon to the grade of Brigade General of Volunteers, and an order for the removal of General Harney.

This order Mr. Lincoln sent to Col. Blair, together with the following letter:

"WASHINGTON, D. C., *May 18th*, 1861.

"HON. F. P. BLAIR:

"MY DEAR SIR: We have a good deal of anxiety here about St. Louis. I understand an order has gone from the War Department to you, to be delivered or withheld in your discretion, relieving General Harney from his command. I was not quite satisfied with the order when it was made, though on the whole I thought it best to make it; but since then I have become more doubtful of its propriety. I do not write now to countermand it, but to say I wish you would withhold it, unless in your judgment the necessity to the contrary is very urgent. There are several reasons for this. We had better have him a *friend* than an *enemy*. It will dissatisfy a good many who otherwise would be quiet. More than all, we first relieve him, then restore him; and now if we relieve him again the public will ask, 'Why all this vacillation?'

"Still, if in your judgment it is *indispensable*, let it be so. Yours very truly,

[Private.] "A. LINCOLN."

"Colonel Blair pocketed the letter and the order. He fully entered into the spirit of Mr. Lincoln's letter, and talked frankly with Lyon, under the seal of confidence, regarding it. It was determined the order should not be handed to Harney, until it should be criminal to longer withhold it. On the next day appeared the arrangement between Price and Harney; and under the circumstances, Colonel Blair concluded to give Harney an opportunity of more completely testing his policy. He was not disposed to part with Harney, if he could avoid it. He admired the man in his military capacity, and thought, if he could once divest himself of the influences surrounding him, he would do well enough. But day by day events multiplied, and the Arsenal was thronged with messengers from every quarter of the State, complaining of the organization of the '*Missouri State Guard*' under the Military bill, and the depredations committed by the Secessionists. Colonel Blair endeavored to rouse Harney to a just appreciation of the demands of the occasion, but that officer could not agree with the policy of the Colonel." *

The agreement between Generals Harney and Price was one by which the State authorities pledged themselves to maintain order in the State, to protect all parties in their rights, and to refrain from raising troops under the Military bill. Gen. Harney, in consideration of these pledges on the part of the State authorities bound the General Government to respect the neutrality of Missouri, and merely to use the Federal troops for the purpose of preserving the peace, at the request of the State authorities. The pledges of the General Government were faithfully kept; but, as will be seen from the passage quoted above, the faith of the State was violated daily. The Southern element was rapidly growing bolder and more formidable, and

* Gen. Nathaniel Lyon and Missouri in 1861, pp. 210–211.

it became evident to all that if the Government would maintain its authority in Missouri, it must act promptly and with vigor. The President, on the 27th of May, urged General Harney to insist upon the faithful execution of the pledges of the State, and pointed out to him their frequent violations. In view of all this, Col. Blair came to the conclusion that the removal of Gen. Harney was now indispensable to the success of the Union cause in Missouri, and on the 30th of May, he delivered to Gen. Harney the order for his removal from his command. On the same day, he wrote to the President as follows:

"St. Louis Arsenal, *May 30th*, 1861.

"To the President: On the 16th of May, an order was issued by the War Department, relieving General Harney from the command of the Department of the West, granting him leave of absence.

"By order of the President, this order was sent to me, to be delivered to General Harney when in case the public interest required it. During the time that Brigadier-General Lyon, acting under special orders of the President, was in command of the United States troops at this post, in view of the hostile attitude assumed by the Governor and authorities of this State toward the United States Government, General (then Captain) Lyon, seeing the formidable preparations which were being made by the authorities to commence war upon the United States, and knowing that these preparations had long been on foot, and extended to all parts of the State, felt it to be his duty to strike a decisive blow at the enemy at a time when his forces were relatively so much the larger; so that such a course of action, accompanied with the power to successfully keep it up, would intimidate and subdue the Rebels before they had gained strength or confidence. The capture of Camp Jackson, while it furnished conclusive evidence of the treasonable purpose of those who controlled it, served greatly to intimidate the leaders of the Rebellion. Had it been followed up by a blow struck at the enemy in other parts of the State, the Rebellion would speedily and effectually, at a small cost of life or treasure, have been suppressed in this State; and it was the policy and intention of General Lyon to pursue such a course. In this policy I sustained General Lyon.

"Just at this point General Harney assumed the command, and before the order relieving him reached me he had made an arrangement with General Price, commanding State forces, the purport of which I presume is known to the President. Satisfied that evil results would follow from that arrangement, I should at the time have delivered the order to General Harney, but felt, under the responsibility placed upon me, that it was proper for me to wait and see if any good might come under the administration of General Harney. From that day to this it has been perfectly apparent to me that matters were growing worse, and that said arrangement served only as a cover and a protection to rebels throughout the State. I have to-day delivered to General Harney the order of the 16th of May above mentioned, relieving him, feeling that the progress of events, and condition of affairs in this State, makes it incumbent upon me to assume the grave responsibility of this act, the discretionary power in the premises having been given me by the President, and I make a brief statement of the reasons therefor.

"We have conclusive evidence that extensive preparations within this State are on foot to raise and arm large forces to make war upon the United States Government. From every neighborhood in the Central and South-west portion of the State, men are drilling and arming, and both men and arms will speedily be brought to the State from Arkansas. A large number of wagons have been sent from Jefferson City to the Southern part of the State to transport arms and other munitions of War. For the last ten days I have had most of my time occupied by persons from all parts of the State, who have come here expressly to give information of this state of facts, and ask the aid of the Government to protect Union men.

"Should these things be permitted longer to go on, the Union men would be crushed or driven out from all parts of the State, and the State be completely given over to the hands of the Rebels. Day after day I have made known to General Harney what was occurring in the interior, and I have urged upon him the necessity of taking measures to protect the peaceful part of the people. His answer has been—'I will tell Price about it; I will get Price to correct it;' and he has treated the statements of these men from the interior as untrue or too insignificant to deserve attention. At times he has promised me that he would interpose, but afterward would say that there was no occasion for doing any thing. I ascribe the conduct of General Harney to the influences by which he is constantly surrounded. His friends and advisers are bitter enemies of the Government, some of them pretended Union men, others undisguised Secessionists. Constantly surrounded by these enemies of the Administration, and yielding to the advice and requests of such men, his conduct is such that under him the cause of the Union is rapidly sinking, and that of its enemies rapidly attaining power; and I feel and know that his removal has become absolutely necessary. The preparations of the enemy are now so active and formidable, that I am satisfied the President should order a large increase of United States forces in this State, so that troops may be enlisted and stationed at Jefferson City, Lexington, St. Joseph, Hannibal, Macon City, Springfield, and other points.

"In other States, where there are no domestic enemies, much larger forces have been authorized, while in Missouri, where the enemy is large and powerful, and is being reënforced from the South, the number authorized is inadequate. I therefore urge upon the President that he issue such orders for the increase of the forces in this State as will enable the loyal citizens to protect their homes and the Government from the Rebels. Forces raised in Missouri will be better able to accomplish this purpose than those from other States.

I have reliable information of the disloyalty of many of the United States officers who have been stationed in New Mexico and Utah, and there is reason to believe that they, with such parts of their commands as they may be able to draw after them, acting in conjunction with the Indians, to the South-west of this State, who by emissaries from Missouri and Arkansas have been incited to hostility, and the forces from the South-west will combine in supporting the Secessionists in this State. From abundant information I regard this to be an impending danger, and in view of it I ask, that in addition to authority to increase our force in Missouri, that orders be issued for the coöperation of the United States regulars and State forces in Kansas to be employed in the South-west part of this State and Arkansas, and the Indian Territory. We are well able to take care of this State without assistance from elsewhere, if authorized to raise a sufficient force within the State; and after that work is done we can take care of the Secessionists from the Arkansas line to the Gulf, along the west shore of the Mississippi.

"Very respectfully, your obedient servant,

"FRANK P. BLAIR, JR." *

General Lyon was now in command of the De-

* Upon the receipt of the above letter at Washington, the Post Master General wrote to Col. Blair:

"Yours to the President came to hand and has been read by him. He is persuaded that you were right, and Cameron sustains you. * * * *

"It is a full vindication of you that Harney, after denouncing the Military bill as unconstitutional, proceeded to treat with Price, acting under its authority, who did not, of course, keep faith, but proceeded at once to play out the game intended by the bill itself."

partment of the West, and the effect of the change was at once felt.

As soon as the State authorities heard of the removal of General Harney, the Governor sought an interview with General Lyon, who at once consented to the request, as he was anxious to come to a definite understanding with the authorities of the State. The meeting took place at the Planter's Hotel in St. Louis, on the 11th of June. There were present Gen. Lyon, Col. Blair and Major Conant, on the part of the Federal Government, and Governor Jackson, Gen. Price and Mr. T. L. Sneed, on the part of the State. The interview lasted four hours.

"Governor Jackson demanded that no United States forces should be quartered in or marched through the State.

"General Lyon laid down his views, as a servant of the Government, somewhat to this effect: That if the Government withdrew its forces entirely, resort would be made to secret and subtle measures to provide arms and effect organizations which, upon any pretext, could put forth a formidable opposition to the General Government, and even while arming, combinations would doubtless form in certain localities to oppress and drive out loyal citizens, to whom the Government was bound to give protection, but which it would be helpless to do, as also to repress such combinations, if its forces could not be sent into the State. A large aggressive force might be formed and advanced from the exterior into the State, to assist it in carrying out the Secession programme, and the Government could not, under the limitations proposed, take posts on these borders to meet and repel such force. The Government could not shrink from its duties nor abdicate its corresponding rights; and, in addition to the above, it was the duty of its civil officers to execute civil process, and in case of resistance, to receive the support of military force. The proposition of the Governor would at once overturn the Government's privileges and prerogatives which he (Gen. Lyon) had neither the wish nor authority to do. In his opinion, if the Governor and the State authorities would earnestly set about to maintain the peace of the State, and declare their purposes to resist outrages upon loyal citizens of the Government, and repress insurrections against it, and in case of violent combinations, needing coöperation of the United States troops, they should call upon or accept such assistance, and in case of threatened invasion, the Government troops took suitable posts to meet it, the purposes of the Government would be subserved and no infringement of the State's rights or dignity committed. He would take good care, in such faithful coöperation of the State authorities to this end, that no individual should be injured in person or property, and that the utmost delicacy should be observed towards all peaceable persons concerned in these relations. Upon this basis, in Gen. Lyon's opinion, could the rights of both the General and the State Governments be secured, and peace maintained." *

After this interview the Governor returned to Jef-

* Annual Cyclopædia, 1861, p. 481.

ferson City, the Capital of the State, and the next day, the 12th, issued his proclamation calling fifty thousand of the State militia into active service for the purpose of driving the Federal troops from the State, and protecting the "lives, liberty, and property of the citizens."

General Lyon and Colonel Blair now determined to assert the authority of the Government without further delay, and as the Governor had called on the people of the State to drive them out, they resolved to anticipate him, seize the State Capital, and hold it for the Union.

Accordingly, on the night of the 13th of June, the steamers Iatan and J. C. Swann, having on board fifteen hundred infantry and a battery of artillery, under Col. Blair, who was accompanied by Gen. Lyon, left St. Louis for Jefferson City, which they reached and occupied on the 15th, the Governor and his friends having fled to the interior of the State.

A day or two later Gen. Lyon proceeded up the river to Boonville with Col. Blair's regiment, and occupied the place, driving off the State troops under Price, which tried to resist his landing. The fight was sharp and brief, and the victory decisive.

On the 24th of June, Col. Blair left Missouri for Washington City, to attend the Special Session of Congress which had been summoned by the President to convene on the 4th of July 1861. The *Missouri Democrat* of the 6th of July 1861, thus speaks of the effect of his absence:

"The lack of Colonel Blair's energetic spirit has

been apparent in every attempt at progress made since he left for Washington.

"In the absence of Colonel Blair the General (Lyon) lacks a strong right hand. The adroitness and facility with which he grasped the State then reeling under Secession influence, and pinned the star with increasing firmness to the constellation of the Union, will in due time cause grateful recollections to spring up in the breast of every honest, loyal citizen. Turn which way we will we can find no one who contributed more successfully to this great object than Colonel Blair." *

* This same journal in its issue of June 26th 1861, speaks as follows of Col. Blair:

"Col. Blair left this city on Monday last for the East; the situation of things in Missouri for the moment not calling for his presence at the head of his regiment, he has departed East to render a more valuable service to Missouri and to the whole country. The time that must elapse between this and the 4th of July, on which day Congress will meet, is short enough for the duties he has undertaken to discharge before he will be required to resume his seat in the House of Representatives.

"That he will do 'well and quickly' what is in his hands to do, none can doubt. From the moment that Colonel Blair entered on public life, he has had this confidence from his friends. From that moment he has commanded this respect from his opponents. Boy or man, all have conceded to Frank Blair the will and the ability to meet the responsibilities of every occasion in which it has been his duty to act. With the expansive vigor of a superior intellect, he has developed new powers in every crisis, and risen equal to the demands of every emergency. To-day he fills a higher place in the popular estimation than he has ever filled. He has left Missouri with a greater reputation, a more extended influence, and larger capabilities for good than she has yet enjoyed. It is but just to Col. Blair to record that, on his return to this city in April last, his talents were subjected to a most severe and trying experiment. The grand object before him, at that time, was to arrest the State of Missouri, then trembling on the verge of revolution, and bind her fast to the Union. The means by which this great and patriotic end was to be

Col. Blair reached Washington by way of New York, and while in the latter city he delivered a powerful speech at the Metropolitan Hotel, in which he

accomplished were of the most difficult and delicate nature. They consisted in the organizing and arming in this city of a military force sufficient to protect its loyal inhabitants against armed bands of secessionists, already organized and officered and drilled, and backed up by a traitorous State Government, and a City Government which, if not traitorous in fact, was hostile to the Union and sympathizing strongly with secession. Who does not remember the haughty bearing of the secessionists at that time (so chop-fallen withal and humbled now)? Our Commissioners of Police had discovered that Captain (now General) Lyon, who had only some two hundred men in the Arsenal, had no authority to bring his men outside its walls. They had procured the opinion of a certain traitor lawyer that to do so was unconstitutional. They had posted sentinels around the Arsenal to spy out the movements there, and bring into contempt the national flag, and put under the law of a rebel city police the men who bore it. Brigadier-General Frost, 'who has since melted quite away,' had announced his purpose to plant batteries on the high grounds commanding the Arsenal, and General Harney had decided that it would not be '*prudent*' in Lyon to take any step to prevent it, and that *no such attempt should be made.* St. Louis trembled and cowered beneath the overwhelming power of secession.

"The difficulty of organizing such a military force as Blair desired was three-fold. There was difficulty in overcoming the fears of the rank and file of the Union men, who knew their motions were watched by a sharp and hostile police. There was danger that the first small body of Union men who might initiate the work might be set upon and cut to pieces by the 'Minute Men,' who had garrisoned and fortified with cannon the building on the corner of Fifth and Pine, or by Frost's brigade, who were at that time quartered in the city.

"But another most imposing difficulty to be overcome lay in the hesitation and timidity of many men of influence among the Union men themselves. It was dangerous, said these, to organize; it was rash to arm; it would excite secessionists, provoke attack, draw down upon us the city police, and lead to bloodshed. But all these difficulties were surmounted; it was in the genius of Colonel Blair to overcome them all. He moved right on. His quiet, steady, and unpretending courage inspirited the faltering Union men. His discretion and celerity of action urged prompt and vigorous war measures, and intimated that General Scott was too slow for the occasion.

The first Session of the 37th Congress was opened at Washington on the 4th of July, 1861, in compliance with the proclamation of President Lincoln. Col. Blair was present in his capacity of Representative from Missouri. Before the House proceeded to the election of a Speaker, Mr. Vallandigham offered a resolution that the Clerk be instructed to omit the name of Mr. Blair in calling the roll, as that gentleman was ineligible in consequence of holding a military commission from the United States Government. Col.

overreached both the police and the 'Minute Men,' the organization was perfected with so much secrecy and dispatch that an army seemed to have been created in an hour. It was in this way that Colonel Blair held up and sustained the Union men with one hand, while with the other he smote and discomfited the secessionists.

"The rest is known. The capture of Camp Jackson, that nucleus of the Secession army, which was to take Missouri out of the Union, the most gallant feat in the history of the War, was but one of the results of the wisdom we have been attempting to portray.

"The battle of Boonville, another brilliant feat of arms, whose splendors have covered our little army as with a mantle, might have been won by any officer with less than a tithe of the credit for talents which rightfully belong to Colonel Blair. These victories were won, in fact, last winter and spring, when Frank Blair, and the friends who followed after him in their self-denying work of patriotism, threaded the streets and alleys of St. Louis by night, and met with secrecy in halls and garrets, and collected, and officered, and drilled, and formed, and moulded into shape by slow degrees the Union army of St. Louis, six thousand strong, soon after to be swelled by contributions from the country to nearly thrice that number. * * * The State is safe, and has been saved by a stroke of genius, with little bloodshed, from the horror of a protracted conflict. The indiscretion of a far-reaching sagacity and a lofty courage in a single man has done the work."

Blair then informed Mr. Vallandigham that he was wrong in his statement, as he, Col. Blair, had not been sworn into the service of the United States. Mr. Vallandigham's objection, therefore, fell to the ground.

The House then proceeded to ballot for a Speaker. On the first ballot Mr. Blair, having been placed in nomination, received fifty votes. Before the result was announced, however, he rose and said:

"I think it unnecessary to impose upon the House the necessity of calling even another ballot for the purpose of securing an organization of the House. I beg leave, therefore, to decline my candidacy at this point, and request such of my friends who have voted for me, as desire to do so, to change their votes."

The result was the election of Mr. Grow, of Pennsylvania, for whom Col. Blair had voted.

Upon the organization of the House, Col. Blair was appointed Chairman of the Committee on Military Affairs. In this capacity he reported and procured the passage of most of the measures which enabled the Government to place and maintain its armies in the field. He was unceasing in his activity, and in the short session of the summer of 1861 accomplished an amount of work which is almost astonishing.

On the 13th of July, 1861, he introduced a resolution for the expulsion from the House of General John B. Clark, of Missouri, in consequence of the latter having taken up arms in behalf of the South against the United States, which resolution was adopted.

Col. Blair was a warm supporter of the Administration of Mr. Lincoln during this session. After the battle of Bull Run, he defended the President from the charge that he had forced General Scott to fight the battle against that officer's better judgment.

At the close of the session Col. Blair returned to Missouri, and at once applied himself to the task of raising troops. General Fremont, who had been placed in command of the Western Department, took no steps to meet the danger with which the State was threatened. He was deaf to all the appeals of the Union men for aid, and was more careful of his own interests than of those of the Government. Indignant at such a course, Col. Blair boldly denounced it, and laid the facts of the case before the Government. Fremont unjustly placed him under arrest, but soon found he had made a grave mistake, for Col. Blair's popularity was so great in St. Louis, that the General's high-handed measure created the greatest indignation and excitement amongst the Union men of the place. The newspapers of the city espoused Col. Blair's cause, and his case was at once laid before the President, who ordered his release, a measure which gave great satisfaction in Missouri, where Col. Blair's services were known and appreciated. Fremont again arrested him during the winter, but was finally compelled to release him.

Col. Blair attended the Second Session of the 37th Congress, in December, 1861, and served to its close, acting during that time as Chairman of the Military Committee.

CHAPTER III.

Colonel Blair is Requested to Raise a Brigade in Missouri—Is made Brigadier-General—Stationed at Helena, Ark.—Grant's First Campaign against Vicksburg—Sherman's Expedition against Chickasaw Bluffs—The Landing of the Troops—The Assault of the 29th of December, 1862—Gallant Conduct of General Blair—The Assault a Failure—The Capture of Arkansas Post—General Blair made a Major-General of Volunteers—Assigned the Command of a Division—His Services in the Vicksburg Campaign—Rejoins Sherman on the Big Black—The Investment of Vicksburg—The Assaults of May 19th and 22d—Conduct of General Blair—His Reconnoissance towards the Big Black—The Second Capture of Jackson, Miss.—Is made Sherman's Second in Command—Put in Charge of the Fifteenth Army Corps—The March to Chattanooga—The Battles of Missionary Ridge—The Pursuit of Bragg—The Relief of Knoxville—General Blair is Deprived of his Command.

In consequence of the personal popularity and great influence of Colonel Blair in Missouri, the Secretary of War early in the Spring of 1862, requested him to raise a brigade of volunteers in that State, of which brigade he was to be the regularly commissioned commander. Col. Blair at once proceeded to comply with this request. In the course of a few months his brigade was organized and ready for the field, and on the 7th of August, 1862, he was commissioned Brigadier-General of Volunteers. His brigade was at first attached to the Fourth Division of the Thirteenth Army Corps, commanded by Gen. Frederick Steele, and stationed at Helena, Arkansas.

In the winter of 1862–63, General Grant first conceived the design of attacking Vicksburg, Mississippi. At this time the Federal Army of the Tennessee, commanded by General Grant, lay along the line of the Memphis and Charleston Railway, from the vicinity of Iuka to Memphis; and along the Mobile and Ohio and Mississippi Central Railways, from the Tallahatchie river to the Tennessee. The Confederate army, commanded by General Pemberton, and consisting of the combined forces of that officer and Generals Price and Lovell, held the line of the Tallahatchie and covered the approaches to Central Mississippi. The Mississippi river being open to Vicksburg and in the control of the naval forces of the United States, it was in General Grant's power to turn the left flank of Pemberton's line by a force which should be landed on the left bank of the Mississippi, and compel him to fall back to Vicksburg. Accordingly, about the last of October, General Grant determined to make an early advance upon the enemy. His plan was as follows. A considerable force of cavalry, under Major-General Washburne, was to cross the Mississippi from Helena, Arkansas, march suddenly upon Grenada, Mississippi, and threaten Pemberton's rear. At the same time Grant, with the main army, would move southward from Jackson, Tenn., by way of Grand Junction and La Grange, following generally the line of the Mobile and Ohio Railway; while Sherman, with four brigades of infantry, was to move out of Memphis on the Tchulahoma road, and attack the enemy at Wyatt's simultaneously with Grant's arrival at Waterford. The plan was skilful, and the first part was well and vigorously executed.

Three columns moved at the appointed time. Hearing of Grant's approach, Pemberton prepared to dispute his progress; but abandoned his intention as soon as he learned of Washburne's movement in his rear. Hastily breaking up his camp, he retreated to Grenada without striking a blow, and left Grant in undisputed possession of the line of the Tallahatchie.

The first part of the plan of operations being thus successfully accomplished, General Grant prepared to carry out the remainder. It was his design that a strong force under General Sherman should descend the Mississippi river, surprise and carry the works near the mouth of the Yazoo river, which commanded the approaches to Vicksburg; while he, himself, with the main army should move rapidly upon Vicksburg by way of Grenada and Jackson, driving Pemberton before him and keeping him too closely engaged to allow him to send reinforcements to that city to resist Sherman's attack. He believed that should Sherman fail to capture the city, he could at least secure a lodgment on the shore of the Yazoo with his right wing in communication with the fleet, which he could hold until the main army could arrive and complete the investment of the city.

Sherman left Memphis with the Thirteenth Army Corps on the 20th of December, 1862, accompanied by a strong fleet of gunboats under command of Rear-Admiral D. D. Porter. At Helena, Arkansas, he was reinforced by General Steele's division, of which General Blair's brigade formed a part.

The expedition reached Milliken's Bend, just above the mouth of the Yazoo, on the night of the 24th of December. On Christmas day, Sherman sent a force into Louisiana and destroyed a part of the Vicksburg and Shreveport (Texas) Railway, to prevent any troops being sent against him over that route. On the 26th, the expedition, convoyed by the gunboats, ascended the Yazoo for twelve miles, Morgan's division leading the way, and followed by Steele's, Morgan L. Smith's, and A. J. Smith's, in the order named. By noon on the 27th, the entire command had disembarked on the south side of the Yazoo, near the mouth of Chickasaw Bayou. The whole army then moved towards the enemy's works, and meeting the Rebel pickets, drove them in towards Vicksburg. "During the night of the 27th, the ground was reconnoitred as well as possible, and it was found to be as difficult as it could possibly be from nature and art. Immediately in front was a bayou, passable only at two points, on a narrow levee and on a sand-bar, which were perfectly commanded by the enemy's sharpshooters that lined the levee or parapet on its opposite bank. Behind this was an irregular strip of beach or table-land, on which were constructed a series of rifle-pits and batteries; and behind that a high abrupt range of hills, whose scarred sides were marked all the way up with rifle-trenches, and the crowns of the principal hills presented heavy batteries. The county-road leading from Vicksburg to Yazoo City ran along the foot of these hills, and served the enemy as a covered way along which he moved his artillery and infantry promptly to meet the

Union forces at any point at which they attempted to cross this difficult bayou. Nevertheless, that bayou, with its levee-parapet backed by the lines of rifle-pits, batteries, and frowning hills, had to be passed before they could reach firm ground, and meet their enemy on anything like fair terms.

"Steele, in his progress, followed substantially an old levee back from the Yazoo to the foot of the hills north of Thompson's Lake, but found that in order to reach the hard land he would have to cross a long corduroy causeway, with a battery enfilading it, others cross-firing it, with a similar line of rifle-pits and trenches before described. He skirmished with the enemy on the morning of the 28th, while the other columns were similarly engaged; but on close and critical examination of the swamp and causeway in his front, with the batteries and rifle-pits well manned, he came to the conclusion that it was impossible for him to reach the county road without a fearful sacrifice of life.

"On his reporting that he could not cross from his position to the one occupied by the centre, Sherman ordered him to retrace his steps and return in steamboats to the southwest side of Chickasaw Bayou, and support Morgan's division. This he accomplished during the night of the 28th, arriving in time to support him, and take part in the assault of the 29th." *

Some sharp fighting occurred on the 28th, in consequence of the movements of the Union forces to take up favorable positions for assaulting the hostile works.

* Sherman and his Campaigns, p. 83.

Time was very important. As yet, Sherman had heard nothing from Grant, but supposed him to be moving southward and engaging Pemberton, and he determined, by a vigorous and concentrated movement, to break the centre of the enemy's line, near Chickasaw Creek, and secure a lodgment on the bluffs. The morning of the 29th was appointed for the assault. It was gallantly made, but was unsuccessful.

Gen. Blair bore himself with conspicuous gallantry in this engagement, and won the unqualified praise of his superior officers. The part taken by him is thus described by the correspondent of the *New York Herald*, who witnessed the fight:

"General Morgan, at eleven o'clock A. M., sent word to General Steele that he was about ready for the movement on the hill, and wished the latter to support him with General Thayer's brigade. General Steele accordingly ordered General Thayer to move his brigade forward, and be ready for the assault. The order was promptly complied with, and General Blair received from General Morgan the order to assault the hill. The artillery had been silent for some time; but Hoffman's Battery opened when the movement began. This was promptly replied to by the enemy, and taken up by Griffith's First Iowa Battery, and a vigorous shelling was the result. By the time General Blair's brigade emerged from its cover of cypress forest, the shell were dropping fast among the men. A field battery had been in position in front of Hoffman's Battery; but it limbered up and moved away beyond the heavy batteries and the rifle-pits.

"In front of the timber where Blair's Brigade had been lying was an abatis of young trees, cut off about three feet above the ground, and with the tops fallen promiscuously around. It took some minutes to pass this abatis, and by the time it was accomplished the enemy's fire had not been without effect. Beyond this abatis was a ditch fifteen or twenty feet deep, and with two or three feet of water in the bottom. The bottom of the ditch was a quicksand, in which the feet of the men commenced sinking, the instant they touched it. By the time this ditch was passed, the line was thrown into considerable confusion, and it took several minutes to put it in order. All the horses of the officers were mired in this ditch. Every one dismounted and moved up the hill on foot.

"Beyond this ditch was an abatis of heavy timber that had been felled several months before, and, from being completely seasoned, was more difficult of passage than that constructed of the greener and more flexible trees encountered at first. These obstacles were overcome under a tremendous fire from the enemy's batteries and the men in the rifle-pits. The line was recovered from the disorder into which it had been thrown by the passage of the abatis; and, with General Blair at their head, the regiments moved forward 'upon the enemy's works.' The first movement was over a sloping plateau, raked by direct and enfilading fires from heavy artillery, and swept by a perfect storm of bullets from the rifle-pits. Nothing daunted by the dozens of men that had already fallen, the brigade pressed on, and in a few moments had driven the enemy from the first range of rifle-pits at the base of the hill, and were in full possession.

"Halting but a moment to take breath, the brigade renewed the charge, and speedily occupied the second line of rifle-pits, about two hundred yards distant from the first. General Blair was the first man of his brigade to enter. All this time the murderous fire from the enemy's guns continued. The batteries were still above this line of rifle-pits. The regiments were not strong enough to attempt their capture without a prompt and powerful support. For them it had truly been a march

'Into the jaws of death—
Into the mouth of hell.'

"Almost simultaneously with the movement of General Blair on the left, Gen. Thayer received his command to go forward. He had previously given orders to all his regiments in column to follow each other whenever the first moved forward. He accordingly placed himself at the head of his advance regiment, the Fourth Iowa, and his order—'Forward, Second Brigade!'—rang out clear above the tumult. Colonel Williamson, commanding the Fourth Iowa, moved it off in splendid style. General Thayer supposed that all the other regiments of his brigade were following, in accordance with his instructions previously issued. He wound through the timber skirting the bayou, crossed at the same bridge where General Blair had passed but a few minutes before, made his way through the ditch and both lines of abatis, deflected the right and ascended the sloping plateau in the direction of the rifle-pits simultaneously with General Blair, and about two hundred yards to his right.

"When General Thayer reached the rifle-pits, after hard fighting and a heavy loss, he found, to his horror, that only the Fourth Iowa had followed him, the wooded nature of the place having prevented his ascertaining it before. Sadly disheartened, with little hope of success, he still pressed forward and fought his way to the second line, at the same time that General Blair reached it on the left. Colonel Williamson's regiment was fast falling before the concentrated fire of the rebels, and with an anxious heart General Thayer looked around for aid.

"The rebels were forming three full regiments of infantry to move down upon General Thayer, and were a proportionately formidable force against General Blair. The rebel infantry and artillery were constantly in full play, and two heavy guns were raking the rifle-pits in several places. * * * * *

"When General Blair entered the second line of rifle-pits, his brigade continued to pursue the enemy up the hill. The Thirteenth Illinois infantry was in the advance, and fought with desperation to win its way to the top of the crest. Fifty yards or more above the second line of rifle-pits is a small clump of willows, hardly deserving the name of trees. They stand in a cornfield, and from the banks of the bayou below present the appearance of a green hillock. To this copse many of the rebels fled when they were driven from the rifle-pits, and they were promptly pursued by General Blair's men. The Thirteenth met and engaged the rebels hand to hand, and in the encounter bayonets were repeatedly crossed. It gained the place, driving out the enemy; but as soon as our men occupied it the fire of a field battery was turned upon them, and the place became too hot to be held."

Believing that with reinforcements he could carry the entire position in his front, General Blair hurried to the foot of the bluff to urge in person the despatch of fresh troops to his aid; but the Confederates concentrated such a strong force of infantry and artillery in his front that it became plain that his command would be destroyed before assistance could reach him, and he reluctantly gave the order to retire down the hill. He brought off his troops slowly and successfully, being himself the last to leave the ground.

Not disheartened by the failure of this assault, Sherman resolved to renew the attack on the 30th, but the next morning he found the enemy's lines too much strengthened and their force too much increased to allow him to hope for success, and the attack was abandoned. On the 31st Sherman sent in a flag of truce, asking permission to bury the dead, which was granted. An attack on Haines' Bluff was planned for the 1st of January, 1863, but given up in consequence of a dense fog which made it impossible to move the troops. The expedition, after another disappointment, was then abandoned, the troops were reëmbarked, and the fleet returned to Milliken's Bend, where, a day or two later, Sherman learned that the part assigned to General Grant in the plan for the capture of Vicksburg, had been defeated by the surrender of Holly

Springs to the Confederate cavalry, under Gen. Van Dorn, and the seizure of Grant's communications by them.

General McClernand now arrived and relieved General Sherman of his command. He divided his army into two Corps, the command of one of which was given to General Sherman, the other to General Morgan. Gen. Blair's brigade continued to form a part of Sherman's corps, constituting the first brigade of the first (Steele's) division.

On the 4th of January, 1863, the army of General McClernand embarked in its transports and, accompanied by Admiral Porter's fleet, ascended the Arkansas River for the purpose of reducing Arkansas Post, a strong fortification on the left or north bank of that stream, about fifty miles above its mouth. The attack was opened by the gunboats on the 9th, and under the cover of this fire the troops were landed. The 10th was passed in taking up positions, and the assault was ordered for the morning of the 11th. Sherman was directed to open fire with all his batteries as soon as the gunboats should commence firing, and after a short cannonade to assault the enemy's works with Steele's and Stuart's divisions. He made his attack with vigor and compelled the surrender of the fort with its garrison and armament. Blair's brigade, commanded by General Blair in person, led the advance of Steele's division, and was the first to encounter the enemy. It came in for a fair share of the hard fighting, and, with its gallant leader, won the unstinted praise of the whole army.

After the destruction of the captured fort the expedition returned to its old quarters at Milliken's Bend, where it was soon after joined by General Grant in person, who was followed by his whole army. Then began the final campaign against Vicksburg.

For his gallantry and skill as displayed in the attacks upon the Chickasaw Bluffs and Arkansas Post, General Blair was promoted to the grade of Major-General of Volunteers, to date from the 19th of November, 1862. During the month of April, 1863, Brig.-Gen. David Stuart, who had been commanding a division in Sherman's corps, resigned his commission in consequence of his appointment to the rank of Major-General not being confirmed by the Senate, and General Blair was given his division, which he led through the ensuing campaign.

General Blair participated in Sherman's feint upon the Yazoo batteries by which Grant covered his march down the Louisiana shore to Hard Times Bend. When Sherman was ordered to follow Grant, General Blair was left with his division to hold the position at Milliken's Bend until he could be relieved by troops from Memphis. As soon as these arrived he moved to Hard Times Bend by a forced march, and crossing the river rejoined the army on the Mississippi shore. On the 14th of May, his division, temporarily under Gen. McClernand's orders, bivouacked at New Auburn. He did not rejoin Sherman in time to take part in the capture of Jackson, but acted with General McClernand until after the battle of Champion Hills. He rejoined Sherman with his division and the pontoon train, which was the only one in the entire army, at Bridgeport, at noon on the 17th of May. That night he threw his pontoon bridges over the Big Black, after some slight opposition from the enemy, and his own and Steele's divisions at once crossed over, followed by Tuttle's in the morning. Sherman started off early on the morning of the 18th, and marching rapidly towards Vicksburg, gained the Benton Road on the north side of the city, and thrust his column between Vicksburg and the forts on the Yazoo. He then moved closer to the enemy's works on the north side of the city, halting only when his skirmishers were within musket range of them. Here he threw Blair's division in front of the works, with Tuttle's in support of it, and ordered Steele to follow a blind road to the right until he reached the Mississippi River. The enemy in the Yazoo forts now finding themselves cut off from Vicksburg and exposed to capture, abandoned those defences in the night, and on the morning of the 19th Sherman occupied them, and opened communication with the fleet of Admiral Porter.

Believing that he could carry the town by a prompt attack, General Grant ordered an assault by his whole force on the enemy's works at noon on the 19th of May. The attack was gallantly made, but was a failure. General Blair's division took part in it, leading the advance of Sherman's line, and suffered heavily.

A second assault was ordered by Grant for the 22d of May. This accomplished more than was gained in that of the 19th, but Grant failed to carry the enemy's line. The part borne by General Blair in this desperate engagement will be seen from the following account of the operations of Sherman's corps:

"In Sherman's corps, Blair's division was placed at the head of the road, Tuttle's in support, and General Steele was to make his attack at a point in his front about half a mile to the right. The troops were grouped so that the movement could be connected and rapid. The road lies on the crown of an interior ridge, rises over comparatively smooth ground along the edge of the ditch of the right face of the enemy's bastion, and enters the parapet at the shoulder of the bastion. No men could be seen in the enemy's works, except occasionally a sharpshooter, who would show his head and quickly discharge his piece. A line of picked skirmishers was placed to keep them down. A volunteer storming party of a hundred and fifty men led the column, carrying boards and poles to bridge the ditch. This, with a small interval, was followed in order by Ewing's, Giles Smith's, and Kirby Smith's brigades, bringing up the rear of Blair's division. All marched by the flank, following a road by which the men were partially sheltered, until it was necessary to take the crown of the ridge and expose themselves to the full view of the enemy. The storming party dashed up the road at the double-quick, followed by Ewing's brigade, the Thirtieth Ohio leading, while the artillery of Wood's, Barrett's, Waterhouse's, Spoor's, and Hart's batteries kept a concentric fire on the bastion to command this approach. The storming party reached the salient of the bastion, and passed towards the sally-port. Then rose from every part commanding it a double rank of the enemy, and poured on the head of the column a terrific fire. It halted, wavered, and sought cover. The rear pressed on, but the fire was so hot that very soon all followed this example. The head of the column crossed the ditch on the left face of the bastion, and climbed up on the exterior slope. There the colors were planted, and the men burrowed in the earth to shield themselves from the flank fire. The leading brigade of Ewing being unable to carry that point, the next brigade of Giles Smith was turned down a ravine, and, by a circuit to the left, found cover, formed line, and threatened the parapet about three hundred yards to the left of the bastion; while the brigade of Kirby Smith deployed on the further slope of one of the spurs, where, with Ewing's brigade, they kept up a constant fire against any object that presented itself above the parapet.

"About two P. M., General Blair having reported that none of his brigades could pass the point of the road swept by the terrific fire encountered by Ewing's, but that Giles Smith had got a position to the left in connection with General Ransom, of McPherson's corps, and was ready to assault, Sherman ordered a constant fire of artillery and infantry to be kept up to occupy the attention of the enemy in his front, while Ransom's and Giles Smith's brigades charged up against the parapet. They also met a staggering fire, before which they recoiled under cover of the hill-side. At the same time, while McPherson's whole corps was engaged, and having heard from General Grant General McClernand's report, which subsequently proved inaccurate, that he had taken three of the enemy's forts, and that his flags floated on the stronghold of Vicksburg, Sherman ordered General Tuttle at once to send to the assault one of his brigades. He detailed General Mower's, and while General Steele was hotly engaged on the right, and heavy firing could be heard all down the line to his left, Sherman ordered their charge, covered in like manner by Blair's division deployed on the hill-side, and the artillery posted behind parapets within point-blank range. General Mower carried his brigade up bravely and well, but met a fire more severe, if possible, than that of the first assault, with a similar result. The colors of the leading regiment, the Eleventh Missouri, were planted by the side of those of Blair's storming party, and there remained till withdrawn, after nightfall, by Sherman's orders. General Steele, with his division, made his assault at a point about midway between the bastion and the Mississippi River. The ground over which he passed was more open and exposed to the flank fire of the enemy's batteries in position, and was deeply cut up by gulleys and washes, but his column passed steadily through this fire, and reached the parapet, which was also found to be well manned and defended by the enemy. He could not carry the works, but held possession of the hill-side till night, when he withdrew his command to his present position. The loss in Sherman's corps in this attack was about six hundred killed and wounded."*

Toward the last of May, it being reported to Gen.

* Sherman and his Campaigns.

eral Grant that General Johnston was moving from Jackson to attack him, he resolved to send out a reconnoisance towards the Big Black to ascertain the position and probable designs of Johnston's army. The command of this expedition, by which much valuable information was gained and some important captures made, was given to General Blair. The *Herald's* correspondent thus describes it:

"Information reaching the ears of the commanding general, that Johnston, in possession of a considerable force, was moving towards the Big Black River with an intention of making a demonstration on our army now in the rear of Vicksburg, induced the movement of a sufficient body of troops in that direction, to meet the approaching enemy, if found as reported, and engage him before he could effect a crossing, or at every hazard to repel any attempt he might make to secure a foothold on this side. Accordingly, an expedition was sent out under General F. P. Blair, Jr., composed of men selected from each corps of the army, with their artillery and a command of cavalry. On the 27th of May, the party started on their mission, and marching hastily towards Mechanicsburg, the cavalry in advance, when near that place, fell in with about one thousand men, partly of the Twentieth Mississippi mounted infantry, commanded by Colonel Wirt Adams, and the rest, composed of detachments, all under command of General Adams. A brisk skirmish ensued, resulting in forcing back our cavalry. The infantry was soon formed and thrown forward, and after a brief engagement the enemy left the field in haste.

"This affair being over, the troops pushed forward, scouring the country in all directions, seizing stock, bacon, and every other thing useful to the enemy. The advance marched within twenty miles of Yazoo City, without meeting any force, then struck across the country and returned to take their part in the investment of Vicksburg.

"The facts collected concerning the enemy were, that Johnston had at his call twenty thousand men at Canton, and a similar number at Jackson. This force was composed of very old and young men, all conscripted for the occasion, and were without arms. His serviceable force did not number more than fifteen thousand, though by the inhabitants it is estimated much higher.

"The expedition returned, confident that no fears should be entertained of serious difficulty from the direction of the Big Black, at any rate for some time. His last experience had so intimidated the rebel general that there was little danger of great boldness on his part, and so long as he remainded on the other side of the river, General Grant was informed that he need have no concern about him. Our cavalry was always in movement in that direction, and kept close watch on all his plans.

"The captures made during the expedition amounted to five hundred head of cattle, five hundred horses and mules, one hundred bales of cotton and ten thousand pounds of bacon. All bridges were either burned or demolished, and all forage destroyed. In a word, the country was divested of everything useful to the enemy."

General Blair participated in Sherman's bold movement upon Johnston after the surrender of Vicksburg, and in the second capture of Jackson. His services during the campaign were brilliant and most valuable, and won the highest praise from his superiors. General Grant declared that "Frank Blair is the best volunteer officer in the Army."

At the close of the campaign, General Blair obtained a brief furlough, and went North to attend to matters of a personal and private nature.

He returned to the army in October, and was assigned by General Sherman the charge of two divisions, ranking next to Sherman himself, in command. Grant having ordered Sherman to join him at Chattanooga, General Blair was at once sent off with his corps to Corinth. Sherman joined him at that point on the 11th of October, and directed him to push forward to Iuka with the first and second divisions of Osterhaus and Morgan L. Smith, while he himself (Sherman) remained behind a few days to hasten forward the troops as they came up, and superintend the repairs of the railroad. He joined Gen. Blair at Iuka on the 18th, and a few days later ordered him to drive the enemy out of Tuscumbia, Ala., and occupy the place, which was successfully accomplished by Gen. Blair on the the 27th of October.

On the 25th, Sherman having been given command of the Department of the Tennessee, assigned General Blair to the command of the Fifteenth Army Corps. Blair, as we have seen, having secured Tuscumbia, made preparations for protecting the passage of the army across the Tennessee, but as Sherman on the same day received a message from Grant to drop his work on the railroad, and march rapidly towards Bridgeport, all previous intentions were abandoned, and Sherman at once pushed forward with the advance to Eastport, leaving Gen. Blair to bring up the rear. The Tennessee was crossed at Eastport, and the Army after one of the most remarkable marches of the War, reached Bridgeport about the 16th of November.

General Blair took part in the hard fought battle of Missionary Ridge, distinguishing himself greatly, and fully sustaining the wisdom of General Sherman in selecting him for the command of a corps. He joined in the pursuit of Bragg's forces, his corps leading the advance, and on the 28th of November inflicted great injury upon the Railway between Chattanooga and Atlanta. He also participated in the march to the relief of Knoxville, leading the advance with his corps. He was highly complimented by General Sherman for his service in this campaign, and was regarded by the Army and country generally, as one of the best and bravest commanders in the service. Notwithstanding this, however, at the close of the campaign, he was without sufficient reason suddenly superseded in the command of the corps he had led so gallantly.

Secretary Stanton, acting upon his own authority, issued the order relieving Gen. Blair, and had the effrontery to declare that he did so "by order of the President." As soon as he heard of this, Mr. Lincoln called on Mr. Stanton to demand the revocation of the order, as he had promised the command of the Corps to Gen. Blair. As the campaign was over, however, and the army about to go into winter quarters, he decided to ask Gen. Blair to give up the 15th Corps and take his seat in the new Congress, promising him a new and equally high command the next Spring. Gen. Blair, in deference to the wish of the President, concluded to do this. The conduct of the Secretary of War was most reprehensible in this case, as it was founded solely upon his political hostility to Gen. Blair, with whom Grant and Sherman were both well pleased.

CHAPTER IV.

General Blair is Elected to Congress—Decides to be Guided by the President's Wishes—Letter of Mr. Lincoln—Takes his Seat in the House—Sharp Attacks on him—His Bold Reply—Denunciation of the Abuses of the Government in the Border States—Denounces the Confiscation Bill—A Powerful Argument—Draws upon himself the Anger and Malice of the Extreme Radicals—They endeavor to Injure his Reputation—Charges against him in the House—He Denounces their Author as a Liar—Asks for an Investigation, which is Ordered—Is Triumphantly Acquitted—His Speech in his own Defence—A Powerful Vindication—Malice of his Enemies—He Leaves the House and Returns to the Field—The Radicals try to Deprive him of his Command—Resolution in the House—Reply of the President—General Blair's Persecutors Defeated.

General Blair had risen rapidly in the Army, and as his success had been the result of genuine merit, he had no wish to leave the service permanently, but, yielding to the wishes of his friends at home, he had allowed his name to be presented as a candidate for Congress from St. Louis, in the Fall elections of 1862, and had been triumphantly returned by his admiring constituents. When the time for the meeting of Congress drew near, he was in considerable doubt as to whether his duty to the country required him to leave the service and take his seat in Congress, or retain his commission and remain in the field. Some of his friends were anxious to have him in Congress, and it was intimated that if he would take his seat in that body he would surely be made speaker of the House. Finally, in order to decide the doubt which perplexed him, General Blair decided to be guided by the wishes of the President, and requested his brother, the Hon. Montgomery Blair, who held a seat in Mr. Lincoln's Cabinet as Post Master General, to say as much to the President. Thereupon Mr. Lincoln addressed the following letter to Mr. Blair:

"EXECUTIVE MANSION,
"WASHINGTON, *Nov. 2d*, 1863.

"*Hon. Montgomery Blair:*

"MY DEAR SIR: Some days ago, I understood you to say that your brother, Gen. Frank Blair, desires to be guided by my wishes as to whether he will occupy his seat in Congress, or remain in the field. My wish, then, is compounded of what I believe will be best for the country; and it is, that he will come here, put his military commission in my hands, take his seat, go into caucus with our friends, abide the nominations, help elect the nominees, and thus organize a House of Representatives which will really support the Government in the War. If the result shall be the election of himself as Speaker, let him serve in that position. If not, let him re-take his commission and return to the army for the benefit of the country.

"This will heal a dangerous schism for him. It will relieve him from a dangerous position, or a misunderstanding, as I think he is in danger of being permanently separated from those with whom only he can ever have a real sympathy—the sincere opponents of slavery.

"It will be a mistake if he shall allow the provocations offered him by insincere time-servers to drive him from the house of his own building. He is young yet. He has abundant talents—quite enough to occupy all his time without devoting any to temper.

"He is rising in military skill and usefulness. His recent appointment to the command of a corps, by one so competent to judge as Gen. Sherman, proves this. In that line he can serve the country and himself more profitably than he could as a member of Congress upon the floor.

"The foregoing is what I would say if Frank Blair was my brother instead of yours.

[Signed] "A. LINCOLN."

In accordance with this request, Gen. Blair left the Army just after the relief of Knoxville, and went to Washington. He took his seat in the House on the 12th of January, 1864, as Representative from the St. Louis District.

On the 23d of February, 1864, in reply to certain attacks made upon him by one of his colleagues, Gen. Blair addressed the House at considerable length, administering a scathing rebuke to those who were seeking to lead the Administration into the most unwarrantable excesses, and denouncing and exposing their outrages and frauds in Missouri and Maryland.

On the 5th of February, the bill for confiscating the property of persons in rebellion against the authority of the United States being under consideration, Gen.

Blair addressed the House at considerable length. In the course of his remarks, he said:

"There is some discussion as to the authority of the President under the Constitution to make certain proclamations, giving effect to public sentiment upon this subject. I shall not pause to debate this question. I have heard enough and seen enough to convince me that if any other sanction or guarantee is required, it will not be withheld. If a constitutional prohibition of slavery in all the States and Territories of the Union is considered essential, it will be conceded by the consent of the southern States themselves; and if I am not greatly mistaken, such an amendment will be supported by the Democratic party of the northern States as soon as it is seen that it is desired by the Union men of the South. The President, in my judgment, expressed more clearly the sense of the entire nation in his proclamations than was supposed by either those who most applauded or those who denounced the act. The pledge which he gave to use all his efforts to compensate the loyal owners of slaves, which was ignored by one class and distrusted by the other, was, in my opinion, the pledge of the nation, and will be redeemed. It was an act too grand and noble to be stained by any leaven of injustice or dishonesty.

"If the judgment of the nation in condemning slavery as the cause of the rebellion is correct, and I am not mistaken in the belief that it is irrevocably doomed to destruction, then it is safe to assume that the great obstacle to the restoration of the Union has been substantially removed, and that as our victorious armies advance, driving back into narrower limits the organized armies of the rebels, the States will resume their places in the Union which has rescued them from usurpation, purged by their own consent of that element which alone supplied a motive for disunion.

"I am well aware that many do not assent to this mode of settlement for our difficulties and for the restoration of the Union; but I believe that this is the plan which the people have resolved upon, and which is now working itself out in spite of opposition from men of ability and influence who take a different view of the question. The President has unquestionably marked out this policy, and in so doing has the sanction and support of a vast majority of the loyal people of the country.

"The discussion upon the pending resolution has brought out very distinctly the grounds of opposition to this policy, and disclosed the quarter from which that opposition comes. The proposition is simply to repeal the joint resolution of the last Congress, by which the confiscation of landed estates of persons in rebellion was limited to the life of the offender; but it makes a distinct issue with the President upon one point of the policy he has adopted for his guidance, and which he has made known in the most solemn and authentic manner; and the debate upon it has disclosed a determination upon the part of leading men of his own party to make an issue with him upon all points of his policy, and either compel him to yield or to divide the party which has hitherto supported him.

"To the President is confided the whole military

power of the country to save its Government from overthrow by rebellion. Those who wage war to accomplish that overthrow commit treason. The punishment for that crime on conviction it is expressly declared in the Constitution shall be prescribed by Congress; but it is provided that '*no attainder of treason shall work corruption of blood, or forfeiture except during the life of the person attainted.*' Capital punishment, the death penalty, in this as in other countries, has been in all time applied to treason. The head that plots and attempts the destruction of the Government is always forfeited to the society that looks to its Government for preservation. In England and other monarchies condemnation for treason not only forfeits the head but the landed as well as personal estate of the offender.

"This visited the sin of the traitor upon his innocent heirs, and was the device of monarchs to hedge around their life and crown by superadding to the terror in conspirators the fear of sacrificing the dignities, influence, and wealth of their posterity by the loss of inheritance, imputing it to corruption of blood to degrade a race and name. The motives of monarchs prompting such unjust and cruel inflictions upon blameless and helpless heirs of one condemned to expiate by death the offense imputed to him do not belong to our Republic. It does not, like the crowned head, apprehend that the stroke of an assassin may terminate, with one life, the safety and peace of a people. Nor has it favorites to pamper with the estates of victims when they may conspire to sacrifice as traitors to quiet the fears of a dynasty into whose ear they whisper. Multitudes of illustrious public men have perished and their families been ruined under the Governments from which our laws have been mainly derived, upon constructive, unfounded, or ill-proved charges of treason, originating in the desire of the reigning favorites of the court to destroy those whom they have supplanted, and to create support for themselves and their followers by the confiscation of the estates of rivals whom their intrigues brought to the block.

"It was these horrid tragedies of the English history of treasons that induced the authors of our Constitution to insert so precise a definition of treason; and in providing for its punishment to declare 'it should *not work corruption of blood, or forfeiture except during the life of the person attained.*' The first act of Congress passed in virtue of this article prescribed the punishment of death for treason, and added the exception in the words of the Constitution in superabundant caution to exclude by legislative enactment the consequence of a condemnation of treason which the common law of England had drawn with it as a part of the code of our country.

"The Federalist—the work of Jay, Hamilton, and Madison—a more authoritative commentary on our Constitution than Blackstone's on the laws of England, had pointed to this article as a bar to such Congressional interpretation as was given in the bill submitted for the President's approval at the last session. It was the security given by the Constitution to save the unoffending heirs of condemned criminals from that forfeiture of estates so apt to be voted in heated party times by parliamentary majorities, and so the sages of the Federalist say the clause meant to abate the mischief by the limitation to '*the life of the person attainted.*'

"The President entertained the view of this provision sactioned by Congress and all the jurists of the country up to the passage of the bill presented to him by the last Congress. Then he was constrained to express the opinion contained in the message in which he communicated his reasons for approving that bill, because it was coupled with the enactment of a resolution embodying the terms of the constitutional limitation. But now it is attempted to repeal the resolution which adjusted the conflicting views of the executive and legislative departments in regard to the confiscation act, and if successful in Congress, the demand is to be made of the President that he resign his constitutional convictions, and strike from the law what he deemed essential to make it compatible with the Constitution and his oath to support it. And how is this demand justified? There stands the letter and spirit of the Constitution, an insurmountable obstacle to concession on the part of the President; but the new-fangled doctrinaries seeing the hopelessness of straining the simple terms of the Constitution to justify the extension of confiscation 'beyond *the life of the person attainted,*' nevertheless now urge expedients to accomplish that object.

* * * * * * * *

"The House will bear with me a little, while I examine the details by which the gentlemen and the

President reach the same general grounds of reconstruction.

"The gentleman [Mr. Stevens] begins by asserting that the usurpers have by force of arms become an independent power *de facto.* The gentleman pretends that the President has acknowledged the rebels as belligerents and entitled to the immunities of a foreign Power engaged with the United States in war.

"So far from this being true, the President has manifested dissatisfaction that England and France have, by acknowledging the rebels as belligerents, favored these pirates, although at the same time they disavow the conclusion drawn from it by the gentleman from Pennsylvania, that they are an independent and, as regards the United States, a foreign power.

"The gentleman declares the confederates out of the Union and not subject to the Constitution and the laws of the United States.

"The President, on the contrary, holds that they are in the Union; that he will hold them to it, as liable to all the penalties of treason, under the form and under the restrictions prescribed in the Constitution and laws.

"The gentleman insists that the heirs of rebels can claim no interest in the confiscated estates of parents condemned for treason, although the reversion is expressly reserved for them under the clause of the Constitution that the punishment under condemnation for treason shall not extend to forfeiture of estates except for the life of the person attainted.

"*Per contra*, the President holds that the law which

passed without this saving clause for the heirs violated the Constitution, and Congress inserted the provision to comply with his opinion, which was embodied in a message to the House, giving his sanction to the modified bill.

"Here I stop a moment to inquire whether the President has, '*after careful examination*, come to the conclusion' to retract the opinion declared in this message. If not, why the attempt to repeal the constitutional saving inserted in the act by the last Congress? It looks like an attempt to play into the hand of some rival who would array a party against the President to drive him to surrender his convictions and break his oath to support the Constitution, or, by maintaining his convictions and his oath, draw on the embarrassment of an opposition, disappointed of their scheme of monopolizing inheritances at the expense of the public interests. Certainly nothing could be worse for the Government and the masses of our countrymen than that the great landed estates should fall again into the mortmain of great capitalists. By being divided up in small lease-holds among the laboring soldiers of the war, the result would be either compromises between the lease-holders and the heirs in reversion—the first giving immediate possession of a part of his holding to the heir as a price for the fee simple of what he retained—or the lease-holder during the life of the rebel owner forfeiting it would realize out of the product of his tenement means to purchase a freehold of a portion. This sort of division between industrious lease-holders and heirs would be beneficial to both.

The one would be stimulated to industry and economy, the other by the increased value imparted to the property ultimately returning by subdivision among a multitude of intelligent, active, thriving, though temporary owners, who, once having taken root in the soil, would endeavor by utmost effort to make the means of rendering their possession permanent. The presence of such a population in the rich lands of the South would surely enhance their value. The forfeiting rebel refugee would find an advantage in having a great community interested in his long life, which would result probably in arrangements meliorating his condition.

"But to continue the details which, according to the speech of the gentleman from Pennsylvania, bring him and the President to the same general grounds in closing the conflict.

"The gentleman, assuming that it is a war of foreign States, adds: '*By the laws of war the conqueror may seize and convert to his own use everything that belongs to the enemy;*' and by the enemy he says expressly he means every man, woman, and child who now remain in the Confederate States, including those who are loyal.

"The President in all his proclamations touching this subject shows that he holds sacred the law of nations as expounded by Wheaton; confiscating no lands but such as are forfeited by treason; no personal property even in virtue of conquest, except slaves, who are taken from the hands of the enemy as instruments of warfare, and liberated with a pledge of remuneration to loyal owners for their loss, and indemnity for injuries that they may receive from our armies.

"The gentleman holds that the State governments now under the usurpation, although recognized and established as part of the Union by the Constitution and the laws made in conformity with it, are '*abolished*,' and '*we may hold them in subjection and legislate for them as a conquered people.*'

"The President holds no such doctrine, but directly the reverse. He looks upon the Constitution of the United States, and the constitutions of all the States heretofore recognized by it, as still subsisting, all uniting to establish, as written characters and muniments of title, a right to that eminent domain and political supremacy which the national Government holds over this whole country. The President, in virtue of military power which, as the representative of the supremacy of the United States, he is called by the Constitution to exert to save it and the Government, the State constitutions and their governments, has struck down slavery in certain sections, upon the principle on which the enemies of these States and constitutions are struck down in battle-fields. What has thus perished in the war, ceases to be a part of the institutions which have existence sanctioned by any Constitution, State or national. The President's plan of reconstruction takes this ground in the instructions given to General Steele to carry it out on the petition of the people of Arkansas. In that instruction he lays it down '*that it be assumed at the election*,' (proposed by the people,) '*and thenceforward, that the Constitution and laws of the*

State as before the rebellion are in full force, except that the Constitution is so modified as to declare that there shall be neither slavery nor involuntary servitude except in punishment for crimes whereof the party shall have been duly convicted.'

"The gentleman asserts that '*it is mockery to say that according to any principle of popular government yet established a title of the resident inhabitants of an organized State can change its form and carry on government because they are more holy or more loyal than others.*'

"The President holds that men disloyal and hostile to a Government, dishabilitated by the commission of treason to exercise the rights of citizens, abdicate their place in the Government, and devolve its administration on the loyal portion; and he has ascertained from the precedents in the State governments that a population equal to one-tenth of the whole number existing in any State are adequate to its administration. He therefore, when desired by them, invites elections in the several States freed from the armies of the rebellion, to ascertain whether a title of the loyal population remain to supersede by civil government under the republican constitutions that belong to them, the military administration imposed by the necessities of war.

"The gentleman proposes to supersede popular elections by the loyal people of a State to renew the action of their republican institutions, by the Roman military law for conquered countries, '*væ victis*,' woe to the vanquished, thus ignoring national law as ameliorated in modern times among civilized Christian nations, and abolishing the State governments which the President by his oath of office and the national Government he administers is bound to guarantee.

"The President on his part resolves to respect his own and the good faith of the nation; he recognizes the existing governments held in abeyance for a time by rebel arms, the rights of loyal citizens suffering under them, opens to all such access to the blessings of the Union through a renewal of their allegiance, and tendering to the mass of those who were forced into the rebel ranks by the betrayal of false functionaries wielding the power in the State and national Governments the healing measure of an amnesty—the felon conspirators and agitators, the authors of our calamities, being excluded.

"The gentleman from Pennsylvania assumes '*that if you were to liberate every slave now, and then re-admit them as free States, the moment they had acquired that standing they would reëstablish slavery and enslave every colored man within their limits.*'

"The President denies this; holds that the freedmen are under the protection of the arm to which they owe their liberties, has taken the precaution, with the sanction of Congress, to place them beyond State jurisdiction, and to assure them in the meantime of a safeguard under such an organization, with the national force, as will preclude all apprehension of the danger suggested.

"This parallel, in my opinion, is a fair *exposé*, showing that the gentleman looks to reconstruction on quite a different basis from that of the President. He admits that in details they do not quite agree, but assumes that they come to the '*same general grounds;*' that is, that '*his* (the President's) *plan is wholly outside of and unknown to the Constitution.*' It is thus that he would make the President take the responsibility of the secession, abolition, absolute-conquest doctrine he [Mr. STEVENS] broaches in defiance of national and State Constitutions, the law of the civilized world, and of all humanity. I take my stand on the Lincoln platform."

Having drawn upon himself the hostility of the extreme Radicals by his bold denunciations of their unconstitutional schemes, General Blair soon had proof that they would spare no effort to get him out of the House. On the 23d of March, Mr. McClurg, of Missouri, charged him with having abused his power as an officer of the army, for the purpose of aiding and encouraging unlawful speculations. He promptly denounced the charge as a base and miserable falsehood, and pronounced its author "an infamous liar and scoundrel;" and asked for a committee to investigate the charge, with power to send for persons and papers.

A Committee, consisting of Messrs. Higby, Brutus J. Clay, and Pruyn, were appointed by the Speaker, and the matter fully investigated. On the 23d of April, the Committee made their report to the House, fully exonerating Gen. Blair from the charge brought against him. The following is their report:

"The undersigned, the Special Committee appointed under the resolution of the House of the 23d of March last to investigate the charge made by Hon. J.

W. McClurg, a member of the House from the State of Missouri, against Hon. F. P. Blair, Jr., also a member of the House from the same State, 'of violating the laws in the matter of an alleged liquor speculation, and to inquire into the genuineness or falsity of the alleged order for the purchase of liquor, bearing date June 3, 1863,' respectfully report that they have had the matter so referred to them under investigation from an early day after their appointment, and have given full opportunity to both parties to produce witnesses before them, and taken all the testimony offered on the subject. The depositions of the witnesses thus examined are herewith submitted to the House.

"It appeared satisfactorily in evidence before the Committee that on the 3d day of June, 1863, Hon. F. P. Blair, Jr., then being a major-general in the Army of the United States in actual service near Vicksburg, in the State of Mississippi, together with eight members of his staff, signed a written order or authority to one Michael Powers, representing himself to be an agent of the Treasury Department, and who had offered his services for the purpose, to procure for their own use a very moderate amount of liquors, tobacco, and cigars, the cost of which, in the language of one of the witnesses, (Captain Maguire,) 'certainly would not exceed one hundred and fifty or one hundred and seventy-five dollars.'

"This order, as it appeared before the Committee, was altered after it was delivered to Powers, by adding to and changing the figures, and also by adding at least one new item, (twenty-five boxes can-fruits,) to such an extent that the invoice on the purchase of the articles in St. Louis, and a permit for which was granted by the collector, amounted to $8,651. As a specimen of the alterations one may be referred to, that as to brandy. The original order was for five gallons; by inserting the figure 2 before the figure 5, and adding the word 'each,' it became an order (as nine persons had signed it) for two hundred and twenty-five gallons. The alterations which the Committee believe, from the testimony taken before them, to have been made in the order, will be seen on reference to schedule A hereto annexed, which contains a copy of the existing order, and a statement at the foot thereof of the articles named in the original order as nearly as the Committee can determine from the evidence before them.

"As to the question by whom these alterations were made, the Committee refer particularly to the depositions of Mr. Powers and Mr. Howard, which are among those herewith submitted. Judging from all the circumstances, they were probably made for the purpose of realizing a profitable speculation under cover of the original order. That they were made by Powers, there cannot from the testimony be any reasonable doubt.

"At the time the order was delivered to Powers, there was no law or military regulation in any way prohibiting it.

"The Committee are therefore of the opinion, and do report, that no violation of law was committed in the premises by General Blair, and that the original order was altered and falsified after it had passed from his possession and control, in the manner hereinbefore stated.

"The undersigned, the chairman of the Committee, for himself deems it proper to state that the replies of Mr. Blair in the House to the charges of Mr. McClurg, all of which have been under investigation before the Committee, are not sustained by the evidence, except as to his denial of being engaged in a liquor speculation, and of the genuineness of the order in question. In this statement the other members of the Committee do not concur—the member from Kentucky for the reason that his conclusions from the testimony are the opposite of those of the chairman; and the member from New York (who was absent while most of this part of the evidence was taken) for the reason that he does not consider the subject embraced in the resolution appointing the Committee, and that they are not, in his judgment, called on to express any opinion in regard to it.

"The Committee having thus completed the duties assigned to them, respectfully ask to be discharged from the further consideration of the subject.

"Wm. Higby, *Chairman.*
"Brutus J. Clay,
"John V. L. Pruyn."

Upon the presentation of this report, General Blair addressed the House at some length. The statement made by him was as follows:

"Mr. Speaker, I am as loth as any other member to consume the time so necessary for the public business, but the use which has been made of this affair is of such an extraordinary character, so malicious and unjust to me, that I have been compelled to appeal to my fellow-members for the privilege of making a few observations, and to ask their indulgent attention at this time.

"It is shown by the report which has just been read in your hearing, that when this 'forgery' was committed I was in the service of the country, and in the trenches before Vicksburg, using my utmost efforts for the preservation of our country and to beat down its enemies. When it was made public and circulated far and wide in the newspapers for the purpose of destroying my reputation, I was again absent from my home and in command of the Fifteenth Army Corps, leading its gallant soldiers on the march from Memphis to Chattanooga, to share in that memorable conflict which drove Bragg from his stronghold on the heights of Lookout Mountain and Missionary Ridge, and afterwards to the relief of our beleaguered army at Knoxville.

"I hope it will not be regarded as indelicate or improper for me, under the circumstances in which I have been placed by this gross and unjust aspersion and the consequences which followed, to allude to the fact that I was assigned to that command by General Sherman, whose corps it was, until he was promoted to the command of the army and department of the Tennessee, and that after that most eventful campaign of marches and battles, as glorious as any recorded in our military annals, I was complimented in general orders, and received the thanks of my commanding general for the manner in which I had handled the corps; yet, at the end of that campaign, I found myself superseded in the command.

"Now, sir, if the allegation which had been made against me, when absent and in the service, had been true, it would have formed a just ground for my removal. I should have been unfit to command any portion of the gallant and patriotic troops of my country.

"Finding myself superseded in a command of which I was so justly proud, and unconscious of having committed any offense which should have subjected me to such a mortification, I came here to resume my seat in this House, to which I had been returned by a confiding constituency, and which I had left eighteen months before, at the solicitation of the Administration, to raise and command troops for the defense of the country. But the malignity of those who had originated and propagated this atrocious slander against me was not satisfied with the humiliation I had suffered in the loss of my command; it pursued me into this House. The House will remember the occasion when a member from my own State arose and reiterated this calumny. I repelled it at the time in language decorous and parliamentary, so far as the member himself was concerned, not knowing but that he had been misled by those who had originated and circulated the slander, but at the same time denouncing it as a forgery, perpetrated by a person in the employ of the Treasury Department, who had himself since admitted that the order was altered and was therefore a forgery, and that it was printed in a newspaper which was pensioned by the Secretary of the Treasury. The gentleman, or, rather, the member who made that allegation at that time, having my denial before him, having the admission of the Treasury agent, Bonner, having the published declaration of the surveyor of the port of St. Louis, Mr. Howard, pronouncing it a forgery, and also having the paper in his hand which showed palpably upon its face that it had been altered, came into this House to renew that allegation upon a subsequent occasion, and with that coarseness and brutality which is characteristic of vulgar minds—*

* * * * * * * *

"I say, sir, that this member was not content to reassert the charge against me of having violated the laws of the country, and of prostituting the office I held in the service of the country for the purpose of speculation, but he did it in an insulting and irritating manner, and made every effort to provoke me, in the manner in which he brought it to the attention of the House; and upon that occasion, I say again, I felt myself so indignant at the charge made, and at the manner in which it was made by that member, that I found it impossible to restrain myself, and used language for which I am willing to apologize to the House, but for which I shall never apologize to him.

"Sir, he had the forged order photographed, and brought it thus prepared for circulation to the attention of the House, and proclaimed that he was

* The Speaker at this point called Gen. Blair to order.

ready to distribute them, and that others could be had cheaply at the photographing establishment at which it was taken. I do not know where that photograph was made—whether it was in the Treasury Department or not. I believe they have machinery of that kind there. It is not the first time in the history of the world in which the fine arts have been prostituted to this base and ignoble purpose, that of perpetuating and disseminating counterfeits. I congratulate myself, however, that while the art of photographing has been applied to such purposes, it has also been made useful in the detection of the rogues, criminals, and counterfeiters who have basely prostituted the art. You can find, sir, in any of the police offices of the country a 'rogue's gallery,' in which the effigies of those eminent for their crimes and rascalities are exposed for the purpose of re-cognition and detection. I intend following that suggestion, to enlarge upon the idea. I will have that 'order' re-photographed, and I will have it decorated and garnished with the portraits of the forgers and disseminators of the forgery, so as to perpetuate their memories and villainies in connection with this specimen of their art.

"Now, sir, it is not my purpose to follow these men who have been guilty of this baseness toward me any further. These dogs have been set on me by their master, and since I have whipped them back into their kennel, I mean to hold their master responsible for this outrage and not the curs who have been set upon me. The evidence, sir, shows that this forgery was made public by a Treasury agent who knew at the time that he made it public, that I had no interest whatever in the goods covered by the order; who knew it so well that the goods having been seized he turned them over to their proper owner, because there was no ground for their seizure and confiscation. He turned them over to the man who appeared on the paper to own them, and yet he retained in his hand this paper, to which he had no right, and gave it out for publication after I had been assailed in the newspapers of my city, for speculating in this whisky. He gave it out for publication after he knew the facts of the case and had had his attention called to them, because I had attacked Mr. Chase in a speech in St. Louis and assailed his trade regulation. So, sir, if any officer of the Army, or any member of Congress, or any gentleman feels sufficient interest in public affairs, and in the honest conduct of public business to assail in a public speech its management in the Treasury and the operation of Treasury regulations, he lays himself open to assaults from the Secretary of the Treasury and all the hounds and dogs that he can set upon him, and he is to be hunted and dragged down by false charges and by forgery.

"It is for the House to decide whether one of its members, in the face of the facts which were brought to his knowledge when he first made these charges on this floor, shall be permitted to reiterate in a manner so gross and offensive that which he utterly failed to substantiate when put to the test, and escape without censure. It is for the members of the House to decide whether such a person is worthy of association with them or not.

"When I resumed my seat in this House, I felt myself constrained by a sense of duty to my constituents to ask for a committee to investigate the manner in which the 'regulations of trade' with the States in insurrection have been carried out by the Secretary of the Treasury. But it seems that the Secretary's friends had not the same confidence in a committee of Congress as I have shown, for when I asked for a committee to investigate the charges which had been made against the Secretary, of sacrificing a vast public interest to advance his ambition, his friends upon this floor refused it, and I was assailed in all the newspapers of the country with having made that allegation against the Secretary because he had stopped my 'liquor speculation.'

"Now, Mr. Speaker, permit me to say that when the Secretary of the Treasury was advanced to his present position, although my good wishes were worth nothing to him at the time, yet he had them. I was in favor of his appointment. As a matter of course, that was of very little consequence so far as his appointment was concerned, yet it is a fact well known. It is of consequence simply so far as it shows that I was not inimical at that time to the Secretary. The reason of my change of sentiment toward him was, that I understood that he had authorized the Mayor of Baltimore to proclaim on the streets of that city, on the 19th of April, that he was in favor of letting the States in rebellion 'go in peace,' and because I also took this impression from the tenor of his conversation that it was his opinion and wish that they should be allowed to go in peace. I understood the same thing from the publications made by newspapers in his own State which were regarded as expressing his sentiments. The allegation was made that such was his position, and it was never denied by him. It was accepted as a fact by all.

"I know, *and he will not deny his written and recorded opinion*, that he was opposed to the reinforcement of Fort Sumter. I knew that after Fort Sumter had fallen, he had opposed the calling out of a large and sufficient force to put down the rebellion, and although he and others of the men of his party and my party then (but I hold no party relations *then* or *now* with peace men) were compelled by the war cry that went up after the fall of Sumter to abandon apparently their peace position. Yet Mr. Chase, I soon found, never really abandoned his determination to cut off the Southern States. On the contrary, he has endeavored to work out, by another programme, the very thing he was then in favor of doing—of letting the South go. He is now for making them go, so far as their condition as States is concerned. He is unwilling that they should ever return to interfere with his presidential aspirations.

"Why, Sir, it was perfectly understood in the second session—the long session—of the last Congress, that he favored the annihilation of the State Governments of the South. His friends in both Houses made that proposition; those who had the most intimate relations with him in both Houses made that proposition. And it is pressed in this House again this winter in a disguised and insidious form, and under the pretentious title of 'reconstruction,' but which is in fact intended for the *destruction* of those States; but this being the very crime of which the rebels in arms are guilty, and which the gentleman from Ohio [Mr. Ashley] charges upon them, it is thought convenient to give the operation another name. The bill reported by the distinguished gentleman from Maryland [Mr. Davis], representing the committee on the rebellious States, which, by the way, is composed to a considerable extent of the Pomeroy private circular committee, for I understand that the gentlemen from Maryland [Mr. Davis], from Ohio [Mr. Ashley], and from Missouri [Mr. Blow], are members of both these committees, is a bill which could very properly have come from the Pomeroy committee. It is a bill which should have been entitled 'a bill for the permanent dissolution of the Union, to disfranchise the whites and enfranchise the negroes, to prevent any of the States from coming back in time to vote for Mr. Lincoln for President, and to promote the ambition of the Secretary of the Treasury.' It is a bill which requires the consent of Congress for the readmission of any of these States to the Union.

"The gentlemen proceed in their disfranchising bill upon the pretext that the usurpation of the rebels for the hour has destroyed the States, or that the forces of the United States sent to drive out and overthrow the rebel power which held the State and national Governments in the South alike in abeyance, are to be considered conquering forces, extinguishing the local constitutions the nation is bound to guaranty. Look ing to the root of the matter, the cause of all our disasters, proves that instead of considering the State Governments abolished, Congress would best perform its functions by amending the Constitution of the United States itself, so as to eradicate slavery from our whole system. This simple remedy, which can be attained by adhering to the forms of the Constitution itself, supersedes the revolutionary schemes of those who would convert the States into Territories and assert absolutism over them in regard to their future admission into the Union. The founders of the Government saw the lurking evil in admitting the slave-tolerating clause in the Constitution; they foretold its fatal tendency. Our present Chief Magistrate, before he was thought of for the place he held, predicted that this Government 'could not endure permanently half free and half slave.' And can there be a better solution of the danger than that furnished by the Senate's bill incorporating Jefferson's ordinance of freedom with the fundamental law of the nation? Is it not better than disfranchising States and robbing loyal men of their rights, putting them on a footing with rebels already disfranchised by their bloody treason? Our soldiers invoke the loyal citizens of the South to join their ranks, and patriots everywhere would call on the loyalists of the South to renew the glorious association of free States of the North and South by joining with its armed deliverers in the reëlection of the man who first organized free government over our whole country, and has thus earned the high privilege of inaugu rating the renewed and most auspicious career of the Union."

Having thus vindicated himself from the aspersions of his enemies, Gen. Blair resigned his seat in the House, and sought a command in the field. His enemies having been foiled in their efforts to injure him in the House, now tried to destroy his influence in the army. On the 25th of April, Mr. Dawes, of Massachusetts, offered the following resolution in the House:

"*Resolved*, That the President be requested to communicate to this House whether the Hon. Francis P. Blair, Jr., representing the first congressional district of Missouri in the present House, now holds any appointment or commission in the military service of the United States; and if so, what that appointment or commission is, and when the said Blair accepted the same, and whether he is now acting under the authority of any such appointment or commission."

In response to this resolution, Mr. Lincoln, on the 28th, sent to the House the following message stating General Blair's action in the case:

" *To the House of Representatives:*

"In obedience to a resolution of your honorable body, a copy of which is hereby returned, I have the honor to make the following brief statement, which is believed to contain the information sought:

"Prior to, and at the meeting of the present Congress, Robert C. Schenck, of Ohio, and Frank P. Blair, Jr., of Missouri, members elect thereto, by and with the consent of the Senate held commissions from the Executive as major generals in the volunteer army. General Schenck tendered the resignation of his said commission and took his seat in the House of Representatives at the assembling thereof, upon the distinct verbal understanding with the Secretary of War and the Executive that he might, at any time during the session, at his own pleasure, withdraw said resignation and return to the field. General Blair was, by temporary agreement with General Sherman, in command of a corps through the battles in front of Chattanooga, and in the march to the relief of Knoxville, which occurred in the latter days of December last, and of course was not present at the assembling of Congress. When he subsequently arrived here, he sought and was allowed by the Secretary of War and the Executive the same conditions and promise as allowed and made to General Schenck. General Schenck has not applied to withdraw his resignation, but when General Grant was made lieutenant-general, producing some change of commanders, General Blair sought to be assigned to command of a corps. This was made known to Generals Grant and Sherman, and assented to by them, and the particular corps for him designated. This was all arranged and understood, as now remembered, as much as a month ago; but the withdrawal of General Blair's resignation, and making the order assigning him to the command of a corps, were not consummated at the War Department until last week, perhaps on the 23d of April, instant. As a summary of the whole, it may be stated that General Blair holds no military commission or appointment other than herein stated, and that it is believed he is now acting as major general upon the assumed validity of the commission herein stated, and not otherwise. There are some letters, notes, telegrams, orders, entries, and perhaps other documents, in connection with this subject, which it is believed would throw no additional light upon it, but which will be cheerfully furnished if desired.

"*April* 28, 1864. ABRAHAM LINCOLN."

This plain statement of the President showed that Gen. Blair's course had been both straightforward and patriotic, and the malice of his enemies resolved itself to a resolution that Gen. Blair, by reason of holding a military commission was not legally qualified to serve as a member of the House. Gen. Blair, however, having several months before the passage of this resolution, voluntarily returned to the field, had practically resigned his seat in the House. The intrigues and plots of Congress had no charms for him, and he preferred an open conflict with a manly foe to the pitiful encounters of the House. The malice of his enemies gave him no concern, and their shafts fell harmless from the triple armor of his own rectitude.

President Lincoln, however, seeing that General Blair's enemies were willing that the country should lose his services in order that their own malice might be gratified, resolved to place the General's military position upon a more assured footing, and accordingly renominated him to be Major-General of Volunteers, which nomination was confirmed by the Senate by a bare majority of two or three, so strongly was that body biassed by partisanship.

CHAPTER V.

General Blair returns to the Field—Is given Command of the Seventeenth Corps in Sherman's Army—The Advance to Dalton—Alatoona Pass—Kenesaw Mountain—The Capture of Atlanta—A Hard Campaign—The Pursuit of Hood—"The March to the Sea"—Army Sketch of General Blair—Details of the March—The Occupation of Savannah—The Seventeenth Corps transferred to Hilton Head—Blair's Midwinter March—The Occupation of Columbia—The March through the Carolinas—Occupation of Fayetteville—Battle of Bentonville—Surrender of General Johnston—The March to Washington—The Great Review—General Blair resigns his Commission.

General Blair returned to the field in March, 1864, and was assigned the command of the Seventeenth Army Corps, in Sherman's Army. By this time General Grant had been made lieutenant-general, and had been assigned the chief command of the armies of the Union, and had taken immediate charge of the operations in Virginia, and Sherman had been placed in command of the Military Division of the Mississippi. Sherman's force in the field consisted of three combined armies, namely, the Army of the Ohio, under Major-General John M. Schofield, the Army of the Cumberland, under Major-General George H. Thomas, and the Army of the Tennessee, under Major-General McPherson. The Seventeenth Corps formed a part of the Army of the Tennessee, and during the early winter and spring was quartered in and around Huntsville, Alabama. The entire army under General Sherman's command numbered ninety eight thousand eight hundred men, together with two hundred and fifty-four pieces of artillery.

The task assigned to General Sherman was of the highest importance. The war had been reduced to a struggle at two prominent points — Virginia and Georgia—and while Grant had reserved to himself the management of affairs in the East, he gave to Sherman the largest discretion in the direction of the campaign in the Southwest. Sherman's part in the great programme for closing the war, was to defeat Johnston's army, capture Atlanta, and drive the Confederates away from their rich granaries in northern Georgia. If successful in this, he expected to be able to render valuable service in compelling the South to submit to the authority of the Union. The results of the campaign show that his convictions were founded upon sound reasoning. The movements in Georgia were to be simultaneous with those in Virginia, and on the 27th of April, 1864, orders were issued for the concentration before Chattanooga of all the troops which were to take part in the campaign, and by the 6th of May, Sherman's whole army was disposed along the border of Georgia, directly in front of Dalton.

The Confederate army, forty thousand nine hundred strong, under the command of General Joseph E. Johnston, was posted around Dalton, along the line of the Chattanooga and Atlanta Railway. It was Johnston's plan to reënforce his army from other points farther South, and take the initiative, but his Government hampered him by its folly and weakness until

Sherman's action compelled him to assume the defensive.

Between the Confederate position and that held by General Sherman there lay an impracticable range of mountains, called Rocky Face Ridge, which was passable only at Buzzard's Roost Gap, a narrow mountain pass, through which ran the railroad to Atlanta and a stream called Mill Creek. The enemy had fortified this pass so strongly that there was no hope of Sherman being able to carry it by assault; and that commander determined to turn the enemy's position on the left. This movement was intrusted to the army of the Tennessee. General Blair commanded his corps in this famous flank march, which resulted in the abandonment of the position before Dalton by Johnston, and his retreat to Resaca. From Resaca Johnston was forced back to Alatoona Pass, and from that point to Kenesaw Mountain, and in all the movements which led to these results the Seventeenth Corps bore an honorable part. General Blair participated in the gallant but fruitless assaults of the 27th of June, on the Confederate position at Kenesaw Mountain, and led his corps across the Chattahoochee on the 9th of July.

On the morning of the 22d of July, General Sherman discovered that the enemy had abandoned the strong line of Peach Tree Creek and had retired within the defences of Atlanta, and he at once gave the order for his forces to close in around that city, which was done during the day, McPherson's army moving upon the left of Sherman's line.

General McPherson marched practically along the

line of the Atlanta and Augusta Railway, with the Fifteenth Corps, General Logan, in the centre of his line, the Sixteenth, General Dodge, on his right, and the Seventeenth, General Blair, on his left. On the night of the 21st, General Blair had made a gallant attack on a force of the enemy strongly intrenched on a commanding hill to the south and east of the railroad, had driven it away and secured the position which was of great value to McPherson in his movement of the 22d. In order to make sure of this position, McPherson commenced to fortify it on the morning of the 22d, and moved forward his whole force to the support of the Seventeenth Corps which was already at work on the intrenchments.

While this movement was going on, General Hood, who had succeeded General Johnston in the command of the Confederate army, sallied forth from Atlanta with a strong column consisting of Hardee's and Stewart's Corps of his army, and fell upon the Seventeenth with that fire and vigor for which the onsets of the Southern troops are famous. The attack was entirely unexpected, and it came before all of McPherson's troops were in position. It fell first upon the left division of the Seventeenth Corps, which was forced back for some distance. General Blair was equal to the emergency, however. Bringing his corps rapidly into line on the crest of the hill, he received the enemy with a terrible fire, which drove them back for a moment. They pressed on again, and for four hours the battle went on hotly. The Seventeenth Corps held its ground, until reënforced, against one of the most brilliant and gallant efforts ever made by the Confederates. The battle became general along the whole line of the army of the Tennessee, but its chief weight fell upon the Seventeenth Corps, which was highly complimented by General Sherman for its gallant conduct. Every attack of the Confederates was repulsed, and about five o'clock, the enemy withdrew towards Atlanta.

In this battle General McPherson, commanding the Army of the Tennessee, was killed. He had ridden towards his left alone, for the purpose of directing the movements of his troops, and strayed into the enemy's lines, and was shot.*

General Blair continued to direct the movements

* After the close of the war some evil-minded persons, wishing to injure General Blair, who had given great offence to the Radicals by his Conservative course, put in circulation a report that General McPherson's death had been caused by General Blair's incompetency to command his corps in the battle of July 22d. As the surest way of refuting this slander, General Blair wrote to General Sherman, asking his opinion respecting it. The following is his letter:

"St. Louis, *June* 22, 1866.

"Major-General Sherman:

"*Dear General*—A report was put in circulation soon after the battle before Atlanta, on the 22d of July, 1864, by some irresponsible letter writer, to the effect that the death of Major-General McPherson was the direct result of my mismanagement and improper disposition of the troops under my command. This report is received and reiterated by persons who are displeased with my political sentiments, wherever it promises to give them any advantage.

"Every soldier and officer who served under your orders has a right to appeal to you against any injustice sought to be inflicted on him while under your command; and as I know that nothing will be more unjust and more injurious than this accusation, I ask you to say whether there is any foundation, or even color of truth, in the statement to which I

of his corps in the operations which led to the capture of Atlanta, and after the fall of that city, obtained a temporary leave of absence, and returned to the West-

have referred. I have only to add that it is my intention to publish your reply to this note.

"Respectfully, your friend and obedient servant,

"FRANK P. BLAIR, JR."

To this note General Sherman replied as follows:

"HEADQUARTERS, MIL. DIV. OF THE MISSISSIPPI,
"ST. LOUIS, MO., *June* 23, 1866.

"GENERAL F. P. BLAIR, ST. LOUIS, present:

"*Dear General*—I am this moment in receipt of your note of yesterday, in which you state that certain parties differing from you in political sentiments, have raised the story that the death of our mutual friend, General McPherson, July 22, 1864, resulted from your mismanagement and faulty disposition of troops.

"It seems impossible to fix a limit to the falsehoods that politicians will resort to, to accomplish their ends; but this goes beyond all decency. The truth was, and is, that General McPherson in person, placed in their position the two divisions which composed your corps, the Seventeenth, and instead of refusing the extreme left, he had in person extended it forward, and detached a party still more to the left and front to secure a position from which he proposed to batter the large rolling-mill in Atlanta. Having about that time of the day, say 10 A. M., received from me a note telling him not to extend too far to his left, he left you and came to me, then near the centre of the general line, and urged on me the importance of using Dodge's two divisions, then moving towards that flank, to extend still more your line. I had consented to modify my former orders in part, and he was returning to that flank when he was killed.

"You were in no manner the cause; nor was it your business to alter the disposition of the troops, just as General McPherson had made them himself. You had no reason to apprehend danger to your left or rear: nor from the nature of the ground could you have seen the movement by which the enemy's skirmishers reached the wooded space, in passing which General McPherson was shot.

"Our military maps are now so perfect and public, and the official reports of the facts so full and clear, that I must say it augurs a very bad

ern States, where he advocated the reëlection of Mr. Lincoln to the Presidency. He returned to the army late in October, and resumed the command of his corps, which was then resting at Smyrna camp ground, after the pursuit of Hood's army into Alabama.

When General Blair returned to the army, Sherman had completed his arrangements for the famous "march to the sea," and had divided his army into two wings. The right, to which General Blair was attached, consisted of the Fifteenth and Seventeenth Corps, and was commanded by General Howard; and the left, comprised of the Fourteenth and Twentieth Corps, was given to General Slocum. The Seventeenth Corps consisted of three divisions, commanded by Generals Mower, Leggett, and Giles A. Smith, and was in the best possible condition for the campaign, and devotedly attached to its gallant leader.

Major Nichols, of Gen. Sherman's staff, gives the following description of Gen. Blair, as he appeared at this period:

"One who had never seen General Blair except in the field as a corps commander, would find it difficult to realize that he has occupied so prominent a position in the political arena; for, while it may not be said that he is a born soldier, yet he possesses in a marked degree many of the qualities which constitute a good commander. Under all circumstances he never loses

heart to lay this charge to you, from which, as your common commander, I exonerate you absolutely.

"With great respect,

(Signed) "W. T. Sherman, *Maj.-Gen.*"

that perfect coolness and self-command which render him master of the situation, and inspire the confidence of the soldiers. This imperturbability never deserts him. One day, when the rebels renewed an attack upon his lines with furious vigor, although they had already been repulsed several times, sustaining terrible losses, Blair removed his cigar from his mouth, as he watched their onset, and quietly observed,

"'See the fellows! There they come again, right through the woods. What in thunder do they want?'

"They wanted to carry his line, but they failed; and Blair continued smoking, as if nothing had happened.

"General Blair is one of the most hospitable and popular men of the army. As commander of the Seventeenth Corps, he is identified with the history of the Army of the Tennessee—a gallant, heroic band of men, it may be added, the record of whose deeds yet remains to be written. The General wears a full sandy beard and moustache, which conceal the lower part of his face. His eyes are of a light hazel color, full of humor and good nature—an expression, however, that is somewhat qualified by the overhanging brow, which has a *noli me tangere* air, as much as to say, 'If I must fight, it shall be war to the hilt.' In height, the General is about five feet eleven inches. His frame is finely proportioned; and he makes a good appearance on horseback. He selects excellent horses, and knows how to ride them. In the army he has the reputation of a kind, generous, discreet man, and a brave soldier." *

* *The Story of the Great March*, pp. 97, 98.

Atlanta and Rome having been destroyed, the right wing, under General Howard, began its march from Whitehall on the 15th of November. General Blair's corps formed the left of Howard's column, and led the advance, moving upon McDonough by the direct road from Atlanta, and occupied that place on the 16th. On the 17th, he encamped at Hendrick's Mill, and on the 18th crossed the Ocmulgee and moved towards Hillsborough. Marching rapidly through Gordon, which he occupied on the 21st, he forced the passage of the Oconee at Ball's Ferry, compelling the Confederates to abandon their fortified position at this point, and after securing the crossing, destroyed a considerable portion of the Georgia Central Railway. On the morning of the 26th of November, General Sherman shifted his headquarters from the left wing, and accompanied Blair's corps in person. On the 28th, Blair encamped before Riddleville, and on the 29th, at Station No. 10, on the Central Railway. On the 30th, he moved to Barton, or Station 9½, rebuilt a partially destroyed wagon bridge, laid a pontoon bridge over the Ogeechee, and crossed that river at that point. Pushing on the next day, along the line of the railway, which he destroyed as he went, he reached Millen on the 2d of December, and burnt the depot and a quantity of railroad supplies. Continuing to move along the line of the Central Railway, which he effectually demolished, Gen. Blair, on the 9th of December, still leading the advance of the army, came upon the enemy in rifle-pits, about three and a half miles from Station No. 2. Rapidly throwing his troops into line, he made a vigorous and successful charge upon the pits, carrying them with a rush, and then pressed on in the direction taken by the retreating Confederates. In a short time he came upon a much stronger force of the enemy posted in an intrenched line, with artillery in position. The Southern line was very strong, and the only approach to it was by a narrow road through a thickly-wooded swamp, which seemed at the first glance impassable. Not daunted by this, Blair moved three lines of battle, with a skirmish line in advance, along and on the right and left of the road; the troops wading through the mud, and often through water up to their knees. They made a vigorous attack upon the Confederates, drove them from their original position, and pressed them back steadily during the day from every point at which they attempted to make a stand, until nightfall, when the corps bivouacked at Pooler, or Station No. 1. On the next day, the rest of the army came up, and Sherman's entire force was united before the defences of Savannah, which city fell into his possession on the 21st of December.

After a month's rest at Savannah, Sherman prepared to execute the remainder of his plan for finishing the war, which was to march through the Carolinas and place his army within supporting distance of the Army of the Potomac, in Virginia.

On the 15th of January, General Howard embarked Blair's corps on transports at Thunderbolt, near the mouth of the Savannah River, and proceeded to Beaufort, South Carolina, where he disembarked the troops. Marching rapidly towards the Charleston and

Savannah Railway, General Blair seized it at Pocotaligo Station, driving off the enemy, and establishing himself firmly on the road, drawing his supplies from Hilton Head by way of Pocotaligo Creek. Two divisions of the Fifteenth Corps arrived soon after, and on the 24th of January, every thing being in readiness, General Sherman reached General Blair's headquarters. On the 31st of January, the advance of the army was begun.

General Blair was ordered to force the line of the Salkehatchie, which was held by the enemy in force, at River's Bridge. He executed this task with great promptness and skill, "with Mower's and Corse's divisions of the Seventeenth Corps, the latter under Giles A. Smith, on the 3d of February, by crossing the swamp, nearly three miles wide, with water varying from knee to shoulder deep. The weather was bitter cold. Generals Mower and Smith led their divisions in person, on foot, waded the swamp, made a lodgement below the bridge, and turned the Rebel brigade which guarded it, driving it in confusion and disorder towards Branchville." * On the next day the Seventeenth Corps occupied Midway, on the South Carolina Railway, and at once commenced the destruction of that road, which was continued until the 10th. Then crossing the South Fork of the Edisto at Binnaker's Bridge, Blair moved towards Orangeburg. On the 12th of February, he reached Orangeburg bridge, where he found the enemy posted in intrenchments. He at once drove off this force, and pressed it across

* *Sherman and his Campaigns.* p. 337.

the bridge. The Confederates held the opposite shore with a strong line, with a battery in the centre, their whole line being covered by works of earth and cotton, and under the cover of their fire they succeeded in partially burning the bridge. Determining to force the Edisto here, General Blair moved Giles A. Smith's division close up to the river in front of the bridge, and moved his other two divisions to a point two miles below. Then throwing a pontoon bridge over the river, he crossed Force's division and held Mower's in support. Force at once moved upon the Confederate works, and the enemy abandoned them. General Smith then secured the bridge, crossed the river, and occupied the abandoned works. The whole corps was then united and Orangeburg was occupied by four o'clock in the afternoon. General Blair was ordered by General Sherman to destroy the railroad as far as Lewisville, and to compel the enemy to withdraw across the Congaree and burn the bridges over that stream, which he did on the 14th. On the 17th he arrived before Columbia. A party of his men crossed the Congaree in a skiff, and were the first to enter the city, which was formally surrendered to General Sherman about the same time. The Seventeenth Corps, however, did not enter the town at all, but encamped across the river from it. On the 20th, after Sherman had finished his work of destruction in Columbia, the march was resumed, and on the 21st of February, Winnsboro was reached. From this point, while Slocum, by a feint towards Charlotte, N. C., deceived the Confederates as to Sherman's intentions, Blair, leading the advance of the right wing, crossed the Catawba on the 22d of February, and marched upon Cheraw, which he occupied on the 3d of March, capturing twenty-five pieces of artillery and a large quantity of military stores, which had been sent there from Charleston when that city was evacuated. These he destroyed, together with the railroad and all the bridges within reach. On the 5th of March, having forced the enemy over the Great Pedee, he crossed that river at Cheraw, and led the advance upon Fayetteville, which he reached on the 12th of March, the town having been occupied by the left wing on the previous day. This portion of the march was very trying upon the men, and some idea of its difficulties may be gained from the following extract from the diary of Major Nichols:

"What a noble army we have here! Every day produces fresh and striking illustrations of the men's cheerful acceptance of all the discouraging circumstances of the situation. For instance; a wagon, painfully toiling along the road, suddenly careens; the wheels are submerged in a quicksand; every effort of the mules or horses to 'pull out' only buries the unfortunate vehicle deeper in the mire, and very soon the animals have dug for themselves a pit, out of which many are never extricated alive. The driver sees at once that it is useless to whip and swear, so he dismounts. Then the train guard, who have been resting upon their muskets, watching the proceedings, quietly stack their weapons, and at once plunge into the mud. A dozen of them are at work with shoulders at the wheels and body of the wagon, and finally they lift it out of the hole upon firmer ground. One or two wagons stuck in this way show at once that the road must be corduroyed. Then, with many a jest and an untiring flow of good humor, the men wade into the neighboring swamp, cut down and split the trees, and soon bridge over these impassable places. A few rods further on the head of column arrives at a creek, which in ordinary seasons is ten feet wide, and has a few inches of water running over a hard sandy bottom. Now the water is four or six feet in depth, and spreads out to a width of sixty feet, encroaching upon the softer earth. A bridge must be built. Into the water dash our men without hesitation, for they know the work must be done at once. Waist deep, throat deep, not a dry spot about them. 'No matter for that,' they say; 'we shall be in camp by and by, and then, before our roaring fires, we will rehearse the incidents of the day.'" *

Wilmington having fallen into Schofield's possession, Sherman remained at Fayetteville on the 12th, 13th, and 14th of March, engaged in destroying the public property at that place, and on the 15th the march was resumed towards Goldsboro. On the 19th General Slocum, with the left wing, encountered the whole Confederate army at Bentonville. Sherman at once sent Howard to his assistance with the Fifteenth and Seventeenth Corps. This column reached Bentonville by a forced night march, arriving there in time to take part in the final repulse of the enemy,

* *The Story of the Great March.* P. 233.

who were defeated after a most gallant and determined effort on their part.

Gen. Blair participated in the closing scenes of the war in North Carolina, and when Sherman's army was transferred to Washington City, led his Corps in the march to that city, where he took part in the great review in May, 1865.

While the Army was in Petersburg, General Howard, his immediate commander, sent Gen. Blair, of his own accord, the following letter, which shows the high opinion he entertained of his gallant subordinate:

"HEADQUARTERS ARMY OF THE TENNESSEE,
PETERSBURG, VA., May 7, 1865.

"MAJOR GENERAL F. P. BLAIR,
Commanding Seventeenth Corps:

"MY DEAR SIR.—Hearing that you intend soon to leave the service, I wish to thank you for the genuine kindness and uniform hearty support you have ever extended towards me, from the time I took command, through all the varied and trying circumstances of hard campaigning up to the present time. I take great pleasure and pride in acknowledging your ability and success as a commanding officer, and if I can at any time be of service to yourself I trust you will not fail to call upon me as a friend. With high esteem, I subscribe myself,

"Yours sincerely,
(Signed) "O. O. HOWARD, MAJ. GEN."

From Washington, General Blair conducted the

Seventeenth Corps to Louisville, Ky., where it was formally disbanded on the 11th of July, 1865. On that day he took a formal leave of his command. In his parting address, he recounted their triumphs, thanked them for their heroism and devotion under all circumstances, and for "the reputation which their gallantry had conferred upon him," and declared his readiness to lead his old comrades, if the necessity for so doing should arise, to the relief of the struggling Republic of Mexico. Having discharged this last duty, General Blair resigned his commission as Major-General of Volunteers, and retired to civil life.

CHAPTER VI.

General Blair Favors a Liberal and Generous Policy towards the South—Opposes the Ultra Measures of the Radicals—Denounces the Disfranchisement Law of the Missouri Legislature—Refuses to Subscribe to the Test Oath—Is Refused his Right to Vote—Separates himself from the Republican Party, and Unites with the Democracy—His Nomination as Collector of Revenue Rejected by the Senate—Is Mentioned as a Candidate for the Presidency—Letter to Colonel Broadhead—Comments of the Radicals—Statement by the *Herald*—Speech of Hon. Montgomery Blair—The Convention—General Blair a Candidate—Nominated for the Vice-Presidency—Scene in the Convention—Formal Tender of the Nomination—Speech of General Morgan—Reply of General Blair—Meeting in 14th Street—Speech of General Blair—His Letter of Acceptance—His Visit to the West—His Speech at Omaha—Tribute from the *Buffalo Courier*.

GEN. BLAIR had given his best efforts in behalf of the Union during the four years of the great Civil War, and, as we have seen, his services were both brilliant and important. While the resistance of the people of the South continued, he was in favor of prosecuting the war with the utmost vigor, but when the war was closed by the submission of the South, his plan of operations was changed. He had the sagacity to see that the submission of the Southern people was genuine and honest, and he at once began to urge the adoption of a liberal and generous policy towards them. He had fought for the restoration of the Union and for the supremacy of the laws, and not for the subjugation or destruction of the South, and he was by no means willing to allow the fair promise which peace brought with it to be blasted by the fanatical fury of the extreme men in control of affairs. He returned to Missouri, and endeavored to promote a wise and liberal course on the part of the State Government towards the people of that State who had been aiders of or sympathizers with the Confederates. Fanaticism ruled the hour, however, and he was powerless to do more than protest against what he saw was both unwise and unconstitutional.

The Legislature of Missouri enacted a law disfranchising all who participated in or gave aid and comfort to the Rebellion, and another law forcing a test oath upon all the citizens of the State. These measures received the unqualified condemnation of General Blair as proscriptive and unconstitutional. He declared that since all those who had aided or sympathized with the Rebellion had submitted peacefully to the authority of the General Government, there was no further necessity of harshness towards them, and that it was dangerous to the peace and prosperity of the State to deprive them of the right of suffrage. He refused to subscribe to the test oath, and having presented himself at the polls in St. Louis for the purpose of casting his ballot at one of the elections, was refused the privilege of voting until he should take the oath. Determined to bring the matter to a prompt issue, he brought a suit before the Court for the purpose of testing the Constitutionality of the laws. The case is still before the Supreme Court of the United States, awaiting a decision. When the Reconstruction laws of Congress were passed, he denounced them as despotic, revolutionary, and unconstitutional, and declared that the people of the South would be justified in resisting their execution. He opposed with great earnestness the policy of universal negro suffrage, branding it as an outrage upon the people and a disgrace to the country.

Up to the close of the war he had acted with the Republican party, but when that organization began the excesses which have made its career infamous of late years, he separated himself from it. He had contributed in a marked degree to the organization, growth, and success of that party, because he could not conscientiously unite with the Democracy on the slavery question. "On all points except slavery," says the *Newburyport* (Mass.) *Herald*, a high-toned conservative Republican journal, "he was Democratic, as were his father and brother; and when slavery was abolished, he naturally swung back to his old position. He saw no reason, as thousands of others cannot, for keeping slavery in politics when slavery had long been dead and in its grave. He won a good name in Congress, and showed spirit, patriotism and capacity during the rebellion. Missouri was saved to the Union by Frank Blair; and afterwards in the Southern campaign he was one of the best and most efficient commanders."

He could not now follow the Republican party into the excesses against which both his heart and judgement revolted, and he at once, with characteristic boldness and wisdom, united himself with the Democratic party.

President Johnson, appreciating the services he had rendered the Union, nominated him in March, 1866, to be Collector of the Internal Revenue for the State of Missouri, but he was rejected by a party vote in the Senate.

In the Spring of 1868, General Blair visited the Eastern States, and during this visit delivered the following address in the town of Seymour, Connecticut, on the 3d of April 1868, showing how the Radical Congress has usurped arbitrary powers in the work of reconstructing the Southern States. The speech presents such a fair exposé of the Congressional outrages that we give it entire. He said:

"Discontent was never so universal in our country as at this moment. Even when the civil war excited the nation, there was an enthusiasm on both sides inspiring heroism. The antagonists, who were honest in their convictions, felt a patriotism that lifted every man above complaint or despondency. When the war closed, the great mass of the people of the North were exultant, and even its soldiers in the field of battle where their foes surrendered, yet smoking with blood spilled from kindred veins, proved, nevertheless, that they cherished a generous sympathy for the fallen. They gave even their stores of provisions to the vanquished as the greater sufferers from longer deprivation, and utterly stript of the means of supply. The hearts of the overthrown South were touched by this magnanimity. Grant, with the sanction of Lincoln, who was in the camp when the first battle commenced, gave peace upon the terms of the act passed by the almost unanimous vote of Congress immediately after the war opened: 'Your arms surrendered, your parole given, go home, obey the laws where you reside, and you shall not be disturbed.' Thus was the great rebellion extinguished. Lincoln had previously declared, during its continuance, the purpose for which it was waged and the conditions on which it would be closed. The Provisional Governors, who, as the deputies of the President, are appointed to see the preliminaries, on which the capitulation is thus made on the fields of battle, strictly observed, in this capacity became quasi military and civil instruments to conduct peaceably the people of the South into their old relations in the Union, taking order that they should not be obstructed in restoring their Constitutions and laws to the state before the war, accommodating them to the new conditions imposed by its results. Their function was to let them know that the way was opened to them for this good work, and give them the aid of the General Government. The people of every Southern State instantly addressed themselves to it. They restored their old constitutions in exact accordance with their original principles, and those of the Constitution of the United States. They abolished slavery to fulfil the demands made pending the rebellion in President Lincoln's proclamation as to the terms of surrender, and making this a condition of their restoration to all their rights by amnesty under their renovated Union Constitutions. Mr. Lincoln's pardon of December 8, 1863, excepted from it all above the grade of Colonel, certain civil diplomatic officers in the Confederate service, and those 'who had left their seat in Congress and judicial stations,' and 'all who had resigned commissions in the army and navy of the United States to aid the rebellion;' with these exceptions every man was pardoned who made oath in these words:

"'I will henceforth faithfully support, protect, and defend the Constitution of the United States and the union of the States thereunder; and that I will in like manner abide by and faithfully support all acts of Congress passed during the rebellion with reference to slavery—and so long and so far as not repealed, modified, or held void by Congress, or by decision of the Supreme Court; and that I will in like manner abide by and faithfully support all proclamations of the President made during the existing rebellion having reference to slavery, so long and so far as not modified or declared void by decision of the Supreme Court, so help me God.'

"This was the oath prescribing the conditions of pardon to restore all the rights of rebels not excluded by its exceptions. This was followed by the capitulation given by Grant to Lee under the sanction of Lincoln, who was with the army and in hourly communication with Grant during the series of conflicts which ended the war. This extended the pardon to all who then surrendered, and afterwards to all who surrendered under Johnson, and every successive surrender, and all who gave their parole and took the prescribed oath were entitled to the benefit of the amnesty. This was the ground assumed by General Grant when General Lee was indicted for high treason, and this received the sanction of President Johnson, and upon it the chief commanding the forces of the rebellion was discharged from indictment formed against him by the grand jury for treason, the capitulation and parole, under Lincoln's proclamation, restoring him to all his rights as a citizen, and stipulating that he should remain undisturbed as long thereafter as he obeyed the laws, being construed as equivalent to a pardon. Jefferson Davis himself would have been exonerated, if he had been surrendered with his troops under this capitulation. Not one of the soldiers or officers of the Confederate army can be justly subjected to punishment or any disqualification from their rights of citizenship by any *ex post facto* law passed by Congress or any of the States; nor can any of those persons entitled to avail themselves of the amnesty proclaimed by either President Lincoln or Johnson. The Constitution forbids it, and in every case where the judicial tribunals have been called on to interpose and stay the usurpations of the Rump Congress, and the military power asserting its authority, they have decided to maintain the immunities of the people under the Constitution, and the Executive amnesties and pardons it authorizes.

"Now, under what pretexts can the so-called Reconstruction acts of Congress be maintained against that which the Supreme Court has in its recent decision asserted? The plan proposed by President Lincoln was founded on the assumption that the States attempting secession had no right to secede; that all their proceedings in that direction were illegal and void, and that whatever shape usurpation of State powers might take in overthrowing the relations between the State and Federal authorities, they remained unchanged and ready for resumption as soon as the hostile insurrectionary force was put down. An opinion just pronounced by the Supreme Court during the present term, establishing his plan of operations, presents the constitutional principle that supports it. The Court says: 'We agree that all the proceedings of these eleven States, either severally or in conjunction, by means of which the existing governments were overthrown and new governments erected in their stead, were wholly illegal and void, and that they remained after the attempted separation and change of government, in judgment of law, as completely under all their constitutional obligations as before. The Constitution of the United States, which is the fundamental law of each and all of them, not only afforded no countenance or authority for their proceeding, but they were in every part of them in express disregard and violation of it.'

"Is it not clear from this, that the *de facto* government having been put down by the means and in the mode provided for by the Constitution, the State governments, overthrown by the suppressed insurrection, must necessarily rise up and their citizens and functionaries assume their duties, and be held as 'completely under all their obligations as before,' and with their reciprocal rights? And is not the Constitution of the United States, which is declared by the Court to be 'the fundamental law of each and all of them,' as absolutely applicable and as thoroughly bound to discharge its duties to both the State governments and their people, as if they had never been crushed under an insurrection?

"The greatest sufferers by the rebellion are the unhappy people who refused to countenance it by their votes, although constrained by secret military societies everywhere putting them under duress, threatening life, liberty and property to coerce them. Taken by surprise, they could neither resist themselves, nor would the general Government, although bound to protect, interpose to save them. Yet the majority, in all the States but one, stood out against the secession ordinances; and now almost the whole people claim their rights under the Constitution, in virtue of the amnesty proclamations, and the soldiers laid down their arms, and gave their parole too, under the capitulation which pledged that they should never be disturbed. This was an absolute pardon, sanctioned by Lincoln, and binding the faith of the nation. What right has Congress to deny them their citizenship under the Constitution of the United States, and of their States, which they have been prompt to accommodate to the conditions imposed by the war, and which had been proclaimed to be necessary preliminaries to its conclusion—emancipation, renunciation of the secession ordinances and the Confederate debt?

"The Supreme Court has already pronounced its decree on the efficiency of the President's pardoning power and amnesty in the decision in Garland's case, which is familiar to the whole country. Has Congress any authority to set aside the Executive pardon, made absolute and indefeasible by the supreme fundamental law of the land? Congress, which had the hardihood to grant pardons for offences imposed by its own *ex post facto* laws, offences which it had no right to create, has not ventured in terms to deny the President's power of pardon—under what pretext does it assume to subject to the most grievous punishment millions of people—multitudes of them innocent of a thought to harm the Union—multitudes of them its devout friends, but nevertheless by conscription dragged into the opposing ranks and their means extorted to supply them, betrayed and abandoned by the Government to its and their enemies—how can they justify the punishment of such or any others, absolved by the proclamation of amnesty and special Executive pardons? Yet the whole white race of the South are unjustly sacrificed to the negro race of the ostracized States. The negroes are made the instruments of forcing upon them governments abhorrent to them, constitutions devised by caucus committees in Washington, to bind them forever under negro rule. Is this no punishment to the exalted race that fought the battles that made us a nation independent of foreign rule? Is it no punishment to our whole kindred of the South to have their ablest and best classes disabled by penal, *ex post facto*, unconstitutional statutes, passed to disfranchise them, to deprive them of the suffrage, which is given to the negroes and to disqualify them for all public trusts? The people of the South who created its governments rise and say in written petitions, and in one vote when consulted: 'Continue the military government of our own race which you have put over us, rather than this unnatural, intolerable subjugation.'

"Let it be remembered that negro sovereignty over the South, which in commanding that section has a control even in the North, was never submitted to the people of the North as a question to be decided in the elections. When it was suggested in the Democratic Conventions that the lurking design of establishing negro suffrage was entertained by the Republican party, it was universally denied by its candidates before the people. The present Congress made their programme for the election rest on the amendment to the Constitution known as the fourteenth amendment, reported from Mr. Stevens's committee, recognizing the constitutional right of each Southern State to establish suffrage for itself, but providing in case the negroes were excluded from voting, they should not be counted in the ratio of representation—that is to say, that no State which excluded any class of people from the suffrage on account 'of race, or color, or previous condition,' should be entitled to representation in Congress or the Electoral College based upon the excluded persons. Upon this pronounced principle, voted by the entire Republican party in both branches of Congress, they went before the people, and by adroitly representing that in case the State of Alabama, for instance, containing half a million of blacks, and half a million of whites, should exclude the blacks from suffrage, its voting population of one-half million of whites ought not to have representation in Congress based on the numbers of both white and black, which would give them equal representation with one million of white men in a Northern State—making one white man in Alabama equal to two in any Northern State. It was on this principle that their existing majority in the present Congress was returned. But they had no sooner reached their seats than they violated their pledges and the Constitution together. They enacted negro suffrage universally for the whole South in their reconstruction acts; they made it paramount in all the Conventions to establish the State Constitutions, and in order to give supremacy to this negro vote, they disabled a sufficient number of the white race to give the negro vote the majority. In giving the right of registry of voters to its own agents, the present Congress holds the power, and if re-elected will retain it, to make the vote of the ten States dependent on its will. If this power now assumed by Congress over the suffrage of the States be maintained and transmitted, as it is reported by Kelly, of Pennsylvania, and Sumner, of Massachusetts, and others, it may be, the Government is consolidated in the hands of Congress, with the power of perpetuating itself.

"This was not the sort of reconstruction on which Mr. Lincoln was reëlected, and on which he staked himself in opposition to the Radicals, and went before the nominating Republican Convention—and afterwards made proclamation to the people to enable them to decide it at the polls. Let me briefly point to the steps taken by the President, and with the approval of the people, on this all-essential question of reconstruction; then contrast it with that of Congress. The collision between Congressional Radicalism and the Executive began under Mr. Lincoln. By resolution Congress invited the President to issue his proclamation of amnesty, coupled with the condition of taking the oath to abide by his proclamation of emancipation as a war measure. In his subsequent message to Congress he explained this measure as having for its object reconstruction of the States, saying that he had 'proffered that if in any of the States named a State Government shall be, in the mode prescribed, set up, such Government shall be recognized and guarantied by the United States, and that under it the State shall, on the constitutional conditions, be protected against invasion and domestic violence,' and then, he added, in justification for extending the oath to support the Constitution so as to embrace the declaration 'to abide by his proclamation of emancipation,' this passage in his message:

" 'But if it be proper to require as a test of admission to a political body an oath of allegiance to the Constitution and the Union under it, why not also to the laws and proclamations in regard to slavery? These laws and proclamations were enacted and put forth for the purpose of aiding in the suppression of the rebellion. To give them their fullest effect there had to be a pledge for their maintenance. In my judgment they have aided and will further aid the cause for which they were intended. To now abandon them would be not only to relinquish a lever of power, but would also be a cruel and an astounding breach of faith.'

"This attitude assumed by the President, and which ushered in the year 1864, the whole Republican party, in and out of Congress, heartily assumed. But the views of ambition in Presidential aspirants worked a change before the close of the summer session. Messrs. Wade and Winter Davis, chairmen of the Reconstruction Committees of the Senate and House, worked through Congress a bill which was to withdraw the subject of restoring the relations of the States in the Union from the President and to take the whole matter into the hands of Congress; and, moreover, to withdraw the subject from the people of the States themselves, and dictate in Congress the Constitution of these States. They induced Congress to enact a law prescribing Constitutions to the States, disfranchising whole classes of citizens, making them ineligible for office and incapable of voting, declaring that every person who shall hereafter hold or exercise any office, civil or military, below the grade of colonel, *is hereby declared not to be a citizen of the United States;* and appointing a provisional Governor, who is authorized to call a convention to adopt the constitution thus prescribed to be submitted to Congress for its assent. The President, by proclamation, shall recognize the government thus formed, and none other, as the established government of the State.

"This bill was thrust through the House on the day it was reported. The Senate passed a substitute entirely changing its character; but after attempts to modify in Committee of Conference, the measure—which was in fact the assumption of Congress to ordain the fundamental law for State governments—was accepted and passed as originally reported to the House. The President, in his proclamation laying this bill before the country, with his reasons for not signing it, states that it reached him for his approval less than an hour before 'the *sine die* adjournment of said session.'

"But the President's objection was not to the plan of construction set forth in the bill. It was that Congress had no power delegated to it in the Constitution of the United States to make State constitutions; that under the theory of our Government this power belonged to the people of the States. He says in proclaiming this bill as a measure for the consideration of the country, 'while I am unprepared by a formal approval of this bill to be committed to any single plan of restoration; and while I am also unprepared to declare that the free State Constitutions already adopted and installed in Arkansas and Louisiana shall be set at naught, thereby repelling and discouraging the loyal citizens who have set up the same as to further effort, or to declare the competency in Congress to abolish slavery in States, but am at the same time sincerely hoping and expecting that a constitutional amendment abolishing slavery throughout the nation may be adopted; nevertheless I am fully satisfied with the system for restoration contained in the bill AS ONE VERY PROPER PLAN FOR THE LOYAL PEOPLE OF ANY STATE CHOOSING TO ADOPT IT.'

"In the last words, marked in capitals, as they

deserve to be, the President proclaims the principle on which Congress has made the war with the Executive Department, which threatens revolution. The bill carried through the House in a day, and which the Senate, in Committee of Conference, accepted in an evil hour, and which it was demanded of the President he should sign in less than an hour, was designed to alter the whole frame of our Government. The people of the States originated their State Governments. They conquered their independence of the British Government, and they then created the Government of the United States, to combine and guarantee the republican State Governments. All our governments, local and national, originate with the people. The Davis and Wade bill was designed to reverse the whole system, and enable Congress to create State Govenments and make them what it chose to make them. Mr. Lincoln said, No: I am willing to submit your plan 'as one very proper plan for the loyal people of any State choosing to adopt it.' This did not comply with the Davis and Wade bill. That was peremptory law—compulsory—was absolute subjugation of the people to the will of Congress. The stand taken for this high-handed measure was thus asserted in the preamble of the bill as sent to the Senate. '*Whereas*, the so-called Confederate States are a public enemy, waging an unjust war, whose injustice is so glaring that they have no right to claim the mitigation of the extreme rights of war, which are awarded by modern usage to an enemy who has a right to consider the war a just one.'

"The measure thus derives its principle from the assumption that the rights of humanity had been forfeited by the whole Southern people. This was the starting point of the Radical party. In refusing to sanction it and give a new origin to the State governments, not only unwarranted by the Constitution of the United States, but incompatible with our whole system and incompatible with the idea of free Government, 'founded on the consent of the governed,' the President was subject to violent abuse put forth in an appeal to the people by Wade and Davis, the Chairmen of the Committees of the two Houses, reporting the bill. 'The President (they said), by preventing this bill from becoming a law, holds the electoral vote of the rebel States at the dictation of his personal ambition, discards the authority of the Supreme Court and strides headlong toward the anarchy his proclamation of the 8th of December inaugurates.' 'A more studied outrage on the legislative authority of the people has never been inaugurated.' 'He has already exercised this dictatorial usurpation in Louisiana.'

"They further tell the President 'that the authority of Congress is paramount, and must be respected;' 'that the whole body of the Union men of Congress will not submit to be impeached by him of rash and unconstitutional legislation,' and concludes, if they do, 'they become responsible for the usurpations which they fail to rebuke, and are justly liable to the indignation of the people whose rights and security, committed to their keeping, they sacrifice.'

"In defiance of this elaborate philippic, circulated

by the Radicals all over the country to defeat the nomination of Mr. Lincoln, he with Mr. Johnson received the nomination and were elected by the Republican party by large majorities.

"Towards the close of the next session, Louisiana, under the recommendation of the President, presented her Constitution, and asked admission for her Senators and Representatives. There was a large majority for it, but it was defeated by what is called filibustering, never before resorted to in the Senate—speaking against time—moving simulated amendments—calling the yeas and nays, and at successive intervals moving adjournments, with the yeas and nays, until by this subterfuge the time lapsed for sending the bill to the House and having it passed before the constitutional term of Congress expired. In this dilatory process to defeat the admission of Louisiana, which was continued through the night until the morning hours of the next day, Messrs. Sumner, Wade, Chandler, Howard, and Brown, were the corporal's guard of Radicals who fought the bill to the death; all the rest of the Radicals giving in their adhesion to this opening measure to restore the Union with the advent of Mr. Lincoln's second inauguration, which followed eight days afterwards. These five votes prevented it; the previous question to bring a bill on its passage being denied by the rules of the Senate. These five votes were sufficient, by the abuse of the rules of legislation in one branch of Congress, to defeat representation of the South; to defeat the public opinion of the great body of the people on the question of restoration; to defeat the will of the Republican party expressed in the Convention which nominated Mr. Lincoln in defiance of this precise issue made with him in the Wade and Davis Reconstruction act, which with their manifesto in support of this measure was urged as vindicating the rights of Congress against the usurpations of the Executive, and in defiance of the vast popular majority, which, in reëlecting the President on this very issue, made in his plan for restoring the Union, held even by the majority in Congress that had voted for the Wade and Davis bill as decisive of the nation's will upon the question. It appears, however, that others of the Radicals were still more malcontent than the five Senators already alluded to, and the following paragraph from the *New York Times* (Republican) declares that Mr. Stevens had prefigured for Mr. Lincoln the fate that now attends his successor:

"'Thad. Stevens wishes to impeach and try President Lincoln instead of his successor. The first accusation that he wished to have made was, that the culprit "did erect North Carolina and the other conquered territories into States and relations, giving them Governments of his own creation, and appointing over them rulers unknown to the laws of the United States, and who could not by any such laws hold any office therein." It will be remembered that the celebrated North Carolina proclamation was the work of Mr. Lincoln. It will be remembered that it was Mr. Lincoln who appointed Stanley Governor of North Carolina, and it was Mr. Lincoln who did several and sundry other things herein charged. It is well that the

Senate and the country have been saved from *this* trial.'

"A few days after this memorable contest in the Senate, Mr. Lincoln was inaugurated as President for his second term, and the next month closed the rebellion. He had returned from the scene of its last struggle, walked through Richmond amidst its ruins, and mingled, without the ostentation of a conqueror, with the people, whom he accosted as fellow-citizens, after the surrender. In reaching the President's house in Washington, he told the crowd that gathered around, 'I would much prefer having this demonstration take place to-morrow evening, as I would then be much better prepared to say what I have to say. Just now I am not ready to say anything that one in my position ought to say.' His heart was then laboring with the great design of bringing back, with the peace, the Union the war had suspended. On that next day, when the people assembled around his portico, he delivered from a carefully prepared MSS. his last speech to his countrymen. In his invitation, asking their attendance, he said, 'you know every thing I say goes into print. If I make a mistake, it does not affect merely me or you, but the country.'

"It was thus he prepared the public for the important purpose he had to announce. It was to make an appeal to the American people to make good the pledges that had been given by the Congress, almost without a dissenting voice, that the war was waged, not for the subjugation, but the restoration of the se ceding States with all their rights unimpaired—to make good his proclamation invited by Congress, granting the amnesty on accepting the emancipation proclamation, and all the successive cognate measures, which he, in virtue of his military rights and responsibilities, had pledged himself should be crowned by the consummation of that grand result—the admission of the States with 'their rights unimpaired.' Louisiana had but the month before, with a Constitution complying with all that Congress or the President ever suggested, been excluded by chicanery of five members of the Senate employing the technicalities of the rules and speaking against time in the closing hours of a session to shut the door in her face. Louisiana was the pioneer State, and as the rest became prepared, accommodating their Constitutions to the conditions proclaimed before the close of the war, the President looked to the harmonious coming together of all the States by their voluntary action—with Governments erected by themselves, deriving their authority from the consent of the governed. In his proclamation of dissent to the Wade-Davis bill, he put it on the ground that the bill created a Constitution having neither origin or adoption in the will of the people, though he submitted it to them 'as one very proper plan for the loyal people of any State choosing to adopt it.'

"It was upon this issue that the Radicals split with Mr. Lincoln, and from the mass of the people who elected him in spite of their denunciation of him, in Congress and out of it, which followed. An attempt was made to defeat his nomination by the Convention upon this issue. Another to set it aside by calling another Republican Convention. A third by setting up Fremont as an independent candidate. But all were crushed by public opinion, and his position in favor of restoration was sustained in his election by a vote of nearly half a million majority.

"In the crowning speech of his career, the last appeal to his country, he reviewed the great measure which had been defeated by the contrivances of five indignant Radical Senators, in defiance of the will of the nation and the legislative body of which they were members. He alluded to the attacks made on him as an usurper, &c., by the manifesto of Davis and Wade; the threat of impeachment by Stevens; the intrigues of his rivals proposing various political machinery for his overthrow, in very gentle phrase, saying: 'As a general rule, I abstain from reading the reports of attacks upon myself, wishing not to be provoked by that to which I cannot properly answer. In spite of this precaution, however, it comes to my knowledge that I am much censured from some supposed agency of mine in setting up and seeking to sustain the new State Government of Louisiana. In this I have done just so much and no more than the public knows.' He then gives the history of the plan which General Banks, the Military Governor of Louisiana, had during the war, after consulting the loyal people of the State upon the President's suggestions, subjected to the action of a popular Convention, and made the basis of a State Constitution to adapt it to the renewal of its relations in the Union. He made suggestions, but no exactions, and the 'system of restoration' which the people of Louisiana adopted, was 'one very proper plan for the loyal people of any State choosing to adopt it.' Many chose to adopt it, and insist upon it, with the Wade-Davis plan before them, as well as the President's suggestions. The Government of Louisiana, thus accommodated by vote of its people to meet the results of the war, was approved by the whole of Mr. Lincoln's cabinet, and 'when the message went to Congress,' he adds, 'I received many commendations of the plan, written and verbal, and not a single objection to it from any professed emancipationist came to my knowledge until after the news reached Washington that the people of Louisiana had begun to move in accordance with it.'

"Now let me give in the words of Mr. Lincoln what the people had done, which so affected the little junto at Washington on the arrival of its news.

"'Some twelve thousand voters in the heretofore slave State of Louisiana have sworn allegiance to the laws, assumed to be the rightful political power of the State, held elections, organized a State government, adopted a free constitution, giving the benefit of schools equally to black and white, and impowering the Legislature to confer the elective franchise upon the colored man. The Legislature has voted already to ratify the constitutional amendment recently passed by Congress abolishing slavery throughout the nation. These twelve thousand persons are already committed to the Union and to perpetual freedom in the States, committed to the very things and nearly all the things the nation wants, and they ask the nation's recognition and its assistance to make good that recognition; now if we reject and spurn them, we do our utmost to disorganize and disperse them.'

"He contrasts the design of the Radical faction, who had made manifest their purpose to 'to disorganize and disperse' the Union element, with the manner in which he and his friends met the advances of the twelve thousand voters of Louisiana that sought a welcome in the homes of their fathers. To the men who, like Sumner, Stevens, and the rest, held that the States had committed suicide, that their constitutions were *tabula rasa*, that their people were foreign subjugated subjects, but who yet agreed with him in the idea 'that the sole object of the Government, civil and military, in regard to these States is to again get them into their proper practical relations' in the Union, he said, 'I believe it is not only possible, but, in fact, easier to do this without deciding or even considering whether these States have ever been out of the Union, than with it. Finding themselves safely at home, it would be utterly immaterial whether they had ever been abroad. Let us all join in the acts necessary to restoring the proper practical relation between these States and the Union, and each forever after innocently indulge his own opinion, whether in doing the acts he brought the States from without into the Union, or only gave them proper assistance, they never having been out of it.'

"His doctrine was 'they never had been out,' or could go out, or be put out; but, as a practical man, he was willing to put that question aside; all he asked of those who assumed to be real Union men was 'proper assistance' in bringing about that Union. He wanted them to prove their faith by affording proper assistance to Louisiana. 'We encourage the hearts and nerve the arms of the twelve thousand to adhere to their work, and argue for it, and proselyte for it, and fight for it, and feed it, and grow it, and ripen it to a complete success. The colored man, too, all united for him, is inspired with vigilance, and energy, and doing to the same end. Grant that he desires the elective franchise, will he not attain it sooner by saving the already advanced steps towards it, than by running backward over them? Concede that the new government of Louisiana is only, to what it should be, as is the egg to the fowl; we shall sooner have the fowl by hatching it, than by smashing it.'

"The last business hours of his life were given to this engrossing subject of bringing the States to embrace each other. On the 14th of April, three days after his speech that may be called his legacy to his countrymen, and just before he went to the theatre, he had a cabinet meeting on the policy he had, in conjunction with the people of the South, devised to make the pacification perfect. His biographer, Mr. Barret (formerly the head of the Pension Office, and who seems to have been on intimate terms with him), says: 'At the meeting of the cabinet, 14th April, he was in unusually buoyant spirits; his remaining labors evidently seemed lighter than ever before—his gladsome humor was noticed by his friends.' He then quotes Secretary Stanton's despatch thus: 'April 14.

At a cabinet meeting at which General Grant was present to-day, the subject of the States and the prospect of speedy peace was discussed. The President was very cheerful and hopeful—spoke very kindly of General Lee and others of the Confederacy, and the establishment of government in Virginia.'

"This is very significant of Mr. Stanton, for the President's nearest friends had made it known, soon after his death, that he had observed that his Secretary of War had been intimate, before the election, with those hostile with his policy, to which Mr. Stanton by his despatch would seem again to give in his adhesion. General Grant's presence, too, at this Cabinet, called to discuss Virginia's establishment in her relations with the Union, identifies him with the President's labors for that purpose. General Grant and Mr. Stanton, in their testimony before the Impeachment Committee, corroborate this statement, Mr. Stanton admitting that he prepared the North Carolina proclamation at Mr. Lincoln's request, and General Grant saying that he heard it read in Cabinet in presence of Mr. Lincoln, and that the Cabinet concurred in the policy it initiated, adding that it was the same proclamation in substance, and he believed in language, which was afterwards issued by Mr. Johnson when he became President. He also testified that he approved this programme. Soon after Mr. Lincoln's death, General Grant showed his zeal for the great object he had at heart by making a journey through Virginia and other States, and reporting favorably of their disposition and fitness for restoration, saying that they accepted in good faith the situation in which it was proposed to place them, and suggested an early meeting in Congress of the Southern representation with that of the North. With eagerness and solicitude the President, who had triumphed in the war, had sought to heal the wounds it had made, to give comfort to the broken-hearted, and above all things tending to the blessed consummation, to bind up the broken members of the Union. General Grant—at the crisis when the Junta in Congress, who opened against Lincoln, personally, the war they now prosecute with fiendish malice against his policy—did not countenance, as he does now, their destructive measures. On the contrary, he allied himself with his counsels, which Mr. Lincoln, in his last speech, tells his countrymen, 'every member of the Cabinet fully approved.' What could have drawn General Grant's fealty from the patriotic cause of restoration, as inaugurated by Lincoln's reëlection? It was so fully approved by the voice of the nation that the great body of the Republicans, who had supported the Wade-Davis bill—the antagonist scheme—gave it up. It was based on a denial to the people of the South of the right to make their own constitutions, assuming it for the rump Congress—the Representatives of another section. Lincoln would recognize no scheme for the reorganization of the State government, unless the people chose to adopt it. This was the diverging point between the President and his Radical opponents in Congress. The overwhelming voice of the nation for a time induced the mass of that party to resign their opposition to his principles and measures.

On his death their hostility revived, but it did not manifest itself until the meeting of Congress after the inauguration of Mr. Johnson. His message, exhibiting the acquiescence of the whole South in his predecessor's policy, gave universal satisfaction. The press at home and abroad were full of congratulations on its happy auguries. But the malcontents in Congress, who had enjoyed during the war unlimited power—who had rioted on public plunder—quickly saw that if the happy intercourse between the North and South was restored, and with it law and order and regular business, enormous issues of paper money would cease, enormous contracts and jobs would no more be put up as national stakes to be gambled for—cotton speculations would escape from legislative and judicial manipulation and become business transactions, and our billions of taxation would shrink to modest millions. The regulated Government that once made our country so prosperous is ill-suited to the genius of public men who before the war felt that nothing but bare boarding could be made by Congressional labor, but who now find themselves living in magnificent palaces of their own—discussing openly and complacently the proper moment for changing the Government into one in which the President and Senate shall be chosen for life — while their friends, the contractors, in their respective States, are erecting villas, manufacturing monopolies, banking establishments, and other grand privileged instrumentalities of wealth that dwarf all that the best-directed individual industry can do in competition. Unsettled times suit political operators and adventurers whose skill is their only capital. When such men reach a place in legislative bodies, constitutional rule is to them like a sheepfold against wolves. Hence the eagerness with which they seek to throw them down. The death of Mr. Lincoln was for these wolves like the death of the shepherd. From that moment their hopes revived. During his life they had been driven in despair to filibustering to keep the South out of the fold, now they saw the ten States exposed, only protected by the strength of one man of the section already vanquished by arms. Lincoln's power was derived from his popularity in the victorious States. The men whom Lincoln had kept at bay were themselves the leaders in that section, and against them the Vice-President could not maintain the mastery as the President himself had in the region that elected him to power. Hence the men who seized the opportunity of Lincoln's death, rejoicing in it as opening the way to make spoil of the unresisting States of the South, to use them for the purposes of their ambition and avarice, were glad, as dissembling mourners, to follow the hearse of the dead President throughout the North, pretending homage to the statesman whose whole policy they had attempted to thwart. They had been defeated and rebuked for it by his reëlection, and by that reëlection were called back to accomplish it, in spite of their reluctance. The revenge they dared not try to wreak on the principal by whom they were once repulsed, they resolved to take of his successor, the Vice-President. The acclaim he received for his message, adopting Mr. Lincoln's Union programme, had hardly ceased to ring in his ears when old Thad. Stevens and his subterranean caucus broke their cell and denounced the Presidential plan, repulsed the Southern States which had adopted it, and sent their Representatives home from the Capitol. From that day to this Mr. Johnson ceased to be President, even *de facto*. A part of Lincoln's Cabinet, which he retained, always at heart hostile to Lincoln's policy, betrayed Johnson to the Rump Congress and used the power of his administration to destroy him. The impeachment now is necessary only to satisfy the malice which would have the gratification of a formal removal. Thad. Stevens threatened it against Lincoln to accomplish what is already practically against Johnson. The Rump have exerted almost despotic power from the death of Mr. Lincoln. They have complete command of the army, all orders to be obeyed being derived through Grant and Sherman issuing them, and the civil departments are, with their patronage, almost entirely at their devotion throughout the country as well as in Washington. The laws are made over the President. Johnson could do nothing but fulminate vetoes to make their daring acts in defiance of the Constitution the more conspicuous. They fell on the bronze of Thaddeus and his comrades as Priam's darts from the brazen shield of Pyrrhus. All the miseries of the country for the last three years are attributable to the Jacobins and their committees that have traversed and worried the country. The military government to which the South has been consigned, to give the army the control of both South and North in the election of President and the next Congress under the sham of negro suffrage, is but a blending of Cromwell's and Louis Napoleon's precedent to make an empire out of universal suffrage controlled by the army. No one can mistake the real issue upon which the Radicals separated from Mr. Lincoln, nor will it be denied that whenever it has been fairly placed before the country it has been decided against them. It was thus decided in his renomination and reëlection. Taught by this experience they avoided making this issue in the election by which the present Congress was returned, and actually went into it upon an amendment to the Constitution which conceded the right of the States to determine the question of suffrage for themselves. Having thus fraudulently secured a new lease of power, they promptly violated the principle of their own amendment and passed their reconstruction acts giving universal suffrage in the South to the blacks, and disfranchising as many of the white men as they deemed sufficient to secure negro supremacy in those States. Thus the issue came once more before the people of the North, and in every election which has been held since the passage of these acts the Radicals have been ignominiously defeated, and the attempt to impose negro suffrage rebuked. They nevertheless persist in forcing these condemned measures upon the country. They are determined to maintain them against the clear majority of the people of both sections. Under these acts three millions of ignorant negroes have been made supreme over six millions of the white race in the South, and the Congressional representation and electoral vote thus controlled is relied upon to overcome the majority against the Radicals in the North. Negro supremacy is not confined to the South; it extends itself to the North, and enables a minority to control a majority in both sections. It is clear now that the Rump Congress has constituted itself the supreme power—the entire Government. The President is subjugated and obeys its laws, constitutional or not. The Supreme Court, whilst ready with its judgment on the question of conflicting constitutional power between the Congress and the President, submits to a law passed by Congress made expressly to forbid its discharge of this, its constitutional function. The army takes and obeys leaders given through General Grant and Secretary Stanton, independently of the Chief Magistrate, the Commander-in-Chief, in virtue of a law passed by Congress to strip the President of his direct and express constitutional authority; Grant and Stanton having acted on the principle that their duty made such law their rule, the order of the President to the contrary notwithstanding. This makes Congress absolute. The next step is to make perpetual this absolutism in Congress. This is to be accomplished by the electing, through the negro vote polled under army orders, twenty Senators and some fifty Representatives from the disfranchised States. This accession, even if the Radicals poll only a considerable minority in the free States, will carry the Presidency and a sufficient vote into the next Congress, added to the negro-elected Senators and Representatives, to make the Constitution what the Radicals want it to be.

They may make the President hold for one term of ten years, or for life, and so of the Senators and Representatives. This was the process by which the Governments of England and France emerged from their revolution, establishing republics into empires, with a monarch and a nobility, to substitute a popular sovereignty."

As the time wore on it became known that General Blair would support the candidate of the Democratic party in the Presidential Campaign of 1868, and many of his friends began to advance his name for nomination by the Convention. As the meeting of the Convention drew nearer, General Blair yielded to the solicitations of his friends, and consented to allow his name to the brought before that body. In order, however, that there might be no misunderstanding as to the views he entertained, he made public a letter which he had written to a gentleman in Missouri, in reply to certain questions propounded by the latter:

"WASHINGTON, June 30.

"*Colonel Jas. O. Broadhead.*

"Dear Colonel: In reply to your inquiries, I beg leave to say that I leave to you to determine, on consultation with my friends from Missouri, whether my name shall be presented to the Democratic Convention, and to submit the following, as what I consider the real and only issue in this contest.

"The reconstruction policy of the Radicals will be complete before the next election; the States, so long excluded, will have been admitted; negro suffrage established and the carpet-baggers installed in their seats in both branches of Congress. There is no possibility of changing the political character of the Senate, even if the Democrats should elect their President and a majority of the popular branch of Congress. We cannot, therefore, undo the Radical plan of reconstruction by Congressional action; the Senate will continue a bar to its repeal. Must we submit to it? How can it be overthrown? It can only be overthrown by the authority of the Executive, who is sworn to maintain the Constitution, and who will fail to do his duty if he allows the Constitution to perish under a series of Congressional enactments which are in palpable violation of its fundamental principles.

"If the President elected by the Democracy enforces or permits others to enforce these Reconstruction acts, the Radicals, by the accession of twenty spurious Senators and fifty Representatives will control both branches of Congress, and his administration will be as powerless as the present one of Mr. Johnson.

"There is but one way to restore the Government and the Constitution, and that is for the President elect to declare these acts null and void, compel the army to undo its usurpations at the South, disperse the carpet-bag State governments, allow the white people to reorganize their own governments and elect Senators and Representatives. The House of Representatives will contain a majority of Democrats from the North, and they will admit the Representatives elected by the white people of the South, and with the co-operation of the President it will not be difficult to compel the Senate to submit once more to the obligations of the Constitution. It will not be able to withstand the public judgment, if distinctly invoked and clearly expressed, on this fundamental issue, and it is the sure way to avoid all future strife to put this issue plainly to the country.

"I repeat that this is the real and only question which we should allow to control us: Shall we submit to the usurpations by which the Government has been overthrown, or shall we exert ourselves for its full and complete restoration. It is idle to talk of bonds, greenbacks, gold, the public faith and the public credit. What can a Democratic President do in regard to any of these with a Congress in both branches controlled by the carpet-baggers and their allies? He will be powerless to stop the supplies by which idle negroes are organized into political clubs—by which an army is maintained to protect these vagabonds in their outrages upon the ballot. These, and things like these, eat up the revenues and resources of the Government and destroy its credit, make the difference between gold and greenbacks. We must restore the Constitution before we can restore the finances, and to do this we must have a President who will execute the will of the people by trampling into dust the usurpations of Congress, known as the Reconstruction acts. I wish to stand before the Convention upon this issue, but it is one which embraces every thing else that is of value in its large and comprehensive results. It is the one thing that includes all that is worth a contest, and without it there is nothing that gives dignity, honor, or value to the struggle.

"Your friend,

"FRANK P. BLAIR."

This letter* gave great offence to the Radicals,

* The *New York Herald*, during the session of the Convention published the following interesting account of an interview with General Blair:

"The Missouri delegation being a unit in favor of General Frank Blair for President, and many of the Western men, as well as a strong party in the Soldiers and Sailors' Convention, supporting him, our reporter called on the General yesterday at the Worth House with a view of learning the grounds on which he based his hopes of nomination by the Democratic party. General Blair very courteously stated that he was very willing to make known his principles, although his recent letter should have settled that matter. Our reporter ackowledged having read the letter, but with a view of eliciting a clearer statement asked if the General did not consider, on a reconsideration of the matter, that his views on the reconstruction laws and the duties of the next President in regard to them might not have the effect of frightening many thousands who, although not Radicals, echo General Grant's demand for peace? The General then spoke in substance as follows:—

"I do not think that people would be alarmed at the prospect of undoing the infamous acts of Congress, and I do not believe in lying and double dealing even for the office of President of the United States. It is better that the truth should be known at once. Alarm the people? Why, they are alarmed now. The country is in revolution; the liberties of one-half of the citizens of this country have been destroyed, and that of the other half threatened. Our commerce has been swept from the seas, and the republic is insulted in the persons of her citizens by a government hostile during our war and hostile still. It will not serve the cause of the people by putting in a President with the same set of opinions as the present occupant of the White House. What more could Chase or Pendleton do than Johnson? Nothing more; and the carpet-bag Congress, which will virtually rule the country, no matter who is President (unless means not yet tried are used to prevent it), will merely have a new 'man at the other end of the avenue' to laugh at and override. If the madness of Congress is not checked we will have in the South an Ireland or a Poland, and periodical insurrections will give vent

and they, of course professed to view it as a threat on the part of Gen. Blair. Since the publication of the letter they have been whining through the country about "Blair's revolution" until they have drawn not a little ridicule upon themselves. Gen. Blair, however, was far from threatening a resort to illegal measures. He meant simply that the work of the Radicals in the South, being illegal, could, and ought to be, undone peaceably and by legal means. His brother, the Hon. Montgomery Blair, in a speech recently delivered in Virginia, makes plain the meaning of the letter. Mr. Blair says:

"This is the language called revolutionary, and said to menace. There is no such thought in it. It is an appeal to the ballot, and it is the Radicals alone who talk of war and are making preparations for it. In connection with the elections, General Blair and the Democratic party invoke the judgment of the

to the aspirations of the people for liberty. There are indications, too, that the West will not quietly submit to be ruined by the Radicals much longer. Under these circumstances I think it is only right and proper that the people should know where I stand, and why I am a candidate for the Presidency. I think that the financial and every other question started to blind the eyes of the people and conceal the real issue is of small importance at present. The country must first be saved from the impending ruin and the supremacy of the constitution established before those questions can be properly taken up. The first duty of a Democratic government should be to vindicate American honor in the matter of the imprisonment and punishment as felons of American citizens in England and Ireland on suspicion and without proof. The prisoners should be demanded at the cannon's mouth, with proper apologies and a sufficient indemnity for the outrages.'

"Our reporter, after thanking the General for his ready courtesy, which contrasted very favorably with the conduct of other parties interested in the Presidential nomination, then withdrew.

people on the issue joined with the Radicals on the validity of their measures, and they propose to carry the judgment of the people into effect by the officer elected for that purpose by them. There can be no war unless the Radicals make it to resist the judgment of the people who are or ought to be final arbiters. What, then, does this outcry from the Radicals mean, but that they will resist the judgment asked for by the Democracy. They deceived the people as to their intentions in respect to these measures, and secured their present power in Congress by denying that they contemplated any such abuses of it. They hastened to prostitute it to subvert the civil government and set up military governments in the South, now to be used to defeat the wishes of the people in the North, and then put forward the commander of the army as their candidate, and gave him the army to elect himself, substantially inviting him to seize power, whether elected or not by the people. This conduct shows their determination to forestall and defeat the will of the people. The menace of war which they now make themselves, but falsely impute to their opponents, because the judgment of the people is invoked against them, only illustrates and puts in broad light their determination to hold power at all hazards. That, at least, is what the people believe is their resolve. It is, however, but a brag game. The object is to intimidate the people into acquiescence of their rule. General Grant ominously says, 'Let us have peace' with the same meaning, and they are winding up the session with a distribution of arms among their followers, to give emphasis to the language of Grant and his myrmidons. They alone disturb the public peace. They alone threaten to resist the will of the people in the lawful exercise of their authority to pass judgment on the acts of their unfaithful servants, and restore the Constitution. The Democracy have submitted without resistance to the most glaring violations of the Constitution. Every species of tyranny and outrage which have disgraced the meanest and bloodiest tyrants in the world has been borne with patience, looking to the day of deliverance by the ballot box in November next. Appalled by the prospect of being at last brought to account, these corrupt and ruthless oppressors are attempting to drive the people from the polls and compel a still further submission by arming their followers and threatening war if they shall pronounce against them. But there is no danger. 'The sure way,' says General Blair, with truth, 'to avoid all strife, is to put the issue plainly to the country.' That has been done now. Let the people decide against these usurpers and they will not have a corporal's guard to sustain them. General Grant will not find a soldier, not even a colored soldier, who would resist that judgment. Napoleon, backed by his millions of armed men, cannot withstand the voice of France. Can the carpet-baggers survive the power to which alone they owe their official life. The dictators of the caucus at Washington, like the Bombas of Naples, will become objects of derision, when, with loss of power, they cease to be feared. Their creatures will become yet more contemptible. The transfer of the executive power by the people to the hands of Horatio Seymour, will end the struggle at once in all its forms, to the joy of a once more united, happy, and free people. Nor have I the least misgivings but that this will be done. In the address I made here a year ago I ventured the prediction that the people will repudiate the faithless men whose insane lust of power had driven them to violate every guarantee for liberty. Our Democratic leaders were so discouraged that they made but little effort at the canvass of last year. The result was, nevertheless, that the Radicals were signally defeated. This forced them to fly to Grant, but the elections since he consented to coöperate with them show that people are not to be diverted from their purpose of restoring the Constitution by the influence of his name, or deterred from doing their duty to themselves and their posterity by brandishing his sword before their eyes. They want the assurance of peace which is afforded by the Government of law and not the peace of despotism, or of the reign of terror, of which Grant, following in the footsteps of every other military chieftain, has become the minister."

The Republicans were very unwilling to lose the coöperation of Gen. Blair, and as a means of drawing him back to their organization, secretly tendered him the nomination of Vice President on the ticket with Gen. Grant,* but he declined it. His separation from the Republican party was the result of his honest con-

* Speech of Hon. M. Blair, at Rockbridge, Alum Springs, Va., July 25th, 1868.

victions of duty, and he was not to be drawn back by bribery.

When the Democratic Convention assembled in New York on the 4th of July 1868, it was seen that General Blair's friends were strong in numbers. The Missouri delegation was a unit for him, and his supporters were numerous in the Regular Convention and in that of the Soldiers and Sailors.

On the fifth day of the session, Gen. Blair was formally placed in nomination by Mr. Broadhead of Missouri, who said:

"We have now reached the fifth day of our session without any successful result. I now ask leave to present to the Convention another man for their consideration. I will nominate General Francis P. Blair, of Missouri. It is not necessary in this Convention that I should attempt to repeat his honorable services as a soldier or as a statesman, for they are known to the whole country. Without desiring to disparage the qualifications of any other of the distinguished gentlemen whose names are presented for the consideration of this Convention, I will only say that General Blair is eminently possessed of those qualifications most needed at this time—firmness of purpose, moral courage, and indomitable will. He will not be readily turned from a purpose once deliberately formed, although another coördinate department of the Government may place itself in the way of its performance; and as President of the United States he would preserve, protect, and defend the Constitution; and he would give to it a living meaning which, in the absence of any judicial interpretation to the contrary, gives to the President the right and imposes upon him the duty of refusing to execute unconstitutional laws. (Applause.) If we would meet the demands of this crisis, if we would not shrink from the issues of this hour, we must by some tangible form of action maintain the independence of the Executive. Congressional despotism is the great evil against which we have to contend. It is the fruitful source of all our troubles. It is that which is riving asunder the framework of our government and substituting the views of faction for the requirements of the Constitution. We want a man at the head of the government who knows the duties of the executive station, and knowing, dare maintain them. Such a man is the gentleman whose name I now present to the consideration of this Convention."

The choice of the Convention, however, fell upon Mr. Seymour—a selection which was promptly and heartily endorsed by General Blair.

The Convention met in the afternoon, after a brief recess, for the purpose of nominating a candidate for the Vice-Presidency. It was felt by all that the selection of General Blair would be the wisest and most fitting choice that could be made, and it seemed to be very well understood that he would receive a heavy vote on the first ballot.

When the Convention was called to order, Mr. Sparks, of Illinois, nominated General John A. McClernand of that State; but General McClernand withdrew his name. Hon. Asa C. Dodge, of Iowa, was then nominated by the delegation from that State; and General Thomas Ewing, Jr., of Kansas, by the Kansas delegation. The name of Kentucky being called, General Preston, of that State, an ex-general officer of the Confederate army, rose and said:

"Mr. President, I am instructed unanimously by the State of Kentucky, by its delegates here assembled, to place in nomination a gentleman of great distinction in his State and in the country; one in the prime of manhood, distinguished by his devotion to the Union—having served it both in a civil and military capacity with the utmost honor, and obtained a reputation in the army second to no man of his grade. Kentucky feels that this nomination is due to the great West, and no Southern State has presented any nominee for any place, as you will observe here; but I feel that it is appropriate—for we have entertained different opinions from him—to state that I am instructed now to nominate him in order to testify that we, the soldiers of the South, stretch forward our hands to the soldiers of the North (applause) in the spirit of a noble amity that your resolutions have inculcated. (Applause.) It is with that view, Sir, after consultation with the Northern delegations, and one of the most powerful, that the duty is devolved upon me of making this nomination. I now have the privilege, therefore, of nominating as a candidate for Vice-President of the United States, General Francis P. Blair, of Missouri. (Applause.)"

As General Preston resumed his seat, General Steadman, of Louisiana, rose and said:

"Mr. President: I rise, Sir, as one of the humble

representatives of the United States Army in the late war, holding a seat in the Convention, to second, on behalf of Louisiana, the nomination of my comrade in arms, Major-General Frank P. Blair. (Applause.) When this Convention adjourned, I went immediately to the headquarters of the Soldiers' and Sailors' Executive Committee, on Union Square. I met there some ten or twelve gentlemen, who were distinguished in the army, and consulted them in regard to their choice as a candidate as a Vice-President of the United States, and by a unanimous vote of all who were present, I was requested to say to this Convention, without disparagement to the name of any other soldier that has been presented here, or may be presented, that General Frank P. Blair would be acceptable to the soldiers of the United States Army. (Applause.) In the exhibition of magnanimity that has been made in this Convention by the soldiers of the Confederate army, in coming up and giving a contradiction to the charge of the Radical party that they did not accept sincerely the situation; in casting their votes as they did in this Convention for that distinguished soldier of the United States Army, Major-General Winfield Scott Hancock, they have given renewed assurance of their devotion to the Union, of their willingness to accept the issues of the war by presenting to this Convention, through General Preston—whom I met on the bloody field of Chickamauga—the name of Major-General Francis P. Blair. (Loud applause.) I feel therefore authorized to say that if General Blair is nominated his nomination will meet with a response from every brave and true man that fought on either side, who desires to see peace and prosperity restored to our common country." (Applause.)

General Steadman was followed by General Wade Hampton, of South Carolina, who spoke as follows:

"Mr. Chairman—The only reason I can give why my State has done me the honor to ask me to speak for her on this occasion is, I suppose, that I met the distinguished gentleman whose name has been presented by Kentucky on more than one field. Our State wishes me to say to the soldiers, and in reply to the remarks of the gentleman from Illinois, the distinguished soldier from Illinois, that the soldiers of the South cordially, heartily, and cheerfully accept the right hand of friendship which is extended to men. (Cries of 'good,' and cheers.) We wish to show that we appreciate the kindness and cordiality that has been extended to us by all classes. We wish particularly to make an acknowledgment to the Federal soldiers who have met us so cordially and so friendly. It is due to them, I think, that they should have the second place upon the ticket. It is due to that Convention which so cordially approved your platform; it is due to the South, and I, for my State, most heartily and cordially second the nomination of General Blair."

General Hampton's speech was greeted with loud applause, and when order was restored, the first ballot was taken, the result of which was announced by the Secretary, as follows:

"The vote stands upon Vice-President, as follows: Whole vote of the Electoral College, 317, which were given unanimously for Frank P. Blair, of Missouri."

The following is a table of the first ballot for Vice-President:

	Blair.		Blair.
Alabama,	8	Nebraska,	3
Arkansas,	5	Nevada,	3
California,	5	New Hampshire,	5
Connecticut,	6	New Jersey,	7
Delaware,	3	New York,	33
Florida,	3	North Carolina,	9
Georgia,	9	Ohio,	21
Illinois,	16	Oregon,	3
Indiana,	13	Pennsylvania,	26
Iowa,	8	Rhode Island,	4
Kansas,	3	South Carolina,	6
Kentucky,	11	Tennessee,	12
Louisiana,	7	Texas,	6
Maine,	7	Vermont,	5
Maryland,	7	Virginia,	10
Massachusetts,	12	West Virginia,	5
Michigan,	8	Wisconsin,	6
Minnesota,	4		
Mississippi,	7	Total,	317
Missouri,	11		

Three hearty cheers greeted this announcement, and another scene of enthusiasm ensued. The Chairman hammered with his gavel, and the Secretary informed the delegates that the vote had not yet been announced.

The Chairman—"The unanimous vote having been

cast for Francis P. Blair, of Missouri, for Vice-President, he is declared the candidate of the Democratic party for the Vice-Presidency." (Great cheering.)

A Committee was appointed by the Convention to wait upon Mr. Seymour and Gen. Blair, and inform them of their nominations. As we have said in the sketch of Governor Seymour, this formal announcement was made in Tammany Hall on the evening after the Convention adjourned *sine die.* The hall was thronged with a brilliant audience, among whom were many of the most distinguished statesmen of the country.

The nomination for the Presidency was first tendered to Mr. Seymour, who replied in a few eloquent remarks. Then turning to Gen. Blair, who had by this time advanced to the front of the stage, General Morgan addressed him as follows:

"General Blair: The Committee appointed by the Convention have made it my pleasing duty, sir, to announce to you your unanimous nomination as the Democratic candidate for the Vice-President of the United States—(applause)—and in tendering to you, sir, this nomination, I feel sure that it will not only be hailed with acclamation by your fellow-citizens throughout the United States, but by thousands of your gallant comrades on many a well-fought field—(applause)—and who will once again rally to the stars and stripes and the defence of free institutions." (Applause.)

After the applause which greeted his presence on the stand had subsided, General Blair said:

"Mr. Chairman: I accept the platform of resolutions passed by the late Democratic Convention, and I accept their nomination—(great cheering)—with feelings of profound gratitude, and, sir, I thank you for the very kind manner in which you have already conveyed to me the decision of the Democratic Convention. I accept the nomination with the conviction that your nomination for the Presidency is one which will carry us to certain victory—(applause)—and because I believe that the nomination is the most proper nomination that could be made by the Democratic party. (Applause.) The contest which we wage is for the restoration of constitutional government—(cheers)—and it is proper that we should make this contest under the lead of one who has given his life to the maintenance of constitutional government. (Applause.) We are to make the contest for the restoration of those great principles of government which belong to our race. (Great applause.) And, my fellow-citizens, it is most proper that we should select for our leader a man not from military life, but one who has devoted himself to civil pursuits; who has given himself to the study and the understanding of the Constitution and its maintenance with all the force of reason and judgment. (Applause.) My fellow-citizens, I have said that the contest before us was one for the restoration of our government, it is also one for the restoration of our race. (Applause, long continued.) It is to prevent the people of our race from being exiled from their homes—(cheers)—exiled from the Government which they formed and created for themselves and for their children, and to prevent them from being driven out of the country or trodden under foot by an inferior and semi-barbarous race. (Applause.) In this country we shall have the sympathy of every man who is worthy to belong to the white race. (Applause.) What civilized people on earth would refuse to associate with themselves in all the rights and honors and dignity of their country such men as Lee and Johnson? What civilized country on earth would fail to do honor to those who, fighting for an erroneous cause, yet distinguished themselves by gallantry in that service? (Applause.) In that contest for which they are sought to be disfranchised and to be exiled from their homes—in that contest they have proved themselves worthy to be our peers. (Applause.) My fellow-citizens, it is not my purpose to make any long address—(cries of 'go on')—but simply to express my gratitude for the great and distinguished honor which has been conferred upon me.

"A voice—'You are worthy of it.'

"General Blair.—And from my heart to reiterate the words of thanks that fell from my lips when I arose."

(Renewed cheering, during which General Blair retired.)

The crowd in the street having called for General Blair, he made his appearance before them after the conclusion of the ceremonies in the hall, and was received with deafening shouts of applause. He then spoke as follows:

"Gentlemen: I return you my heartfelt thanks for the kindness with which you have received me here this evening. I value, my fellow-citizens, this unbounded enthusiasm, not because I consider it any personal compliment to myself, but because I see in it what no man can mistake—that the people of this country have aroused themselves, and intend to take back their Government in their own hands (applause), that they intend to redeem themselves (applause) from the rule (a voice—'misrule') of this dynasty that has disgraced and degraded the country. (Great cheering and cries of 'good, good.') That they intend to assert the rights of American citizens which have been taken away from them by the military power of the South (applause), and the rights of American citizens in foreign lands as well. (Enthusiastic cheering.) My fellow-citizens, the Radicals now in power (groans and hisses.) I wish I could groan as loud as all of you. (Laughter.) They have sought, fellow-citizens, to make a new Ireland of America. (Groans.) I know, fellow-citizens, that it is impossible for me to speak so as to be heard in this immense audience. (Cries of 'go on.') I know that standing in such a dense mass as you are now standing in, is not conducive to comfort, and that it will be better for me to desist. (Cries of 'go on.') I therefore again, fellow-citizens, return you my heartfelt thanks for your kindness, and beseech you to make your assault upon the Radicals this fall with the same serried ranks as I now see here assembled before me. I take my seat with the conviction that victory is sure." (Applause, long and loud, during which General Blair retired.)

A few days later, Gen. Blair forwarded to the Committee the following formal letter of acceptance of the nomination of the Convention:

"*General George W. Morgan, Chairman of the Committee of the National Democratic Convention:*

"GENERAL: I take the earliest opportunity of replying to your letter notifying me of my nomination for Vice-President of the United States by the National Democratic Convention recently held in the City of New York.

"I accept without hesitation the nomination tendered in a manner so gratifying, and give you and the Committee my thanks for the very kind and complimentary language in which you have conveyed to me the decision of the Convention.

"I have carefully read the resolutions adopted by the Convention, and most cordially concur in every principle and sentiment they announce.

"My opinion upon all the questions which discriminate the great contending parties have been freely expressed on all suitable occasions, and I do not deem it necessary at this time to reiterate them.

"The issues upon which the contest turns are clear and cannot be obscured or distorted by the sophistries of our adversaries. They all resolve themselves into the old and ever recurring struggle of a few men to absorb the political power of the nation. This effort under every conceivable name and disguise has always characterized the opponents of the Democratic party, but at no time has the attempt assumed a phase so open and daring as in this contest. The adversaries of free and constitutional Government, in defiance of the express language of the Constitution, have erected a military despotism in ten of the States of the Union, have taken from the President the power vested in him by the supreme law, and have deprived the Supreme Court of its jurisdiction. The right of trial by jury, and the great writ of right, the *habeas corpus*—shields of safety for every citizen, which have descended to us from the earliest traditions of our ancestors, and which our Revolutionary fathers sought to secure to their posterity forever in the fundamental charter of our liberties—have been ruthlessly trampled under foot by the fragment of a Congress; whole States and communities of people of our race have been attainted, convicted, condemned, and deprived of their rights as citizens, without presentment or trial or witnesses, but by Congressional enactment of *ex post facto* laws, and in defiance of the constitutional prohibition, denying even to a full and loyal Congress the authority to pass any bill of attainder or *ex post facto* law. The same usurping authority has substituted as electors in place of the men of our own race, thus illegally attainted and disfranchised, a host of ignorant negroes who are supported in idleness with the public money, and are combined together to strip the white race of their birthright through the management of Freedmen's bureaux and emissaries of conspirators in other States. And to complete the oppression, the military power of the nation has been placed at their disposal in order to make this barbarism supreme. The military leader, under whose prestige this usurping Congress has taken refuge—since the condemnation of their schemes by the free people of the North, in elections of the last year—and whom they have selected as their candidate, to shield themselves from the result of their own wickedness and crime, has announced his acceptance of the nomination, and his willingness to maintain their usurpations over eight millions of white people at the South, fixed to the earth with his bayonets. He exclaims, 'Let us have peace!' 'Peace reigns in Warsaw,' was the announcement which heralded the doom of the liberties of a nation. 'The empire is peace,' exclaimed Bonaparte when freedom, and its defenders expired under the sharp edge of his sword. The peace to which Grant invites us is the peace of despotism and death. Those who seek to restore the Constitution by executing the will of the people condemning the reconstruction acts, already pronounced in the elections of last year (and which will, I am convinced, be still more emphatically expressed by the election of the Democratic candidate as President of the United States), are denounced as revolutionists by the partisans of this vindictive Congress. Negro suffrage (which the popular vote of New York, New Jersey, Pennsylvania, Ohio, Michigan, Connecticut, and other States has condemned as expressly against the letter of the Constitution) must stand, because their Senators and Representatives have willed it. If the people shall again condemn these atrocious measures by the election of the Democratic candidate for President, they must not be disturbed! Although decided to be unconstitutional by the Supreme Court, and although the President is sworn to maintain and support the Constitution, the will of a fraction of a Congress, reinforced with its partisan emissaries sent to the South, and supported there by the soldiery, must stand against the will of the people and the decisions of the Supreme Court and the solemn oath of the President to maintain and support the Constitution! It is revolutionary to excute the will of the people! It is revolutionary to execute the judgment of the Supreme Court! It is revolutionary in the President to keep inviolate his oath to sustain the Constitution! This false construction of the vital principle of our Government is the last resort of those who would have their arbitrary reconstruction sway and supersede our time-honored institutions. The nation will say that the Constitution must be restored and the will of the people again prevail. The appeal to the peaceful ballot to attain this end is not war—is not revolution. They make war and revolution who attempt to arrest this quiet mode of putting aside military despotism and the usurpations of a fragment of a Congress asserting absolute power over that benign system of regulated liberty left us by our fathers. This must be allowed to take its course. *This is the only road to peace. It will come with the election of the Democratic candidate, and not with the election of that mailed warrior whose bayonets are now at the throats of eight millions of people in the South, to compel them to support him as a candidate for the Presidency, and to submit to the domination of an alien race of semi-barbarous men. No perversion of truth or audacity of misrepresentation can exceed that which hails this candidate in arms as an angel of peace.*

"I am, very respectfully,
"Your most obedient servant,
"FRANK P. BLAIR."

After the close of the Convention, Gen. Blair made a visit to the far West, on business connected with the Pacific Railroad, and while at Omaha, Nebraska, on the 16th of July, was serenaded by a party of enthusiastic admirers, to whom he spoke as follows:

"I am here to acknowledge the compliment you have paid me. I assure you that I value the compliment. I am well aware that it is not paid to me as an individual, but rather as one of the representatives of that cause to which you have shown yourselves so devoted. (Applause.) It is a cause, my fellow citizens, worthy of your greatest devotion and of your highest enthusiasm. It is the cause of free government and constitutional government in this country, and I am satisfied, my friends and fellow citizens, from the enthusiasm and feeling manifested here to-night and elsewhere where I have been, that this cause is destined to a great and glorious victory in the next election in November. (Great applause.) I feel, my fellow citizens, that we are destined to achieve a great victory in behalf of our free government and free constitution. I feel to-day, not alone from this manifestation, but from all we have seen during the past year in the elections where the policy of the radical party has been condemned by overwhelming majorities of people of the United States—(cheers)—and notwithstanding this condemnation by the people, these reckless people, who achieved power upon a totally different issue from that which is now before the people, have in defiance of the popular will, in defiance of the votes of the people, of whom they were simply the representatives, urged forward these measures to a completion in the hope that they could bind the hands of the people of this country and wrest from them the power forever. (Applause.) Yes, my fellow citizens, they have by these measures put under foot all the people of our race in ten of the Southern States; they have bound a million of people to the earth with their bayonets, and they have put on the top of them this hideous black barbarism—(applause)—and, my fellow citizens, feeling that they have lost the confidence of the white race, both North and South, they propose to overcome the charges cast against them at the North in the free States during the last year by the minority of the South, whom they have made supreme over the white race there, and the question comes up for your decision—for the decision of the whole of the people of this country—will you permit a minority in both sections composed of the white race. (Cheers.) That race, my fellow citizens, that glorious race of people whose history is the record of intellectual progress among mankind, the only race that have ever shown themselves capable of establishing and maintaining free government. (A voice. The Blair family, I suppose.) The Blair family will be found on the side of the white race. (Cheers.) The Blair family can never be deterred from taking that stand by any man who wishes to assail the fair white race of this country by a mixture with the blacks. (Applause.) My fellow citizens, it is not my intention to detain you by any lengthened remarks. (Cries of 'Go on.') I knew very well that what I had to say would not please a certain set of people, and I will say further that I did not intend to please them. (Loud cheers.) If any one is displeased that we, the Democrats, intend to restore the government and the constitution, they may make their decrees now, for I tell you that after November next you will not be able to hear one of them speak. (Applause.) But I am for giving them the largest liberty of speech. I do not intend nor desire that they should be gagged as they are now endeavoring to gag eight millions of our people in the South. I do not think it will be the policy of the Democratic party when it comes into power and re-establishes the government to proscribe free speech anywhere in the country. It has always been their policy to give the largest liberty to all men to use the most perfect freedom of speech, for without it we cannot maintain our free institutions. But these things are exceedingly distasteful to our Radical brethren. Throughout the South, they put the gag in the mouth of those people whom they have trod under the military heel. Men are arrested, thrown into prison and tried by military commissions, in defiance of those constitutional guarantees of the rights of free speech, right of trial by jury and the right to be tried before his peer and the judicial tribunal for any alleged offence. Where are those rights now? They have been stilled, trodden down, and yet we find men in this country who can stand up and defend those acts of atrocity. (Cheers.) My fellow citizens, I thank you for your attentive audience. This is a gratifying spectacle to any man who loves liberty and the constitution. This enthusiasm is a sure harbinger of our success next November. (Cheers.) And that success, under the lead of the distinguished gentleman who has been chosen by a Democratic convention as your candidate for the Presidency, is certain to restore to you the constitution handed down to you by your fathers. Gentlemen, I again thank you. (Cries of 'Go on.') I find it impossible, my fellow citizens, to make my voice reach the confines of this immense crowd, and, thanking you from my heart for the kindness which you have shown me to-night—thanking you still more for the enthusiasm you have shown for that cause in which I am now engaged along with you, I now retire." (Loud cheers.)

At Leavenworth, Kansas, on the 31st of July, 1868, General Blair addressed the State Democratic Convention and the citizens generally assembled in mass-meeting, as follows:

"Fellow-Citizens of Kansas: I congratulate myself on my good fortune in having to address so large and enthusiastic an audience as I now behold. I do not assume to myself that this is a personal compliment to me. I am too well aware that, on the contrary, your presence here to night is rather due to your devotion to the great cause in which we all are engaged, and in that sense I accept it as a greater compliment than if it was a mere personal ovation. The cause to which we are devoted, and of which I am one of your representatives, is one worthy of your most profound devotion. It is a cause in which the enthusiasm which I see here to-night, so far as I have observed, has prevailed throughout the country. It is the cause of popular rights, the cause of civil government, the cause of constitutional liberty. It is the cause, the worthiest of all for which man has arrayed himself in times past, and it will become you—it will become all of us—to evince our devotion to that cause which has showered upon the nation so many blessings since its foundation. This cause is in peril; this cause has received from the party in power the most violent shock; it has been undermined, and is almost on the point of being overthrown. But the people of the country are rallying to defend this cause, the holiest and best in the world, and in their might I confide, in their strength I am willing to abide. They alone can rescue this nation from the impending peril, and it is for you, and for all citizens of this country who love democratic institutions, to come up as one man and sustain the best and holiest cause in the world. (Applause.) I do not speak merely empty rhetoric on this subject. I could advert, and I will advert, to the particular transactions by which this cause has been brought into peril. I call your attention to the aggressions which have been made by the Radical party, calling themselves Republicans, upon the fundamental principles of our Government, those great, underlying principles on which all civil liberty depends. They have sought, by various measures which the Constitution has prohibited, to entrench themselves in power in this Government. They, losing the confidence of their own race—losing the confidence of the white people, have sought to give the power in a portion of the States of this Union to another element—the black race—hoping, after losing the confidence of the white race, to maintain and perpetuate their supremacy by giving political power in ten States of this Union to the black race. (Applause, and cries of 'Shame! shame!') Now, my fellow-citizens, I take the broad ground that the white race is the only race in the world that has shown itself capable of maintaining free institutions and a free government—(Applause); that nowhere, in any country or at any time, have the black people shown themselves capable of establishing or maintaining a constitutional government, or any other kind of government. (Prolonged cheers.) Yet the people of the Southern States have been disfranchised, and the ignorant blacks—the same people that the Republican party has declared were imbruted by slavery—whom we all know to be ignorant—whom we all know to be semi-barbarous—whom we all know have never been capable of creating, establishing, or maintaining a free government, are made to predominate in all those States. Not only are they made to predominate in the Southern States, but the three or four millions of semi-barbarous blacks have the entire control of those States, and send twenty Senators to the United States Senate, while the four millions of white people of New York send but two Senators. It would take

New York, Pennsylvania, Ohio, Indiana, Illinois, Missouri, and enough of the other great States of the Union put together, containing twenty millions of white people, to counterbalance the three or four million blacks in the South; so that the negroes are not only put above the white people of the South, but above the white people of the North also, and three or four millions of blacks are made equal in the Senate of the United States to more than twenty millions of the free white people of the North. (Cheers, and cries of 'shame.') Fellow-citizens, we all very well know that this is a political trick to keep what is known as the Radical party in power. They don't believe in it themselves. They voted it down in the State of Kansas by 10,000 majority, but notwithstanding the people have voted down negro suffrage in this State, your two Senators and Representatives still insist upon sustaining the State governments erected on the negro vote of the South. You don't understand the danger in which our institutions are from the ignorant blacks and vagabond carpet-baggers of the South. (Prolonged applause, and cries of 'Yes, we do; and we'll save the country yet.') The people have never assented to these so-called reconstruction acts. In the election of 1866, so far from presenting that issue, they dodged it—they presented an entirely different issue. The issue they submitted then was what is known as the fourteenth amendment to the Federal Constitution, which conceded to all the States the right to regulate suffrage for themselves. That was the issue upon which the last Congressional election was held.

After they had attained power by admitting the doctrines on which the Democratic party always stood, they went to work to disfranchise the white people of the South and enfranchise the blacks, denying to the States the rights which were contained in the Fourteenth amendment. As soon as they showed their hands, the elections of 1867 declared against them. In New York, Ohio, Pennsylvania, Michigan, California, Oregon, Connecticut, and in enough States to carry the election, the people decided against them. But the Senators and Representatives from those States refused to obey the will of the people. They put it at defiance, and went on with their reconstruction; and now declare they have fixed it, and that it is not in the power of the people to undo what they have done. And because in a letter I wrote pending the nominations in New York, I took the ground that the will of the people must be executed, they proclaimed me a 'revolutionist' anxious to reinstate the rebellion. The idea that any one should undertake to undo what has been done by this great Congress—this Rump, this fragmentary Congress—(cheers)—who got into power by deceiving the people on false issues, is monstrous in their virtuous eyes. After their action has been condemned by 10,000 in Kansas, by 50,000 in New York, by as many in Ohio, by 30,000 in Michigan, and by overwhelming majorities of the people wherever there has been an expression of their will, it is revolution to favor the execution of the will of the people—Frank Blair is a 'revolutionist' and wants to inaugurate another rebellion! (Cheers and laughter.) I say the

Southern States were never out of the Union—that is the doctrine we hold to and fought for four years; but now the Radical party has taken the exact position that Jeff. Davis and other leaders of secession took at the commencement of the war. (Applause and cries of 'that's so.') I tell you I have no animosity toward the negroes, and those who are pretending to be their friends are their worst enemies. Every one knows, from my history, that when the negroes were in slavery I was an advocate for their emancipation. I advocated it at the worst times, and in the worst places. I advocated it when the present pale-faced Radicals of Missouri did not dare to lift up their heads. (Prolonged cheers.) And now I say that unless the negroes submit to the intelligent guidance of the powerful white race, their fate will be that of the Indians—they will be exterminated. The negroes can only be happy and prosperous as long as they are guided by the intelligence of the white race. (Cheers.) Whenever it is sought to disfranchise the intelligence of the country and make it subordinate to the ignorance of the country—whenever it is sought to subordinate the white race of the country to the black barbarism of the negro—the prosperity of the country is at an end. (Applause and cries of 'that's so.')

"But I come back to the proposition with which I started, that the Radical party has done these things in defiance of the will of the people. Have the people ever indorsed negro suffrage? (Never.) Did you not condemn it in this State? Was it not condemned in all the States of the Union at the last election? and shall the Radical party persist in pressing it upon the people, that it shall be the rule? And when, as I have already stated, I said in New York, that if the Democratic party should carry these elections; if the people should elect a Democratic President, this pretended reconstruction should be undone; and if these miserable carpet-baggers in the Senate were in the way of its being done, the people will find a way to execute their will; those miserable creatures who have undertaken to forestall the popular will, say that any one who undertakes to execute the will of the people is a revolutionist. (Applause.) Look at the attitude of these men. Who are the revolutionists? Who has put at defiance the popular will? Who has taken away the powers of the Executive as granted to him by the Constitution? Who has curtailed the jurisdiction of the Supreme Court of the United States? Who has done all this? Why the Radical party. (Cheers and cries of 'That's so.') Who has put ten States of this Union under martial law in time of profound peace? The Radical party in Congress. Who has taken away from the President the constitutional powers granted him as Commander-in-Chief of the army and conferred it on their candidate for the Presidency? The Radical party. Who hold eight millions of white people of the South pinned to the earth with bayonets? The Radical party. General Grant was selected as the candidate of the party because they knew they were beaten on their principles, and because he alone, with his great personal popularity, was supposed to be able to arrest the tide that was about to overwhelm them;

because with the almost omnipotent power now given him in ten States of this Union, they thought he could control the votes to their own advantage. Is this man, who has bayonets at the throats of eight or ten millions of the people, the proper representative of the people? (Not much.) And are those who seek to turn aside those bayonets and give the law and the Constitution control, revolutionists? I tell you now all their attempts to subjugate this people will be overthrown. The success of the Democratic party at the coming election is foregone. It is ordained of Heaven. It is a thing already consummated almost, because the people of this country are not the men to surrender their liberties. (Never, never.) Nor can the eminent services or prestige of General Grant mislead them. (Applause.) I desire to speak of General Grant with the greatest respect for his services to his country. I shall never allow myself to speak of him otherwise than with the greatest respect. I don't think we gain any advantage by misrepresenting him or his services.

"A Voice—We have not heard from him yet.

"General Blair—No, and you are not likely to hear from him—(applause)—but as he is a candidate for the highest position in the world, he is subjected to a fair criticism on his conduct and language. I call your attention to the report made by General Grant when sent by President Johnson to the South to investigate the condition of affairs there. He then stated that the people of the South had submitted to the terms imposed upon them by the Government, and that they were fitted to return to the rights of citizens in the Union. Since that time he has seen proper to change his attitude on this question. I do not impugn his motives, but we are all at liberty to look at the facts. When the Radicals were keeping the States out he recommended their admission. I know very well from General Grant's former position that he has no amity for the negro. Neither has General Sherman nor General Sheridan. They have no hatred towards the people of the South. Look at the terms General Sherman gave Johnston at the surrender in North Carolina. It all goes to show that these military leaders, who are all now arrayed against the Democracy, in their hearts believe in the doctrines of the Democratic party. They did then and they do now. But I will tell you the secret—what has brought them to the Radical party. It is their military instinct, which tells them that the Radical party is in favor of a despotism in this country, and without having any affinity for the negro, or hatred for the white people of the South, they felt that the Radicals were in favor of erecting a despotism, and they knew full well that that would give additional consequence to military men. That is the secret of these men arraying themselves against Democracy, against constitutional liberty, and against the civil institutions of our country. (Continued applause.) We have honored these men as no nation ever honored its heroes before. We have given them the loftiest positions, but they are not content; they would make themselves dictators over all the country. And now is the time for you to show yourselves as ready and capable of prostrating these would-be dictators as you were in prostrating the rebellion. (We are ready.) I know you are ready. I know that while you cherish the services they performed for the Government, you are not inclined to surrender your own birthrights—the birthright of a citizen and freeman. (Applause.)

"A Voice—What about the Copperheads?

"General Blair—I think these Radicals have made the name 'Copperhead' respectable by their great treason against the Government. I think that whatever of prejudice may have existed against those who were called 'Copperheads' during the war, because of their sympathy for a people who, however wrong, have made themselves memorable for all time, will have been forgotten and their sins will have been forgiven, when the Radicals, who have undertaken to destroy the liberties of the whole people, to subvert our institutions, to put down the great principles upon which civil liberty alone can be sustained, who sought to perpetuate their power by appealing to the ignorance of a degraded race of beings, will be held up as examples for continual execration. (Applause.) The Radical party will be overthrown. The people are in no temper to submit to the domination of a party who seek to maintain themselves by calling to their aid this ignorant and barbarous race of men. (Applause.) I may be accused of appealing to your prejudices. I do not appeal to your prejudices. I appeal to history. I appeal to that which ought to guide every statesman. It is impossible to make a nation prosperous by giving the reins of power into the hands of a race of people who are incapable of guiding any nation. You have repudiated that doctrine—(Yes, and will do it again)—and you ought to do it forever. (Applause.) A man is unworthy himself, if he is classed as a white man, who will put the black man over his own race; and no one but a demagogue would do it. If the Radicals felt secure in their position they would be content to appeal to their own race of people for support, to the people who had created this Government, who maintained it and carried it forward to unexampled prosperity. They would be content to appeal to the intelligence of the white race. But no, they know they have forfeited the confidence of the white race. They are conspiring against the most cherished institutions of our country. They are giving the franchise to that ignorant race whom they know to be incapable, and at the same time, are disfranchising the intelligent white people of the country, and their doom is sealed. (Applause.) But fellow-citizens, there are others here from whom it is your right to hear. (Cries of 'Go on,' 'go on.'] There are gentlemen here who have been but recently nominated for high positions in your State —gentlemen who I believe will be elected by the people of the State—and they have a right to be heard, and you have a right to expect that I will give way for them. Having claimed your attention for the length of time I have, I now surrender it to men from your own State, after thanking you for your very kind attention to me."

At St. Joseph, a few days later, in reply to a serenade from the citizens, Gen. Blair said:

"GENTLEMEN OF ST. JOSEPH: In addressing the large and enthusiastic audience before me I shall not insult you by calling you 'fellows,' or by advising you to throw a man in the river, who happens to differ in opinion regarding the sentiments expressed, as I understand has been done by a distinguished military gentleman in this place upon a recent occasion. I believe this to be a free country, and that the people will treat those with respect who respect the people. Our objection to the principles of our adversaries in this great political campaign is that they assume too dictatorial a tone towards the people. They denounce me as a revolutionist—say that I wish to inaugurate another rebellion—because I say it is time for the rule of the bayonet to be checked. (Great applause.) The people of the State of Missouri and the people of the whole country, are tired of being bound to obey the dictates of their military commanders. We believe it is time for the will of the people to be carried out. This will be done. (A voice—'We'll fix that in November.') Yes, we will settle that in November, and we will do it peaceably by the ballot. The people are now fully aroused and none of these men will dare to defy the will of the people. Those who attempt it will come to grief, and it is time they should come to grief. Unless checked they will go on until they establish negro suffrage over this State and the Northern States, as they already have in ten States of this Union. They will extend a military despotism over all the States and negro supremacy, as far as the people will allow it. This fragmentary Congress, and the carpet-baggers that have got into the Senate under the auspices of this Rump, have already attempted to degrade the white men of all the States to a condition of inferiority to the negro. This is the main issue. The people have decided in all those States where they have enjoyed the privilege of a free vote, that this thing cannot be; and I tell you that the will of the people shall be carried out in spite of the designs of these ambitious men who have trampled the Constitution under their feet, and a Republican form of government shall be guaranteed to the people of the Southern as well as of the Northern States. But we are told that even if the Democratic party elect their President, and a majority of the House of Representatives, that these carpet-baggers who assume to constitute a majority of the Senate, will defeat legislation, and will impose this ignorant and semi-barbarous race of negroes upon the country as the superior of the white man. Let them dare to do it, and they will find that the more than one million majority of voters who are opposed to this scheme will make it impossible for them to perpetuate such an atrocious outrage upon American citizens. The people have risen in their might every where, from Maine to California, and have by their votes, said they will not have this negro supremacy kept up in this country. They will not be shaken in this purpose to turn aside the bayonet that is still kept pointed at the throats of the white men of the South. Neither will the Radical party in its hopeless minority, be able to defeat the will of the people. I feel an abiding confidence in the success of the Democratic party to-day, because it is right. Thanking you, gentlemen, for your very kind and attentive audience, I bid you farewell."

The nomination of Gen. Blair has given entire satisfaction to all Conservative men throughout the country. His high qualities of head and heart, together with the brilliant military reputation won by him during the war, have made him a favorite with all. In place of any estimate of our own, we subjoin the following summary of his character, taken from the *Buffalo Courier*, of July 10th. It is so just and complete that we prefer it to any comments of our own:

"What moderate, discerning, patriotic Republican, conscious of the mediocrity of Grant in all that concerns affairs of State, and of the inane shallowness of Colfax in every thing, can ignore the services of 'Young Frank Blair' in Missouri? He came, so to speak, from the political loins of Andrew Jackson, who sent for his father, Francis P. Blair, senior, to edit the Jacksonian organ at Washington, at the time when Calhoun and the nullifiers had struck hands with the consolidationists to drive 'Old Hickory' from his post as the steadfast defender of the Union and the laws. Mr. Blair, the father, still lives in honored competence at Silver Springs, Maryland, just outside of the District of Columbia, and his farm is yet the political homestead of the brothers Frank and Montgomery, the latter the valued and trusted cabinet minister of Abraham Lincoln; the former the undisputed and heroic savior of Missouri from the secession conspiracy. Francis P. Blair, Jr., inheriting all the patriotism and political sagacity of his father, early threw himself into the better politics of Missouri. At the outbreak of the war he represented the Union element of the State in Congress, and by his honesty and regard for the rights of adopted as well as native-born citizens, had won from the German population of St. Louis a confidence which he never betrayed, and which gained for the army of the Union a class of its earliest and truest soldiers. There is not either an honest Confederate or Federal in Missouri to-day who presumes to doubt that, but for young Frank Blair, the greatest State west of the Mississippi river would have gone as a unit for secession. We have not at hand the complete data to make up General Blair's brilliant military record. We remember, however, that in one of the first months of the war he was at the head of a regiment he had raised, and assisted in driving Sterling Price and the Confederate army beyond the confines of Missouri. In August, 1862, he had earned a brigadier-generalship and a prominent place among the leaders of that great army of the Southwest which clove the heart of the rebellion and at last issued with Sherman in the Carolinas. Gen. Frank Blair was thus, from the beginning of the war to its end, one of those heroes to which the rough school of border warfare gave birth. There were few fields, indeed, between St. Louis and Richmond in which he was not a brilliant and prominent officer. When the great army of the West made its triumphal march into Washington at the close of the war, he was at the head of one of its most magnificent *corps d'armée.* He entered the national capital as a conqueror, where his father but a short generation before had appeared as an obscure but valiant editor, summoned to do battle with his pen for the Union and Constitution. The gallant General, though already conscious of his great inherited power in statecraft, from the moment of the breaking out of the war abandoned the field of politics, except in so far as, to cope with the secession wiles of Gov. Claiborne Jackson, the methods of the politician were necessary. It was not till the true purposes of the war had been perverted and extreme Radicalism had seized on the spoils of victory, that we find General Blair taking formal issue with the Radical party. He has since been as earnest for the perfect restoration of the Union by peaceful and conciliatory measures, as formerly he was prompt in its vindication by the sword. In his nomination no political caucus made use of his name and fame to serve factional ends. He was the spontaneous choice of both the soldier and civilian elements of the Democratic party, and his strength at the West will be found to equal that of Governor Seymour in the East. The prominent qualities of General Blair are sagacity, personal devotion, coolness and daring in the field of battle, and that conservative knowledge of time and tide which makes him as prompt to resist Jacobinism as to oppose secession. He has also a chivalric element in his character which has often won him friends out of the ranks of his enemies. Wade Hampton, 'the Southern Murat,' and the best soldiers of the Confederate army, now hail his nomination with such a heartiness of enthusiasm as only could come of that respect which springs up between brave enemies in hard-fought fields. With the name of Francis P. Blair on our banner, who shall say that the Democratic party is not the party of the Union? and if service to the country be a test of fitness for high office, will our opponents care to put Colfax, the plausible speaker, in the scale of comparison with Blair, the Western soldier."

www.ingramcontent.com/pod-product-compliance
Lightning Source LLC
LaVergne TN
LVHW021322110826
845150LV00003B/643

* 9 7 8 1 4 2 5 5 5 6 5 6 3 *